I0004683

Free Yourself from Microsoft and the NSA...
Learn Linux and Libre Office!

David Spring M. Ed.

Free Yourself from Microsoft and the NSA...

Learn Linux and Libre Office!

Copyright, David Spring M. Ed.

Collegeintheclouds.org

FreeyourselffromMicrosoftandtheNSA.org

September 2013

Dedication

This book is dedicated to 8 freedom pioneers...

Gary Kildall... 1942 -1994

Gary was a computer programmer who in 1975 invented both the DR DOS operating system and the BIOS Computer Start Up Program. Gary is often called the "father of the personal computer." The original MS Windows operating system, called MS-DOS was a virtual copy of DR DOS – making Microsoft the biggest copyright violator in history. We cover more about Gary Kildall in Chapter 1, Section 3.

Thomas Penfield Jackson... 1936 – 2013

Judge Jackson presided over the 1998 – 2000 trial of US versus Microsoft and wrote a 207 page "Findings of Fact" which document many of the events we discuss in this book. Judge Jackson ruled that Microsoft had repeatedly violated the Sherman Antitrust Act and therefore should be broken up. His decision was overturned by a corrupt Court of Appeals. But his Findings of Fact still speak truth to injustice today.

Edward Snowden

In June 2013, Edward Snowden released NSA documents which changed the course of this book. These NSA documents reveal a massive spy program by the NSA, with the help of Microsoft, and provide additional evidence that support my claims of an NSA "open back door" to the Windows operating system. Edward confirmed my research that the NSA is spying on us. In this book, we explain how they spy on us.

Glenn Greenwald

Without the courage and determination of Glenn Greenwald, Edward Snowden's story would have been buried by a wall of NSA propaganda. It is a frightening thing that we currently have so few real reporters willing to speak truth to injustice. We must all more closely examine where we are getting our "news" from.

Richard Stallman

Computer programmer, founder of the GNU project and the Free Software Foundation, and advocate for the public and scientific benefits of free software programs. GNU stands for GNU is Not Unix. Unix is a closed source operating system. GNU is basically just a joke that only a computer programmer would understand. It means GNU/Linux is a free operating system.

Linus Torvalds

Computer programmer and developer of the free open source Linux operating system which is at the heart of the Linux Mint distribution. Linus built the Linux operating system in 1991 and decided to give it away so that everyone would benefit. Linus currently develops and maintains the Linux "core" program for the Linux Foundation in Beaverton, Oregon.

Clem Lefebvre

Founder of the **Linux Mint** project – which is the Linux distribution closest to Windows XP and Windows 7. "It is extremely important to us that people are happy with their computer. Our goal is to bring people what they need, what they want and what they ask for. People should not be forced to migrate to something new just because someone else thinks they should."

Aaron Swartz...1986 - 2013

Inventor of RSS (Really Simple Syndication) and advocate for the principle that science and innovation, paid for with public tax payer dollars, belongs in the public domain. Aaron called this basic human right "the freedom to connect." Aaron said "There is no justice in following unjust laws. It is time to come into the light and oppose the private theft of public knowledge. Sharing knowledge is a moral imperative."

It is because of their devotion to the free exchange of knowledge that we still have the ability to free ourselves from the chains of Microsoft and the NSA.

Free Yourself from Microsoft and the NSA...
Table of Contents

Preface: Could All the Conspiracy Theories be True?

> **"This wholesale invasion of Americans' and foreign citizens' privacy does not contribute to our security; it puts in danger the very liberties we are trying to protect**." Daniel Ellsberg June 10 2013

Welcome to the open source community and to our comprehensive step by step guide on learning how to install and use free open source tools (software) on your computer. Open source means the software is free and can be shared by anyone with anyone for any purpose. Open source is like a public library...free and open knowledge shared with the community for the common good. Free as in Freedom. No patents, no hassles, no barriers, no limits!

If you are concerned about Microsoft handing over your data to the NSA, we are here to offer you a safer more secure option. If you have had enough of Windows 8 viruses and the Blue Screen of Death and the never ending stream of model changes and price increases, we are here to offer you a less expensive and more reliable alternative. Our goal is to explain why you should install the free open source tools called Linux and Libre Office on your home, school and work computers – and then provide you with specific instructions on how to use these free open source tools to free yourself from the chains of Microsoft and the NSA.

In June 2013, former NSA agent Edward Snowden confirmed that Microsoft works closely with the NSA. This book provides the shocking hidden details of that relationship and explains why it harms everyone from social activists to small business owners. If you are concerned about Microsoft handing over your data to the NSA, we are here to offer you a safer more secure option. If you have had enough of Windows 8 viruses, the Blue Screen of Death and Microsoft's never ending stream of model changes and price increases, we will show you how to switch to a less expensive and more reliable alternative.

Our goal is to explain why you should install the free open source tools called Linux and Libre Office on your home, school and work computers – and then provide you with specific instructions on how to use these free open source tools to free yourself from the chains of Microsoft and the NSA. But this book is about much more than simply learning Linux and Libre Office. Knowledge is power. If you really want to be free then it is important to learn the truth. Only the truth can set us free. The truth in this case is rather shocking. The truth is that there is a group of very wealthy powerful people who want to control the entire world – and to gain complete control, they intend to control both the internet and all of our computers. This book provides concrete evidence that at least some of the "crazy conspiracy theories" are true.

The shocking details revealed in this book include:

...Microsoft was "given" an exemption from the Sherman Antitrust Act in trade for giving the NSA access to all Windows computers.

...The NSA has access to every file on every one of the world's two billion Windows computers – and has had this access since 1998!

.... The NSA used the "open back door" to Windows computers to launch a "cyber-attack" against Iranian nuclear power and oil plants in 2009 using an NSA created super virus called Flame.

... In early 2010, the Flame Super Virus escaped and began infecting commercial computers all over the world – and played a key role in causing the largest environmental disaster in the world – the BP Gulf Oil Spill.

... The Flame virus and its many cousins, which attack computers by pretending to be "Windows Updates," have now infected millions of computers.

... As bad as all of this is the worst is yet to come. Microsoft's latest operating system, Windows 8 comes with an extremely dangerous startup program called "UEFI: which is not only capable of remotely controlling every part of your computer – it is also capable of crashing the entire world economy! In April 2014, Microsoft will end support for Windows XP computers – leaving hundreds of millions of Windows users unprotected from Flame and other viruses. In just a few simple steps, you can protect your existing computer and the data stored on it. Now is the time to learn the full story about the relationship between Microsoft and the NSA so that you can protect yourself from the coming crash.

Who is this guy and why is he saying this crazy stuff?
Because many of the claims in this book may sound crazy, I would like to briefly explain who I am and why I wrote this book. Up until recently, I was a website consultant, community college instructor and a loyal user of the Microsoft Windows operating system and Microsoft Office word processing program. However, in 2012, Microsoft made a radical change to the Windows operating system when it replaced Windows XP and Windows 7 with an entirely different system Microsoft called Windows 8 and which they now call Windows 8.1 Blue. This new system is extremely difficult to learn and use – and it has several "features" which severely limit your freedom. I was therefore in the process of writing a book called "Learn Linux and Libre Office – A Cure for the Windows 8 Blues" in order to give people an alternative to Windows 8.

Important Questions about Unusual Aspects of Windows 8

This research into strange aspects of Windows 8 and Windows 8.1 led me to seek out answers to a series of questions. These questions and their answers revealed several hidden connections between Microsoft and the NSA.

First, why has Microsoft been allowed to continue their monopoly of computer systems even after two federal judges found Microsoft guilty of repeatedly violating the Sherman Antitrust Act? The Microsoft Monopoly exemption occurred at the exact same time Microsoft gave the NSA access to all Windows computers. In fact, the Microsoft Monopoly exemption was granted by the same judge who later became the FISA court NSA judge! Could it be that our government secretly agreed to allow the Microsoft monopoly to continue in exchange for Microsoft giving the NSA access to all Windows computers?

Second, why would Microsoft risk their company and offend their users by moving away from a popular operating system like Windows 7 to an extremely unstable and complex operating system like Windows 8? There were many strange things about Windows 8 that did not make sense. For example, why is the Windows 8 operating system actually two different operating systems with two different control panels and two different versions of the Internet Explorer web browser and two different sets of user interfaces? An operating system this complex has never existed before. Neither Windows XP nor Windows 7 had more than one control panel or more than one web browser. Also, why are our user names and passwords for Windows 8 now stored on a database at Microsoft rather than inside of our own computers as was the case with Windows 7? Such an invasion of privacy has never occurred before.

Third, why with Windows 8, was Microsoft forcing all computer manufacturers to move away from a simple computer startup program called BIOS to a new complex and unstable startup program called UEFI? Why should Microsoft even care what program computer manufacturers use to startup our computers? Why was the development of UEFI done in secret? Where did UEFI come from? Who created it? When was it created and what is its purpose? And why is UEFI ten times the size of BIOS if its only function is to tun on the computer and then hand the process over to the operating system?

Windows 8/UEFI/Secure Boot places digital handcuffs on your computer to make it much more difficult for you to add Linux to your computer... Imagine a world in which Microsoft controlled every aspect of 90% of the world's one billion computers. This is worse than a monopoly. It is corporatocracy.

Fourth, why does the UEFI startup program include a controversial feature called "Secure Boot"? Since its inception, Secure Boot has raised alarm bells among computer users because it gives Microsoft almost total control over our computers by preventing us from loading any program which is not approved by Microsoft. Members of the open source community have called this strange process "Restricted Boot" (see cartoon below). Where did secure boot come from? Who created it and what is its purpose?

Fifth, does Secure Boot included a "Windows 8 Kill Switch" which Microsoft (or the NSA) could use to kill your computer? Not only did the answer turn out to be yes, but the kill switch appears to be the main purpose of Windows 8!

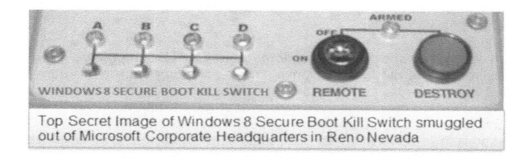

Top Secret Image of Windows 8 Secure Boot Kill Switch smuggled out of Microsoft Corporate Headquarters in Reno Nevada

Sixth, how does the Windows open back door work?
It has been clear to many computer users that since 1998 Microsoft has used an **"open back door"** to make "updates" to our computers. This back door was created when Microsoft introduced Internet Explorer 4 and embedded this web browser into the Windows 98 operating system. I wanted to know how this back door worked, whether it could be turned off (it can't) and what kind of changes it could make in your computer – even without your permission. What was the connection between the open back door and the increasing number of Windows Updates containing malicious code which crash Windows computers?

Seventh, what was the Flame virus and how is the Flame virus related to Windows Update problems? In June 2012, Microsoft admitted that a super virus named **Flame** was using the open back door to remotely attack Windows computers. This led me to research several more questions: What is the Flame virus? Who created it? When was it created? What is its purpose and how does it work? Also why have Microsoft's monthly updates gone crazy during the past year? Why are there so many reports of these updates crashing computers? Are these security patches related to the Flame virus and/or the NSA?

Eighth, did the NSA Flame virus cause the BP Oil Disaster?
Researching the history of the flame virus led to even more disturbing questions about the relationship between Microsoft and the NSA. Several newspaper reports confirmed that in 2009, Microsoft played a key role in the NSA attack on Iranian Nuclear and Oil Facilities via the development of the Stuxnet and Flame super viruses. Then, in 2010, the Flame virus escaped and began crashing not just Iranian oil facilities but lots of other oil facilities around the world.

I discovered evidence that the Flame virus led directly to the BP Gulf Oil Spill – the worse environmental disaster in the history of the world.

In the weeks before the BP disaster, the Windows computer system froze leading to a lack of control over safety equipment. Symptoms indicate the Flame virus caused the computer crash which led to the explosion.

Ninth, is it possible that the Cyber War and the War on Terror are both fake? I discovered evidence that the so-called Cyberwar is fake. There have been cyber attacks. But they have not come from either the Iranians or the Chinese. Instead, there is evidence that nearly all computer attacks on US computers are initiated by the NSA - in order to create the illusion of a cyberwar. I also discovered evidence that the War on Terror is fake. There is no Al Qaeda. What passes for Al Qaeda is merely a branch of the CIA. Nearly all terrorist attacks appear to have originated with the CIA in order to create the illusion of a war on terror.

Al Qaeda appears to be simply a front for the CIA and CIA paid operatives. The ground to air missiles being used by these fake Al Qaeda groups were given to them by our own US government.

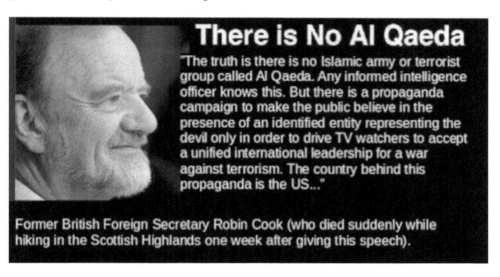

There is No Al Qaeda

"The truth is there is no Islamic army or terrorist group called Al Qaeda. Any informed intelligence officer knows this. But there is a propaganda campaign to make the public believe in the presence of an identified entity representing the devil only in order to drive TV watchers to accept a unified international leadership for a war against terrorism. The country behind this propaganda is the US..."

Former British Foreign Secretary Robin Cook (who died suddenly while hiking in the Scottish Highlands one week after giving this speech).

American tax payers appear to be funding both sides of the war on terror.

Pallets stacked with US $100 bills arriving in Iraq in 2004. (photo: Scott Applewhite/AP)

By June, 2013, I had uncovered some very disturbing answers to all of the above questions. Answers to all of these questions are provided in more detail in Chapters 1 and 2. Even before the Snowden revelations, I came to the conclusion that the real purpose of Windows 8, UEFI, Secure Boot and the open back door to the Windows operating system has little to do with what we have been told and more to do with Microsoft and the NSA taking over total control of our computers. I was in the process of finishing this book exposing the problems of Windows 8 and outlining the connection between Microsoft and the NSA.

Then on June 6, 2013, the incredible Edward Snowden articles exposing the relationship between Microsoft and the NSA appeared.
We now know, thanks to the Snowden revelations in June 2013 that Big Brother is downloading not only all of our phone calls and emails – but every document in every Windows computer. One slide in particular indicated that in 2007 Microsoft helped the NSA jump start a secret mass surveillance program called PRISM.

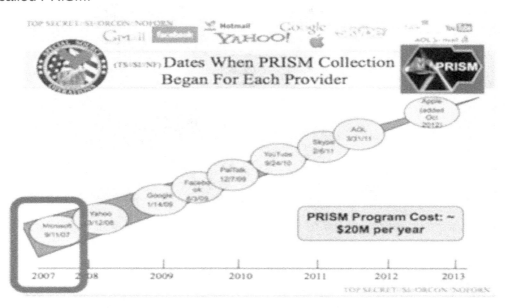

I was already aware that in 2007, shortly after joining the Prism program, Microsoft launched a parallel program to provide the NSA with a "kill switch" on all Windows 8 computers via a new secret startup program called UEFI with an ominous feature called Secure Boot. After the Snowden revelations, I realized that the most important aspect of this book was to warn people about the dangers of Windows 8, UEFI and Secure Boot and provide computer users with a way to regain control over their computers by helping them switch to the Linux operating system. Thus, I changed the name of the book from "Learn Linux and Libre Office – A Cure for the Windows 8 Blues to "Free Yourself from Microsoft and the NSA – Learn Linux and Libre Office."

The goal of this book is two fold: first to help you become more aware of the problems of using the Microsoft operating system – and especially the problems associated with Windows 8, UEFI and Secure Boot – and to provide you with step by step instructions on how to add and use the Linux operating system and the Libre Office word processing program.

As in the Wizard of Oz, we are told to ignore the man behind the curtain as our own government ignores international law and kidnaps the elected President of Bolivia and holds him prisoner while they search his plane for a person whose only crime was leaking the truth to the American people. The truth is that we are all being spied on and these massive spy programs are a clear violation of the 4th Amendment to the US Constitution.

"The 4th and 5th Amendments to the Constitution of my country, Article 12 of the Universal Declaration of Human Rights, and numerous statutes and treaties forbid such systems of massive, pervasive surveillance."
Edward Snowden, June 12 2013

As a reminder, here is what our US Constitution has to say about freedom of speech and the right to privacy.

AMENDMENT I... Congress shall make no law respecting an establishment of religion, or prohibiting the free exercise thereof; or abridging the freedom of speech, or of the press; or the right of the people peaceably to assemble, and to petition the government for a redress of grievances.
AMENDMENT IV...The right of the people to be secure in their persons, houses, papers, and effects, against unreasonable searches and seizures, shall not be violated, and no warrants shall issue, but upon probable cause, supported by oath or affirmation, and particularly describing the place to be searched, and the persons or things to be seized.

What Snowden is saying and what I also believe is that our allegiance should not be to a corrupt government or to any immoral laws. Rather we should uphold the Constitution of the United States and we should support the Universal Declaration of Human Rights.

Does the NSA control the Ministry of Truth?

As in the book 1984, power crazy people control the media. They control business. But their real objective is not merely to control knowledge and money – but to control people. How they control us is through something called the **shock doctrine** which is an endless war – a war against people, a war against our environment and a war against the truth. Because knowledge is power, these wealthy people want to control the internet. One way they control the transfer of knowledge is by waging a war against reporters and whistleblowers. Another way they plan to control the transfer of knowledge is by controlling all of our computers. They do this by controlling the backdoor to the Windows operating system on more than one billion Windows computers around the world. The best and easiest thing you can do to defeat their plan and to free yourself is by learning Linux, Libre Office and other free open source tools.

Try to imagine you are living in a world very different from what we were raised to believe, a world even worse than Orwell's 1984. Imagine a world in which the war on terror is fake. In this book, we provide evidence that the goal of the NSA is not to control terrorism – but to control and enslave people around the world. There are no weapons of mass destruction – only weapons of mass distraction. Imagine the possibility that the cyber war is fake. In this book, we provide evidence that the NSA not only has developed super bugs to attack other nations, but that it is also using those same super bugs to launch fake attacks on businesses here in America to make it look like there is a cyber war – when in fact the NSA is behind BOTH SIDES of the war – just like in the book 1984.

Imagine a world where nearly everything you read in the newspaper and watch on TV news is fake. Imagine a world in which elections are sold to the highest bidder and political parties are simply friendly faces for Big Brother. The evidence is all around us. Think about the bank deregulation of 1999 with the repeal of the Glass Steagall Act – which led to the economic collapse of 2008 – which led to the multi-trillion dollar bailout of the "too-big-to-fail-and-too-big-to-jail" Wall Street banks. This bailout was accomplished by robbing trillions of dollars from the American people. The robbery is still going on.

Lies of the NSA

If you have any doubts left at all that our own government is lying to us about NSA spying, please watch the following three minute Youtube video produced by ProPublica. http://www.youtube.com/watch?v=eptZuXkUGmI

Oregon Senator Wyden asks a direct question: "Does the NSA collect data on millions of Americans?" James Clapper in an obvious act of perjury replied "No Sir." What is most amazing about this lie is that James Clapper still has a job. Meanwhile, the NSA war machine uses fear to manipulate us.

NSA SHOCK DOCTRINE WARNING SCALE
SEVERE DANGER... Bombs will explode any minute!!!   Hide under your bed and trust us to protect you.
HIGH RISK OF IMMINENT ATTACK (or maybe an attack in the next week or so... especially if you live in Detroit)   Contact your Congressperson and ask them to vote for more funding for the NSA. Call now while you still can!
ELEVATED RISK OF SOMETHING BAD PERHAPS HAPPENING SOMEWHERE IN THE NEXT MONTH...   Stay indoors and report anyone wearing a suspicious backpack. Avoid traveling in a car, train, plane or boat.
ATTACK STILL POSSIBLE... BUT OK TO GO SHOPPING...   Internet Chatter no longer indicates an attack will happen soon. Feel free to go into debt. How about buying a new computer?

In August 2013, our government announced the closing of 22 US Embassies and issued a world wide travel alert for the entire month of August - warning Americans not to travel – during the biggest travel month of the year. Supposedly this warning is due to the threat of a possible terrorist attack from Al Qaeda based on unknown information from a "very credible source."

AUGUST 2013... NSA ISSUES GLOBAL TERROR ALERT!

"There is an awful lot of chatter out there... The NSA allows us to gather the chatter. If we did not have these programs, then we simply would not be able to listen in on the bad guys."
Senator Saxby Chambliss
August 4 2013

Supposedly, the timing of this threat is related to the end of the holy month of Ramadan and Laylet al-Qadr, or the Night of Power, one of the holiest moments on the Muslim calendar. In August, 2012, Iran supposedly used this day to launch a cyber attack on Saudi Oil computers. However, in this book, we provide evidence that the Saudi computer attack on the "Night of Power" in August 2012 was launched by our own NSA. Iran had nothing to do with it. There are several problems with this new warning from the NSA. First, the timing has nothing to do with Muslim Holidays and everything to do with funding the NSA. The warning came just days after Congress almost voted to defund the NSA spying program.

As for the "credible un-named source" one wonders if that refers to James Clapper – the head of US Spying who recently admitted to lying to Congress in the "least truthful" way - or was it the CIA paid taxi driver who warned about "weapons of mass destruction" a few years ago?

On August 5, 2013, the Colbert Report aired the following clip on the Global Terror Warning: http://www.colbertnation.com/the-colbert-report-videos/428327/august-05-2013/global-terror-warning

Americans just need to avoid "this" area!

The real purpose of the attack – or threat of attack – is to scare the American people into providing hundreds of billions of additional tax dollars to the NSA.

NSA Attack on the First Amendment Freedom of Speech
On August 8, 2013, there was another shocking attack on the 1st and 4th Amendments. The email service used by Edward Snowden, Lavabit, was shut down by the NSA for refusing to hand all of their data over to the NSA. Until they were shut down by the NSA, Lavabit had 350,000 users – all of whom no longer have access to their email accounts. The NSA justifies this abuse with what they call the "Three Hop" Rule which they claim gives them the right to all of the data of anyone who has any relationship to anyone who has any relationship to an NSA suspect. Since Snowden might have some relationship to a terrorist and since the 350,000 Lavabit users are on the same email database as Snowden, the NSA gets to download all of the data of all 410,000 people.

> **"This experience has taught me one very important lesson: without congressional action or a strong judicial precedent, I would *strongly* recommend against anyone trusting their private data to a company with physical ties to the United States."**
> Ladar Levison, Founder of Lavabit

Below is a link to one of the most shocking videos I have ever watched:
http://www.youtube.com/watch?v=Ui3KpztUzVg&feature=c4-overview-vl&list=PL50BDB9BCCFAF09CA

Levison added: "What I'm opposed to are blanket court orders granting government access to everything. If the American people knew what our government was doing, they would not be allowed to do it anymore. What we have seen in recent years is their willingness to use those laws in ways personally I consider to be unconstitutional, unethical and immoral."

Edward Snowden, speaking from Moscow correctly noted, "America cannot succeed as a country where individuals like Mr. Levison have to relocate their businesses abroad to be successful." The next day, another US email encryption provider, Silent Circle, shut down. Another US "secure" email service, Hushmail, caved and handed over their database to the NSA. Once people realize that their data is not safe with Hushmail, they too will go out of business. The lesson here is that the only safety for your data is by moving your cloud data and email service to servers which are located outside of the United States.

> **"If you run a business, and the FBI or NSA want to turn it into a mass surveillance tool, they believe they can do so, solely on their own initiative. They can force you to modify your system. They can do it all in secret and then force your business to keep that secret. Once they do that, you no longer control that part of your business. In a very real sense, it is not your business anymore. It is an arm of the vast US surveillance apparatus, and if your interest conflicts with theirs then they win. Your business has been commandeered."**
> Security Expert Bruce Schneier August 30 2013

Economic Suicide

The problem with NSA surveillance is that our entire economy depends upon email privacy for efficient communications. For the past 20 years, the one bright spot of the US economy has been our lead in technology and cloud computing. However, businesses and individuals do not want their data handed over to their competitors. They have seen how the NSA handed over Airbus data to Boeing. Businesses will increasingly migrate their data to places they view are safer. The systematic takeover or closure of companies such as Lavabit, Silent Circle, Hushmail, Microsoft, Google, Apple, AOL and all other "partners" of the NSA mean that all of these companies will eventually be driven out of business – because their business model cannot succeed when their potential customers know they are being run by and for the NSA. All of their employees will lose their jobs. Some economists have estimated that American technology businesses could lose over $100 billion in cloud computing contracts worldwide over the next three years as businesses move their data overseas to avoid the NSA. However, cloud contracts are just the tip of the iceberg. As people around the world realize that companies such as Microsoft and Apple cannot be trusted to protect their data or their privacy, the total economic loss to the US will be in the trillions of dollars and **millions of US technology workers will likely lose their jobs – all thanks to the cyber monster called the NSA.**

> **"The U.S. government, in its rush to spy on everybody, may end up killing our most productive industry. Lavabit may just be the canary in the coal mine."** Jennifer Granick Stanford Center for Internet and Society

On August 21, 2013, the German Federal Office for Security in Information Technology (BSI) warned citizens to **avoid Windows 8 for being "an security risk."** An English summary of the article is at the following link. http://www.testosteronepit.com/home/2013/8/21/leaked-german-government-warns-key-entities-not-to-use-windo.html

"Users of Windows 8 surrender control over their machine the moment they turn it on. For that reason, experts at the BSI warned the German Federal Administration and other key users against deploying computers with Windows 8"

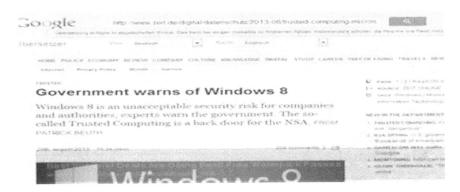

Rüdiger Weis, a professor at the Beuth University of Technology in Berlin, and a cryptographic expert, told *Die Zeit* <u>in an interview</u> that Microsoft wanted to completely change computing by integrating "a special surveillance chip" in every electronic device. Through that chip and the processes of Windows 8, particularly Secure Boot, "users largely lose control over their own hardware and software."

With the 2008 bank bailout, the largest robbery in history occurred right in broad daylight. Since then, tens of millions of jobs have been transferred to sweatshops in China while entire American cities like Detroit have been destroyed and driven to bankruptcy. Will we now fall victim to an NSA induced recession?

Political Suicide
At the same time that the NSA is bringing down internet companies, it is also destroying freedom of the press. Reporters have been threatened with jail time for refusing to hand over their sources to the US government. In Great Britain, the government just forced the news agency, The Guardian, to destroy the hard drive containing information leaked to them by Edward Snowden. If we no longer have privacy or freedom of speech, how can any group critical of the government organize? How can any whistleblower safely contact any reporter? How can human rights groups get information from victims of human rights abuses? How can any client safely and privately communicate with any attorney? How can any patient privately consult with any doctor?

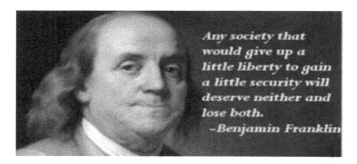

Any society that would give up a little liberty to gain a little security will deserve neither and lose both.
–Benjamin Franklin

Legal Suicide... The End of the Rule of Law?
Also in August 2013, online open source legal firm, Groklaw, announced that they too are shutting down explaining that the work they do is simply not possible if they are under the control of the NSA. The American Civil Liberties Union and several other freedom groups have filed lawsuits trying to restore our 4th Amendment right to privacy.

**War is Peace
Freedom is Slavery
Ignorance is Strength**

George Orwell 1984

Perhaps the most shocking of all of the revelations in August 2013 occurred with the release on August 20, 2013 of the 85 page FISA Court opinion which found that the NSA had violated the Bill of Rights "tens of thousands" of times. http://www.scribd.com/doc/162016974/FISA-court-opinion-with-exemptions Written by FISA Court judge John D. Bates on October 3, 2011, on page 16, the court noted that the NSA has repeatedly lied to the court about what it was doing:

> "This Court is troubled that the governments revelations regarding NSA acquisition of internet transactions make the third instance in less than three years in which the government has disclosed a substantial misrepresentation regarding the scope of a major collection program... repeated inaccurate statements made in the governments submissions... frequently and systematically violating (the FISA Court orders)." On Page 77, the court added: "The measures proposed by NSA for handling (emails of millions of Americans) tend to maximize rather than minimize the retention of non-target information."
>
> On Page 78, the court noted: "Each analyst... is left to apply the proposed minimization measures alone, from beginning to end, and without the benefit of his colleagues' prior review... the governments proposed measures seem to enhance rather than reduce the risk of error... In sum, the NSA collection results in the acquisition of a very large number of Fourth Amendment protected communications that have no direct connection to any targeted facility and thus do not serve a national need."

Basically, FISA court judge John D. Bates had assumed the government was telling the truth and then he found out the government was not telling the truth. In fact, the NSA had been keeping the FISA court in the dark since court oversight began in 2006. Judge Bates found that the NSA had violated the Fourth Amendment rights of Americans "tens of thousands of times" each year using the NSA's own study (see page 41). In fact the actual number of violations may be in the hundreds of millions of times each year as we now know that the NSA is doing much more than they told Judge Bates.

On August 23 2013 we found out how the NSA got around restrictions placed on it by the FISA court was by paying its "Prism Partners" (including Microsoft) millions of dollars to do its dirty work for it. The NSA paid and continues to pay millions of dollars to cover the costs of major internet corporations involved in the Prism surveillance program after a court ruled that some of the NSA's activities were unconstitutional. The material provides the first evidence of a financial relationship between the tech companies and the NSA. It is still not clear why it is okay for private companies like Microsoft to do things the NSA is not allowed to do. http://www.theguardian.com/world/2013/aug/23/nsa-prism-costs-tech-companies-paid

Also this summer, it was revealed at a Congressional hearing that the NSA has begun assembling scores of new cyber "offensive" and "defensive" teams, the agency's most concrete step toward preparing the Pentagon and intelligence agencies for a new era of cyber warfare and computer conflict. These teams consist not only of NSA spies but also private corporate contractors.

Top Secret NSA Operations Center

"The confluence of circumstances enabling mass surveillance has the potential to permanently imperil Americans' civil liberties. How we respond will determine whether we continue to function as a democracy."
Heidi Boghosian, executive director of the National Lawyers Guild.

Microsoft Blackmails Windows XP Users
The NSA wants total control over our computers. Their plan to gain access to all of our computers requires that Windows users "upgrade" from Windows XP to Windows 8. To make this happen, in April 2013, Microsoft announced that they will discontinue support for Windows XP beginning in April 2014. Since then, they have used a series of malicious Windows updates to sabotage Windows XP and Windows 7 computers in an attempt to force uses to replace their current computers with Windows 8.

The only protection from these attacks is to turn off "Automatic Windows Updates" and install Linux as a dual boot. Sadly, Microsoft has sabotaged the Windows operating system in order to make it more difficult to install Linux as a dual boot – but we will show you how to get around these obstacles. The only way to take back control over your personal or business computer is to learn how to install and use Linux and Libre Office.

December 5 2013 Update... Connecting the Dots between Microsoft Backdoors, NSA Corruption and the Bitcoin Ponzi Scheme

In the past three months since I published **Free Yourself from Microsoft and the NSA**, there has been a steady stream of increasingly shocking revelations about the extent of NSA spying in the US and around the world. NSA operatives have been caught spying on their wives and girlfriends. The NSA has also been caught spying on dozens of world leaders including Angela Merkel, the elected leader of Germany and the Pope in the Vatican, the leader of the Catholic Church. http://news.panorama.it/cronaca/papa-francesco-datagate

In this brief update, we will look at evidence of several shocking links between Microsoft, the NSA and Bitcoin indicating a diabolical plot to manipulate, undermine and corrupt the development of alternative digital currencies. As financial analyst, Greg Mannarino recently said, "We already have a digital currency. It is called the US dollar." It appears that the NSA wants to insure that no credible alternative to the US digital dollar arises. They therefore created and sabotaged Bitcoin in order to give alternate digital currencies a bad reputation.

I realize what I am about to describe may seem difficult to believe. But these are only the latest of many examples of Microsoft and the NSA doing things that are very evil in order to gain control over the entire planet. In fact, the NSA makes the Mafia look like a gathering of Sunday school teachers. The NSA's goal, from a February 2012 document, as confirmed by Snowden releases on November 22, 2013, is to extract all data on "anyone, anytime, anywhere" by influencing (corrupting) the "global encryption market." This goal is evidence of the NSA's evil intentions.
http://www.nytimes.com/2013/11/23/us/politics/nsa-report-outlined-goals-for-more-power.html?_r=0

The full extent of the NSA's diabolical plot was first brought to light on September 5, 2013 when Glenn Greenwald (and several others) exposed a new batch of top secret NSA documents with articles in the Guardian, the New York Times and ProPublica. The following three articles describe a $4 billion16 year NSA bribery and kickback scheme called Bullrun which has severely corrupted encryption standards used to secure financial and other sensitive records.
http://www.theguardian.com/world/2013/sep/05/nsa-gchq-encryption-codes-security
http://www.nytimes.com/2013/09/06/us/nsa-foils-much-internet-encryption.html?_r=0
http://www.propublica.org/article/the-nsas-secret-campaign-to-crack-undermine-internet-encryption

The Bullrun program is much bigger and much more dangerous than the NSA PRISM program exposed in June 2013. The following is from the actual 2010 NSA memos which describe Bullrun:

"For the past decade, NSA has led an aggressive, multipronged effort to break widely used Internet encryption technologies." This NSA plot "actively engages the U.S. and foreign IT industries to covertly influence and/or overtly leverage their commercial products' designs" to make them "exploitable."

In other words, the NSA bribes companies like Microsoft with hundreds of millions of dollars every year in order to insert flaws into their computer programs. In November 2013, it was revealed that the NSA has hacked into more than 85,000 Windows computer networks around the world. http://www.nrc.nl/nieuws/2013/11/23/nsa-infected-50000-computer-networks-with-malicious-software/

This raises the question of how the NSA is gaining access to these computer networks. One method is the backdoor key Microsoft gave the NSA in 1998, as I describe in detail in my book. However, the Bullrun program means that the NSA is also using deliberately flawed encryption programs to gain access to computer networks. The NSA refers specifically to using encryption keys in their 2013 budget request as being needed to "influence policies, standards and specifications for commercial public key technologies." Public key technologies are the most commonly use of encryption methods. A public key is like a password. For example, if the password to your bank account is TakeMyMoney, the encrypted version of your password might be XQ4%zv20#49. A public/private key combination is used to translate the password back into TakeMyMoney. At the heart of all "key" programs are random number generators that make it hard for hackers to translate the encrypted password unless they possess the all-important keys.

Encryption is the Achilles heel of internet and computer security. Without encryption there is no security. It is therefore essential to understand the history of how NSA corrupted crucial NIST (National Institute of Standards and Technology) encryption standards if we have any hope of getting back to internet security. Thanks to Snowden, we now know that in early 2006, the NSA insisted on adding an unsafe "elliptic curve based random number generator" created by the NSA to three other more secure encryption methods that had already been researched and approved before the NSA take over. The corrupted standard is in NIST Special Publication 800-90. On May 29, 2006, a pair of researchers in the Netherlands authored a paper showing that this NSA created elliptic curve based random number generator was insecure and that attacks against it could "be run on an ordinary PC." http://s3.documentcloud.org/documents/786216/cryptanalysis-of-the-dual-elliptic-curve.pdf

The math used by the Netherlands researchers was rather complex. A less complex explanation of the danger of this bad NSA encryption method was presented in August 2007 by two junior Microsoft employees at an internet security conference in Santa Barbara California. .
http://www.wired.com/images_blogs/threatlevel/2013/09/15-shumow.pdf

This presentation occurred at almost the exact same time that Microsoft joined the NSA's PRISM program and made dangerous modifications to the UEFI computer startup program (described in detail in my book). While there are many families of elliptical functions, all of them suffer from the same problem described by these researchers. Basically, elliptical curves are either too complex to be used for encryption without certain restrictions (such as limiting the elliptical curve function to integers) - or they are not random if there are restrictions.

The NSA must have had a purpose in mind in putting such a bad encryption method into the national standard list of approved encryptions. I therefore started researching applications that used this bad NSA encryption method. One application was the Windows operating system. Despite the fact that it was known to be insecure, Microsoft added this NSA fake encryption method to Windows Vista in February 2008. Even though the NSA flawed process was not the default encryption method, adding it to the Windows operating system made it much easier for the NSA to attack Iranian Windows computer systems later that same year. The NSA also likely used this same method to attack over 50,000 other Windows computer networks around the world in the next two years. The number is now over 85,000 compromised computer networks per a leak of top secret NSA documents released on November 23, 2013.

"The malware can be controlled remotely and be turned on and off at will. The 'implants' act as digital 'sleeper cells' that can be activated with a single push of a button. According to the *Washington Post*, the NSA has been carrying out this type of cyber operation since 1998."
http://www.nrc.nl/nieuws/2013/11/23/nsa-infected-50000-computer-networks-with-malicious-software/

Another program that adopted the flawed NSA encryption scam was **Bitcoin**, the world's largest and most successful digital currency program. In fact, several lines of evidence indicate that Bitcoin was developed by the NSA between 2006 and 2008 – around the same time that the NSA sabotaged the NIST encryption standards. The domain name registration for Bitcoin was in August 2008 and the first paper was published in November 2008. The production of the first bitcoins was in January 2009. The NSA elliptical encryption method was and still is used to verify the authenticity of bitcoin ownership as one of the final steps in transferring ownership of bitcoins. This is despite the fact that the weakness of elliptical random number generators had been exposed in 2006 and again in 2007. Why would Bitcoin use a flawed encryption method produced by the NSA?

On October 28, 2013, an article appeared in Bitcoin Magazine claiming that Bitcoin got "lucky" because it used a Koblitz ellipse curve rather than the normal pseudorandom ellipse curve (secp256k1 rather than secp256r1). But using a K curve rather than the R curve does not reduce the danger of the function.

In fact, the article cited several examples of how the original programmer for bitcoin, Satoshi Nakamoto, got very "lucky" in avoiding less than obvious computer programming problems in the design of bitcoin. For example, the article explains that had the maximum number of bitcoins been 210 million instead of 21 million, Bitcoin could not be represented in floating point notation making bitcoin programming much harder. But rather than being lucky, these complex mathematical coincidences are strong evidence that Bitcoin was not designed by a single lucky person – but by many extremely smart mathematicians and computer programmers over a period of several years. Not many high tech organizations hire both mathematicians and computer programmers. And if they did, they would not be likely to choose the NSA flawed encryption method. In other words, the strange design of Bitcoin has the fingerprints of the NSA all over it.

The 2013 Bitcoin magazine article, which spoke so glowingly about how smart and lucky the founder of Bitcoin was, led me to dig deeper into the history of Bitcoin. The mythical founder of Bitcoin was named Satoshi Nakamoto. In his posts, he used a fake name and a fake German email address (satoshin@gmx.com). He claimed to be from Japan. But he spoke perfect English. He also wrote words using the British spelling (for example, colour rather than color). While careful steps were taken to hide the actual location of the emails, a detailed analysis of his 500 posts to the Bitcoin forum indicated that **Satoshi lived in the US East Coast time zone** – which just happens to be the time zone where NSA headquarters are located. In addition, Satoshi often took an unusually long time - averaging two weeks - to respond to forum posts. This indicated that a group of people would prepare a response and then have it approved by senior officials before actually posting responses to the forum. Finally, despite being on the East Coast of the US, Satoshi registered the bitcoin domain name on a server located in Finland.

All of these red flags aside, the biggest clue indicating that the NSA was and is behind Bitcoin comes from following the money. With the rise in the value of Bitcoins, Satoshi now has nearly $200 million dollars' worth of bitcoins. Yet he has never cashed any bitcoins in for dollars. Just as bitcoin was gaining widespread acceptance, Satoshi suddenly stopped posting altogether and simply disappeared. **What kind of person or group of persons would be willing to turn their backs on $200 million?** The NSA is the only group with the money, math and computer skills needed to pull of this Bitcoin scam. No one has ever actually met this amazingly smart, lucky and/or generous computer programmer called Satoshi. Yet he was able to do what entire teams of programmers have failed to do – establish a digital currency now worth an estimated $21 billion.

Doesn't this story seem fishy to you? To me, it reeks of the foul stench of the NSA. The NSA aka Satoshi, set up a website, bitcoin.org in August 2008 at just about the same time that the NSA started their PRISM program and the UEFI program. This was also only one month before the bank bailout that was the beginning of the ongoing theft and destruction of the US dollar. It was almost like those in high places could see this crash coming.

In November 2008, one month after the bank bailout, on the Bitcoin website, the NSA published a "white paper" under the Satoshi alias, explaining how Bitcoin works. (see http://bitcoin.org/bitcoin.pdf). This white paper is also very unusual. There are only a few references with the latest reference being from 2002. So why did it take Satoshi over six years to publish this white paper? In the paper, they (he) boldly state: "We have proposed a system for electronic transactions without relying on trust." The problem with this statement is that **all human transactions are based on trust relationships** – except of course for the NSA where the slogan is to trust no one!

But even if this person or group of persons had revealed themselves, so that it would be possible to determine where bitcoin really came from and what the motives of the developers were, there are many other very suspicious things about bitcoin. The choice of the NSA flawed elliptical encryption method was just the first red flag. Another major red flag is how bitcoins are initially generated. In a real digital currency, the generation of the currency would be tied to something of real value – such as gold, or silver or homes or even just a hard day's work. This is not the case with bitcoins. They are generated by handing your Windows based computer over to some hidden third party who then uses your computer to "solve math problems." The first person to solve the current problem gets 50 bit coins. Because the math problems increase in difficulty over time, it takes more and more and faster and faster computers to solve the problems. This is called "bitcoin mining." But the real mining is the data mining of the NSA. The system they have set up to draw innocent people into this trap is diabolical in the way that it takes advantage of the human weakness for greed to encourage people to hand over their computers to the NSA in order to get a fake digital reward.

Who is behind the curtain?
The final bit of evidence is to follow the money. Who is currently using and promoting bitcoin? One group is drug dealers. Sadly, the world's largest drug dealers are the CIA and NSA. This is a primary source of their hidden income. Another group promoting bitcoin is the military (such as the US Air Force). For those not familiar with the NSA, it is actually a branch of the military and has a very close relationship with the Air Force. Why else would the Air Force get involved in promoting a digital currency based on an NSA flawed encryption method? But ultimately, Bitcoin is not about making money. It is about controlling digital currency. This is why the NSA is willing to walk away from a quick $200 million in profits. It is clear that the NSA has the digital keys to break Bitcoin any time it wants. If and when Bitcoin finally crashes, look for the NSA to be the "man behind the curtain."

Bitcoin is only one of several diabolical plots being carried out by the NSA. On November 8, 2013, computer safety guru, Eugene Kaspersky, gave a talk in Australia in which he acknowledged that the Windows Flame and Stuxnet super viruses had infected Russian Windows computers controlling everything from nuclear power plants to their space station. Watch http://www.youtube.com/watch?v=6tlUvb26DzI#t=1620

Eugene notes of the Microsoft Windows program: "Windows network for the scientists.... they come to the space station with UBS's which are infected. I am not kidding!.. These kinds of networks are not safe by design... Unfortunately, they have the very same computer as you! The attack is a virus. It can spread. If it infects an Australian power plant, I call it collateral damage. It is very possible that other nations which are not in conflict will be victims of cyber attacks on their critical infrastructure. Cyber space has no borders."

We discuss the NSA/Microsoft development of these super bugs in detail in our book. The only good news is that governments around the world are starting to realize the need for independent branches of the internet which are not under the direct control of the NSA. This has already led to a major drop in business for US technology corporations – all of which are subject to control by the NSA. The cost to the US economy of NSA spying is in the hundreds of billions of dollars – with thousands of jobs being lost.

Oregon Senator Ron Wyden recently remarked, **"If a foreign enemy was doing this much damage to the economy, people would be in the streets with pitchforks."**

Meanwhile, there have also been several toothless bills introduced into Congress to create the illusion that something will be done to reign in the NSA. None of these bills deal with the real problem which is that the NSA and Microsoft are taking over billions of computers in the world through the very dangerous UEFI – NSA startup program. The only solution to the criminal activities of Microsoft and the NSA is to shut both of them down for good.

The solution to the currency problem is to replace the corrupt Federal Reserve with a debt free currency in accordance with the US Constitution (see the NEED Act by Dennis Kucinich). Alternately, States could establish a public bank like the Bank of North Dakota (see Ellen Brown and the Public Banking Institute).

Until the NSA is shut down, things are likely to get worse. The Editor of the Guardian stated that they have only released one percent of the Snowden documents. So read this free book and stayed tuned for more updates. http://freeyourselffrommicrosoftandthensa.org/

David Spring M. Ed.
December 5, 2013

How this book is organized

This book is divided into ten chapters. Each chapter has four sections. The first chapter covers the rise of the Microsoft Monopoly and its hidden connections to the NSA. The second chapter covers the frightening consequences of this collusion between Microsoft and the NSA. The third chapter covers some of the major drawbacks of Windows 8. I want to make sure you are aware of all of the drawbacks of Windows 8 in order to inspire you to take the time to follow through with the rest of the book and actually install Linux on your computer. The fourth chapter covers the history of open source alternatives. The fifth chapter reviews how to download and use Linux Mint in a virtual box inside of your normal Windows computer. This will allow you to see how easy it is to use Linux and Libre Office without making any major changes to your current computer. The sixth chapter explains why and how to back up your computer and how to "dual boot" Linux with Windows. This may seem hard to believe but Microsoft is deliberately trying to crash your computer and prevent you from using Linux. You will see that Linux is not only easier than Windows, it is also much faster. The remaining chapters cover additional free open source programs to use with Linux to free yourself from Microsoft and the NSA.

This book is the text portion of our complete ten week 40 hour online course on using Linux and Libre Office. Each chapter covers one week in our ten week course. Each of the 40 sections covers one hour in our online course. Our course also includes 40 videos demonstrating the skills discussed in each chapter, 40 activities to help you master these skills and 10 video conference classroom sessions, one hour per week for 10 weeks. If you are interested in taking our complete online course on using open source tools or learning more about our programs, visit our website, **collegeintheclouds.org** or email us for information on the next course offering. We have also posted this book on our book website, **freeyourselffrommicrosoftandthensa.org** in case you want to read the book online or refer your friends to it.

Other Books and Courses by David Spring

This book is the first book and course in our six book, six course series for sharing knowledge. In our books and courses you will learn how to use several free knowledge sharing tools including the Linux Operating System, Libre Office for word processing, Joomla for website management, VirtueMart for Ecommerce and Moodle for Elearning.

For more information about all six of our books and their related courses, visit our main website, collegeintheclouds.org. Here you will also find links to our Youtube channel with videos covering all of the topics in our books and courses. If you have any questions, feel free to post them on our website forum!

http://collegeintheclouds.org/forum

Are you ready to learn the power and freedom of Linux and Libre Office? Let's get started!
David Spring, M.Ed.
September 11, 2013

Before moving on to Chapter One, we should first cover this basic question... What is Linux?
Linux is a free computer operating system that works on almost any computer. Linux runs 90% of all super computers – because it is the fastest in the world. Linux runs 80% of the all stock markets – because it is the safest in existence. Linux runs 70% of all smart phones - because it is simple and easy to learn. Linux runs 60% of all Internet servers - because it is very dependable. Linux runs 50% of all tablets - because it is the most versatile operating system.

Linux is so versatile that it can run almost any Microsoft Windows program – including MS Office. Most important, Linux does not allow the NSA to access to the data on your computer. In short, Linux is the foundation for our global economy and the largest shared technology in history. **Linux is also a free open source alternative to the Windows 8 Blues!**

How do you pronounce Linux?
This is an interesting question. Computer programmers tend to **pronounce Linux as Len-X.**
This is because Linux is derived in part from the UNIX computer operating system and UNIX is pronounced You – Nix. So Len-X is close to You-Nix.

Chapter 1... How Microsoft became a Branch of the NSA

Knowledge is power. It is important to become aware of the huge risk facing computer users as a result of the merger of Microsoft and the NSA. This chapter describes the evolution of the ominous relationship between Microsoft and the NSA - and how these two monsters have merged to form a super monster.

Microsoft joins the evil empire.

This chapter is divided into four sections.

1.1 Hidden Links between Microsoft and the NSA
We begin with the Snowden revelations and summarize the current state of the merger of Microsoft and the NSA by exposing several hidden relationships between them.

1.2 Why Linux is More Secure than Windows
This section explains why Linux is the world's most secure operating system – secure enough to offer us protection from Microsoft and the NSA.

1.3 Emergence of the Evil Empire
This section details the horrific history of Microsoft in the years leading up to their merger with the NSA.

1.4 US Protects Microsoft Monopoly in trade for NSA Backdoor
This section describes the trial of Microsoft in 1998 that led to the ruling that Microsoft must be broken up – and how a sweetheart deal was arranged to allow the Microsoft Monopoly to continue – in trade for becoming a branch of the NSA.

1.1 Hidden Links between Microsoft and the NSA

> **"Big government and Big Business have morphed into Big Brother."**
> Bill Moyers June 10 2013

Whistleblower Edward Snowden reveals that Microsoft is helping the NSA spy on computer users

As I explained in the Preface, I had uncovered some disturbing facts about Windows 8 and was in the process of finishing a book about those problems when on June 6, 2013, a 29 year old computer analyst named Edward Snowden – who had worked for the US National Security Agency (NSA) for the past four years and had worked for the "US intelligence community" for the past eight years - released Top Secret evidence that Microsoft has been working with the NSA to spy on US and foreign citizens.
http://www.guardian.co.uk/world/2013/jun/06/us-tech-giants-nsa-data

EDWARD SNOWDEN
NSA Whistleblower

This is the truth. This is what is happening. This is an architecture of oppression. I don't want to live in a society that does these sorts of things. Edward Snowden June 6 2013

I understood immediately that the Snowden revelations were the missing piece of the puzzle I was trying to solve. They provided crucial answers to most of my remaining questions and confirmed answers I had already gotten. For example, one could argue that the reason for the open backdoor to the Windows operating system, created in 1998, was to reduce pirating of bootleg copies of the Windows operating system in China. It has long been known that 80% of all Windows programs used in China are not authorized by Microsoft. So it made sense that Microsoft would want to create a way to stop these illegal programs from working. I also learned that Microsoft had written the latest versions of UEFI and Secure Boot in about 2007.

On the surface, it might appear that the purpose of UEFI and Secure Boot was to control pirating of Microsoft programs in China. The trouble with this theory is that the Windows open back door, UEFI and Secure Boot did not work very well to control pirating. Both programs created many more problems than they solved. So why were they there?

The Snowden evidence (and in particular the Top Secret NSA slide presentation) revealed a completely different and much more sinister purpose to the open back door, the UEFI start program and the Secure Boot control program. It was pretty clear that the company Edward Snowden worked for in Hawaii was nothing but a front for the NSA which has an annual budget of over $8 billion. It is also clear that the purpose of the NSA office in Hawaii, and what Edward Snowden was doing in Hawaii, was to spy on the Chinese using the various tools of the PRISM program. What was less clear was the role that the Microsoft open back door played in all of this.

An important clue about Microsoft's involvement with the NSA is the NSA slide which indicates that Microsoft joined the PRISM program at its inception in 2007. The reason this is important is that 2007 is also the year that Microsoft took over the EFI computer startup program and changed its name to UEFI. Shortly thereafter, in 2008, Microsoft added the controversial "Secure Boot" feature to UEFI. The timeline and the purpose of the NSA PRISM program fit in exactly with the "features" of UEFI and Secure Boot. Could it be that the PRISM program was the hidden fist behind the UEFI and Secure Boot glove?

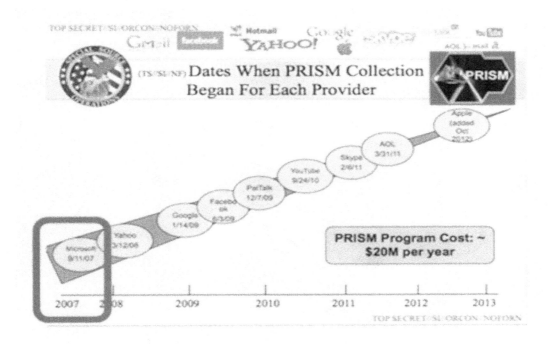

This NSA slide confirms that PRISM does not merely collect emails but can also go into a person's computer and collect stored data from the hard drive:

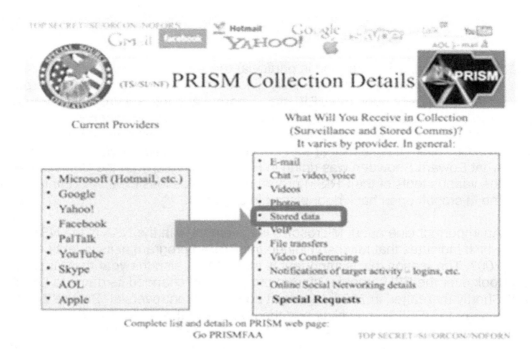

The fact that the NSA is able to gather stored data from the hard drives of computers means that the NSA possesses a "key" approved by Microsoft in order to access the files and programs inside of our computers through the Windows open back door. I had feared that people would say I was crazy to assert that Microsoft had given a key to allow the NSA access to Windows computers. The above slide was the proof I needed to support the research I had done linking Microsoft to the NSA before the Snowden revelations.

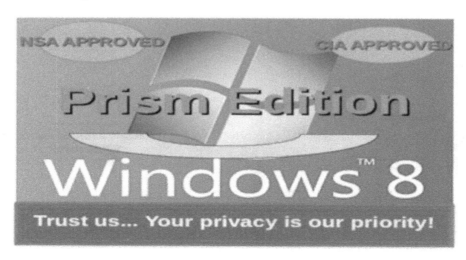

How the NSA downloads documents from Windows Computers
On July 31, 2013 Glenn Greenwald released documents provided by Edward Snowden on a top secret NSA program called Xkeyscore (aka XKS) which is used to download and store documents from your Windows computer. http://www.theguardian.com/world/interactive/2013/jul/31/nsa-xkeyscore-program-full-presentation

In 2008 Xkeyscore used over 700 servers at 150 sites around the world. This NSA mass surveillance program is much larger now.

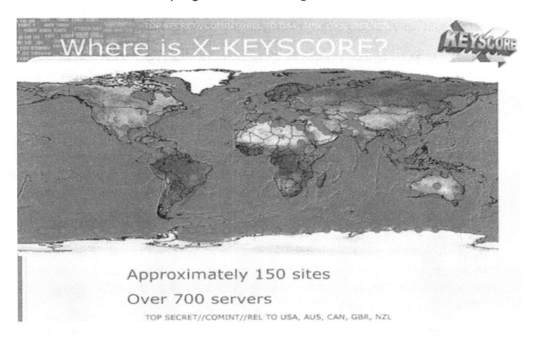

Hundreds of thousands of analysts – mostly working for private consulting firms - can download all of your data with no prior authorization required and no legal warrant from any court is required. How do they do this? First, the analyst opens the Xkeyscore database and clicks on a link called "show me exploitable machines."

This is narrowed down by country and then by other factors called selectors.

A top secret 2010 guide explains that analysts can begin surveillance on anyone by clicking a few simple pull-down menus designed to provide both legal and targeting justifications. Once options on the pull-down menus are selected, their target is marked for electronic surveillance and the analyst is able to review the content of their communications. A simple pull down menu called "Foreign Factors" allows any analyst without any supervision to click on a button and select one of a dozen reasons to target anyone. Once the analyst has the computers they want to target, they can search for all Word documents inside of the Windows computer. The documents are sorted by file names just as you see them when you are looking for files.

The Three Hop Rules includes Everyone in the US
However, the "Three Hop" rule revealed by the NSA at a Congressional hearing in July 2013 confirms that the NSA not only targets those outside of the US, but also those in contact with those outside of the US (the first hop) and those who are in contact with those who are in contact with those outside of the US (the second hop) and those who are in contact with those who are in contact with those who are outside of the US (the third hop). So if someone outside of the US "friends" a person who is a friend of a friend of yours on Facebook, you are added to the list of targets.

In addition, if you live within 100 miles of any US border, you are also a target as the "border" is loosely interpreted to be 100 miles deep! In short, the targets now include at least 99% of the US population. The opportunities to blackmail people and especially elected representatives (ala Hoover) are staggering. Another NSA whistleblower indicated that the NSA has targeted nearly every member of Congress.

NSA Surveillance
Did you hear about the three-hop rule?
"Think of it this way. Let's say the government suspects you are a terrorist and it has access to your Facebook account. If you're an American citizen, it can't do that currently (with certain exceptions—(though many people beg to differ))—but for the sake of argument. So all of your friends, that's one hop. Your friends' friends, whether you know them or not—two hops. Your friends' friends' friends, whoever they happen to be, are that third hop. That's a massive group of people that the NSA apparently considers fair game."
The Atlanticwire.com

Not only is everyone now under surveillance, but the data collected by the NSA is given to all kinds of groups... including private corporations!

NSA Blanket Spying on all Americans is Unconstitutional

The reason blanket searches of all Windows computers are illegal is that it is a clear violation of the 4th Amendment of the US Constitution – which requires a warrant before any single search can be made.

4th Amendment to the US Constitution... The right of the people to be secure in their persons, houses, papers, and effects, against unreasonable searches and seizures, shall not be violated, and no warrants shall issue, but upon probable cause, supported by oath or affirmation, and particularly describing the place to be searched and the persons or things to be seized.

The 4th Amendment in the Bill of Rights requires that a warrant describe the exact place to be searched, the exact persons or things to be seized as well as "probable cause" that a crime has been committed before a search is started.

Of course, the NSA claims that they did get a court warrant. Below is a copy.

FISA Kangaroo Court Automatic Search Warrant Form	? X
Effective Date of Warrant	September 11 2001 to whenever
Requesting Agencies	NSA, CIA, DHS and/or FBI
Group to be searched	The American People
Probable Cause	They might be terrorists
Places to be searched	All Windows Computers

TOP SECRET

OK   RUBBER STAMP NOW

In fact, in 2012, the government asked for 1,800 FISA warrants, including blanket warrants, and the court approved all of them. Sadly, the number of innocent Americans spied on was in the millions. So much for "judicial oversight."

When the Founding Fathers wrote the Fourth Amendment, they didn't intend for secret courts to approve secret searches based on secret testimony by secret witnesses with secret judgments resulting in secret sentences to secret prisons.

How long has Microsoft been secretly sending our data to the NSA?
The answer to this question came on June 10 2013 from an article published by Matthew Aid called "Inside the NSA Ultra Secret China Hacking Group" in the journal Foreign Policy. This article claims that a sub-group of the NSA called TAO has "successfully penetrated Chinese computer and telecommunications systems for **almost 15 years.**"
http://www.foreignpolicy.com/articles/2013/06/10/inside_the_nsa_s_ultra_secret_china_hacking_group?page=0,0

Matthew Aid has spent more than 25 years documenting the history of the NSA and in 2009 wrote a book called "The Secret Sentry: The Untold History of the National Security Agency."

"The Office of Tailored Access Operations, or TAO, has successfully penetrated Chinese computer and telecommunications systems for almost 15 years."

According to Matthew Aid's interviews with former NSA officials, TAO's mission includes hacking into Chinese computers and "stealing the data stored on the computer hard drives." This confirmed that TAO started in 1998 – shortly after Microsoft created the open back door to the Windows operating system.

One could look at the fact that Microsoft created an open back door in 1998 and TAO began hacking Chinese computers in 1998 as a remarkable coincidence. However, at exactly the same time, in 1998, a special key was added to the Windows operating system called **NSAKEY.** This code was discovered in 1999 after Microsoft programmers failed to remove it from a version of Windows.
http://www.washingtonsblog.com/2013/06/microsoft-programmed-in-nsa-backdoor-in-windows-by-1999.html

> According to Andrew Fernandez, chief scientist with Cryptonym of Morrisville North Carolina, the result of having the secret key inside your Windows operating system is that "it is tremendously easier for the NSA to load unauthorized security services on all copies of Microsoft Windows, and once these security services are loaded, they can effectively compromise your entire (Windows) operating system".

Back when the NSA Key was discovered in 1999, Microsoft claimed it was all an innocent mistake and that they were not giving the NSA access to the Windows operating system. However, the NSA slide show released by Edward Snowden in June 2013 makes it very clear that Microsoft has been directly involved with the NSA since at least 2007. In addition, if you read the history of the TAO, you will see example after example of how they were able to access the hard drives on computers in China and elsewhere beginning in 1998. It is obvious that TAO was able to accomplish what they did by using the Windows open back door and the NSA key to the Windows operating system.

Even if one believes that the Windows open back door and the NSA Key and the TAO program are all just a coincidence, there are dozens of other examples we will describe in this book which also indicate a hidden connection between Microsoft and the NSA. These hard to explain events include the continuing existence of the Microsoft Monopoly even after being found guilty of multiple violations of the Sherman Antitrust Act between 1996 to the present.

Another important example is the secret development of UEFI and Secure Boot – beginning with the start of the Prism program in 2007 and continuing to the present day. We will show that at roughly the same time, from 2007 to the present, Microsoft helped the NSA develop the Stuxnet and Flame viruses used to attack Iran.

In addition, Microsoft has been paid hundreds of millions of dollars to be the technical advisers to the Department of Homeland Security and recently received a $600 million dollar 3 year contract with the US Department of Defense.

What does DOD's Microsoft deal mean for federal IT?

The Defense Department and Microsoft have heralded their recently announced, $617 million joint enterprise licensing agreement as a game-changer in military IT. Like multiyear enterprise licensing agreements made by the individual military services in the past, the deal aims to offer more effective, efficient and agencywide access to Microsoft products. This time around, the agreement involves multiple components and was reached in an era of fiscal pressure.

The JELA, as Pentagon officials are calling it, reflects the increasing focus on enterprise IT and ongoing budget worries, officials say. But what does it mean for the way DOD leaders buy technology and for the broader federal IT market?

According to DOD officials, the agreement is more than a run-of-the-mill government IT buy. "Shrinking budgets, a determined cyber threat and a need for enhanced information security

Many other articles have confirmed this rather frightening relationship between Microsoft and the NSA - the world's largest software corporation and the world's most unethical spy agency in 2007 and again in 2009.

NSA, Microsoft Worked Together on Windows Vista Security

The U.S. agency best known for eavesdropping on telephone calls had a hand in the development of Microsoft's (MSFT) Vista operating system, Microsoft confirmed Tuesday.

The National Security Agency (NSA) stepped in to help Microsoft develop a configuration of its next-generation operating system that would meet U.S. Department of Defense (DoD) requirements, said NSA spokesman Ken White.

NSA Helping with Windows 7 Sec |

The National Security Agency is a life-long friend of Windows and Microsoft.

NPR reports that the National Security Agency (NSA) has been working with Microsoft to improve the security measures of Windows 7. The NSA has been involved with the new operating system since its inception, showing that the agency is committed to getting more involved with the private sector in regards to cybersecurity. The agency revealed its involvement yesterday during a hearing held in Washington.

The NSA Death Star of Data Bases... Ten times bigger than the Pentagon!
The scale of the data collected by the NSA with the cooperation of Microsoft has been incredible. In just the 30 day period between March 1 2013 and March 30 2013, the NSA collected 3 billion pieces of intelligence on more than one hundred million Americans. These revelations have made it clear that the purpose of the Microsoft back door to our computers is not merely to provide updates and hinder pirates – but also to assist the government in spying on us. It is obvious that the main purpose of Windows 8, UEFI and Secure Boot is to permit Microsoft and the NSA to gain an increasing level of control over all of our computers.

The World's Largest Spy Center being built in Utah...

The NSA Utah Spy Center is the world's largest, most expensive data storage center - linked to 20 listening posts in the US and more overseas. This NSA Utah data center is also linked to more than 70 Department of Homeland Security "Information Sharing Fusion Centers" in the US.

These fusion centers do the same thing as the NSA... spy on innocent people.

Intelligence gathering over time has added the formation of many public-private intelligence sharing partnerships. One of many joint NSA/corporate partnerships is the Domestic Security Alliance Council (DSAC). This group includes many large corporations such as Bank of America, Boeing, Google and Microsoft. In summary, the mission of the NSA and DHS has shifted from counter terrorism to the vague phrases "cyber warfare" and "all hazards." Data collected and stored by the NSA is not used merely to stop terrorists. In fact, much of it is used to put down peaceful political protests in the US (such as Occupy Wall Street) and create terror in other countries (such as China, Pakistan and Iran).

"These systems allow analysts to listen to whatever emails they want, whatever telephone calls, browsing histories, Microsoft Word documents. And it's all done with no need to go to a court, with no need to even get supervisor approval on the part of the analyst." Glenn Greenwald Opednews.com July 29 2013

Placing public security in the hands of private for profit corporations
The private spy firm Booz Allen, where Edward Snowden worked, is growing at an alarming rate. Their revenue (nearly all from the federal government) grew from one billion dollars per year in 2000 to five billion per year in 2010.

There are now actually commercial companies selling spying tools to allow you or anyone else to spy on your neighbors and start your own version of the NSA.

In should be obvious by now that the Windows operating system is not safe. But in the next section, we will look at why the Linux operating system is secure.

1.2 Why Linux is More Secure than Windows

> **"Comparing the security of Linux with that of Microsoft Windows is not very instructive. Microsoft has done such a terrible job with security that it is not really a fair comparison."**
> Bruce Schneier Open Source and Security 1999

My concern is not so much that Microsoft would shut down all of the Windows computers – but rather that a group of rogue hackers – or some rogue government - will use the vulnerability created by Microsoft to shut down all of the Windows computers - crashing the economy of the US or the entire world.

Warrant? You want to see my warrant? We don't need no stinking warrant... We got a key to your computer!

Given the Snowden revelations, you might wonder whether it is possible to free ourselves from mass surveillance by the NSA even if we switched from Microsoft to Linux. It is true that the NSA will still be able to monitor our internet and phone activity.

But in switching to Linux, the NSA will no longer be able to reach right inside of our computers. The NSA will not be able to copy data that is in our computers, they will no longer be able to look at our personal files and they will no longer have the power to shut down our computers or alter the programs in our computers. The primary reason Linux is more secure than Windows is because Linux does not have an open back door which allows anyone other than you to stop or modify your computer without your permission. So moving to Linux is at least a partial step in the right direction.

Open Source is a more secure developmental model
A second reason open source is more secure than Microsoft is that it is a bottom up, community driven development model rather than a top down corporate driven development model. Throughout history, very little innovation has come from the top down. The top mainly want to protect the status quo. They are set up to actively discourage change and innovation.

Meanwhile, open source is bottom up in that programmers are coming up with solutions for their own problems. They then share these solutions with others and the whole community benefits and moves forward in a rapid cycle of innovation – all due to a developmental model which encourages multiple points of view.

In a 2007 presentation sponsored by Google, Linus Torvalds, the originator of the Linux operating system, used the following diagram to illustrate the difference between open source and closed source program development:

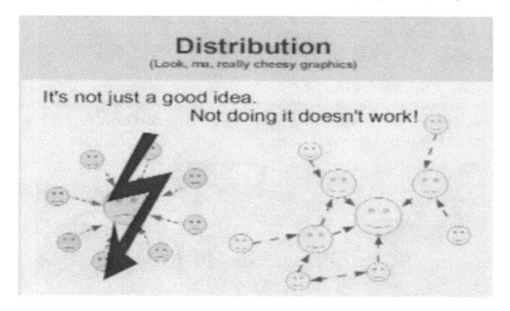

http://www.youtube.com/watch?v=4XpnKHJAok8

Linus explained that open source program development creates more branches to the tree which leads to more checks and balances, better decisions, more efficient merging of new ideas and a stronger, faster and more secure program. You build a better community by empowering everyone in the community.

A family is always stronger and more secure than any individual.

Open source programs like Linux do not have to worry about bloating their programs with complex code intended solely to maintain a monopoly. They are free to write simple codes that are easier to make compatible with other software and run faster in your computer. The result is that Linux uses eight different "security modules' which protect your computer from hacker attacks.

How the Linux Security System Works
The Linux operating system consists of a "core" which is surrounded by up to 8 security modules to which are attached dozens of application extensions like the Firefox Web Browser or the Libre Office Word Processing program.

8 different security modules or 8 walls to protect the Linux Core

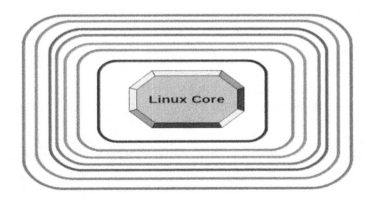

Even if a hacker is able to break through one of the security walls, they simply run into another security wall. Because different "families" of Linux operating systems uses different combinations of walls, the diversity of Linux operating systems makes it difficult for hackers to break into a Linux computer.

Doesn't Linux use a security system developed by the NSA?

In 2001, the NSA developed a security module which was eventually incorporated as one of 8 security modules available in the Linux core. This has been misreported in the press as indicating that the NSA somehow controls Linux. However, this module is simply a "permissions" system which has three levels of permissions to gain access to the Linux core. Moreover, it is only one of eight different security modules which protects the Linux operating system. It is nothing like the NSA Key which allows the NSA to directly access the Microsoft Windows operating system and change programs inside of your computer.

Security Competitions... Linux 2, Apple 0, Microsoft 0

There has only been a couple of official competitions comparing the security of Linux with Microsoft and Apple. The first was held at a Hackers conference called CanSecWest in 2008. The competition, called Pwn2Own, offered free computers and a cash prize to anyone who could hack into an Apple, Microsoft or Linux computer that was placed in public view at the conference. On the second day of the three day competition, one of the 400 attendees was able to crack the Mac security system – winning $20,000 and an Apple computer. On the third day, another hacker was able to crack the Microsoft computer – winning $10,000 and the Windows computer. No one was ever able to crack the Linux computer.

Linux triumphant: Chrome OS resists cracking attempts

Summary: Linux, once again, proved to be far more secure than most other operating systems as Google's Linux-based Chrome OS shrugged off its attackers at the $3.14-million Pwnium cracking competition.

 By Steven J. Vaughan-Nichols for Linux and Open Source | March 8, 2013 -- 16:11 GMT (08:11 PST)

This competition was repeated in March 2013 – but this time with over $3 million in prizes available. Both the Apple and Microsoft computers were hacked. But even with millions of dollars in prizes at stake, no one was successful in taking down the Linux-based Chrome OS. Linux remains the best choice for security-conscious desktop users. What is impressive about this result is that two different versions of Linux operating systems were able to withstand three days of highly motivated attacks of some of the world's best hackers. http://www.zdnet.com/linux-triumphant-chrome-os-resists-cracking-attempts-7000012331/

Why is Linux so much secure than Microsoft?
There are many problems with the Microsoft business model. One of them is that Microsoft wants (needs) access to your computer to make sure you are not using a pirated version of their software. They therefore allow programs to be changed or disabled without "root" access. One of the first steps in installing a Linux operating system on your computer is creating a unique password that only you know. This is called the "root" access password. Without this password, there is no way to add or change any of the programs. However, Windows programs can be installed or uninstalled without the consent of the administrator (that is you) and without any root password. This seems to be related to the Microsoft policy of keeping an open back door to your computer.

Community Security Development is Stronger than Top Down Security
Security development is much more robust in an open development model than in a closed secret model. Linux is safer because it is open source. On September 15, 1999, one of nation's leading security experts, Bruce Schneier wrote an important article, called Open Source and Security, which explains why open source programming will always result in a more secure system than closed source programming. Bruce uses the term "algorithm." You can think of this as being the passwords by which programmers protect programs from hackers. "Cryptographic" refers to processes for securing data such as encryption.

Before an algorithm can really be considered secure, it needs to be examined by many experts over the course of years. This argues very strongly for open source cryptographic algorithms... If an algorithm is only secure if it remains secret, then it will only be secure until someone reverse-engineers and publishes the algorithms.
Bruce Schneier Open Source and Security 1999

What Bruce points out in this article is that open source development provides more feedback to close the weaknesses in a security system. Bruce has written many books and articles on this subject since 1999 and I encourage you to visit his website and read some of them here: http://www.schneier.com/

The problem with the Microsoft model is that it is done in secrecy. There is very little feedback and no checks and balances. It therefore results in programs which are easily hacked. This is why I have maintained throughout this book that the entire Microsoft business model is fatally flawed. The Microsoft Monopoly model may make billions of dollars. But it results in extremely poor – and even dangerous - products such as Windows 8, UEFI and Secure Boot.

NSA Paying Foreign Governments to illegally spy on Americans

On July 31 2013, yet another Snowden release confirmed that the NSA pays GCHQ, the largest spy agency in Great Britain, $100 million per year to spy on US citizens as one more way to evade US laws against this practice. http://www.theguardian.com/uk-news/2013/aug/01/nsa-paid-gchq-spying-edward-snowden

How Corporations and Government Collude to Circumvent our Civil Rights

"There are two types of laws in the U.S., each designed to constrain a different type of power: constitutional law, which places limitations on government, and regulatory law, which constrains corporations. Historically, these two areas have largely remained separate, but today each group has learned how to use the others laws to bypass their own restrictions. The government uses corporations to get around its limits, and corporations use the government to get around their limits...Our elected officials are often supported, endorsed and funded by these corporations as well, setting up an incestuous relationship between corporations, lawmakers and the intelligence community. The losers are us, the people, who are left with no one to stand up for our interests."
Bruce Schneier July 31 2013
http://www.bloomberg.com/news/2013-07-31/the-public-private-surveillance-partnership.html

There are many more problems with Windows 8 which will cover in the next chapter. But hopefully you are getting the idea that Windows 8 is nothing at all like any previous version of Windows. It has been quite a wild year for anyone using Microsoft Windows. But from the signs of recent developments (described later in this book), things will only get worse in the coming year. Remember, you only have until April 2014 – less than one year - to figure out what you are going to do to replace your Windows XP operating system. And if you want to take back control over your computer, you have less time than that. So keep reading... and may the source be with you!

What's Next?
The next section begins with clarifying what an operating system is and then provides a brief history of what has happened to the Windows operating system and how we have gotten to where we are today. It is the part of the book I wrote before learning about the Snowden revelations on June 6, 2013.

1.3 Emergence of the Evil Empire

> **"We need to slaughter Novell (DR DOS) before they get stronger....If you're going to kill someone, there isn't much reason to get all worked up about it and angry. You just pull the trigger. Any discussions beforehand are a waste of time. We need to smile at Novell while we pull the trigger."**
> Microsoft senior manager, David Cole, sent out an email defining a plan to sabotage a competing operating system, DR DOS: September 30, 1991.

This is a book I never thought I would have to write. However, the fatal flaws of the new Windows 8 operating system (now known as Windows 8.1 Blue) and the UEFI – Secure Boot Start program - have compelled me to explain why the Linux operating system is a much safer and more reliable option. If an honest history of personal computers is ever written, the one year period from June 2012 to June 2013 will go down as a "turning point" in the change from the Windows commercial operating system to the Linux free open source operating system. In a later chapter, we will describe the advances made by Linux during the past year. But as great as these improvements have been, it would not have mattered without an even greater decline in the safety and function of the Windows operating system over the past year.

For nearly 20 years, I was a pretty loyal Microsoft Windows user. From 1985 to 2004, I was an Adult Education instructor at Bellevue College in Washington State – just a few miles from Microsoft corporate headquarters in Redmond Washington. More recently, I have taught courses in web design and computer programming at Seattle Community College. I also do web design and consulting for dozens of small business owners. Over the past 28 years, I have taught thousands of students – including hundreds of students who work at Microsoft. I was influenced by my own negative experiences with Windows 8 and Windows 8.1 Blue. But I am not writing this book based merely on those experiences, I am writing it based on my experiences with my thousands of students. I am certain that Windows 8 is so difficult to learn and use that many of my former students will never be able to get past the obstacles Windows 8 puts in their way. I want to provide my students and others like them with an easier, safer, less expensive and more reliable alternative.

My experience with Microsoft goes all the way back to floppy discs and the Microsoft Disc Operating System – also known as MS-DOS that were popular in the 1980's. I have also used nearly every version of Windows.

30 Years of Microsoft Hits & Misses.... 1983 to 2013

1983 MS-DOS	1985 Windows 1.0	1988 Windows 2.0	1990 Windows 3.0
MS DOS	WINDOWS	WINDOWS	Microsoft Windows
1992 Windows 3.1	1995 Windows 95	1998 Windows 98	1999 Windows 99
Microsoft Windows	Windows 95	Windows 98	Windows 99
2000 Windows ME	2001 Windows NT	2002 Windows XP	2003 Windows 2003
Windows Me	Windows NT	Windows	Windows 2003
2007 Windows Vista	2010 Windows 7	2012 Windows 8	2013 Windows 8.1
Windows Vista	Windows 7	Windows 8	Windows 8.1

I had a negative experience with Windows Vista. So I continued using Windows XP until Windows 7 came out. For the past four years, I have used Windows 7 with Office 2010. I use it 8 hours a day 6 days a week to write articles and build websites. So until the summer of 2012, I was a pretty typical and loyal Microsoft Windows user.

What is an operating system?

Operating systems are the foundation of every computer. They are the interface between computer hardware and computer software. They affect how fast your computer processes data and how organized the data is after it is processed. Operating systems also have a great effect on the appearance of your computer screen, how easy it is to use your computer and whether or not your computer will be safe from attacks from viruses and hackers.

There are three major types of operating systems for personal computers. The most common is the Windows operating system. The second most common is the Apple operating system. And the third most common is the Linux operating system (which includes the Google Chrome operating system).
Within the Windows operating system, there are several versions – with the two most popular being Windows XP and Windows 7. Currently over 600 million people use the Windows XP operating system and another 800 million use the Windows 7 operating system.

Both the Apple OS and the Google OS are related to or based on the free open source Linux operating system. In fact, the most popular laptop computer sold by Amazon, the Google Netbook is based on the Linux operating system. So millions of people are already using the Linux operating system– even if they don't know it!

A Brief History of Personal Computer Commercial Operating Systems
Much of the following history was taken from legal documents associated with several lawsuits including US v Microsoft (1994), Caldera versus Microsoft (1996), US v Microsoft (1997), US v Microsoft (1998) and Comes v Microsoft (2007). We cover the history of open source operating systems in Section 3. Here we cover how the Microsoft Monopoly was created by sabotage another much better commercial operating system. http://thismatter.com/articles/microsoft.htm
http://www.albion.com/microsoft/findings-1.html#pgfId-1031833
http://techrights.org/wiki/index.php/Petition_text_-_overview

See the book by Wendy Rohm called "The Microsoft File: The Secret Case Against Bill Gates," published by Random House, September 1998.
Also see:
http://news.bbc.co.uk/2/hi/science/nature/159742.stm
http://lists.essential.org/1998/am-info/msg04680.html
http://www.kickassgear.com/Articles/Microsoft.htm
http://online.wsj.com/article/SB904177645701365500.html
http://www.maxframe.com/DR/Info/fullstory/ca_sues_ms.html

1973 – 1993 Microsoft Dirty Tricks Destroy Doctor Dos
In 1942, Gary Kildall "the father of PC software" was born in Seattle Washington. In 1972, he graduated with a PHD in computer science from the University of Washington. One year later, in 1973, Gary developed a program called CP/M (Control Program for Microprocessors). This was the first operating program for personal computers. In 1976, Gary started a company called Digital Research, Inc to promote this new operating system which he called DR-DOS (Digital Research Disc Operating System).

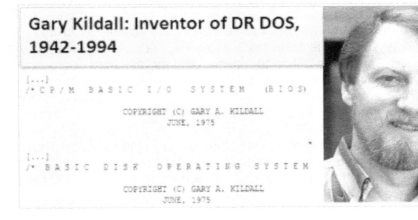

Gary Kildall: Inventor of DR DOS, 1942-1994

[...]
/* CP/M BASIC I/O SYSTEM (BIOS)
COPYRIGHT (C) GARY A. KILDALL
JUNE, 1975

[...]
/* BASIC DISK OPERATING SYSTEM
COPYRIGHT (C) GARY A. KILDALL
JUNE, 1975

CP/M (aka DR-DOS) quickly became the dominant personal computer operating system in the late 1970's and early 1980s –selling nearly one million copies. Gary also developed a system called BIOS (or Basic Input Output System) which he used to start DR DOS. BIOS is a program on a chip which is separate from the hard drive and is still used today to start most computers.

In November 1977, Bill Gates visited Gary Kildall and obtained a license to use CP/M for $50,000 in cash. In July 1980, IBM contacted Bill Gates because they needed an operating system for their newly planned personal computer. Gates supposedly told IBM to contact Kildall. However, IBM and Kildall were unable to agree on terms for a CP/M license. Some believe this was because IBM got a "better offer" from Bill Gates. Others believe the fix was in all along.

Three Reasons to Believe the IBM Deal with Microsoft was Rigged
Why would one of the world's most important companies - IBM – developing one of their most important products, the Personal Computer (aka the PC), make a deal to produce an operating system for the PC with a tiny software company that had never produced a single operating system? Some have pointed out that Bill Gates mother, Mary Gates, was good friends with IBM President John Opel and she asked him to meet with her son. While this is a nice story, it is not how major corporations do business. What is rarely pointed out is that Bill Gates Senior was a corporate attorney for technology based law firm. As such, he likely understood that IBM might face "monopoly" charges if they tried to control both the hardware and the software for the PC. IBM was under under a 1956 Consent Decree which in turn was based on a 1935 Sherman Antitrust Judgment against IBM. IBM was also litigating a 1969 Monopolization case against it – a case that was not resolved until 1982.

> "IBM had excluded competition in many ways, including by systematically acquiring control over potential competitors and patents made by others... The principal objects of the (consent) decree are to extirpate the practices that have caused monopolization and to restore workable competition in the market."
> http://www.justice.gov/atr/cases/f0800/0814.htm

With the US Justice Department hanging over their heads, who could IBM trust to help them control this new market? Not Gary Kildall – who was demanding over 10% of the sales price of the PC to use his operating system. Meanwhile, Bill Gates was willing to make a deal for less than one percent of the sales price. Never mind that the deal involved an operating system that Bill Gates did not even own! It seems that an inside deal was rigged all along to have Microsoft pirate Gary Kildall's operating system for IBM.

The basis for this theory is that in April 1980, a programmer named Tim Paterson with a company called Seattle Computer Products created a clone or mirror of CP/M which Tim called QDOS – which stood for Quick and Dirty Operating System.

In July 1980, Bill Gates Junior met secretly with IBM representatives to provide an operating system for a new computer which IBM had not even made yet. Then, on January 6, 1981, Microsoft paid $25,000 for the right to sub-license this system. Then on July 27, 1981, just before the public launch of the IBM PC, Microsoft bought QDOS outright from Paterson for $50,000.

Microsoft then gave IBM a license to use QDOS for free – but retained the right to charge IBM competitors for use of this new operating system. So MS-DOS began its monstrous life as a clone of DR-DOS – a pattern that Microsoft has continued with many of its other products. Gary Kildall was livid. He later said: *"Here we were, in good faith, in negotiations with IBM and they (Bill Gates and Microsoft) came in with a complete rip-off."*

In his autobiography, Kildall called MS-DOS "plain and simple theft" because its first 26 system calls worked exactly the same as DR DOS.

This history was described in a chapter of a 2004 book by Harold Evans called "They Made America: From the Stream Engine to the Search Engine.". Below is a quote from an article describing this book:

"Evans related how Paterson "[took] 'a ride on' Kildall's operating system, appropriated the 'look and feel' of [Kildall's] CP/M operating system, and copied much of his operating system interface from CP/M."
http://www.theregister.co.uk/2007/07/30/msdos_paternity_suit_resolved/

The Evans book led to a defamation lawsuit by Paterson – who claimed that his system was not the same as DR DOS. However, the federal judge in the case, Thomas Zilly, found in favor of Evans stating "truth is an absolute defense to a claim of defamation." The Judge also agreed that Paterson copied DR DOS, including the first 26 functions, although Paterson renamed several of these. For example, Kildall's "Read Sequential" function became "Sequential Read" in MS DOS while "Read Random" became "Random Read".

The IBM Personal Computer...introduced to the public on August 12 1981

For the first few years, the IBM PC initially came out to the public without any operating system. To settle a legal threat from Gary Kildall, IBM offered both MS DOS and DR DOS as options. But IBM priced MS DOS at $40 and DR DOS at $250 – leading to a big consumer preference for MS DOS. Despite the fact that IBM gave Microsoft a huge price advantage, use of DR DOS continued to be a significant factor as, due to several ongoing improvements made by Gary Kildall, DR DOS was a much better operating system than MS DOS.

1991 Microsoft uses Monopoly power to kill DR DOS
In the summer of 1991, Gary Kildall sold DR DOS to Novell, a manufacturer of high end servers and network systems. Microsoft recognized that this was a threat to their emerging monopoly and immediately tried to buy Novell. When Novell refused to be bought and instead appeared to be working out a deal with IBM to promote DR DOS instead of MS DOS, Microsoft responded in the fall of 1991 by sabotaging their own operating system. The goal of this sabotage was to fool manufacturers and developers into thinking that DR DOS was not reliable and was not compatible with the Microsoft operating system.

According to court documents in the Caldera v Microsoft 1996 lawsuit, here is how Microsoft managers carried out this plot:

First, contrary to standard industry practice, Microsoft refused to give Novell – or anyone doing business with Novell and DR DOS – a beta copy of their next version called Windows 3.1. Second, Microsoft falsely stated that they did not test DR DOS and thus could not insure it was compatible with Windows 3.1. Third, and most important, in December 1991, a Microsoft programmer named Aaron Reynolds inserted a secret encrypted code into the final Windows 3.1 beta – a marketing release for computer manufacturers, reviewers and developers – that triggered a fake error message whenever a computer was running DR DOS with Windows.

Microsoft sent out thousands of copies of this sabotaged Windows 3.1 beta program knowing it would cause reviewers and computer manufacturers to think there was a problem with DR DOS. This plot remained hidden until a lawsuit against Microsoft in 1996 by Caldera, which had bought DR DOS from Novell. Below is a summary of the evidence:

On September 27 1991, a senior manager at Microsoft, Brad Silverberg, sent an email to Jim Allchin, another manager at Microsoft with concerns about DR DOS:

"After IBM announces support for dr-dos at Comdex...my best hunch is that they will offer dr-dos as the preferred solution...they will also probably continue to offer msdos at $165 (drdos for $99). drdos has problems running windows today, and I assume will have more problems in the future."

In plain English, Microsoft was worried that IBM might be having second thoughts about giving too much power to Microsoft and had made a sweetheart deal with Novell to undercut Windows by offering DR DOS at a lower price than Windows. Strangely, at the time and contrary to the claim in the above email, DR DOS did not have any problems running Windows. But that was about to change.

Jim Allchin sent Brad Silverberg a reply email:

> "You should make sure it has problems in the future. :-)".

On September 30, 1991, another Microsoft senior manager, David Cole, sent out an email defining a plan to sabotage DR DOS:

> "We should surely crash the system... The approach we will take is to detect DR DOS 6 and refuse to load. The error message should be something like 'Invalid device driver interface."Maybe there are several very sophisticated checks so competitors get put on a treadmill... aaronr had some pretty wild ideas... The less people know about exactly what gets done the better."

Mr. Cole, Mr. Silverberg, and other Microsoft senior managers went on to discuss how they would conceal the sabotaging code from the press and hide these efforts from the public. The plan was to blame the problems on DR DOS.

In the next two months, Windows programmer, Aaron Reynolds, aka aaronr, did the dirty work of planting the secret cyber bomb inside of Windows 3.1 which was released to thousands of developers and computer manufacturers in December 1991. The damaging code was encrypted – the only lines of encrypted code in Windows 3.1. But the author of the code left one line unencrypted. That line was AARD – the letters Windows developer Aaron Reynolds used to tag his code.

The function of the encrypted code was a mystery until 1993 when software sleuth Andrew Schulman broke the code and discovered its true purpose. He wrote an article about it for Dr. Dobbs Journal. Mr. Schulman found that the code searched for two tiny differences between MS-DOS and DR-DOS, and when it discovered these differences, it froze the computer.

On February 10 1992, an internal Microsoft memo by Brad Silverberg that was released in the 1996 lawsuit explained the purpose of the malicious code:

> "What the guy is supposed to do is feel uncomfortable when he has bugs, suspect the problem is DR-DOS and go out and buy MS-DOS and not take the risk."

Later that year, Microsoft disabled the bug when it released Windows 3.1 to the public. However, by this point, the harm to the reputation of DR DOS had already been done. Sadly, the Microsoft sabotage plan convinced computer manufacturers to not ship DR DOS causing DR DOS sales to plummet.

At the 2006 Comes versus Microsoft trial, the plaintiffs introduced the following email from Microsoft Manager, Jim Allchin dated September 18 1993.

> "We need to slaughter Novell (DR DOS) before they get stronger....If you're going to kill someone, there isn't much reason to get all worked up about it and angry. You just pull the trigger. Any discussions beforehand are a waste of time. We need to smile at Novell while we pull the trigger."

The attorney for the 2006 Comes versus Microsoft case went on to say... "Microsoft is not just an aggressive competitor. It is a competitor who is willing to break the law to destroy competition. "

On July 11 1994, at the age of 52, Kildall suddenly died. It was reported that he "fell in a bar and hit his head." It was also reported that he "had a heart attack" but the autopsy was unable to determine the exact cause of death. Kildall was buried at Evergreen Washelli cemetery in North Seattle.

1993 Microsoft uses Monopoly power to kill Word Perfect
The next challenge to the Microsoft Monopoly was a word processor called Word Perfect – which until 1993 had a higher market share than Microsoft Word. One of the purposes for the constant model changes in Windows was to create incompatibility with Word Perfect. Novell, which owned Word Perfect, recently brought a lawsuit against Microsoft for this predatory practice.

As evidence that Microsoft used model changes to give Word and Office an advantage, Novell produced a 1994 email from Bill Gates that states:

> "I have decided that we should not publish these extensions. We should wait until we have a way to do a high level of integration that will be harder for likes of Notes, WordPerfect to achieve, and which will give Office a real advantage . . . We can't compete with Lotus and WordPerfect/Novell without this.".... Bill Gates 1994

The failure to publish the extensions meant that Word Perfect was not compatible with Windows 95 when it was released in 1995 – and that led to the death of Word Perfect as shown on the following chart:

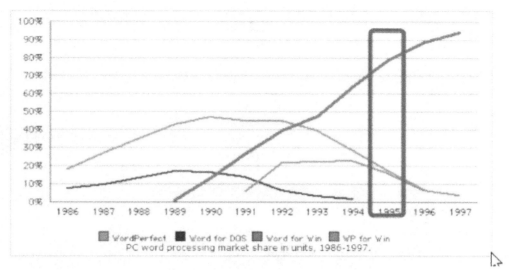

Market Share of Word Perfect versus Word 1986 to 1997
Graph from Stan Liebowitz, University of Texas at Dallas
http://lowendmac.com/musings/08mm/rise-of-microsoft-monopoly.html

1995 to 1998 Microsoft declares "war" on Netscape Navigator
In the early 1990's, Microsoft employed similar predatory tactics to eliminate competition from several other popular programs which competed with Office. But none of these attacks compared to what was coming next. In 1995, Microsoft began what was called the "Browser Wars" on a tiny company called Netscape. It was a bit like the US going to war against Grenada as it was not really a war at all. Rather it was more like a Mobster Hit against a small grocery store clerk.

Web browsers are used to help people navigate the internet. Today, the three most common web browsers are Microsoft Internet Explorer, Google Chrome and Mozilla Firefox – a web browser which used to be called Netscape Navigator. The internet began in 1992 and one year later, in 1993, the first graphical web browser for the general public was released by students at the University of Illinois. The web browser was called Mosaic.

In 1994, members of the Mosaic team formed a new company called Netscape, to produce a commercial version of Mosaic. In December 1994, Netscape introduced Navigator which quickly became very popular.

Microsoft did not introduce Internet Explorer until August 16 1995 with the release of Windows 95.

Between 1995 to1997, Microsoft waged an all-out war on Netscape which resulted in Internet Explorer becoming the dominant web browser – despite the fact that Navigator was much better in terms of accurately displaying websites:

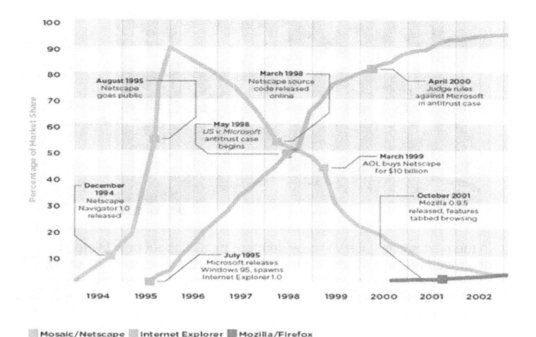

Mosaic/Netscape ▓ Internet Explorer ▓ Mozilla/Firefox

http://www.wired.com/special_multimedia/2008/mf_chrome_browserwars_1610

1996 Caldera versus Microsoft

On July 24, 1996, the new owner of DR DOS, called Caldera, sued Microsoft for illegal conduct which "destroyed competition in the computer software industry."

The 1996 Caldera lawsuit was based on the 1994 US government lawsuit which found that Microsoft exclusionary contracts violated federal laws. In the 1995 Microsoft consent decree, Microsoft agreed to stop its predatory practices – but continued to use them. The 1996 Caldera lawsuit called the federal consent decree "too little, too late...No single organization should have absolute power."

Caldera noted that DR-DOS sales doubled from $15 million in 1990 to $30 million in 1991. Its sales in the first quarter of 1992 soared again, to $15 million in just the first three months – an annualized rate of $60 million. But by the final quarter of 1992, DR DOS sales collapsed to just $1.4 million – an annualized rate of just $6 million - effectively destroying DR DOS.

The Caldera lawsuit also described a Microsoft misleading practice called "Vaporware." In May 1990 Microsoft issued a press release promising that MS DOS 5 would soon offer features similar to DR DOS 5. The actual MS DOS 5 was delivered in June 1991, a year after it was promised. Even then, it lacked the comparable features. Thus, the term vaporware meant promoting a software product which does not actually exist in order to maintain market share.

In the next section, we will provide more details about how Microsoft destroyed real innovators such as Netscape. But what must be understood is that this was not a competition with a level playing field among equals. It was blackmail and corruption intended to maintain the Microsoft monopoly with the Windows operating system.

MISSION (NOT) IMPOSSIBLE...
This computer will self-destruct on April 8 2014...Your mission, should you decide to accept it is to learn how to use free open source tools. You will not need to know computer programming. But you will have to click on a couple of buttons! You nation and your computer are counting on you...
Good luck... And may the source be with you!

The only good news is that Windows 8 is so bad and so difficult to use that it will finally open the door to customers demanding that manufacturers install Linux as an option on the computers that they sell.

1.4 US Protects Microsoft Monopoly in trade for NSA Backdoor

> **"Microsoft enjoys monopoly power"** and used that power to **"set the price of Windows substantially higher than that which would be charged in a competitive market — without losing so much business as to make the action unprofitable."**
> Judge Thomas Penfield Jackson November 1999 Findings of Fact

In this section, we will review the legal actions between Microsoft and the US Department of "Justice". These actions resulted in the US government protecting the Microsoft Monopoly – despite numerous violations of the Sherman Anti-trust Act - in trade for Microsoft giving the NSA a backdoor to the Windows operating system.

1994 US versus Microsoft (aka Microsoft Act I)

On July 15, 1994, just four days after the sudden death of Gary Kildall, the US Department of Justice (DOJ) sued Microsoft for its predatory actions in using its monopoly position to destroy DR DOS and Word Perfect. Sadly, the DOJ also worked out a 'sweetheart deal" Consent Decree with Microsoft. However, in February, 1995, trial court Judge Stanley Sporkin rejected the sweetheart deal. He found Microsoft guilty of violating several sections of the Sherman Antitrust Act and ordered Microsoft to stop requiring computer manufacturers to enter into straightjacket exclusionary contracts. Microsoft appealed claiming the judge was biased against them. In June 1995, the Court of Appeals reversed the trial court's decision, sided with Microsoft and replaced Judge Sporkin with Judge Thomas Penfield Jackson – who was instructed to sign the toothless sweetheart deal that Microsoft had worked out. This deal failed to punish Microsoft for past destructive actions – as long as they promised not to do it again! The ink wasn't yet dry on the agreement when Microsoft was again destroying competitors.

1997 US versus Microsoft (aka Microsoft Act II)

In 1997, the US Department of Justice sought to have Microsoft held in contempt for violating the 1995 Consent Decree – noting that Microsoft was using the same straightjacket exclusionary contracts to destroy Netscape as they had used to destroy DR DOS, Word Perfect and many other companies. Despite the Federal District Court's entry of a preliminary injunction on December 11, 1997, Microsoft publicly announced on December 15, 1997 that any computer maker that did not agree to license and distribute Internet Explorer could not obtain a license to use Microsoft's Windows operating system. Microsoft apparently knew that the "fix was in" and whatever the trial court decided would be overturned by the Court of Appeals. In early 1998. the Court of Appeals reversed the trial court and Microsoft was again free to do whatever it wanted.

1998 US versus Microsoft (aka Microsoft Act III)
On May 18, 1998, the tactics used by Microsoft to kill Netscape led to a lawsuit brought by twenty states against Microsoft. On November 5 1999, federal judge Thomas Penfield Jackson issued more than one hundred pages of findings. This summary of what Microsoft did to Netscape Navigator is a chilling account of the dangers of allowing any company to have monopoly power over any market.
http://www.justice.gov/atr/cases/f3800/msjudgex.htm

Bill Gates laughs and jokes while testifying at the US Versus Microsoft trial on August 27 1998

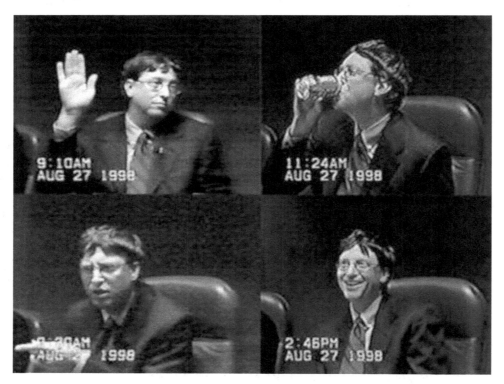

Did Bill already know that the "fix was in" regardless of what happened at this trial? Watch the video of his comments and decide for yourself.
Bill Gates was on the stand for about 6 hours. You can see the first three hours Bill Gates evading questions on Youtube from the following links:
http://www.youtube.com/watch?v=m_2m1qdqieE
http://www.youtube.com/watch?v=TyM7RpU6cHc
http://www.youtube.com/watch?v=8WSvNRnjr94
In the third video, Bill asks the attorney to define the word "definition."
For a quick overview of Bill's comments, see the following 5 minute video:
http://www.youtube.com/watch?v=eKcPx2jD5to

At the trial, Microsoft produced video tapes which it later had to admit had been falsified. During the trial, Intel Vice President, Steven McGeady quoted Microsoft Vice President Paul Maritz as stating that Microsoft's intention was to "cut off Netscape's air supply" by giving away a clone of Netscape Navigator for free. Driving Netscape out of business cost Microsoft hundreds of millions of dollars – and eventually even billions of dollars.

Netscape Revenue 1995 to 1998

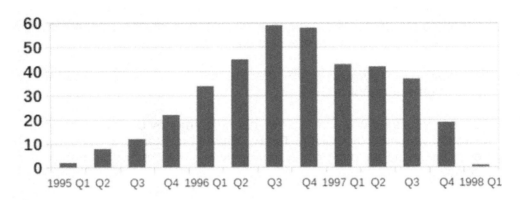

Netscape's air supply was their revenue. Microsoft was able to use their monopoly power to completely shut off Netscape's revenue in less than 3 years.
http://www.justice.gov/atr/cases/f1900/1999.htm

The judge found that "Microsoft enjoys monopoly power" and used that power to "set the price of Windows substantially higher than that which would be charged in a competitive market — without losing so much business as to make the action unprofitable." Microsoft then used the artificially inflated price of Windows to offset their huge losses on Internet Explorer. The court also found that Microsoft used variable pricing schemes to reward computer manufacturers who helped it maintain its monopoly and punish manufacturers who offered competing products.

The court also found that in the summer of 1995, Microsoft also placed obstacles in the path of Netscape in order to make it difficult for Netscape to develop a web browser which was compatible with Windows 95. In two meetings in June 1995, Microsoft openly warned Netscape leaders to not compete with Internet Explorer – using both threats and bribes.

When Netscape continued to develop Navigator, Microsoft withheld crucial information from Netscape for three months – until October 1995 – making it impossible for Netscape to make a browser compatible for Windows 95 until after the crucial Christmas buying season.

This was similar to the tactics Microsoft had used earlier to destroy DR DOS and WordPerfect. In addition, in violation of the 1994 Consent Decree, the court described in detail how Microsoft used their monopoly position along with a combination of bribery and blackmail to arrange "exclusive contracts" to use and promote Internet Explorer with 30 leading internet companies and the top 20 computer manufacturers. Interestingly, the combination of all of these exclusive contracts, sweetheart deals and blackmail schemes likely cost Microsoft billions of dollars.

An Important Question: Why did Microsoft spend billions to control the browser market?

The judge concluded that the reason Microsoft destroyed Netscape was to control the market for internet applications. However, this point of view does not make any sense for several reasons:

First of all, even today, 15 years after the trial, there is very little money to be made in browser applications.

Second, Netscape was not making that much money compared to what Microsoft was already making. Today, all web browsers are given away for free. Why would anyone want a monopoly in a market that did not make any money?

Third, browser development was undergoing rapid changes due to the ever changing nature of websites that the browsers needed to load. This rapid change is still going on today. The overhead cost of supporting browsers was and still is extremely high. So the browser market has huge costs and very little return on investment.

The judge thought that Microsoft simply wanted to maintain a monopoly on everything and that Netscape Navigator might at some point be able to compete with the Windows operating system. But this is nonsense because browsers are completely different from operating systems. It made sense for Microsoft to kill DR DOS because DR DOS was a direct threat to the Microsoft Windows monopoly. It also made sense for Microsoft to kill WordPerfect because WordPerfect was a direct threat to Microsoft's most profitable product – MS Office.

But it made no sense at all for Microsoft to spend hundreds of millions of dollars – even billions of dollars - and break numerous federal laws - in an effort to take over the browser market.

Why did Microsoft give up several extremely profitable monopolies in order to obtain an unprofitable monopoly?

One of the most puzzling aspects of Microsoft's actions in 1996 was their willingness to make deals with AOL in order to kill Netscape. On March 20, 1996, AOL entered into an exclusive partnership with its leading competitor Microsoft to promote Internet Explorer.

This was a deal which Bill Gates had strongly opposed just two months earlier in January 1996. So what changed between January and March of 1996?

> <u>Microsoft accorded AOL free desktop placement that undermined its own MSN.</u>
> The March 12 1996 agreement prohibited AOL from expressing or implying to subscribers or prospective subscribers that they could use Navigator with AOL. Nor did it allow AOL to include, on its default page or anywhere else, instructions telling subscribers how to reach the Navigator download site. In order to gain AOL's acceptance of these restrictions,

This deal is extremely unusual because Microsoft had also spent hundreds of millions of dollars building MSN – which was a direct competitor to AOL. Unlike the browser market, people were willing to pay hundreds of dollars per year for internet provider email service. Even a 5 year old could see that it would be much better to monopolize the internet provider market than to monopolize the browser market. Still, Microsoft agreed to promote AOL right on the Windows start screen in order to get AOL's agreement to promote Internet Explorer to their customers. Why either company would agree to promote their primary competitor in order to kill Netscape is a question which deserves to be looked at more closely. If this was only about monopolies and money, Microsoft never would have promoted AOL at the expense of MSN.

1997 Microsoft Blackmails Apple
Microsoft went even further in their quest to destroy Netscape by blackmailing their number one operating system competitor, Apple. From 1995 to 1996, Apple promoted Netscape by including it as the default web browser on every computer they sold. In early 1997, Microsoft threatened to discontinue the Apple version of Office unless Apple switched to the Internet Explorer web browser.

This would have cost Microsoft hundreds of millions of dollars, destroyed Apple and angered millions of Apple computer users – and certainly lead to an anti-trust lawsuit. Instead, in July 1997, Apple fired their President Gil Amelio, (who had opposed caving in to Microsoft), and replaced him with Steve Jobs – who promptly agreed to Microsoft's demands by switching from Netscape to Internet Explorer. Why would Microsoft endanger even their highly profitable Office monopoly to go after a market which made no money?

The next year, in March 1998, Steve Jobs terminated Apple's Open Doc program, making Apple even more dependent on MS Office. Why would Steve Jobs do such a thing less than one year after Bill Gates used MS Office to blackmail Apple into promoting a browser that Steve Jobs knew was inferior?

With Apple canceling Open Doc, Microsoft Office was left without substantial competition until the emergence of Open Office in October 2001. Meanwhile, Microsoft showed no interest in the emerging search engine market – which was soon taken over by Google. This was another highly profitable market. Why didn't Microsoft go after Google like they went after Netscape? Going after Netscape at the expense of these four other much more profitable markets would eventually cost Microsoft billions of dollars. So why did they do it? Why was Microsoft so motivated to destroy Netscape?

Why did AOL buy Netscape for $4 billion and then continue to promote Internet Explorer – essentially throwing away $4 billion?
On November 24, 1998, in an extremely surprising move, AOL purchased Netscape for over $4 billion in AOL stock. However, even after this purchase, AOL continued to promote Internet Explorer - over Netscape Navigator, a product which AOL now owned.
The claim was that AOL "needed its relationship with Microsoft." The fact is that Microsoft had brought in fewer than one million of AOL's ten million customers in 1998. The other nine million AOL got on its own. Adding Netscape as a market base and promoting Netscape would have given AOL millions more customers than they got from Microsoft. It therefore appears that the purpose of spending $4 billion to buy Netscape was to drive Netscape out of business – no matter the cost! Why did AOL do this? Certainly AOL had no interest in helping Microsoft achieve a browser monopoly... Or did they?

What caused Microsoft to change its mind about the importance of browsers?

In early 1995, Microsoft thought so little of the browser market that they had only 6 programmers working on Internet Explorer 1. By 1999, they had more than one thousand programmers working on Internet Explorer 4. In January 1996, Bill Gates was strongly opposed to making a deal with AOL. Then in March 1996, he suddenly changed his mind. What happened that caused this sudden change?

Why did Microsoft decide to place Internet Explorer inside of the Windows operating system?

This was even stranger than trading four highly profitable markets and spending a billion dollars on a worthless market. It is even stranger than AOL spending more than $4 billion on the same worthless product and then killing it. Beginning in 1997, Microsoft came up with a plan to put Internet Explorer right inside of its most important product – the Windows operating system. Up until this point, Internet Explorer had been a separate program from the Windows operating system. Installing Internet Explorer into the Windows operating system bordered on insanity for several reasons.

First, Windows is the most important part of the Microsoft monopoly. It is the foundation for the rest of the monopoly. Historically, the core of the operating system is kept separate from all other programs in order to protect the core. All other programs are added as modules to the core. Putting any optional coding in the core increases the file size of the core and slows down loading of the core and reduces the performance of the entire system.

Second, putting a web browser into the core places the entire operating system at risk from web based hacker attacks because it opens a back door which exposes the core to direct attack by hackers. Installing Internet Explorer in the core made it easier for malicious viruses to penetrate the system via Internet Explorer to infect non-browsing parts of the system. No one in their right mind would even consider doing this.

Third, placing Internet Explorer in the core created huge additional coding compatibility problems. Putting a complex web browser in the core jeopardized the stability of the operating system. Specifically, it increased the likelihood that a browser crash would cause the entire system to crash.

Fourth, putting Internet Explorer in the core of the Windows operating system also meant that users could not remove Internet Explorer without crashing the Windows operating system. Microsoft took this step despite numerous objections from their own computer manufacturers.

Fifth, merging Windows with Internet Explorer also meant that businesses who did not want their employees using the internet were denied a means of preventing employees from using the internet. Before this point, it was easy for employers to simply delete internet explorer from business computer.

But once Internet Explorer was placed inside of Windows, it could no longer be removed. So Microsoft offended computer manufacturers, and even their most important business customers just to get Internet Explorer in the core of the Windows operating system and thereby create an open back door. How strange is that?

Nevertheless, for the new version of Windows, code named Chicago and later named Windows 98, Internet Explorer 4 was placed in the core and released to the public on September 30 1998. Windows 98 was supposed to be released several months earlier so that computer makers would be able to take advantage of the Christmas selling season. But at great financial harm to Microsoft and computer manufacturers, Windows 98 was delayed for several months in order to place Internet Explorer 4 in the core. So this crazy integration decision was made even at the cost of putting Windows 98 out of the 1998 Christmas buying season.

In addition, Microsoft programmed Windows 98 to continue using Internet Explorer – even if the user tried to make Netscape Navigator the default browser! In particular, a new feature called Windows Updates required the use of Internet Explorer. These updates (the open back door) introduced even more security risks and privacy risks.

What was the real reason for this insane decision to put a web browser inside of the world's most common operating system?
Microsoft must have had a very important reason to take such huge risks. For years, I thought the reason they took all these crazy steps was to use the open back door to stop pirates from bootlegging Windows and Office. The problem with this theory is that the open back door did not actually stop or even slow down bootlegging. In addition, it did not explain what was about to happen next.

A Bonus Clue... The Monopoly Game is rigged in Microsoft's Favor
On April 3, 2000, Judge Thomas Penfield Jackson issued his conclusions of law, finding that Microsoft was a monopoly and had violated Sections 1 and 2 of the Sherman Antitrust Act. On June 7, 2000, Judge Jackson ordered a breakup of Microsoft. Microsoft would have had to be broken into two separate units, one to produce the operating system, and one to produce other software components such as Internet Explorer and Office. This would have prevented Microsoft from using a monopoly in some areas to create a monopoly in other areas.

Microsoft once again wins in the Court of Appeals!
Microsoft immediately appealed the decision. This is when things suddenly changed – and really got interesting. The federal court of appeals in Washington DC – the same group that had overturned the 1995 trial court and replaced Judge Sporkin (by claiming he was biased against Microsoft) with Judge Thomas Penfield Jackson - found that Judge Jackson was also biased against Microsoft.

They therefore remanded the decision to a new judge to determine a new penalty. Perhaps this is why Bill Gates was not worried during the trial. He knew the fix was in and whatever happened at the trial would be overturned on appeal.

There were many glaring problems with this decision by the Court of Appeals. Most important, the court of appeals did not find a single fault with any of Judge Jackson's Findings of Fact! Thus, there was no showing of either bias or harm. Things got even stranger after this. On September 6, 2001, just five days before 9/11 and the attack on the World Trade Center, the US Department of Justice announced that it was no longer seeking to break up Microsoft and would instead seek a lesser antitrust penalty. Microsoft then drafted a toothless settlement proposal. This was like allowing a bank robber to write up their own penalty.

Then on November 2, 2001, the Department of Justice reached an agreement with Microsoft to settle the case by basically accepting Microsoft's proposal – a proposal which meant next to nothing in the way of changes for Microsoft. A year later, on November 1, 2002, the new judge who had been appointed by the Court of Appeals, **Judge Kollar-Kotelly** accepted the proposed toothless settlement.

Judge Colleen Kollar-Kotelly first made fame in November 2002 by letting Microsoft walk – despite the trial court's ruling in 2000 that Microsoft was a monopoly which had repeatedly violated the Sherman Antitrust Act. Judge Kotelly just a few months earlier in May 2002 had been appointed Presiding Judge of the US FISA court. Judge Kotelly went on to grant Microsoft and the NSA nearly unlimited rights to spy on hundreds of millions of Americans.

Judge Colleen Kollar-Kotelly – The Judge from Microsoft and the NSA

To add insult to injury, Judge Kotelly put "Microsoft Board Members" in charge of monitoring the toothless agreement. Not surprisingly, these Microsoft Board Members have failed to find any further violations.

Nine states (California, Connecticut, Iowa, Florida, Kansas, Minnesota, Utah, Virginia and Massachusetts) did not agree with the settlement, arguing that it did not go far enough to curb Microsoft's anti-competitive business practices. They therefore appealed the decision. However, on June 30, 2004, the DC appeals court unanimously approved the settlement, rejecting objections that the sanctions were inadequate.

So after having three times been found to be in violation of the Sherman Antitrust Act (in 1994. 1997 and again in 1999), with over one hundred pages of Findings of Facts about criminal acts on the books against them, Microsoft was given a free ride. Microsoft could continue to use its monopoly power to destroy any potential competitor.

Andrew Chin, an antitrust law professor at the University of North Carolina at Chapel Hill, who had assisted Judge Jackson in writing the Findings of Fact, later wrote that the settlement gave Microsoft **"a special antitrust immunity.. under terms that destroy freedom and competition... Microsoft now enjoys illegitimately acquired monopoly power."** In a 2005 Wake Forest Law Review article, he wrote **"Judge Kotelly's final judgment more closely resembled articles of surrender than a negotiated treaty."**

Why did the Department of Justice and the Court of Appeals allow Microsoft to continue with their monopoly?

How does the game of Monopoly always end? It ends with one person getting a monopoly which they then use to take all of the money - while everyone else goes broke. This is why monopolies are illegal. It is because monopolies ALWAYS eventually destroy any economy and any society which allows them to continue unchecked. Today, 15 years after the Netscape trial, Bill Gates is the richest man in the world – with over $70 billion. At the same time, our economy is in shambles with record unemployment, and record home foreclosures - all while banks are robbing us blind. Our political system is in even worse shape with elections sold to the highest bidder. Corporation lobbyists are writing their own laws and there is a revolving door between greedy corporations and a corrupt government. How is this possible? Keep reading. It is about to get much worse.

May 2002 Judge Kotelly appointed Presiding Judge of the FISA Court

On May 19 2002 Chief Justice Rehnquist appointed Judge Kotelly to serve as Presiding Judge of the United States Foreign Intelligence Surveillance Court , which is a 7-year appointment. The FISA Court is the Court that oversees the conduct of the NSA. The Presiding Judge is the only judge on the eleven judge panel who is actually told what the NSA is doing.

2004 Corrupt Judge Colleen Kotelly secretly approves NSA spying

In October, 2001, George Bush issued a top secret order allowing the NSA to start a "warrantless" domestic spying program – in direct violation of the 4th Amendment. Bush asked phone companies and data companies to voluntarily comply. Almost all did. In March 2004, attorneys at the Justice Department become aware of what was going on and demanded it be stopped. In June 2004, the head of the NSA, General Hayden, held secret meetings with the head of the FISA court, Judge Kotelly to come up with a way to continue the President's Surveillance Program (or PSP) despite the objections of the Justice Department – who had the audacity to suggest that the NSA needed a "warrant" to spy on millions of innocent Americans.

On July 14, 2004, Judge Kotelly signed a "blanket warrant" allowing the NSA to spy on almost anyone. Her ruling was a secret not just to the public and Congress, but to all of Kotelly's ten fellow judges on the FISA court. On May 24, 2006, Judge Kotelly signed another order, this one authorizing the bulk collection of phone metadata from U.S. phone companies. Judge Kotelly gave both Microsoft and the NSA a free ride. What are the odds that something this shocking would happen by random chance?

> **"It is a kangaroo court with a rubber stamp."**
> Russell Tice, Former NSA Analyst referring to the FISA Court that approved all NSA warrants in 2012. June 6 2013

June 2013... An Answer Emerges

In June 2013, a whistleblower named Edward Snowden produced several Top Secret documents created by the National Security Agency (NSA) showing that the NSA was working with several corporations to spy on Americans. The lead corporation was Microsoft. Another cooperating corporation was AOL. One slide in particular told a very frightening story. The notes for the following slide state: "98 percent of the PRISM data is based on Yahoo, Google and Microsoft. According to this NSA training presentation, the data was taken "directly from the servers of these three companies."

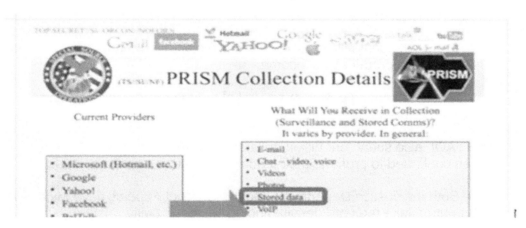

Other documents confirmed that these companies made modifications to their systems to allow all of their data to be accessed by the NSA.

> If the NSA targets an individual, it virtually take over that person's data "so the target's computer no longer belongs to him, it more or less belongs to the U.S. Government". Edward Snowden Interview June 2013

I looked at this NSA slide for a long time. Then I began to wonder about how long Microsoft had been involved in deals with the NSA. I also began to wonder about the "NSA KEY" which had been placed in the Windows operating system in 1998 and discovered in 1999.

I began to wonder why the Internet Explorer open back door had been placed in the Windows operating system despite all of the problems it created for Microsoft and continues to create for Microsoft. Could it be that Microsoft and AOL conspired with the NSA to take out Netscape Navigator? Why would the NSA want to take out Netscape?

Suddenly, it dawned on me that perhaps I had been looking at Microsoft's actions all wrong. Perhaps it was never about money. Perhaps it was about **something more important than money: control of the internet.** Specifically, it was about NSA control of the internet. Perhaps the NSA felt that control of the internet was too important to leave to a few college kids from the University of Illinois.

This was not about creating a financial monopoly. It was about **creating a political monopoly.** It sounds pretty crazy. But what other explanation is there? I decided to call this crazy theory the **Microsoft NSA Conspiracy Theory**. Many people won't believe this. But I am hoping they will at least think about it. I also decided to set up a website with an open public forum devoted to discussing this topic and any additional evidence that might emerge to support or refute this theory.

What I am hoping is that if you do not believe this theory, you will provide a reasonable alternate explanation for the following facts:

#1: Microsoft spent billions of dollars and violated numerous laws to control a market which produces no income.

#2: Microsoft made deals with several of their rivals to assist them in controlling this worthless market.

#3 : AOL also spent four billion dollars to control this worthless market – and then continued to promote their leading competitor's product.

#4: Both the Justice Department and the Court of Appeals gave Microsoft a Get out of Jail Free card despite finding Microsoft guilty.

The website is called **Microsoftnsaconspiracy.org**. I look forward to hearing your comments and suggestions!

Unlike the Supreme Court, the FISA court hears from only one side — the government. A single judge signs most surveillance orders, which totaled nearly 1,800 in 2012. None of the requests from the NSA were denied and none of the FISA court findings were ever made public. Congressional oversight has also been meaningless. The FISA court signs a one-paragraph form once a year stating that the NSA's process "contains the required elements."

As for the NSA, they now spy on 150 countries and have more than 700 server farms around the world. Seventy percent of the federal government's intelligence budget now goes to private contractors. Far from overseeing the agencies, members of Congress court them, hoping to obtain business for companies that contribute generously to their campaigns. Instead of protecting democracy, Microsoft and the NSA are destroying democracy.

As further proof that leaving the backdoor to the Windows operating system is a bad idea, in the next chapter, we will look at the harm it has inflicted on Microsoft customers in just the past year. Below is what will be left of the Bill of Rights if the NSA is allowed to continue spying on innocent Americans.

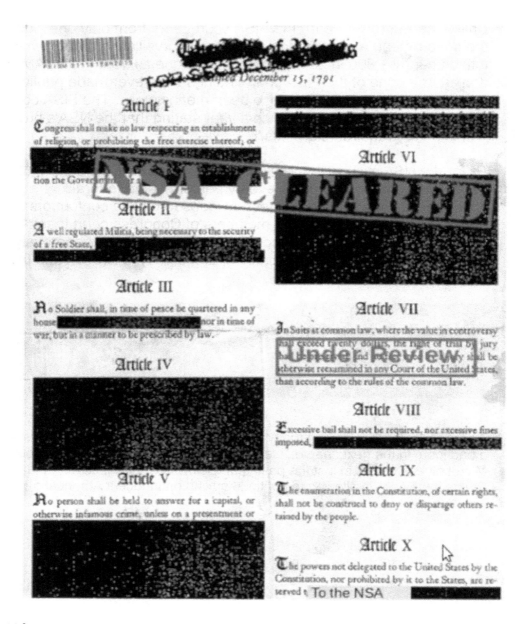

The Bill of Rights

TOP SECRET *Ratified December 15, 1791*

NSA CLEARED

Article I

Congress shall make no law respecting an establishment of religion, or prohibiting the free exercise thereof; or

▓▓▓▓▓▓▓▓▓▓▓▓▓▓▓

tion the Gover▓▓▓▓▓▓ or a

Article II

A well regulated Militia, being necessary to the security of a free State, ▓▓▓▓▓▓▓▓▓▓▓▓▓▓

Article III

No Soldier shall, in time of peace be quartered in any house ▓▓▓▓▓▓▓▓▓▓▓ nor in time of war, but in a manner to be prescribed by law.

Article IV

▓▓▓▓▓▓▓▓▓▓▓▓▓▓▓▓▓▓▓▓▓▓

Article V

No person shall be held to answer for a capital, or otherwise infamous crime, unless on a presentment or

▓▓▓▓▓▓▓▓▓▓▓▓▓▓▓▓▓▓▓▓▓

Article VI

▓▓▓▓▓▓▓▓▓▓▓▓▓▓▓▓▓▓▓▓▓

Article VII

In Suits at common law, where the value in controversy ~~shall exceed twenty dollars, the right of trial by~~ jury **Under Review** ~~and no fact tried by a jury shall be~~ otherwise reexamined in any Court of the United States, than according to the rules of the common law.

Article VIII

Excessive bail shall not be required, nor excessive fines imposed, ▓▓▓▓▓▓▓▓▓▓▓▓▓▓▓▓

Article IX

The enumeration in the Constitution, of certain rights, shall not be construed to deny or disparage others retained by the people.

Article X

The powers not delegated to the United States by the Constitution, nor prohibited by it to the States, are reserved : To the NSA ▓▓▓▓▓▓

What's Next?

In the next chapter, we will take a closer look at the consequences of Judge Kotelly's decision to let Microsoft continue with their predatory monopoly and her equally devastating decision to rubber stamp NSA spying on all Americans. Creating this twin headed monster – and allowing it to continue to exist – has caused far more damage than anyone could have ever imagined.

Chapter 2... Super Bugs, Cyber Wars, Disastrous Updates and Blackmail

This chapter summarizes the consequences of the merger of Microsoft with the NSA. Thanks to the "open backdoor" in the Windows operating system, any person or any business with a Windows computer is now faced with the ever present danger of super viruses and cyber warfare.

This chapter includes the following four sections:

2.1 Super Bugs and Cyber Wars
The section reviews how super bugs were created by the NSA to attack Iran – but then escaped into the wild and now are attacking Windows computers around the world.

2.2 The Flame Virus and Windows Update Disasters
On the first Tuesday of every month, Windows computer users are faced with a decision. Do I accept the Microsoft Updates and risk crashing my computer? Or do I take my chances with the hackers?

2.3 Microsoft Blackmail Warning: Upgrade or Die!
Microsoft has said that on April 8 2014, they will pull the plug on 600 million Windows XP users – because they want you to buy Windows 8. We will give you a better option.

2.4 UEFI: The Microsoft - NSA Kill Switch
Windows 8 comes with a new start program called UEFI – which includes a hidden kill switch controlled by Microsoft and the NSA.

2.1 Super Bugs and Cyber Wars

> **"Should we shut this thing down?"** Mr. Obama asked, according to members of the president's national security team who were in the room. Told it was unclear how much the Iranians knew about the code, and offered evidence that it was still causing havoc, Mr. Obama decided that the cyber attacks should proceed. - From a 2012 New York Times article about a top secret White House meeting in August 2010.

Should we shut this thing down?
This question should be asked about the relationship between Microsoft and the NSA. Instead, it was asked about the first major cyber attack in history – launched in 2009 and 2010 by the US against Iran – using the NSA open back door to the Windows operating system. In this chapter, we will look at the consequences of Judge Kotelly 2002 decision to allow the Microsoft Monopoly to continue combined with her 2004 decision to allow the NSA unlimited power to spy on all Americans. Because we will be getting into areas which some might think of as "conspiracy theories" we will first consider the question of whether our government ever lies to us. We will then look at how the NSA used the Windows open back door to develop "super bugs" to attack computers in Iran in 2009 – and what happened after these super bugs escaped and began infecting corporate computers around the world in 2010. There is substantial evidence that one of the NSA super bugs led directly to the world's worst environmental disaster – the BP Gulf Oil Spill. We will then review how these super bugs began taking down personal computers of millions of Windows users in 2012 – a problem which still exists today and is getting worse with every passing month.

Does our government ever lie to us?
On March 12 2013 at a Senate Intelligence Committee hearing, Oregon Senator Ron Wyden asked Director of National Intelligence James Clapper: "Does the NSA collect any type of data at all on millions or hundreds of millions of Americans?" Clapper, who was under oath committed perjury by saying "No Sir."

In June 2013, Clapper admitted he did not tell the truth and gave a series of excuses – claiming he responded in the "least untruthful manner." Nevertheless, for a public official to lie to Congress and the American people is a felony. At the very least, Clapper should have been fired. He should also spend some time in jail. If we cannot trust public officials to tell Congress the truth when they are under oath, why should we believe anything they tell us when they are not under oath? Sadly, this is not the only example of our government lying to us.

In the book "1984" George Orwell predicted that a fake "permanent war" would be used to manipulate people into accepting a loss of all of their freedoms. Could our own government be capable of spreading false information to manipulate the American people? We know that in the early 1960's, the CIA developed plans to attack targets in the US and then blame the attacks on Castro as a pretext for an invasion of Cuba. We also know that in 1964, the Gulf of Tonkin incident was faked in order to justify the Vietnam War. These are just a few of hundreds of examples of our government lying to us to maintain power. For more, read "**A Peoples History of the United States**" by Howard Zinn

Oil Wars, Shock Doctrine, and Weapons of Mass Distraction
The corporate controlled leaders of the US have long coveted the Iranian Oil Fields. In April 1953, the CIA spent millions of dollars to overthrow Iran's democratic elected Prime Minister, Mosaddegh and replace him with a puppet dictator- the evil Shah of Iran. In October 2002, this same CIA wrote a report called the National Intelligence Estimate, claiming that Iraq had "weapons of mass destruction." The source for this information turned out to be a con man and former Iraqi taxi cab driver with the code name "Curve Ball."

CORPORATE PRESS: WEAPONS OF MASS DISTRACTION

This fake "weapons of mass destruction" claim led to the Iraq War – costing trillions of dollars and killing over one million people – but allowing our corporations to take over the Iraqi Oil Fields. More recently, US corporations have taken over Libyan Oil Fields. But the real prize is still Iran.

In June 2008, Naomi Klein wrote a book called **The Shock Doctrine: The Rise of Disaster Capitalism.** In this book, she provides several examples of how the US government has used fear and fake disasters to manipulate the US public into supporting actions that were against their own best interests. Is the current Cyber War another example of disaster capitalism? Let's look at the facts.

Open Back Doors and Broken Windows
As we have covered in the previous chapter, the security problems for Windows actually started in September 1997 when Microsoft first came out with Internet Explorer 4. Unlike Internet Explorer 1, 2 and 3 (which were essentially copies of the Mosaic web browser), Internet Explorer 4 was directly tied into the Windows operating system. This open backdoor is how Microsoft delivers "automatic Windows security updates" whenever you are online.

In June, 2013, Edward Snowden released a series of Top Secret slides created by the NSA (National Security Agency) confirming that another purpose of the Windows open back door– and maybe even the main purpose of the open backdoor - is to spy on everyone. But when Microsoft left the backdoor to all of our computers open, this caused and still causes a huge security risk for all of us who own Windows computers. The risk is that Super Viruses will eventually be able to use the same backdoor used by Windows Updates and the NSA to get inside of our computers and cause all kinds of havoc.

2007 to 2010 NSA Develops Flame and Stuxnet Viruses to attack Iran
In May 2012, Russian cyber security experts discovered a super bug named **Flame** that they described as being the largest super bug ever built. Flame works by going through the Windows open back door and is capable of recording audio, video, screen shots, keyboard activity, network activity and altering programs and files on the Windows C drive. Flame is capable of wiping out a computer's hard drive using a module called Wiper to delete pictures, documents and programs.

On June 19, 2012, the Washington Post published an article claiming that the Flame virus was developed by the NSA "at least five years prior" - meaning about 2007. The plan started as a proposal by General Cartwright which was approved by George Bush in 2006. The code name for the secret project was Olympic Games and the purpose of Flame was to collect intelligence in preparation for a cyber attack on Iranian nuclear facilities. The Flame spying of Iranian computers began in 2007 and was used to provided detailed information on Iranian computers and facilities. The actual attack used a much smaller super bug called Stuxnet. The first attacks on Iran by Stuxnet began in June 2009 and grew larger in 2010 under Obama.

"Flame was designed to masquerade as a routine Microsoft Update." http://articles.washingtonpost.com/2012-06-19/world/35460741_1_stuxnet-computer-virus-malware

Unfortunately, according to a June 1, 2012 article in the New York Times, in the summer of 2010, the Flame virus broke free from Iran, got onto the internet and began attacking computer systems around the world. This led to a top secret meeting at the White House in August 2010 to address this problem.

"Should we shut this thing down?" Mr. Obama asked, according to members of the president's national security team who were in the room. Told it was unclear how much the Iranians knew about the code, and offered evidence that it was still causing havoc, Mr. Obama decided that the cyber attacks should proceed.

In March 2013, US Cyber Command and National Security Agency chief General Keith Alexander told Congress that 13 of his 40 Cyber Command teams are focused on "offensive operations." According to Edward Snowden, here is how the NSA plans and launches offensive cyber attacks on other nations:

Stage One: Intercept all data... more than two trillion intercepts per year.
Stage Two: Data Mining... through several trillion files of data.
Stage Three: Vulnerability Assessment.. Look for weakness in the cyber security of other countries in order to develop cyber sabotage plans.
Stage Four: Design & Implement Attacks on other countries. **Acts of War!**

On June 12, 2013, James Bamford posted an article on wired.com explaining how the NSA developed a super bug to bring down computers in Iran in 2010. http://www.wired.com/threatlevel/2013/06/general-keith-alexander-cyberwar/ "The cyber weapon that came to be known as **Stuxnet** was created and built by the NSA in partnership with the CIA and Israeli intelligence... Armed with that intelligence, network exploitation specialists then developed software implants...that mapped out a blueprint of the network and then secretly communicating the data back to the NSA."

Both the Stuxnet and Flame super bugs worked only on Microsoft Windows computers. The two bugs served different purposes. Flame was used to extract data about the Iranian networks and record conversations through computer microphones without the Iranians knowing they were being spied on. Stuxnet was used to take control of the Iranian computers and use them to attack crucial settings within the Iranian infrastructure. But with both viruses, clearly, the NSA was using the Windows back door and the Microsoft NSA Key to attack Iran.

Did Iran really launch a cyber war counter attack?
According to many articles in the US Press, there is a cyber war going on between the US and Iran. The US press and NSA claim that within two years of the Stuxnet attack by the NSA, the Iranians were able to copy the Flame super bug with their own super bug and send it back to infect computers in Saudi Arabia and the US.

In August 2012, a devastating virus was unleashed on Saudi Aramco, the giant Saudi state-owned energy company. The malware infected 30,000 computers – erasing three quarters of the company's stored data, destroying everything from documents to email to spreadsheets and leaving in their place an image of a burning American flag. Then a series of denial of service attacks took American's largest financial institutions offline in September through December 2012.

All of these recent cyber attacks have been blamed on Iran. However, there are three problems with this claim that the Iranians are attacking us. First, the Iranians strongly deny that they are attacking computers in the US or anywhere else. The Iranians know that any attack on US would lead to increased funding for the NSA to launch even more attacks on them. They would be entering a battle they could not possibly win. After all, the US military spends $1,000 billion per year while the Iranian military spends only $10 billion per year.

Second, the super virus being used is the less powerful Flame virus. As a consequence, every one of the cyber attacks has resulted in only minor damage to US computers. No blown up nuclear power plants. No destroyed hydroelectric dams. Not even a minor power outage. Just a series of headlines about how we are being attacked by the Iranians – and sales of tens of thousands of replacement Windows computers! If the attacks were really coming from Iran, why did they not use the Stuxnet virus – which is capable of causing much more harm than the Flame virus?

Third and most important, the Flame virus which attacked Saudi Arabia contained a section of code which referred to the Persian Gulf as the **"Arabian Gulf."** The term Arabian Gulf is used primarily by the US Military – never by the Iranians!

Since about 2009, various branches of the US armed forces have issued directives to their members to use the "Arabian Gulf" when operating in the area. https://en.wikipedia.org/wiki/Persian_Gulf_naming_dispute

In Iran, it is considered an insult to the long history of their country to refer to the Persian Gulf as the Arabian Gulf. A Saudi historian said "from a scientific and historical point of view, it has been called the Persian Gulf since Alexander the Great." The United Nations has ruled that only the name Persian Gulf should be used. Iran is so concerned about this name that it has banned airlines who do not use the term Persian Gulf when flying in Iranian air space. In May, 2012, Iran even threatened to sue Google Maps for failing to use the term "Persian Gulf."

Imagine if your worst enemy sent you a bad email which included a severe insult to your mother. You could copy the email and send it back to them. But would you leave the insult to your mother in the Reply email? No one would leave such a harmful insult in the code when it could easily be removed. Therefore, for all of the above reasons, it was not Iranians who attacked the Saudi Arabia computers.

How the NSA benefits from creating a Fake Cyberwar
Cyber War leads to increased funding for the NSA. If the NSA wants increased funding from Congress, the best way to get it is to scare Congress into believing that there is a cyber war going on. But there are other benefits. The attack on Saudi Arabia likely led to the sale of 30,000 more Windows computers. The fake Cyber War has also led the Saudis into seeking closer cooperation with the NSA. It also leads to huge business opportunities for NSA affiliated security firms as corporations rush to have their corporate data protected. Most of all, an atmosphere of Fear, Uncertainty and Doubt (FUD) creates political support in the US for expansion of the NSA surveillance programs. The NSA is the biggest benefactor of this fake cyber war (both financially and politically). This is why the NSA - with the cooperation of Microsoft - has created a surveillance monster.

One of the Top Secret documents released by Snowden was Presidential Policy Directive 20 – a memo from President Barack Obama directing U. S. intelligence agencies to draw up a list of targets for U.S. Cyber Attacks.

April 2010 BP Gulf Oil Spill is the Worst Environmental Disaster in History... Thanks in part to Microsoft Blue Screen of Death

At 11 pm EST on April 20, 2010, a date that will live in infamy, BP's Deepwater Horizon Oil Rig exploded killing 11 workers and spewing millions of gallons of toxic sludge into the Gulf of Mexico killing birds, fish and other wildlife from Louisiana to Florida. The spill took three months to contain and will take more than 30 years (if ever) to clean up. The economic loss, just to BP is over $42 billion and the actual cost to the American people and to the environment is beyond calculation. While companies such as Halliburton were blamed for an inadequate well seal, the real initial cause of the 2010 Gulf Oil Spill as been largely covered up by the corporate media. There is now no question that computer problems associated with the Microsoft Windows operating system were to blame. The only question now is whether the Flame virus – and by extension the NSA – were also to blame.

On July 23 2010, at a government hearing to determine the cause of the oil spill, the oil rig's chief electronic technician, Mike Williams – who miraculously survived the explosion – described the events leading up to the disaster. The full details of his testimony are listed on the following web page.
http://techrights.org/2010/10/12/deepwater-update/

Mike Williams testimony sounded exactly like what happens today whenever a Windows computer is attacked by the Flame Virus. According to Mr. Williams, for months, the computer system on the ill fated BP oil rig had been locking up, producing what the crew called the "blue screen of death." (Note: The Blue Screen of Death most commonly occurs on Windows computers after a faulty update). When the computers were down, the safety equipment did not work and the well could not be monitored.

Five weeks before the explosion, in March 2010, Mike Williams had been sent to the oil rig to fix the computer problem. Mike testified, "The computer screen would just turn blue. You'd have no data coming through."

Mike explained that with the computer frozen, the drillers did not have access to crucial data about what was going on in the well. Mr. Williams described the Windows computer system as "a very unstable platform" and "bad software" that was the root cause of most of the drilling problems. This buggy Windows based control system left drillers blind when it crashed daily and was responsible for safety system bypasses that eventually destroyed the well seal and led to the explosion. On page 42 of the hearing transcript, Mr. Williams stated:

> **"For three to four months we've had problems with this computer simply locking up. [sometimes it was a blue screen, sometimes a frozen display] … We had ordered replacement hard drives from the manufacturer. We had actually ordered an entire new system, new computers, new servers, new everything to upgrade it from the very obsolete operating system that it was using."**
> http://techrights.org/2010/10/12/deepwater-update/

Thus, according to Mr. Williams, the computer problems began in January 2010. Between the manufacturer and the rig, they could not get the bugs worked out of the new operating system. They couldn't get the old software to run correctly on the new operating system. Microsoft Updates – instead of fixing the problem actually made the problems worse.

Did the NSA created Flame virus play a role in the BP Gulf Oil Disaster?

In the following pages, we provide many examples of what happens when the Flame Virus leads to faulty Windows Updates. Having personally experienced this problem, it sounds to me like the wild Flame virus is exactly what caused the problem. We know that the Flame virus was first introduced in Iran in 2009. NSA officials did not notice it had escaped into the wild until the summer of 2010. But it is entirely possible that the Flame virus escaped into the wild as early as 2009. In support of this theory, Iranian computer programmers claimed that the Flame virus had attacked their OIL FIELD COMPUTERS in addition to their nuclear facility computers. "The (Flame) virus penetrated some fields – one of them was the oil sector," Gholam Reza Jalali, an Iranian military official told the country's state radio.

The 2010 Gulf Oil Spill has severely harmed not only the economy of the Gulf Coast – but also the entire US economy as the cost has been passed along to the American people in the form of higher gas prices.

The Microsoft- NSA open back door and the unstable Windows operating system was at least in part to blame for the worst environmental disaster in the history of the world. This is what happens when the world puts up with a computer monopoly and looks the other way as it becomes "partners" with the NSA.

The War on Terror...How many Americans are actually terrorists?
According to a 2004 report by the ACLU, the Department of Homeland Security forced Blue Cross of Michigan to do a detailed search of the records of 6 million of their members. There were 6,000 false positives – people the computer thought might be terrorists. However, after further research of all 6,000 people, the number of actual terrorists that were found were ZERO. So in my opinion, the odds of an American being an actual terrorist is less than the odds of being struck by lightening. It is certainly not worth sacrificing the US Constitution and the Privacy rights of all 300 million Americans. Al Qaeda appears to be simply a front for the CIA and CIA paid operatives. The ground to air missiles being used by these fake Al Qaeda groups were given to them by our own government.

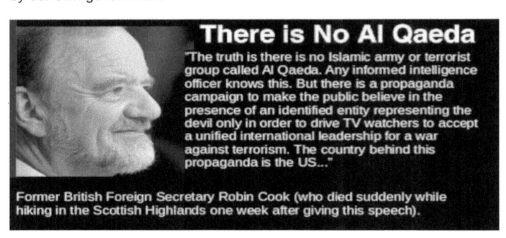

There is No Al Qaeda

"The truth is there is no Islamic army or terrorist group called Al Qaeda. Any informed intelligence officer knows this. But there is a propaganda campaign to make the public believe in the presence of an identified entity representing the devil only in order to drive TV watchers to accept a unified international leadership for a war against terrorism. The country behind this propaganda is the US..."

Former British Foreign Secretary Robin Cook (who died suddenly while hiking in the Scottish Highlands one week after giving this speech).

Now that we have linked the NSA – Microsoft connection to the Cyberwar and to the world's worst environmental disaster, in the next section, we will look at how the Windows back door has created havoc for millions of personal computers.

2.2 The Flame Virus and Windows Update Disasters

"Flame was designed to masquerade as a routine Microsoft Update."
http://articles.washingtonpost.com/2012-06-19/world/35460741_1_stuxnet-computer-virus-malware

June 2012: The Flame Super Virus creates an unsolvable security problem for every Microsoft PC
On June 2012, Microsoft issued a public warning that the Flame super virus was using "Microsoft Updates" to attack Windows computers in the US.

Imagine you are a hacker and you learn that Microsoft has created an open backdoor to every Microsoft PC in order to apply their updates and make sure you aren't using a bootleg copy of Windows. Wouldn't you want to go through this backdoor and see what is in the house? This is what happened with the spread of the Flame virus in the summer of 2012. Below is a summary of the Flame virus and how it works and what Microsoft is doing to try to control it.

The infamous Flame virus can infect Microsoft PCs by tricking them into believing its malicious payload is actually an update from Microsoft. Flame gains access to your computer by making copies of security certificates for Microsoft Updates.
Though they appear to be digitally signed by Microsoft, the certificates are actually cooked up by the people behind Flame, thereby tricking PCs into accepting them as legitimate. Microsoft revealed that the Flame virus can use the fake certificates to spoof Microsoft's own Windows Update service. As such, Windows PCs can receive an update that claims to be from Microsoft but is in fact a launcher for the malware.

Once infected, a PC thinks the file that loads Flame is actually a Windows Update from Microsoft. Flame uses a certificate that chains to the Microsoft Root Authority and improperly allows code signing. So when a Windows Update request is received, Flame provides a binary signed certificate that appears to belong to Microsoft. The unsuspecting PC then downloads and executes the binary file, believing it to be a legitimate Windows Update file. The binary is not the Flame virus itself but a loader for Flame – which then spies on the infected computer(s).

The Flame virus employs a man-in-the-middle attack to steal data, listen in on audio conversations, and take shots of screen activity. If this sounds a lot like what Edward Snowden says the NSA is doing, it is because it is. To try to control this super virus, Microsoft issued a series of Security Patches as described below. But these only made a bad situation much worse.

June 2012 Microsoft introduces a Jekyll and Hyde Monster of an operating system called Windows 8
Also in June 2012, Microsoft introduced a new operating system called Windows 8. One purpose of this new operating system is to make Windows more "mobile friendly." However, another lesser known purpose of Windows 8 is to add new security measures called UEFI and Secure Boot to combat pirates and bootleggers (and apparently to also increase the ability of the NSA to control computers in China and elsewhere).

We will discuss these security features and problems in greater detail in a later chapter. However, it is important to know that Windows 8 is radically different, not only from Windows 7, but also from any other operating system that has ever existed.

One of the many things that make Windows 8 so different is that it consists of two different operating systems that have been patched together. First, there is a new Metro operating system which controls many of the security functions in addition to the mobile functions. Second, there is a modified version of the Windows 7 Desktop operating system. The problem with trying to tie these two operating systems together is that Windows 8 has two of nearly everything – including two different control panels and two different versions of Internet Explorer. These different programs cause unexpected conflicts - which means that Windows 8 can be extremely unstable.

June 2012 Windows 8 Crashes during first Media Launch
This is why Windows 8 has been freezing up and crashing computers ever since the first day it was introduced on June 18, 2012 at a presentation in Los Angeles.

To see this problem in action, watch the following two minute video posted on June 19, 2012 and now seen by more than 3 million people: http://www.youtube.com/watch?v=N1zxDa3t0fg

Windows 8 freezes in its first introduction to the world.

During the official presentation of the new Microsoft Surface tablet, former Windows Vice President Steven Sinofsky opens up the Metro version of Internet Explorer – using the new Windows 8 operating system - and the system froze. Not even repeatedly jabbing on the device's home button - the touch-sensitive area with the Windows logo on the long side of the tablet - would bring the tablet back to life. Ironically, the line Sinofsky had to deliver while holding the dead tablet was "I can browse smoothly."

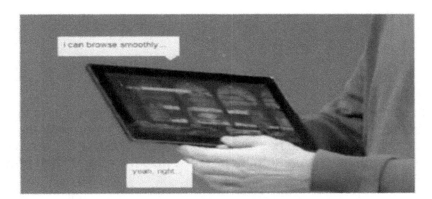

This public demonstration of the instability of Windows 8 should have been a warning to all of us. The public launch - when sales of Windows 8 would officially begin - was originally scheduled for September 2012. It was delayed until the end of October in a last ditch effort to resolve the major problems before selling Windows 8 to the public. But even in November, there were widespread reports on public forums of Windows 8 crashing computers (including my own computer). On November 12 2012, the head of Microsoft, Steven Ballmer, announced that that Windows chief executive, Steven Sinofsky, was leaving Microsoft for unspecified reasons.

August 2012 the Flame Super Virus Continues to Spread

By August 2012, the Flame virus had spread from industrial and oil rig computers to personal computers. The most worrisome thing about these super viruses is how they get into our computers in the first place. They enter via an "official" update to the Windows operating system. A user thinks they are simply downloading a legitimate patch from Microsoft, only to install Flame instead. Flame spreading through Windows updates is more significant than Flame itself. My first personal experience with the Flame virus began with the August 2012 automatic update from Microsoft. At the time, the media claimed that the Flame virus only infected a few hundred computers and was part of a "cyber war" trying to stop the Iranians from developing nuclear weapons. Supposedly, in order to put a monkey wrench in Iranian computers, our own government created the Flame Super Bug. However, once in the wild, Flame quickly began infecting millions of computers – including my own. It took me many months to get rid of this virus.

Patch Tuesday Updates turn into Black Tuesday Nightmares

As most Windows XP and Windows 7 users know, Microsoft releases updates and security patches on the second Tuesday of every month. This was originally known as Update Tuesday or Patch Tuesday.

But because some of these patches have caused millions of computers to crash (due to unforeseen compatibility problems with other programs), the second Tuesday of every month has also become known as Black Tuesday – where Windows computer users around the world hold their breath and pray as they push the update button.

Patch Tuesday is often followed by Crash Wednesday

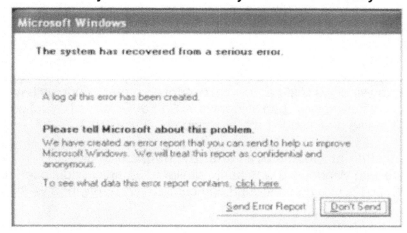

August 2012 was a really bad month for Microsoft, including security problems in a common controls library (this is the library associated with the Internet Explorer open back door). The issue is that when the computer downloads a Windows Update and has to restart to configure, the configuration fails and you get a message stating "reverting configuration", then windows restarts. After restarting, the configuring windows message appears again and fails again hence you get stuck in a never ending loop.

September 2012 Hacker Gang boasts of unlimited supply of super viruses
On September 7, 2012, Computer World published a rather frightening article explaining that an elite hacker gang called Elderwood had exploited eight Internet Explorer (open back door) flaws and were planning on attacking many more.
http://www.computerworld.com/s/article/9231051/Elite_hacker_gang_has_unli mited_supply_of_zero_day_bugs

November 2012 The Stuxnet Super Virus Spreads to large corporations
In November 2012, Chevron admitted that it had become the first US corporation to have a similar virus called Stuxnet infect its computers. While Stuxnet was meant to destroy things, Flame was designed to spy on people. In addition, the open door super viruses continued to plague personal computers as is shown by the following blog post from November 19, 2012.

"I think I got the flame virus (Windows 7). I have been onto the Microsoft support page and followed various "cures" all to no avail. I have been into control panel and gone through the windows troubleshooting advice and it tells me that it has found and fixed problems with my Windows update and installed 9 updates. When I click to restart I get the same failure message. It seems to recycle the startup procedure 3 times before it eventually gets to my desktop page, and when I look at my update history there is a long list of failed installations."

November 2012 Microsoft Public Launch of Windows 8

In late October 2012, Microsoft came out with an offer where we could "upgrade" from Windows 7 to Windows 8 for only $40. But because my computer is so important to my work, I wanted to try Windows 8 out on a trial basis before I made the leap. My caution was based in part on my negative experience with Windows Vista and in part on the fact that Windows 8 worked in a completely different way than Windows 7. So I downloaded a trial version of Windows 8. I also downloaded a trial version of Office 2013.

Windows 8 is still not reliable even after the public launch

My experience with Windows 8 was eerily similar to an article published on November 20, 2012: http://tech.fortune.cnn.com/2012/11/20/windows-8-killed-my-pc/

Below is a quote from this article:

"I'm not the first person to have issues migrating from Windows 7 to Windows 8. A number of users have taken to social media outlets like Twitter and Facebook to vent their frustration. Many report that their systems have completely crashed as a result of the upgrade... The Microsoft engineers told me the issues I was having were unique and would probably only impact PC users who have the exact same configuration as my computer, which they estimated to be around 200,000 computers. I found it hard to believe that the world's largest chip maker, Intel, and the world's largest PC manufacturer, Lenovo, had anything on the market today that couldn't talk with Windows 8 – that would be ridiculous, right? If Microsoft doesn't get its act together, it could soon face a revolt that could put the company on the path to technological irrelevance."

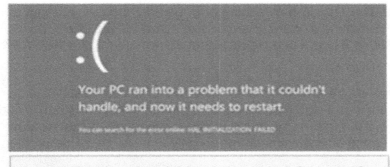

Windows 8 Blue Screen of Death

Black Tuesday Updates merge with Windows 8 problems

Beginning in December 2012, Black Tuesday disasters became more frequent.

On Black Tuesday in December 2012, the monthly Windows updates again crashed my computer – along with millions of other computers around the world. My computer was still suffering from the deadly August 2012 Windows Super Virus (Flame) update and I assumed this was the underlying problem. However, with every monthly Windows Update since, my computer has grown progressively more ill. The following comments were posted on a forum along with dozens of reports of Microsoft users complaining that the December 2012 update crashed their computers:

> "Windows update is telling me there is ONE more update MS12-078 – Critical must be downloaded and installed. I am terrified about doing that and restarting the machine, rather wait for Mayan prophecy to prove itself true this Friday but if there will be no end of this world, what shall I do to prevent Windows from crashing my computer and ending my world?"
>
> "Windows recently installed new patches. Upon reboot (I was sleeping and never saw it, I am now stuck in Windows update" configuration hell. The computer just reboots over and over (even after I try to get it into safe mode) and I get the error message that windows "update did not configure properly. Windows is reverting to last configuration." I cannot get past this. I am stuck in this never ending nightmare."

Black Tuesday Problems continue in January 2013

On January 8 2013, Microsoft released patches for 12 vulnerabilities in Windows, but did not come up with a fix for the Internet Explorer (IE) bug that cyber criminals have been exploiting for at least a month. That vulnerability was one of several exploited by an elite hacker group "Elderwood."

Below are just a few of the hundreds of posts about Windows updates crashing computers in January 2013.

"I am SCREWED!!! The darn machine performed an update overnight and now I can't get anything to work. Every single screen FREEZES!!! I have conference calls in 2 hours and I cannot prepare for anything. THE WORST update ever."

"Hopefully there will be a fix for this 'fix'. I need the folks at MSOFT to do something about it and fast. Updates are supposed to help, not hurt. Tried a system restore. But then my system goes and uploads the latest window update when I go to shut the system down only to have the same problem again."

Microsoft doesn't seem to be listening!

"Any suggestions to those of us who are stuck in this reboot cycle? I've tried everything and the problem seems to be getting worse. This latest update has rendered my desktop unusable! I keep getting a blue screen of death.

"Yesterday morning OMG Windows managed to get through the "let me decide what to install" and decided for me! My computer is now dead for good."

"My computer tried to patch Windows 8... but that crashed my computer. After that, it failed to reboot. Further checking revealed my hard drive died. So much for my new Windows 8 computer! No wonder PC sales are down!"

"Frankly I doubt hackers could do as much damage as Microsoft did with this poorly written update … I'll take my chances with the Hackers. I'll let some other Poor Saps be Microsoft's unpaid Beta Update Testers …"

"Well, add me to the list. I have a HP with Windows 8 I got it for Christmas. At first, it worked great!! Then I kept getting the blue screen of death and it says to go online. When I try to go online, a few seconds later my computer goes blue screen of death again! (Sent from my IPAD because I can't use my computer)."

The updates have completely ruined both my mother's and my boyfriend's PCs. WELL DONE MICROSOFT!!! Now we all need new computers."

"After updating last night automatically, my whole Windows 8 system is screwed up. Start screen is glitched permanently, with the tiles showing the wrong image, the charm bar doesn't even show any icons, and the volume bar has completely disappeared. I've restarted multiple times, no dice. My new computer is dead in the water. **I am seriously considering switching to Linux because Windows 8 simply does not work."**

This is what happens to computers once their operating system stops working!

"I have had several updates sitting in the queue, but was reluctant to install after the update in December caused me to pay $150 in computer recovery fees. But the system was running so poorly, I finally gave in and attempted install of a few updates last night. I have experienced no less than 10 blue screen of death events since. I have started in safe mode and attempted several restores. There are still 16 "critical" updates uninstalled and I am not willing to try them again."

Blue Screen of Death at an airport

In March, 2013, the Windows updates went from bad to worse

"Personally I have suffered at the hands of the ill-conceived Microsoft Software Empire for too many years. This latest upgrade from Windows 7 to Windows 8 is horrendous. It brought my computer to a crawl. Rebooted several times and even had to conduct a hard reboot. I have removed the Windows patches. Still my computer won't work."

Microsoft "recalls" a patch after it does more harm than good

In February, 2013, Microsoft issued Windows Security Update KB2823324 that addressed a vulnerability that an attacker can exploit. If you were gullible enough to install this update on Black Tuesday in February, Microsoft advised you in an obscure security blog post on April 12 2013 that you should manually uninstall the patch *whether your machine got toasted or not. There's a fair chance the patch will send your computer into an endless cycle of the Blue Screen of Death.*

Microsoft said that users should uninstall this security update because it caused "system errors." Microsoft has not specified exactly what "system errors" are being caused by this update. But according to numerous reports, the April 2013 update is causing more than errors — many computers are unable to boot because of it!

Below are some forum posts on the April 2013 Windows Update.

"April 2013 update ruined my pc, now it won't boot correctly, won't restore from ANY restore points. I have wasted 2 days on this and I am thoroughly pissed. Posted from my iPod: nothing else works on any of my windows pc's! "

"Patch Tuesday always sends me into a cold sweat. I have read so many horror stories attributing to the updates. Trouble is you feel compelled to install them! The April 2013 Patch Tuesday was a disaster for my computer. The computer was working normally until I tried to boot it this morning. It will boot OK to a normal looking screen, but then the screen gets display glitches, and neither the mouse nor the keyboard will work after that. I tried multiple reboots and different system restore points, but none of them will fix the problem. Pray for me."

"April 2013 update has been an absolute flop. Came into the room to find my PC shutting down. Logged in and nothing but application errors. Everything on startup died. None of my office suite loads! This is an absolute joke. Never again will I install a Windows update. **Linux is looking better all the time.**"

This was the second time in two months that Microsoft had to pull a bad security patch. http://www.infoworld.com/t/microsoft-windows/microsoft-withdraws-kb-2823324-second-botched-automatic-update-year-216325

Then, at the end of April 2013, a United States Department of Labor website was hacked. Clicking on the site caused a computer running Windows with Internet Explorer 8 to download malicious software. The super virus takes advantage of a "remote code execution flaw" in Internet Explorer..

May 2013 Microsoft issues Mega Update... 31,000 updates in a single day!

May 2013... Microsoft issues first ever Mega Update!

I will never forget the May 14 2013 Windows Update. On Black Tuesday in May 2013, Microsoft unleashed their most ridiculous update ever. While the press claimed that there were only 33 updates, anyone with a Microsoft computer knew better. I was stunned by the notice on my screen which stated that there were **more than 31,000 updates being installed on my computer.**

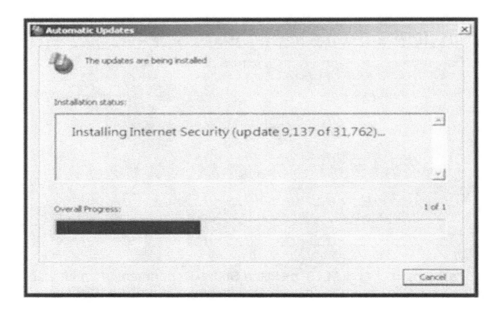

> Why have there been so many disastrous Windows updates in the past few months? It is as if Microsoft is deliberately sabotaging all of our computers to force us all to upgrade to Windows 8. Or is it just the open back door?

The urgency of finishing the Linux book became even more apparent as the problems with Microsoft seem to be getting worse over time. After the May update, I turned off Windows updates to prevent any further damage to my computer. But I knew this was not a long term solution because over time, my own computer would become more vulnerable to attack. This is because Windows has a fundamental security flaw. In order to leave it open to Microsoft updates – the same door is also open to hackers – and there is no way to really close it even if you turn off updates. Now I was rushing to finish the book on Linux in order to protect my own computer!

June 2013 Another Patch Tuesday causes more crashed computers
The June 11 2013 updates included a patch of its certificate handling infrastructure and patches for code which could allow information disclosure, denial of service and remote code execution. Another patch fixed 18 flaws in Internet Explorer. All had the tag "Exploit code likely," indicating some very serious problems. Here are a few June forum posts from pcsupport.about.com:

> "The computer updated automatically installing these patches. Then it won't start even after 5 attempts of auto repair. It tells me the PC cannot start because of a patch. Luckily I have installed Linux in case Windows does not work."
>
> "The latest MicroSuck update has completely crashed my laptop. Thankfully I run Linux on my two pcs. MS 7 is being wiped off my laptop as I type."
>
> "This update this morning wiped my PC! I lost all the folders that were on my desktop including thousands of pictures of my children! Can anyone help me?"
>
> "I did the June update and shut my computer down and I lost data that was on my computer after the restart. I am furious. I am sick and tired of this."
>
> "I had the same problem. I used Linux Mint 15 live CD to save my files to an external Hard Drive."
>
> "The first time I encountered this "Microsoft-approved virus" called Internet Explorer 10 update it broke my updater AND caused my system to slow down by about 20X so I called MS and had to pay $99. What a waste! They did nothing. Now every time I go to bed my system tries to reinstall this virus and breaks everything. It's beyond obnoxious that it keeps screwing up my system (with a half hour shutdown and lengthy boot up just to unsuccessfully retry the update), it's totally hopeless that it CALLS THIS SCREWED-UP STATE A SUCCESSFUL UPDATE!"

May 2013 Cyber attacks against US corporations on the rise.
According to the New York Times, a new wave of cyber attacks is striking American corporations, prompting warnings from federal officials, including a vague one issued by the Department of Homeland Security. This time, officials say, the attackers' aim is not espionage but sabotage, and the source seems to be in the Middle East. The targets have primarily been energy companies, and the attacks appeared to be probes, looking for ways to seize control of their processing systems. The attacks are continuing. The Department of Homeland Security said it needs to expand its cyber security force by 600 hacking specialists to keep pace with the rising number of threats.

June 2013 Whistleblower Edward Snowden reveals Microsoft is working with NSA to spy on Windows computer users
Reading the Top Secret reports released by Edward Snowden sent chills down my spine. I had just completed studying the new Windows Startup program called UEFI with Secure Boot and I was just about finished writing this book to expose this major scandal. However, Edward Snowden helped me understand that I had only just been looking at the tip of a rather ugly iceberg. I spent many more days and nights do further research on the connections between the NSA and Microsoft. It lined up exactly with my research on UEFI, Secure Boot, Windows 8 and the open back door.

July 2013 Patch Tuesday confirms more holes in Windows
Microsoft released more patches. All were critical vulnerabilities. The company has closed a total of 34 holes in Windows, Internet Explorer, Office and many other products, among them the Windows kernel vulnerability that has affected the Windows privilege system for over a month.

"July 2013 patches break networking. Beware! Anyone know of a fix? System restore isn't working.. This update has been a MASSIVE pain. It has has crashed 3 different software programs. Not good Microsoft."

"After installing the July updates I've run into massive problems. Some applications no longer want to open and I can not successfully system restore."

"July 9 2013 patches installed last night. Now my machine boots with a random BSOD. I cannot even get into safe mode, nor system recovery, nor any of the usual ways to try to fix Microsoft's mess. All of them results in a BSOD!"

"MS is is using Windows Updates to crash Windows 7 to try to force us to buy Windows 8. My desktop running on XP freezing every 20mins….I should have learned from the terrible updates earlier this year to not install them anymore!"

"Random Blue Screen Of Death (BSOD) after 18 patches from Tuesday, July 9, 2013. Cannot look at the debug file, cannot stop the problem from the BSOD."

Many people have claimed that the August 2013 Microsoft Updates were the worst on record. The only solution left is to simply turn off Microsoft Updates and install Linux as a backup or primary access system to your files.

How to Turn Off Windows Updates
At some point, the risk of Windows Updates crashing your computer will be greater than the risk of hackers crashing your computer. When you reach this point, the following are steps you can take to turn off Windows Updates. These steps apply mainly to Windows 7 and Windows XP. If you have a Windows 8 computer, the updates are the least of your problem. My advice is to take the Windows 8 computer back where you got it and ask for a refund.

How to turn off Windows Updates in Windows 7
Open the Control Panel and click on Windows Update. Then click on Change Settings. In the section called "Important Updates" use the drop down arrow to select "Never check for updates." Then click OK.

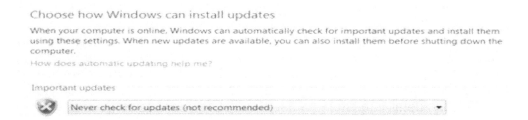

How to turn off Windows Updates in Windows XP
There are two different methods that may or may not work.
First Method: Open the Control Panel and click on System. Then click on the Automatic Updates tab. Then unselect the "Keep my computer up to date" box. (Alternately you may need to select "Turn off automatic updating." Then click OK.

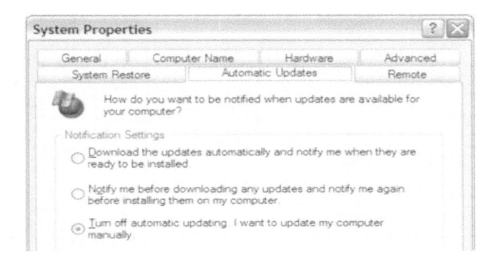

Second Method: Open the Control Panel and click on Administrative Tools. Then click on Services. Look for the service called Automatic Updates. Select it.

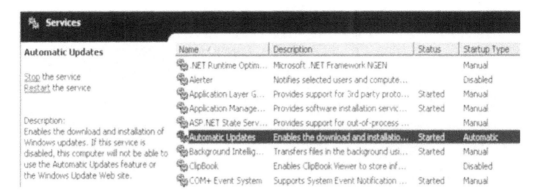

Then right click on it and select Properties. Then change the "Startup Type" to Disabled. Then click OK.

If you turn off Windows Updates, it is important to keep backups of your data and to install Linux in a dual boot so that you can access your data even if (when) your Windows operating system ever crashes. These topics are covered in detail in a later chapter. But first, let's turn to some of Microsoft's other shady dealings.

2.3 Microsoft Blackmail Warning: Upgrade or Die!

> ## "You would be a fool to use anything but Linux."
> Thomas Bushnell, Google Technical Projects Director, April 29, 2012

On April 8, 2013, Microsoft announced that they will eliminate security support for Windows XP on April 8, 2014. This will leave more than 600 million Windows XP users without a safe and viable solution to operate their computers. I knew that many of my students used Windows XP and I worried about what would happen to them – and hundreds of millions of other XP users - when Microsoft pulls the rug out from underneath them in April 2014. For me, this announcement was the final straw. I began writing this book to help my students learn how to switch from the Windows operating system to the free Linux operating system.

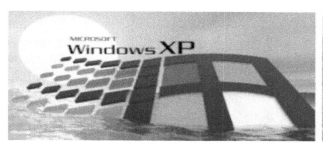 

What will these hundreds of millions of XP users do when their computers are brought down by hackers in April 2014? Some may fork over $500 to get Windows 8 and Office 2013 installed on their current computers.

Steve Ballmer, the head of Microsoft, explains to Wall Street stock investors that ending support for Windows XP in April 2014 is an "unprecedented opportunity" to force hundreds of millions of people to "upgrade" to Windows 8 – at $500 each!

It is clear that the main reason Microsoft is discontinuing Windows XP Support is to force XP users to pay for Windows 8. Others may get so mad that they will fork over $1,000 to move to an Apple computer. But what about the millions of people who are just scrapping by and barely have enough money for food and shelter?

It was evident to me that my students would be vulnerable to computer attacks and therefore forced to "upgrade" to Windows 8.

The Windows XP Train Wreck coming in April 2014... The Ultimate Computer Crash! Even those who do have the money to pay Microsoft for Windows 8 will be in for a rude awakening – because Windows 8 is nothing at all like Windows XP or Windows 7. Instead, Windows 8 is riddled with problems that will likely cause many users to seek out other solutions to their computer needs.

To encourage XP users to "upgrade" to Windows 8, Microsoft announced that they are offering a "15% off" special deal on upgrading to their Windows 8 operating system and Office 2013.

Hopefully, having read our book this far, you now have a better understanding of why we should all make the move to the Linux free open source operating system instead of paying the Microsoft blackmailers. I am certain that even if Windows 8 got all of their reliability problems worked out and did not crash computers, most of my students would simply not be able to handle the complexity of all the new Windows 8 commands – let alone feel comfortable having an open back door to the NSA inside of their computers. .

The Search for a Better Alternative Begins
After learning that Microsoft was going to pull the rug out from under hundreds of millions of Windows XP users, I began a quest in search of other better options. One option would be to spend $1,000 or more on an Apple computer. The problem here is that many people cannot afford to spend an extra thousand dollars. That is why they were still using Windows XP instead of Windows 7. In addition, Apple is a monopoly linked to the NSA just like Microsoft.

For the first time, I began to seriously consider free open source programs as the only other available option.

Open source software is free of any patent restrictions and often comes at no cost.
Image: http://blogs.op5.com/study-open-source/

I was aware that the number one selling laptop at Amazon.com, the Google Chromebook, used the Linux operating system (which Google calls Chrome OS). The Chrome book is made by Samsung and sells for just $250. It weighs just 2.4 pounds, has a battery life of 6.5 hours, uses USB 2 and 3 ports and has a reliable and fast 16 GB Solid State Drive – with additional capacity provided by USB flash drives. When asked why Google chose to use the Linux operating system on their internal computers and on their Chrome OS, the Google Technical Projects Director Thomas Bushnell said it was about security. He said that Google was a target for hackers and that the Linux operating system was the safest operating system in existence.

"You would be a fool to use anything but Linux."
Thomas Bushnell, Google Technical Projects Director, April 29, 2012

But the Chromebook is pretty limiting. Google Chrome is limited to using Google Docs. What I was looking for was a solution which would work on any computer and run any program. Since the Google Chrome operating system was based on the Linux Ubuntu operating system, Linux Ubuntu was my next stop. I tried four versions of Ubuntu. But they all had serious problems with their filing system.

Ubuntu looks like the Apple interface and the Google Chrome interface because the Apple operating system and the Google Chrome operating system are close cousins of the Ubuntu operating system. But all of these operating systems have filing systems which are more difficult to use than the Windows filing system. I really wanted something that was as close as possible to Windows so that my students would not have to face a steep learning curve.

Linux Mint... A free open source version of Windows XP and Windows 7
Then I tried a free open source program called Linux Mint Mate. I was stunned. The Start Menu and filing system not only worked almost exactly like Windows XP and Windows 7, in many ways it was better!

Linux Mint comes with a free open source word processor called **Libre Office 4.** Libre Office is better than Microsoft Office 2013 and can work with all of my Word and Excel and Power Point documents. It even works with PDF and HTML documents. Libre Office 4 comes pre-installed on Linux Mint 15 Mate – along with hundreds of other free open source programs! I knew immediately this was the option that could help my students and anyone avoid the Windows 8 nightmare that would befall them in April 2014. I began writing this book on how to install and use Linux Mint 15 Mate and Libre Office.

Windows 8 Blues... coming soon to a store near you
The same day as the ridiculous Microsoft May Mega Update, Tuesday, May 14, 2013 Microsoft announced that they would be coming out with a patch for Windows 8 called Windows 8 Blue and they would give away Windows 8 Blue free to anyone who had the misfortune of buying Windows 8. In the announcement, Microsoft executives admitted that Windows 8 suffered from major problems. But they promised to post a free patch in their store to fix these problems. They assured us that this patch would bring back the Start Button (or at least what they called a "Start Tip") and the ability to log directly into the normal desktop screen rather than the new Metro Tiles screen.

The problem with this "solution" is that it does nothing to fix the underlying structural problems of Windows 8. In an effort to make Windows more tablet friendly, Microsoft has destroyed the entire structure of Windows 7 and replaced it with a tinker toy. The tinker toy will remain – even if you log into the desktop version of the tinker toy.

Windows 8 differs radically from Windows 7. It is not just that it relies on a tile-based Start screen rather than the traditional start button and Start menu. Or that it has two completely different interfaces – the traditional desktop screen which comes up for some applications and the tile based screen which comes up for other applications. It is the entire structure of Windows 8 that is the problem. The differences between Windows 8 and Windows 7 can be seen in the fact that Microsoft issued 739 major updates to Windows 8 in the first six months after it was released!

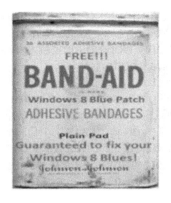

In short, anyone unfortunate enough to be inflicted with a Windows 8 heart attack is being offered a box of band aids. They will eventually figure out that Windows 8 Blue is no better than Windows 8 Black. Offering victims of the Windows 8 Blues a free band-aid will do nothing to solve this problem. The only real solution this leaves us is to move to an operating system that actually works.

The very next day, May 15, 2013 Microsoft issued another "XP Upgrade to Windows 8 or Die" Warning.

Where will you be when Windows XP support ends?

15 May 2013 1:14 PM

Small businesses, we know you love Windows XP. It's been good to you. But it's 12 years old, and the time has come to start bidding it a fond farewell. The unfortunate fact is that it's out of date and support for it will end on April 8, 2014 – less than a year from now. Are you ready?

What does end of support mean? It means no security updates. No free or paid assisted support options, and no updates to online content. Using new hardware and software will become increasingly difficult and incompatible.

Microsoft is really pulling out all of the stops to force people to give up Windows XP. After the May 2013 Black Tuesday disaster, I knew I needed to work harder on finishing this book showing people how to move to Linux. There were two major problems. The first was that documentation on Linux has been written almost exclusively by computer programmers – who make using Linux much harder than it needs to be. I resolved to create a new kind of Linux manual - one that was written in plain English and included simple steps with a lot of screen shots showing my students which buttons to push and in which order.

2.4 UEFI: The Microsoft-NSA Kill Switch

"We call Windows 8.1 'Windows Prison Edition' because it's designed to require people to send data to Microsoft servers, and of course, Microsoft will hand over any of that data to the US government on request. It puts the users in prison,"

Richard Stallman July 2013

In this section we will cover what is perhaps the most frightening part of the Microsoft-NSA program to take control over our computers. It is a new program called UEFI. It can be more accurately thought of as the Microsoft-NSA Kill Switch. Microsoft has required that this sinister "feature" be added to all Windows 8 computers.

Microsoft has created many obstacles to prevent you from adding to Linux
As I continued my research, a much bigger problem emerged. Sadly, Microsoft does not want people to use Linux. Microsoft seems to be doing everything they can to keep their corporate monopoly. They want the money that will come from forcing XP users to pay $500 each to change to Windows 8. There are 600 million Windows XP users in the world today and Microsoft wants all 300 million to spend $500 each to "upgrade" to Windows 8 and Office 2013. That is $300 billion dollars that Microsoft stands to lose if folks ever learn that they can get a much more stable and reliable word processing system for free.

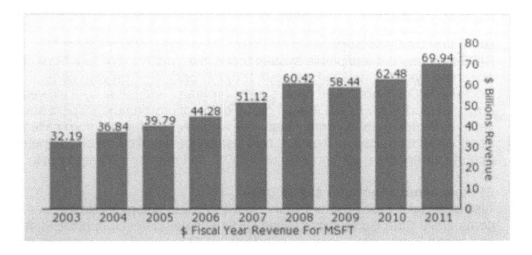

In 2012, Microsoft revenue was $72 billion.
The Windows operating system is the key to maintaining the Microsoft computer monopoly. So Microsoft has placed all kinds of malicious roadblocks, obstacles and traps to prevent people from using Linux.

What is a Start Up Program?

To understand what the problem with UEFI and Secure Boot is, it is helpful to know a little bit about how computers start up. When you push the POWER ON button on your computer, this initiates a Start Up program. Historically, the universal startup program was called BIOS which stands for **Basic Input Output System.** This Start Up program is installed by the computer manufacturer. BIOS determines what program boots next and in what order. Typically, the next program to boot is the Windows Boot Manager. This starts Windows which then can be used to start Windows based programs such as MS Office. There are free open source versions of all of these things as shown below:

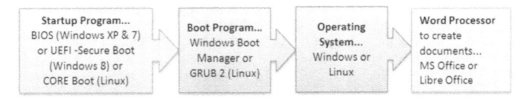

BIOS versus Core Boot

BIOS is a very old and stable system that allows you to have four or more operating systems installed into four or more "partitions" on your computer. Because BIOS is not a free open source program, and because it slowed down the performance of Linux, a group of Linux programmers spent several years developing an extremely fast, safe and free Startup program called Core Boot. While Core Boot is free and could easily be installed on all computers, manufacturers have continued to use BIOS until Windows 8 came out in 2012.

EFI turns into a monster called UEFI

Also during the past 12 years while Core Boot was being developed, a commercial Start Up program called UEFI was being developed. UEFI stands for Unified Extensible Firmware Interface. UEFI is based on a program called EFI which was an attempted by Intel to update BIOS. EFI did not have the Secure Boot "feature" and neither did UEFI until about 2008. UEFI has been criticized for not solving any of the problems of BIOS. Like BIOS, UEFI requires two separate drivers – one for the firmware and one for the operating system. This makes UEFI slow and difficult to work with.

But the biggest complaint about UEFI is that it placed control for programs in the hands of computer manufacturers such as HP and software companies such as Microsoft rather than in the hands of the computer owner (you).

In fact, for computer users, Secure Boot is like putting on a pair of handcuffs. This does not stop hackers from attacking your computer – because hackers are experts at removing handcuffs. But it does make it harder for you to work with your computer – because now you need to learn how to remove the Secure Boot handcuffs before you can install Linux.

Windows 8/UEFI/Secure Boot places digital handcuffs on your computer to make it much more difficult for you to add Linux to your computer... Imagine a world in which Microsoft controlled every aspect of 90% of the world's one billion computers. This is worse than a monopoly. It is corporatocracy.

One of the new "features" of Windows 8 is something called "Secure Boot." While it does very little to protect your computer, it does make it much more difficult to add another operating system, such as Linux to your computer. Beginning with UEFI version 2.2, UEFI added a new feature called Secure Boot. This uses a special key, which is nothing more than a digital image, to be activated before any operating system, or any other program can be loaded into the computer.

There are several absurd things about this feature. First, Secure Boot is not a very secure system. This is because digital images are easily copied. Recall that fake digital images were used by Flame to attack Microsoft Security Updates. We are now all well aware that this digital signature system does not work. Second, generic keys are already in existence to bypass the system. It seems that everyone has been given a key to your computer except you! Third, Secure Boot adds huge costs to computers because manufacturers have to pay private companies to have Secure Boot and UEFI installed. For all of these reasons, Core Boot is a much less expensive and more effective security system. Core boot lets you control the final configuration. This is not only the most secure system – it is also the easiest system for the end user... which is you.

Despite all of these issues, and despite the fact that Secure Boot is an optional feature of UEFI, Microsoft has required all computer manufacturers to use UEFI with Secure Boot on all of their Windows 8 computers. If Microsoft was really concerned about speed or security, they would have insisted on using Core Boot.

So the insistence on UEFI with Secure Boot seems to have only one purpose – to make it difficult to impossible to install Linux on your computer – in order to maintain the Microsoft Windows monopoly (and/or to help the NSA). To make matters worse, Microsoft has insisted that manufacturers use a special key controlled by Microsoft – rather than a key controlled by the manufacturer. This gives Microsoft total control over your computer – not just the backdoor and the front door – but also the Startup program. This is a very frightening development.

One of the worst of these monopolistic predatory practices is forcing computer manufacturers to sign exclusive agreements to prevent manufacturers from loading a free Linux operating system into computers which have the Windows operating system. Because many users find it difficult to add an operating system to their computer, a far better option would be to have it come pre-installed on all computers so that all users would have to do to activate it is to click on a button. The question is why computer manufacturers have not already added Linux to the computers they sell. After all, Linux is free and can easily be installed in computers by the manufacturer. They could then sell their computers for a hundred dollars cheaper with a fully functional operating system. This would also give their customers a choice. If they also want the Microsoft Windows operating system, they could pay an extra hundred dollars for it. But they would not have to buy Windows just to get the computer they want. Microsoft prevents this from happening by forcing manufacturers to sign restrictive licensing agreements.

Can't we just turn off Secure Boot?
You can – sort of. You can switch from Secure Boot mode to legacy mode. But this is not the same as going back to the old BIOS Start Up program that starts all Windows XP and Windows 7 computers. You still have the UEFI program controlling whether your Windows 8 computer starts and the kill switch is still there. There are reports of folks switching to the UEFI Legacy mode only to have Microsoft switch the mode back to secure boot at the next Microsoft Update. And there is no way to close this backdoor to your computer because as we now know, Internet Explorer is tied into the Windows operating system. Finally, the UEFI code is ten times bigger than the BIOS code. What do you think all of that extra code is all about?

But isn't UEFI some nice program that was created by a non-profit group?
Since UEFI with Secure Boot is capable of destroying the entire world economy, it is worth understanding how this nuclear weapon came into being. Microsoft claims to be an innocent bystander in the creation of Secure Boot. But the facts tell otherwise. According to the UEFI official story, around the turn of the century, Intel wanted to update the BIOS Startup program to help their chips start up faster. So they used an "open source" operating system called BSD to create a new Startup program called EFI (Extensible Firmware Interface).

There are several things fishy about this official story. First, BSD stands for the Berkeley Software Distribution. It was created in the early 1990's at the University of California at Berkeley and is a free open source operating system. Fast forward to 2000. Intel wants a better Startup program. Does it make any sense that a hardware company like Intel would try to write any software program – much less a program that controls the Startup of every computer? This is like Microsoft deciding that they were going to start making their own computer chips!

Besides if Intel had really wanted a modern fast Startup program, they could have simply have used the <u>free open source Core Boot program</u> that was being developed by the Linux community. In addition, EFI was not that fast or that smart. It was slower than Core Boot because it used the same complex driver process that BIOS used. At any rate, according to the official story, in 2005 Intel gave up on the EFI project and donated the EFI code to the UEFI Forum – a non-profit group that suddenly appeared like magic out of the middle of nowhere whose mission it was to create a modern Startup program. Naturally, Intel and Microsoft were on the Board of this new nonprofit organization.

The UEFI verification or signing mechanism is identical to the Microsoft Windows signing mechanism – a process that has already been attacked and compromised by the Flame virus.

In 2006, UEFI made version 1.0 which was not much different than EFI. But it was important enough for Bill Gates to give a Key Note Speech about UEFI:

"These are changes across the board, in terms of how hardware and software work together. If we think about boot, we're finally moving away from the old BIOS to this unified extensible firmware interface and that gives us new flexibility and capability." **Bill Gates WINHEC 2006 Keynote Speech**

UEFI version 1.0 in 2006 was not that different from BIOS. In particular, it did not include secure boot. Neither did version 2.1 which was released on January 7, 2007. So what the heck was Bill Gates talking about in his 2006 speech? Could it be that Bill knew something completely different was in the works? Beginning in 2008, just a few months after Microsoft joined the NSA PRISM program, strange things began to happen. The biggest change was with version 2.2. With version 2.2, the purpose began to change, the tools began to change and even the code began to change. Suddenly instead of being merely an update to BIOS, UEFI became a nuclear weapon with the addition of Secure Boot. The UEFI manual grew to be nearly 2,200 pages. Who could have done that? Pay no attention to that man behind the curtain (who also happens to be the richest man in the world). Then UEFI version 2.3 was released in April 2011 – just 6 months before the "developer" release of Windows 8 at a Microsoft Developer conference in September 2011. The Secure Boot contracts and certificates were not released until 2012. This seemed to be an attempt to hide the real nature of Secure Boot until the release of Windows 8.

Evidence that Microsoft created UEFI and Secure Boot

Microsoft has denied having been involved in creating the UEFI and Secure Boot Twin monsters. However, there are four convincing facts which refute their claim.

First, UEFI file names use back slashes for separators. Microsoft is the only company in the world which uses backslashes in their file names. All other programmers use forward slashes.

Example of Unix Forward Slash File Naming:
/home/davidspring/Documents/file.txt
Example of the same file with Microsoft Backward Slash File Naming:
C:\Users\davidspring\Documents\file.txt

The open source community uses forward slashes to define file names. This is because Linux and BSD are both based on Unix and Unix uses Forward slashes for file names and backward slashes for the "escape" function. But there is one company in the world that is arrogant enough to write their own computer languages which uses backward slashes for file names. The company who uses backward slashes for file names is Microsoft. And the UEFI file names? Well, they all now use backward slashes. This is very odd because the "official" story claims that UEFI was based on BSD and BSD uses forward slashes!

Security experts are mad at Microsoft for insisting on programming with backward slashes as it creates a huge security risk. This is because all URLs use forward slashes – including web pages which protect sensitive business data. One example of this danger occurred in 2004. Active Server Pages (ASP) is a Microsoft programming language. In 2004, it was discovered that ASP has a huge security flaw associated with back slashed file names.

> "By using a backslash instead of a forward slash you could access secure ASP.NET resources that normally required authentication. So, if accessing www.example.net/secure/private.aspx is supposed to be a protected web page requiring authentication, anyone who wants to could still access the file by entering the URL as www.example.net/secure\private.aspx. Even if you set NTFS permissions to block anonymous users, ASP.NET still allowed access." **Mark Burnett, Hacking the Code and Stealing the Network**

It is clear that in writing UEFI with back slashed file names, Microsoft has not learned its lesson about what a dangerous practice this is. They have now tied insecure back slashed file names to the most dangerous computer weapon ever produced.

This is why I maintain that UEFI and Secure Boot should be avoided at all costs. There is nothing safe about either of these "features." Computer manufacturers should replace UEFI and Secure Boot with Core Boot – which of course uses the standard and secure forward slash file names.

In any case, the fact that UEFI has been changed to back slashed file names is clear evidence that the two latest versions of UEFI were actually written by Microsoft programmers. It is also clear that Secure Boot was written by Microsoft and added to UEFI at the very last minute. It is also clear that Secure Boot was written specifically for Windows 8. Thus, Microsoft's finger prints are all over the crime scene. And make no doubt about it – UEFI with Secure Boot is a crime against humanity. It doesn't take Sherlock Holmes to figure out where UEFI really came from or what the real purpose of Windows 8 is.

Second, the UEFI security signing mechanism is identical to the Microsoft Windows security signing. I do not mean similar. I mean IDENTICAL. Many sections of UEFI code even begins with the word "win."

Third, the versions of UEFI since Microsoft joined this project are completely different from the version of UEFI which existed before Microsoft joined the project. As just one example, the original versions of UEFI did not have secure boot and made no mention of anything like secure boot in their plans.

Fourth, before Microsoft joined the project, the source code for EFI was open and publicly available. After Microsoft joined, a cloak of secrecy covered the project. No one knows for sure exactly what is in the bloated UEFI code – which is ten times bigger than either the BIOS code or the Core Boot code.

The Secure Boot Kill Switch is different from the Windows 8 "Apps" Kill Switch that has been discussed in the media
A Kill Switch is a program which can remotely delete software and edit code without the user's permission. There are at least two known Kill Switches on the Windows 8 operating system – these are the Secure Boot Kill Switch and the Apps Kill Switch.

There has been some confusion in the media about which Microsoft Kill Switch is the most dangerous. I want to make it clear that I have no problem with the new Windows 8 Apps Kill Switch which is capable of destroying any programs you purchase through the Microsoft Apps Store. Anyone who buys an app through the Microsoft Apps store deserves to have their programs nuked without warning. The Apps Kill Switch does not kill your entire computer and does not prevent you from installing an alternate operating system. In fact, all it takes is a comparison of the silly programs at the Microsoft Apps store to the 40,000 free programs at the Linux store to get people rushing out to download Linux.

We have managed to get a picture of the Windows 8 Secure Boot Kill Switch:

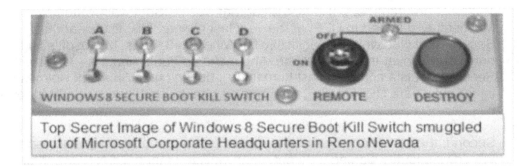

Top Secret Image of Windows 8 Secure Boot Kill Switch smuggled out of Microsoft Corporate Headquarters in Reno Nevada

You can see that the **Windows 8 Secure Boot Kill Switch** comes with four safety locks to prevent accidental discharge. This is very similar to the safety mechanisms for any other nuclear device. Before activating the kill switch, the staff member (with super key security clearance) would first have to disable all four safety locks. They then would turn the kill switch to the ON position before activating with the big red button affectionately known as the Doomsday Machine. Naturally Microsoft has promised to only use this device against pirated copies of their software. Members of the open source community have complained that UEFI and Secure Boot will prevent users from adding Linux.

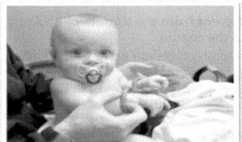

(Because secure boot is enabled by default on all Windows 8 computers), "it is a bit like if everyone is born with handcuffs on and only if you pay a certain amount of money you get released."
Red Hat Developer
Matthew Garrett

Want Freedom? Say no to UEFI and demand Core boot.

Microsoft claims that that Secure Boot is needed for safety reasons. However, if Microsoft was even remotely concerned about safety, they would not leave the back door open to all Microsoft operating systems. Microsoft had already created problems for "dual booting" a Linux operating system with Windows 7. We will discuss these problems further in the section on dual booting. But it is apparent that Microsoft is doing everything in its power to maintain its monopoly.

Microsoft Windows has since 1997 had known malicious features... features to spy on the user and restrict what the user can do, which are in fact digital handcuffs, and it has known back door security problems whereby Microsoft can change anything about your program remotely.

However, these attempts at censorship may backfire for Microsoft. As users become more aware that Microsoft is trying to limit their ability to use open source operating systems this may actually increase the interest in using them. Users will realize that the way to take back control over their future is to first take back control of their computer.

Secure Boot adds a new verb to the English Language: Brick
Thanks to Secure Boot, a new verb has been added to the English Language. It is brick – as in "Secure Boot just bricked my computer." The verb comes from the noun "brick" which is a heavy useless block. Sadly, if you try to do anything Secure Boot does not like, it might shut down your computer and prevent it from turning on again – turning your computer into a heavy useless block aka a brick. There are now numerous reports of UEFI and Secure Boot bricking computers that attempt to install Linux. Microsoft's solution to the bricked computer problem is to buy a new official key from Microsoft. Perhaps this is the new Microsoft business model.

Microsoft Secure Boot Super Key Special Offer!

Has your Windows 8 computer stopped working because you tried to install Linux on it? Gee, that's too bad. Well, have we got a deal for you... for a mere $99 you can get a genuine Microsoft authorized **Super Key** guaranteed to unlock any Windows 8 computer and allow you to install anything you want on it!

Only $99!

Just like the key we gave to the NSA!

Buy today and get 2 super keys for the price of 1

Limited Time Offer While Supplies Last. Laptop and extended warranty not included. Taxes and software are extra. Not available in all areas (prohibited in countries with anti-monopoly laws). Additional terms and conditions may apply. See your local dealer for details.
The term "**Super Key**" is a registered trademark of Microsoft Corporation, Reno, Nevada. Any other use of the words Super or Key will be persecuted to the fullest extent of the law.

In a later chapter, we will show you how to turn of secure boot. There are many reports that some computer manufacturers simply turn off Linux operating systems. These include Lenovo, Toshiba and Samsung. But even turning off Secure Boot and Microsoft Update is just a temporary fix – since Microsoft still retains control over every computer with Windows 8/UEFI/Secure Boot installed on it. The only real solution is to not buy a computer with Windows 8 installed on it and demand that computer manufacturers use Core Boot instead of UEFI/Secure Boot. Even though Windows 8 is the greatest attack on our freedom since the East India Corporation came up with the Stamp Act – a move that started the American Revolution – do not expect much help from our government. A better solution is to file and run for office at the next election.

In the meantime, the best thing you can do to take back control of your computer is finish reading this book and learn how to install and use Linux and Libre Office on your own computer. We will review the best available solutions to all of these Windows 8 problems in later chapters. The reason this book is so long is not because Linux is hard to learn. Rather it is because of all the Microsoft traps.

The Secure Boot Trap is challenged in Court

On March 26, 2013, an 8,000 member group in Spain called Hispalinux filed a complaint against Microsoft protesting that the new "Secure Boot" feature in Windows 8 was simply another attempt to maintain the Microsoft Monopoly by making it more difficult for folks to add Linux to their computers.

> "UEFI Secure Boot with Microsoft keys is "designed to block non-Microsoft software. This is not a side-effect. It is its main purpose and is spelled out as such in Microsoft's own documentation... One of the options allowed by UEFI is the digital signature of drivers and applications, permitting complete control over the start-up system. Microsoft, as the sole owner of the private key, which matches up with the public key held in the memory of computers running Windows 8, is the only party that can authorize (sign) the software components in UEFI, the only party that can sign the boot of the operating system, and the only party that can sign the communications between the operating system and UEFI. To attain this goal, Microsoft has to use all its influence and power in the market to force computer and component manufacturers to accept its monopoly in the key generation system."
> Hispalinux Lead Attorney Jose Lancho

In June 2013, the American Civil Liberties Union filed a lawsuit against the NSA for violations of the 1st and 4th Amendments to the US Constitution. Hopefully, this book will help more people understand the connection between Microsoft and the NSA and help them take steps to free their computers from this attack on their privacy.

Everything to gain and nothing to lose

It is important to understand that you do not need to give up your current operating system or word processing programs to install open source tools on your computer. You can have Linux and Windows open at the same time and switch back and forth between them just like switching back and forth between your web browser and a Word document. You can even use open source tools like Libre Office to work with, save and send Word documents. And you can use the Linux operating system to run Windows programs. In fact, nearly anything that you currently do using expensive Microsoft programs you can do better, easier and safer using free open source tools.

We will show you how to safely install and use open source tools so you can test them side by side with whatever you are currently using -and decide for yourself whether you want to jump permanently to open source. Open source tools put you in control of your computer and your life. No more patches, no more upgrades, no more hassles! In other words, you have nothing to lose and everything to gain by learning more about the many benefits of open source tools. Once you give it a try, you will probably wonder why you waited so long. That is how we all feel the first time we are exposed to open source programs.

Many organizations have seen the writing on the wall and already made the move from Windows to Linux.

The International Space Station announced in May 2013 that they will switch dozens of computers from Windows XP to Linux in order to get a more "stable and reliable" computer operating system.

What's Next?

The above are just a few benefits of Linux over Windows. In the next chapter, we will describe many more reasons for using the Linux operating system instead of Windows 8. If you are in a hurry to get started adding Linux to your computer, you can skip the next chapter and move directly to Chapter 4. But if you really want to understand the inner workings of Windows 8 and Linux, there is a lot of important information in the next chapter that is worth knowing.

Chapter 3... Why we must end the Microsoft Monopoly

We must end the Microsoft Monopoly before it ends us.

Chapter 3 includes the following four sections:
3.1 Top Ten Reasons to use Linux instead of Windows 8
3.2 Why Windows 8 Blue will not fix the Real Problems
3.3 The Fatal Flaw of the Microsoft Windows Monopoly
3.4 The Real Cost of the Microsoft Monopoly

In the first two chapters of this book, we pointed out several major problems of Windows 8 – none of which have been "fixed" by Windows 8.1 Blue. These problems include Microsoft's collusion with the NSA to create an open back door to all of our computers. This open back door also created a security nightmare which has led to a constant stream of super bugs, "updates" and computer crashes. As if this was not bad enough, Windows 8 has added two more problems by attempting to create the world's first "dual" operating system (having two separate control panels) and imposing a monstrous startup program called UEFI with a horrific add on called Secure Boot. These two programs are simply a friendly face put on the "Microsoft-NSA" Kill Switch – which gives Microsoft and/or the NSA complete control over any computer that has this startup program installed on it. The only way to avoid this problem is to not buy a Windows 8 computer.

Sadly, staying with Windows XP or Windows 7 are no longer viable options either. Microsoft has announced that they will stop security support for Windows XP on April 8 2014. But the reality is that Windows Updates themselves are no longer trustworthy. Microsoft is so insistent that we all "update" to Windows 8 that they appear to be deliberately sabotaging their own updates and crashing Windows XP and Windows 7 computers in an effort to force folks to buy a Windows 8 computer. Thus, there is only one option for folks who want to get back control over their computers. That option is to keep using your current computer – hopefully with the BIOS startup program - and turn off Windows Updates. Then, to retain access to your data in the event of a Windows crash, add Linux in a "dual boot" configuration and switch over to using Linux as your primary operating system.

Because Microsoft has placed many obstacles in your way in an effort to prevent you from adding Linux to your computer, in this chapter we will provide several more reasons you should add Linux to you computer. Even if you are not concerned about Microsoft or the NSA killing your computer. This chapter provides a summary of the many huge benefits you will get by adding Linux to your computer.

3.1 Top Ten Reasons to use Linux instead of Windows 8

> *"I hate Windows 8. Hate it with a passion. A passion as hot as a thousand suns. The problem with Windows 8 is that Microsoft decided to shove a highly inefficient touch-based user interface onto millions of PC users using non-touch desktops and notebooks... forcing people sitting behind desktops and notebooks to change their work flow on a whim is simply asking too much. And believe me, after trying for months to like Windows 8, I still hate it."* Adrian Hughes Forbes Magazine
> http://www.forbes.com/sites/adriankingsleyhughes/2013/03/14/why-windows-8-is-the-first-windows-release-i-absolutely-hate/

In this section, we will review 10 important reasons to make the switch to Linux rather than shelling out another $500 for Windows 8 and Office 2013. Hopefully after reading this article, you will have a better understanding of why we should all make the move to the Linux free open source operating system.

#1: Linux costs less... In fact, it is free!
In Chapter 2, we pointed out the "impending doom" of the Windows XP operating system in April 2014 and the fact that replacing Windows and Office with the newer versions will cost about $500. Meanwhile Linux Mint with Libre Office is free.

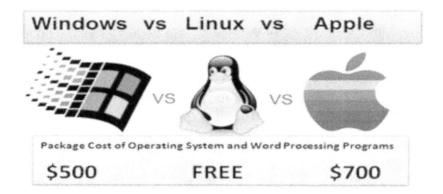

Let's say, you buy a new computer every couple of years. By this point, you have been through the ringer of MS DOS, through Windows 95, 98, ME, 2003, XP, Vista, 7 and now Windows 8. You have also been through many versions of Office. Each time Windows destroys your computer, you pay several hundred dollars for an upgrade that often worked worse than the version you could no longer use because it was "no longer supported." Folks are starting to add up the cost of all of these new versions. In most cases, it comes to more than $200 per year just for software! If you have a family and several computers, or a small business with several computers, the cost quickly exceeds $1,000 per year.

Microsoft typically sells $70 billion in software every year – and makes more than $20 billion in profit every year! But instead of passing along some of these savings to their customers, Microsoft is now increasing prices in a very hidden way by moving to a "software as a service" (SAAS) model whereby you only rent their software for a month or a year at a time instead of buying it. Ironically, for all the money we are sinking into these over-priced products, we are getting a product that is worse than an open source option we can get for free. My mom had a saying: "Fool me once, shame on you... fool me twice, shame on me."

#2: Linux is more dependable than Windows 8

We have already given many examples showing that Windows 8 is an unstable system with numerous technical problems which cause it to freeze or crash causing the Blue Screen of Death. The reason Windows 8 is so unstable is that Microsoft is trying to combine a "metro" Operating System with a traditional "Windows 7" desktop Operating System. These are fundamentally incompatible objectives and as incompatible as trying to combine water with oil. The Windows 8 operating system ends up not work well for either mobile or desktop usage. The Windows 8 underlying programming is so different from the Windows 7 desktop structure that Windows 8 has been plagued with a series of technical crashes right from the initial public launch. These are in addition to the ongoing technical problems with viruses and crashes that have plagued all past versions of Microsoft Windows.

Linux Mint 15 Mate Start screen and menu

Linux Mint Mate does not suffer from any of these technical problems. You will therefore be able to get your work done without worrying about your computer crashing and losing all of your data. The following are all more examples of how undependable Windows 8 really is.

Windows 8 still has Boot Loop problems
Problems have continued to plague Windows 8. A whole list of Windows 8 crash problems is posted on the following website:
http://crashctrl.com/2013/02/surface-pro-known-issues-bugs-quick-fixes/
This is the sarcastic comment from a computer repair analyst:
"Ah, woe be unto you. For you have fallen into the Secure Boot Loader loop due to a Firmware Panic. I weep for you. Please note that the terms Secure Boot Loader Loop (SBLL) and Firmware Panic are both arbitrary terms that I created to attach to these hardware failures. I feel they are the best description available with the information at hand. Microsoft has not stated what is actually happening when SBLL occurs. Most assume it is a dead SSD but who knows?"

#3: Linux is much safer...Windows 8 leaves important security information on text files which hackers can easily access
Windows 8 leaves identity and security information exposed to hackers. Linus Mint doesn't. You are therefore less likely to suffer from identity theft or being attacked by viruses if you switch to Linux Mint. The reason Windows computers are so easily attacked is because they are designed to be attacked.

Hackers Love Windows 8!

Why Windows is much more likely to get Viruses than Linux
The biggest problem with Windows is that Microsoft leaves the "back door" open to your computer so that they can reduce pirating (and help the NSA). The back door is a link between Windows and Internet Explorer. Because this backdoor is open, hackers have learned how to go in the same backdoor that Microsoft uses to access your computer for updates. This is why Windows computers are so vulnerable to viruses, ad ware, and spy ware. It has been estimated that the average Windows computer is infected within 40 minutes of going online. This is also why you need antiviral programs if you are using Windows. Linux does not leave the backdoor open because they do not care where you got your copy of Linux from.

But there are other features that make Linux more dependable than Windows. For example, Linux uses folder, file and program authorization management. There are thus several levels of security in Linux. In Windows you can do pretty much anything to the system. You can go inside the system folder and delete whatever you want: Windows won't complain even if you delete critical files. Linux doesn't allow that. Every time you request to do something that has to do with the system, an administrator password is required. Many important files are hidden from view and you have to turn off file hiding even to see them. This means that viruses can't delete or modify what they want in the Linux system as easily as they can in the Windows system.

#4: Linux is Faster... Windows 8 runs slow because it has bloated software
Check out the following comparison of three different tablet systems:

Tablet	Total Space	Free Space	OS Took	% Free
Apple IPad 2	32 GB	28 GB	4 GB	88%
Asus Android 3	32 GB	28 GB	4 GB	88%
MS Surface	32 GB	15 GB	17 GB	46%

(note that the Asus Android uses a version of the Linux operating system)

The Windows 8 operating system uses an incredible 17 GB of disc space – over 4 times more than Apple or Android. This is why Apple and Android are many times faster than Windows 8. In addition, the MS Surface needs twice the working RAM as the Asus Android, (2 to 4 GB instead of 1 to 1 GB) but is much slower at everything. In other words, Apple and Android use 4 GB while Windows 8 uses 17 GB. This is a real problem if you are looking at video games and want to avoid latency issues. No dedicated gamer is going to want a slow, bloated operating system.

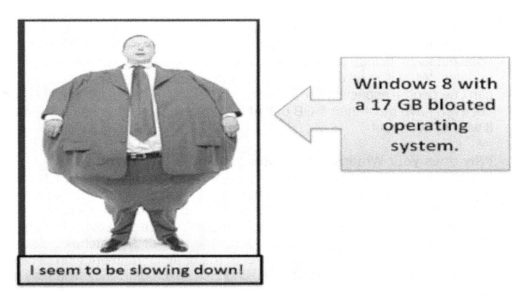

I seem to be slowing down!

Windows 8 with a 17 GB bloated operating system.

Growth of Microsoft Windows File Size over Time

Microsoft Windows has not always been so huge. Below is a table showing the increase in file size over time using data from Wikipedia.org.

Windows Version	Years	Recommended RAM (MB)	Recommended Space on Hard Drive (MB)
Windows 3.1	1992 to 1994	1	15
Windows 95	1995 to 1997	8	50
Windows 98	1998 to 1999	24	500
Windows ME	2000 to 2001	64	2,000
Windows XP	2002 to 2006	256	2,000
Windows VS	2007 to 2008	1,000	15,000
Windows 7	2009 to 2011	2,000 MB	20,000
Windows 8	2012 to now	4,000 MB	20,000

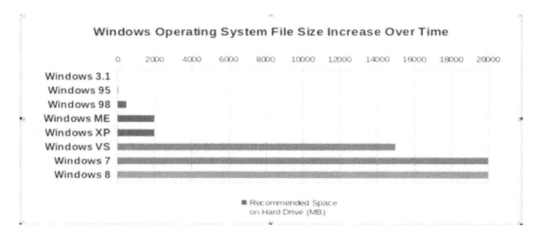

Why has Windows grown so much bigger than any other operating system? And why is Windows 8 so much bigger than earlier versions of Windows? This does not even include the file size expansion due to all of the monthly updates. What is in all of this secret Windows coding? No one knows. But it can't be good – especially for someone with an older computer that likely does not even have more than 1 GB of RAM. On many older computers, Windows 8 will not even run!

Why does your Windows computer get slower day after day?

But as slow as Windows is when it is new, it gets even slower over time. Windows has a number of design flaws, resulting in it becoming slower and slower and not lasting very long. You've probably heard more than once someone say "My computer is getting sluggish". There are several things that cause Windows computers to slow down. One is all of the patches intended to protect the open backdoor from hackers. The other is fragmentation because Windows does not do a good job of using disc space efficiently. You may think this is just how computers work. Well, try Linux and you'll be surprised. Five years from now, your system will be just as fast as the day you installed it.

#5: Windows 8 Touch Screen causes Gorilla Arm...

Windows 8 Touch Screen causes ergonomic fatigue and injuries when used on a desktop or laptop. The ideal position for humans at work is eyes up and hands down. Linux Mint allows you to use your computer efficiently with your hands down at your side resting on the keyboard and your eyes looking straight ahead at the vertical monitor. Using Windows 8 touch with desktops and laptops requires lifting your arms to perform difficult hand motions on the touch screen straining your back and arms. Using Windows 8 touch with tablets forces your eyes and head to look down, straining your neck. In a recent study, researchers at the Harvard School of Public Health looked at whether using a tablet in various seating configurations can cause head and neck strain.

They found that using a tablet on your lap for extended periods may raise the risk of neck and shoulder discomfort and potentially musculoskeletal problems because it forces the user to look down at a steep angle. This causes head and neck flexion and is a particularly hazardous for users who are doing a lot of typing. Using touch-screen computer tablets strains muscles in the head and neck more than a desktop or laptop computer would.

The ideal work configuration is eyes up and hands down.

Reaching up to a lap top with a vertical touch screen strains arms and wrists.

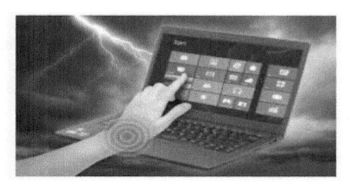

The worst work configuration is head down... it is a pain in the neck!

The ideal solution for getting work done is a vertical screen and a horizontal keyboard. This is why laptops and desktops are easier to use and less tiring. It is because they use a vertical screen for the eyes and a horizontal keyboard for the hands. Putting your hands on a vertical screen or putting your eyes on a horizontal tablet will eventually cause fatigue and chronic stress. In other words, traditional laptops and desktops are better than tablets and touch screen laptops and desktops. New is not always better. Apple's Steve Jobs once said he'd never launch a touchscreen laptop because of what he called "gorilla arm". "We've done tons of user testing on this," he said back in 2010, "and it turns out it doesn't work. Touch surfaces don't want to be vertical. It gives great demo, but after a short period of time you start to fatigue, and after an extended period of time, your arm wants to fall off." Studies have shown that users of desktop touchscreens report a "significant increase of discomfort in the shoulder, neck and fingers; and that the electric signals from shoulder muscles tell the same story." "We concluded that the more frequent use of their hands and fingers in unsupported – arms were off the chair armrests – and stretched arm postures, which was necessary to perform touch gestures on the display, could be the main cause of their greater body discomforts," says Gwanseob Shin of the Urban Institute of Science and Technology. This problem was also covered in the January 2013 issue of Scientific American: http://www.scientificamerican.com/article.cfm?id=why-touch-screens-will-not-take-over

"In late 2012 Microsoft broke from the pack. It made a billion-dollar gamble that personal computing is taking a new direction. The gamble was Windows 8, and the direction is touch. At first, you might think, "Touch has been incredibly successful on our phones, tablets, airport kiosks and cash machines. Why not on our computers?... I'll tell you why not: because of "gorilla arm." There are three big differences between these handy touch screens and a PC's screen: angle, distance and time interval...You're not just tapping big, finger-friendly icons. You're trying to make tiny, precise movements on the glass, on a vertical surface, at arm's length."

The public might dismiss Steve Jobs as just someone saying bad stuff about Microsoft. But when ergonomics experts start writing in Scientific American, the public is going to at some point find out that Windows 8 Touch laptops are a fundamentally flawed design. There is no "patch" for such a glaring flaw.

#6: Windows 8 Hand Gestures are Error Prone
Windows 8 introduces a bunch of complicated finger gestures that are very erratic and easy to get wrong. I often have to do the same motion three times to get it to work. If something doesn't work, users don't know whether they did the gesture wrong, or if the gesture doesn't work in the current context, or if they need to do a different gesture entirely. This makes it hard to learn and remember the gestures. And it makes actual use highly error-prone and more time-consuming than necessary.

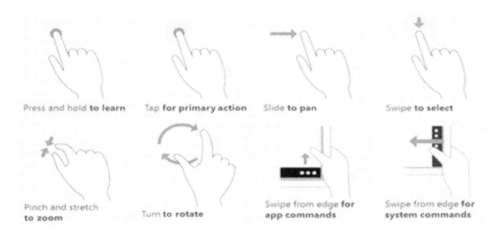

Press and hold to learn   Tap for primary action   Slide to pan   Swipe to select

Pinch and stretch to zoom   Turn to rotate   Swipe from edge for app commands   Swipe from edge for system commands

Above are eight of the Windows 8 new hand gestures

It was the erratic nature of the hand motions and hidden hot corners that got me worried about whether my students would be able to learn Windows 8. I think many of them will not be able to do these hand motions because they are hard to memorize and do not always work. Many are not even going to get a touch screen as they prefer to use a mouse and keyboard. So the new Metro interface did not make any sense at all. If you want to use your mouse and keyboard to open or close almost anything, you need to learn about what is hidden behind the new hot spots in the four corners of your computer screen. You also need to learn more than a dozen shortcuts using a combination of keys on your keyboard. You also need a lot of patience. The interface is littered with swipe ambiguity, where similar (or identical) gestures have different outcomes depending on subtle details in how they're activated or executed.

The following is a real Windows 8 command to open an application: To reveal the list of currently running applications: you need to first swipe from the screen's left edge, and then immediately reverse direction and do a small swipe the other way, and finally make a 90-degree turn to move your finger to a thumbnail of the desired application. The slightest mistake in any of these steps gives you a different result. For example, start swiping from the right to the left and you will either scroll the screen horizontally or reveal the charm bar, depending on exactly where your finger first touched the screen. This is simply a very bad design that as users give up will drive them away from Microsoft and force them to look for other options. Below is an example of how Windows 8 replaces simple commands with complex finger motions.

Welcome to the Windows 8 Touch Screen Help Center!

Please follow these three simple steps
to open an application using your touch screen:
First, do a long horizontal "swiggly swipe" from the screen's left edge,
followed by a short vertical swipe in the downward direction (see image):

Second, do a quick clockwise "circle swipe", then draw an X in the middle of it
and push down on the middle of the X.
You can remember this motion with the simple phrase
"A circle and a dot, X marks the spot" (see image):

Third, draw a happy face with two big ears and a double chin (see image):

Hopefully, your app will start. If not, please install the free Linux Mint operating system. You can then open applications by clicking on the words
"Click here to open applications".

#7: Linux comes with a fully functioning Word Processing program.
Linux comes with a fully functioning Word Processing program called Libre Office – which can be used to open, edit and send Microsoft Word documents. Microsoft Windows does not come with anything – as Microsoft Office costs hundreds of dollars EXTRA.

#8 Linux offers hundreds of additional free tools
Linux Mint also comes with a software center which allows you to download hundreds of additional free tools with just the click of a button.

This is one of the biggest advantages of Linux over Windows. If you want to add special abilities to your computer, you do not need to buy them – as thousands of free programs can be added to your Linux operating system with just the click of a button. These free programs include image editors such as GIMP, desktop recorders, video players and video editors. All of these tools are nicely organized by category – with reviews – in the Software Manager.

#9: Linux brings your old computer back to life
Because its code is so bloated to begin with and gets even worse over time with all of the patches, Windows uses much more hardware power just to make it work. But for most users, who surf the web, read and write emails, there is really no need to be buying a new computer every three years. Linux runs very well on older computers – making them faster than the day they were new.

#10: Linux Promotes Personal Freedom
Linux and "Open Source" software are "free". This means their license is a "free license", and the most common is the GPL (General Public License). This license states that anyone is allowed to copy the software, see the source code, modify it, and redistribute it as long as it remains licensed with the GPL.

What is so important about freedom? Imagine if Microsoft doubles the price for a Windows or Office license to $1,000 per year per computer. Or imagine if the NSA decides to shut down your computer. If you're tied to Windows, there's nothing you can do. You and your business are stuck with a single monopoly and Microsoft can charge whatever they want and you will have to pay it.

With Open Source, if a particular project or support company dies, or even takes their project in a direction you do not like, all the code remains open to the community and people can keep improving it. If this project is especially useful to you, you can even do this yourself. You're free to do whatever you want with open source software.

Hopefully, the past three chapters will help you better understand why Microsoft's days for dominating the world's computer operating systems are numbered. They might be able to hide the truth for a little while. But the Windows 8 operating system is so bad that at some point, users will start looking for other solutions.

3.2 Why Windows 8 Blue will not fix the Real Problem

"**Frankly, I think the new Start button will only make experienced Windows users angry - very angry. It's certainly going to confuse the living daylights out of a lot of otherwise sane Windows users. In spite of what you may have read in some well-known publications, there simply is no Start menu in Win8.1. No way, no how - all we get is a Start button, and it's a sham... The bottom line: Windows 8.1 "Blue" is more of the same nonsense.**" Woody Leonhard, infoworld.com
htp://www.infoworld.com/t/microsoft-windows/windows-blue-microsoft-blows-it-219820?page=0,2t

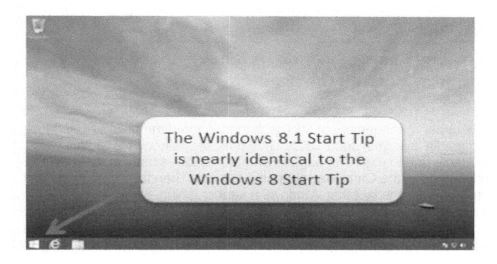

The Windows 8.1 Start Tip
is nearly identical to the
Windows 8 Start Tip

In May 2013, the new head of the Microsoft Windows 8 program claimed that Microsoft had fixed over 700 problems since Windows 8 first came out in October 2012. She also said that Windows 8.1 Blue would address many of the remaining issues. In this chapter, we will explain why Windows 8.1 Blue does not address the real problems of Windows 8 – because the whole Windows 8 concept is fundamentally flawed. In June 2013, I downloaded the latest version of Windows 8 to demonstrate these problems. But before we get into the details, I want to make it clear that the ONLY solution to the Windows 8 problems is for Microsoft to abandon the entire thing. Microsoft needs to do what Apple has done and what Linux has done and create separate operating systems for mobile devices and desktop computers. In trying to be everything for everyone, Windows 8 winds up doing nothing well for anyone. Microsoft also must get rid of the Windows back door, UEFI and Secure Boot. But because of its "deal" with the NSA, this is simply not going to happen.

Microsoft not only has a structural problem with their Windows 8 operating system, but they also have a structural problem with how decisions are made at Microsoft. First, the Microsoft upper management ignored the advice of their own computer programmers in scraping the Windows 7 desktop structure (and a separate mobile system). Then they ignored the advice of thousands of beta testers who pointed out nearly every problem we are now covering in this book.

Many users of Windows 8 have not been very happy with all the problems.

The upper management at Microsoft then ignored the failure of Windows 8 at the media launch in June 2012. They released Windows 8 while it was still unstable and loaded with bugs in October 2012 – simply to try to take advantage of the Christmas shopping season. Then they tried to blame other programs for the fact that Windows 8 kept crashing. Now we find out that they have also sold out their customers by giving the NSA access to Windows computers! To "fix" these problems, they are claiming that adding back a "Start Tip" will make everything better. But Windows 8 Blue is simply putting lipstick on a pig.

Beneath the lip stick, there is still going to be a terribly dysfunctional pig of an operating system. And I mean that literally. Windows 8 takes up an incredible 10 GB right out of the box. This does not include the Office word processing program or any of dozens of other programs which come by default with Linux. Windows is 400% bigger than either Apple or Linux. Windows 8 is a slow pig that eats up all the resources on your computer – thus slowing down everything else.

Obviously adding even more patches on this pig with Windows 8 Blue is only going to make the problem worse. Now for the details about the real problems with Windows 8 that will not be fixed by Windows 8 Blue.

Problems Not Fixed by Windows 8.1 Blue
In the last section we pointed out ten major problems of Windows 8 – none of which are fixed with Windows 8 Blue.
#1: Linux costs less... In fact, it is free!
#2: Linux is more dependable than Windows 8
#3: Linux is much safer...Windows 8 leaves important security information on text files which hackers can easily access
#4: Linux is Faster... Windows 8 runs slow because it has bloated software
#5: Windows 8 touch screen causes Gorilla Arm.
#6: Windows 8 hand gestures are error prone
#7: Linux comes with a fully functioning Word Processing program.
#8: Linux offers hundreds of additional free tools.
#9: Windows 8 slows down and crashes older computers.
#10: Windows 8 limits your freedom
We will now look at four more problems which Windows 8.1 does not fix.

#1: The Windows 8.1 Start Tip has the same problem as Windows 8
Below is the new Windows 8.1 Blue Desktop screen with the new Windows 8.1 Start Tip in the lower left corner just to the left of the blue "e":

The problem with this Windows 8.1 Start Tip is that when you click on it, it takes you to the Windows Metro screen and a completely different operating system than is used on the desktop. This new Start Tip is nearly identical to the Windows 8 Start Tip which was in the same place and also took you to the metro screen.

By contrast, the Windows 7 Start button kept you on the desktop screen and brought up a well-organized menu of programs. These programs would also open in the desktop screen and could be overlapped – allowing you to move quickly between programs.

#2: There is no way to permanently disable the hated Metro screen:

Above is only about one third of the Metro screen. To see the rest of it, you have to use the scroll bar on the bottom.

#3: Going back and forth between a metro screen and a desktop screen will drive you crazy

Windows 8.1 still require that you go back and forth between the Metro screen and the original desktop screen to open and use programs and applications. For example, if you are working on a Word document and you want to open an application, or even the control panel, you need to first left click on a hidden hot corner (or Start Tip) to go back to the metro screen. You then need to right click on another hidden portion of the metro screen to open up the All Applications link. You then need to left click on this **All Apps** link to get to the **APPS** screen below.

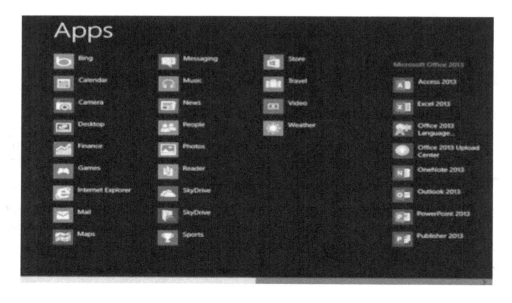

You then need to use the scroll bar at the bottom of the screen to scroll through dozens of applications to find the one you are interested in. You then need to right click on that application to open it. Once open, it is very difficult to close the application because often there is no Exit button. Even if you do figure out how to close it, instead of going back to the list of applications – which is where you came from, you are taken back to the desktop screen. Let's say, you clicked on an application only to find it was not the application you needed. So you close it. Ideally, you would expect to be taken back to the list of applications so that you could immediately open another application. But because you are taken back to the Desktop, you now need to repeat all of the above steps to reach a new application. By this point, you have likely forgotten why you even wanted the application – and you have also lost your train of thought about that Word document you were working on. When users can not view two or three applications and documents on the desktop simultaneously, they must keep information from the desktop in their short-term memory while they activate another window on another screen.

All of this switching back and forth between screens is a problem because human short term memory is very poor. But in addition, whenever they want to switch windows they will have to take their mind off of their primary focus and devote attention to bringing up another screen. This is simply not a very efficient way to do multitasking. Other problems include hidden "hot corners", lucky charms, "flat screens" and a variety of other pop ups that come and go without any rational basis. These problems will drive former Windows users completely crazy. At some point, many will start looking for something else – anything else.

#4: Microsoft has made it difficult for independent gaming programmers to build apps for Windows 8

Several gaming manufacturers are so upset with Windows 8 that they have announced that they are moving their games to Linux. Part of the problem for builders of computer games is that the bloated nature of Microsoft code slows down their computer games. The other part of the problem is that Microsoft demands a 30% cut of all the games sold which work with Windows 8. Some developers of popular games got so fed up with the new bloated code in Windows 8 that they moved their games to the free Linux operating system. On February 14, 2013, Gabe Newell, co-founder of video game company Valve, said: "Windows 8 is a catastrophe for everyone in the PC space."

Gabe Newell announcement: Windows 8 is a disaster... We're moving our games to Linux! Any questions?

In another interview, Newell stated:

"Windows 8 was like this giant sadness. It just hurts everybody in the PC business. Rather than everybody being all excited to go buy a new PC, buying new software to run on it, we've had a 20+ percent decline in PC sales — it's like "holy cow that's not what the new generation of the operating system is supposed to do." There's supposed to be a 40 percent uptake, not a 20 percent decline, so that's what really scares me. When I started using it I was like "Oh my god..." I find [Windows 8] unusable... Steam users have been asking us to support gaming on Linux. We're happy to bring rich forms of entertainment and our community of users to this open, customer-friendly platform."

That is why Newell is now moving his Steam game empire to Linux.

Note: Gabe Newell spent over a decade working at Microsoft on Windows before cofounding the Valve (Steam) Gaming platform. So he is an expert on the Windows operating system. If Windows 8 is unusable for Gabe, what chance does the average user have of making it work?

We're moving to Linux... You're welcome to join us!

Now that we have covered many of the problems not fixed by Windows 8.1 Blue, in the next chapter, we will expose the real underlying problem with Windows 8. It is a problem which can not be fixed.

3.3 The Fatal Flaw of the Microsoft Windows Monopoly

I just got a new computer which came with Windows 8 preinstalled on it. I have one question... How can I get rid of Windows 8? A user question posted on one of many blogs dealing with Windows 8 problems.

Questions about Windows worth thinking about

Have you ever wondered why the Microsoft Windows operating system is so much larger (and so much slower) than the Linux or Apple operating systems? And why is it that Windows is so much more susceptible to viruses and hacker attacks? And why does the Windows operating system need dozens to hundreds of "updates" every month – while Linux can go six months without any patches? Why is it that Microsoft makes such a lousy operating system even though it has tens of thousands of full time programmers? Why it is that Windows 8 has such an insane structure? Why do we even need a deeply flaws Secure Boot when we already have a free open source Core Boot? Why am I so confident that Windows 8 Blue will not be able to address the most important flaws of Windows 8?

The fatal flaw is the Microsoft Monopoly Business Model

To answer these questions, we need to understand that the structure of the Microsoft way of doing things is totally different from the Linux way. I understand the Microsoft way because, from 1985 to 2004, I had hundreds of Microsoft students attend my courses at Bellevue College. I have spent thousands of hours talking with Microsoft employees. I probably know more about what is going on at Microsoft than most of the employees at Microsoft. Some of those students were responsible for coming up with creative ways to stop pirates from making bootleg copies of Windows. Imagine that was your job. What would you do? How would you stop the pirates?

Sell copies of Microsoft Windows for $10 each... We cannot do that... It would be against the "Pirate Code" - which says that one pirate should not steal business from another pirate... On the other hand, the Pirate Code says nothing about copying... Me thinks we have found a loophole!

The answer is that it is impossible to stop pirates from copying Windows because it is a digital program which is easily copied. All you can do is add complex keys and other gimmicks which prevent pirated versions of Windows from working. But for every gimmick you come up with, the pirates can come up with a counter gimmick.

So all the gimmicks really do is add more bloated code to the already bloated code of Windows. This is a huge reason why Windows is so much more bloated than Linux. Linux does not care if you copy their operating system – in fact they encourage it. But Microsoft does care about copies. So Microsoft uses a series of gimmicks to throw monkey wrenches in the path of the pirates.

The First Major Gimmick... Internet Explorer 4 and the open back door
The pirating problem got much worse for Microsoft in the 1990's as the internet itself was used to spread pirated copies of Windows as well as information on how to attack Windows. So Microsoft decided to turn Windows from a stationary target to a moving target. In 1996, Microsoft came out with **Internet Explorer** – which was their first attempt at a web browser. The first three versions were separate programs which ran on Windows. In fact, the first three versions of Internet Explorer were actually "borrowed" from Netscape. But a strange thing happened with **Internet Explorer 4** when it was added to Windows 98. Suddenly, instead of being a separate program, Internet Explorer was now an integral part of Windows – and has been ever since.

Internet Explorer 1, 2 & 3 were separate programs outside the operating system. But Internet Explorer 4 was placed inside the operating system. WHY?

Think about this. Why would anyone in their right mind tie the web browser code directly to the operating system code? Linux doesn't do this. There is no doubt that tying these two things together makes the programming for each much more difficult – and slows down both the browser and the operating system. With all of these drawbacks, Microsoft must have had a very good reason for doing this. Some mistakenly thought that Microsoft was trying to monopolize the browser business. But this was not the case at all. At the time, browsers were being given away for free. There was and still is very little money to be made by monopolizing the browser business. The initial motivation for Microsoft to link Internet Explorer to Windows was because they wanted to maintain the Windows monopoly. The only way to do this was by adding Internet Explorer integration to Windows. Allow me to explain how this whole process works. It is important to know because this is the "back door" which I refer to throughout this entire book.

Facts that confirm Microsoft relies on an open back door to your computer
If you start with the understanding that the most important thing for Microsoft is money – which means protecting the Windows monopoly, then this will start to become more obvious. Let's look at a couple of important facts:

Fact #1: You cannot uninstall Internet Explorer from Windows
This is true of Windows XP, Windows Vista, Windows 7 and Windows 8. You can "turn Internet Explorer off" from the Windows feature list – which hides Internet Explorer but does not remove it.

Many users (and especially programmers) have noted that the most vulnerable part of any Windows operating system is Internet Explorer. Because most of them hate Internet Explorer, there is a natural tendency to try to get rid of it. But if you actually succeeded in getting rid of it, you would crash Windows. This is in part because Windows relies on the core engine which runs Internet Explorer.

Fact #2: Microsoft Updates come in through Internet Explorer
Have you ever wondered what all the updates are about? Microsoft calls them security updates. But many of these are not at all about protecting your computer. They are about protecting the Microsoft Windows monopoly. The idea is to constantly keep changing your Windows settings (creating a moving target) to prevent pirated copies of Windows from fully functioning. Without these constant updates, there would be no Microsoft Windows monopoly.

Fact #3: Each version of the Windows operating system is tied to a particular type of Internet Explorer
One of the many problems of trying to continue to run Windows XP is that it will not work on any version of Internet Explorer past Internet Explorer 8. Why is this? Some have claimed that Microsoft is doing this deliberately to try to force Windows XP users to upgrade to Windows 7 or Windows 8. This could be. But I think there is a different more fundamental reason. I think it is because the security functions of Windows and the security functions of Internet Explorer are tied together at the hip. This is why Windows XP can run the latest versions of Mozilla Firefox and Google Chrome web browsers but cannot run the three latest versions of Internet Explorer. In other words, instead of Microsoft being entirely evil, they could simply be stuck between a rock and a hard place. This is simply the only way they can maintain their monopoly.

Fact #4: The structure of Windows 8 makes it more obvious that there is a direct connection between the operating system and Internet Explorer
Windows 8 is actually two different operating systems which have been tied together. For the sake of convenience, I will call these the **Metro Mobile operating system** – which runs the Metro screen and functions – and the **Windows 7 Desktop operating system** which runs the desktop functions. The reason integration is so bad between the desktop and the metro screen is that <u>they are completely different operating systems</u>. What Microsoft has done is create a Jekyll and Hyde combination of two separate operating systems and then tried to hide this fact with one log in screen. Windows 8 Blue cannot "fix" this problem because it is an inherent part of the structure of Windows 8.
Windows 8 = Metro NSA Operating System + Windows 7 Operating System

There are many ways this is revealed. First, you can have either the metro screen or the desktop active – but you cannot have both! When you first log in, you are forced to visit the Metro Mobile Operating System. Windows 8.1 will allow you to go directly to the desktop. But all it is really doing is allowing you to choose the desktop operating system when you first boot up your computer.

Second, the file structure is different for the two operating systems. If you go deep into the Windows 8 Desktop Explorer File Manager, you can still see that many of the functions say "Windows 7" on them. This makes it pretty clear that the desktop is still Windows 7. However, many of the functions of Windows 7 have been removed and placed in the Metro Mobile operating system. This includes all of the applications and the search functions and the security functions. This is why you are forced back to the Metro screen before you can go to the Applications screen or the Search screen. Third, many of the abilities in Windows 7, such as the ability to control the size and location of open windows, are missing in the Metro Mobile operating system. One of the most obvious problems here is the inability to overlap open program windows. Or you can see all of one application, but only part of another. You cannot overlap any applications or get is an application and the metro screen side by side or the metro screen and the desktop side by side.

Fourth, the Metro Operating System uses a different version of Internet Explorer. The clearest indication that these are separate operating systems is that they use two different versions of Internet Explorer! Below is the **Metro NSA Operating System version of Internet Explorer.**

Click on the Internet Explorer icon in the Metro screen and you get the Metro version of Internet Explorer. Note that the browser screen opens in full screen mode with the URL box at the bottom.

Windows 7 Desktop Operating System version of Internet Explorer

Change from the Metro Mobile operating system to the Windows 7 operating system by clicking on the Desktop icon in the Metro Start screen. Then click on the Internet Explorer Icon on the desktop and you get the Windows 7 version of Internet Explorer complete with the traditional navigation buttons. To remove any doubt at all about whether these are separate versions of Internet Explorer, leave the Windows 7 Internet Explorer running and while on the desktop hover over the upper left corner hot spot. This will bring up a small icon showing the Metro Mobile version of Internet Explorer is still running.

I hope that now you are starting to get the picture that we are dealing with two completely separate operating systems with two completely separate versions of Internet Explorer!

Fifth, with Windows 8, you cannot perform many functions – including resetting your password, unless you are online

This is one of the most sinister and least known "features" of Windows 8. We covered this in our first chapter. But ask yourself... why should Microsoft care about what your password is? And why would they want to store your password on their database? With Windows XP and Windows 7, you have complete control over your user account and your password for your computer. Just click on Change your Password. Then type in your current and new password. There was no need to be online to change your password with Windows 7 and Microsoft did not care what your password was. After all, it is your computer, isn't it?

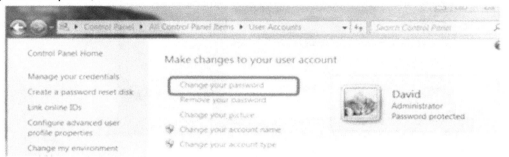

However, with Windows 8, you must be online to change your password. Even to get to the password screen requires following some very hidden steps. First, you need to start Internet Explorer. Then you need to click on one of the left side hidden hot corners to bring up the Five Magic Charms. Then you need to click on the bottom charm, called Settings. Then you need to click on a link called Change PC settings. This takes you to the new Metro Control Panel. Then you click on Users. This takes you to the Windows 8 Metro Operating System User Account screen:

Notice that your account with Windows 8 is now tied to your email address.

Next, click on Change your Password. If you are not online, you will see this warning:

Change your password

Sorry, we couldn't connect to Microsoft services right now. If this problem persists, search for "network problems" on the Start screen.

However, if you are online when you try to reset your password with Windows 8, you are taken to the following password reset screen:

Change your Microsoft account password

David Spring

Old password

Forgot your password?

New password

Reenter password

The Latest Microsoft Gimmick: Secure Boot is really "Protect the Microsoft Monopoly" Restricted Boot

Also in 2012, it became clear that it would not be easy to move from Windows 8 to a Linux operating system because Windows 8 is using a new "feature" called Secure Boot to control which operating systems are loaded onto your computer. Microsoft is forcing computer manufacturers to use special "keys" controlled by Microsoft to be installed on all computers. Windows 8 is not about mobile computing or the metro interface. All of that is pure distraction. Windows 8 is gaining total control over your computer. This is why Windows 8 has introduced a way to control the log in process on your computer's front door. This is also why Windows 8 requires manufacturers to use the Secure Boot locking mechanism on all of their Windows 8 computers. It is to give Microsoft total control over every computer so that Microsoft can shut down any Windows 8 computer which does not have the official Microsoft keys. This is what some have called the Windows 8 Kill Switch. Of course, for this plan to work, Microsoft also has to get people to stop using Windows XP. So Phase 2 of the plan is to shut down support for Windows XP on April 8, 2014. Shortly thereafter, someone (cough, the NSA, cough) will unleash a virus which will put an end to all of the bootlegged copies of Windows XP. The fact that this will take down 600 million computers is beside the point. It is the profit that counts. This is profit not only for Microsoft, but for computer manufacturers who will get to sell millions of additional computers - because Windows 8 is so bloated that it won't run on those old XP computers.

This still leaves Windows 7 computers. These do not have the Microsoft Kill Switch and they will continue to be supported by Microsoft Updates until 2020. Gee, I wonder if the bootleggers will figure out a way to make bootleg copies of Windows 7? Oh, wait, they already have! In that case, I wonder if Microsoft (aka the NSA) will stand idly by and watch hundreds of millions of bootleg XP computers be turned into bootleg Windows 7 computers.

If you were Microsoft, what would you do? I have an idea. Why not send out updates that wipe out the Windows 7 computers too? It doesn't have to happen all at once. It can be a little change here and a little change there. Pretty soon the Windows 7 computers start to slow down and die and then then everyone will have to get a Windows 8 computer. Eventually, Microsoft (aka NSA) will have total control over whether or not every computer even starts.

All of the examples shown above – and many more - are why the Windows 8 system is fundamentally flawed and cannot be fixed. They can make some minor cosmetic changes. They can even give you the choice between entering the Metro Mobile operating system first or the Windows 7 Desktop operating system first. What they cannot do is turn two different operating systems into one.

This means that all of the functions and applications must be accessed through the Metro screen and that commands and functions which work on one of these operating systems will not work and may not even be accessible on the other. What all of this complexity will do however is help maintain the Microsoft Windows monopoly – because it is so complex that pirates will have trouble bootlegging and copying it – at least for a while. What Microsoft fails to understand is that in making it too difficult for pirates, they have also made using their software too difficult for their own customers. Once these customers really understand how difficult it is to learn and use Windows 8 – and how insecure it is – they will run in droves towards Apple and Linux. And if the fact that Microsoft now controls even the password on your computer doesn't get you to move to a less invasive operating system, then nothing will.

Why the Microsoft Total Domination Plan will fail

Unfortunately for all of us, this Windows Secure Boot plan is doomed to fail. The Flame virus has shown hackers how to break the Microsoft digital image signature key used with Windows Updates. This same digital image key is used to lock down computers with the Windows 8 Secure Boot. It is only a matter of time until the only ones who do not have a key to every Windows 8 computer are the people who bought Windows 8 computers.

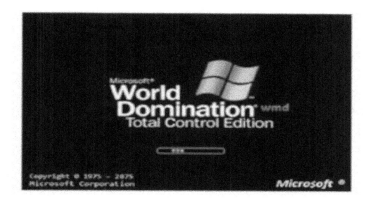

Now Microsoft is not going to use their Kill Switch to shut down every Windows 8 computer. They only want to shut down bootlegged copies of Windows 8. But in creating this nuclear weapon of the computer age, Microsoft (aka NSA) has created a monster that they will not be able to control. Imagine some hacker group gets ahold of this nuclear Kill Switch. They can and will use it to take down every Windows 8 computer. All that is required is to change the keys to the Secure Boot Start program and Windows 8 computers will refuse to start. This is like the landlord having the ability to change the keys on your house. A good landlord will not lock you out of your house – but a bad landlord will . Your computer is the home for all of your data. Computers are not only the home for your data - they are the home for the essential data of every business in the world. Imagine what would happen to the world's economy if someday all of the world's computers were to suddenly shut down.

Three warning signs your Windows 8 Computer has been hacked.
Despite all of the Microsoft gimmicks designed, all these gimmicks have done is add more ways that hackers can attack your computer. Therefore, as a public service, we are providing three sure fire signs you can use to tell if your Windows computer has been hacked. First, if you notice the Microsoft now fails to authorize programs it used to find acceptable, you may have a problem:

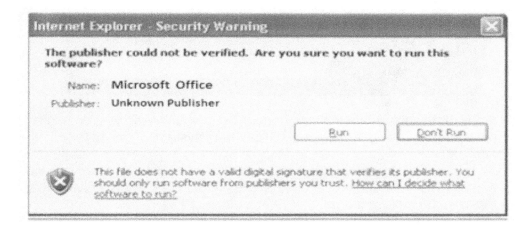

Second, if there seems to be an abnormally high number of security updates on Patch Tuesday, you may have a problem:

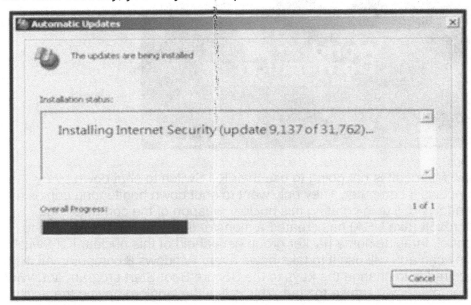

Third, if you see additional users who you do not recognize on your Windows 8 log in screen, it is very likely that Microsoft security has been compromised.

A suspicious Windows Login screen:

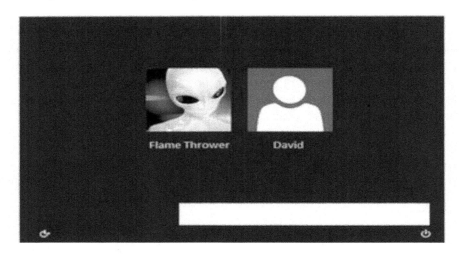

If any of these three things start happening to your Windows 8 computer, please reboot using a more secure operating system!

As bad as this disaster would be. There is an even greater threat created by the Microsoft Monopoly – and it is already happening. We will review this threat in the next section.

3.4 The Real Cost of the Microsoft Monopoly

I prefer dangerous freedom over peaceful slavery.
Thomas Jefferson

We have now reviewed more than a dozen benefits of the Linux operating system over Windows 8. Given the functional benefits of Linux and the fatal flaws of Windows 8, it is difficult to imagine anyone going with Windows 8 if they really understand all of its flaws. By now, you should understand why Windows 8 is completely different from Windows XP or Windows 7. Still, it is likely that Microsoft will be able to fool millions of people simply with the huge force of their billion dollar per year advertising campaigns. The only question is how many people they will be able to fool before folks find out what a flawed product they are getting with Windows 8. Now, we will look at Microsoft's plan to convince us that we should spend $500 on Windows 8 and MS Office 2013... and signs that word is already starting to get out that Windows 8 is a disaster. We will also look at some of the more hidden costs of the Microsoft monopoly.

Sales of Windows 8 are 50% less than same period sales of Windows 7
A Bloomberg report on March 14 2013 claimed that Microsoft has only sold 1.5 million Surface tablets. This includes one million Surface RTs (the cheaper version with an operating system that is even worse than Windows 8)... I wonder how many Surface RT buyers know that they will be very limited in the programs they can run? This limitation is pretty well hidden on the MS Surface website. 1.5 million Surface tablets was only half the number Microsoft expected to sell in the first six months.

Meanwhile, in the same six month period, Apple sold 45 million Ipads. So **Apple is outselling Microsoft 30 to 1 in the tablet market.** The total market was over 150 million tablets sold. So MS has gotten less than 1 percent of the market – despite a record one billion dollar advertising campaign. One Microsoft analyst summed it up this way: *"Things (at Microsoft) were bad at the beginning of the year and they are getting worse."*

Net Applications, a research firm that uses an objective basis for determining operating system usage, recently reported that the Windows 8 adoption rate is worse than Vista – which had previously held the record as Microsoft's worst product. At 6 months, the Windows 7 adoption rate was 12% and Windows Vista was at 4.5%. Windows 8 still hasn't hit 4%:

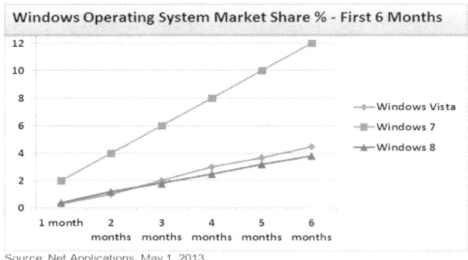

Source: Net Applications, May 1, 2013

What is the current market share for Windows 8?

According to data from Net Applications, in June 2013 Windows XP had 37% of the market compared to Windows 7 which had 44%. Windows Vista had 4.6% and Windows 8 finally moved over 5% - still the worst beginning performance of any Microsoft operating system. As a whole, Windows accounted for 92% of all traffic while Apple Mac OS X captured 7% (leaving only 1.3% for Linux). Windows XP is losing market share at a rate of about one half percent per month. This means that Windows XP will still be above 30% of the market in April 2014. With a total market of 2 billion computer users in the world, what will these 600 million Windows XP users do on April 8 2014 when their "security updates" end and their only replacement choices are Windows 8 or something else?

Steve Ballmer loses $340 billion in 10 years and $34 billion in a single day

On Thursday, July 18 2013, Microsoft revealed for the first time that it had lost $900 million due to weak demand for Windows 8 and poor sales of its Surface tablet. The next day, Microsoft stock fell 11.4 percent for a total loss of $34 billion. Microsoft still has about $88 billion in cash. Revenue is still about $80 billion per year and profit is about $20 billion per year. However, company value as determined by stock price has plunged from $605 billion in 2000 to $265 billion in August 2013 for a loss by Microsoft shareholders of $340 billion. This decline in stock price came despite Microsoft trying to raise its stock price by buying back $50 billion in stock during the past 5 years. Given the outrage over Microsoft's close relationship with the NSA, it is likely that Microsoft value will continue to decline in the future.

Can Microsoft Marketing convince us to buy a fatally flawed product?

According to Forbes Magazine, Microsoft plans to spend a record $1.5 billion dollars trying to convince us to buy Windows 8. While spending this massive amount of money, the Microsoft marketing department will tell us that Windows 8 is an improvement on Windows 7 because it is "touch screen friendly" and therefore works better on tablets. They will tell us that Windows 8 is simply Microsoft becoming more like Apple. There is also a plan to introduce Microsoft Blue this summer as an updated version of Windows 8. The name "Windows Blue" seems to be yet another blunder by Microsoft as it will likely just remind Windows users of their past bad experiences with the Windows Blue Screen of Death (see example below).

August 2 2013 Update Microsoft Sales go from bad to worse

In August 2013, Microsoft reported that it actually spent more on advertizing last year than it made in Surface sales. Anytime a company spends more on advertising a product that it gets back on sales, there is a major problem. Microsoft's response is that they will spend yet another billion on advertising. But word is getting out that Windows 8.1 Blue and Surface are both terrible products. What is needed is not more advertising – but better products. Despite all of these problems, the CEO of Microsoft is optimistic about the success of Windows 8. In October 2012, at a Windows 8 launch event in New York, Steve Ballmer pointed out that 670 million computers will need upgrading in the next few years and that 400 million more will be sold annually (all thanks to Windows crashing all of our computers).

At $500 per computer to Microsoft for Windows 8 and Office, that is a lot of money. If Steve Ballmer is right, the real cost of all of these upgrades to Windows 8 and Office 2013 will be close to $200 billion – or $50 billion per year each year for the next four years.

I have a different point of view. I work with real students in the real world. I have seen how they struggled with Windows 7 and everything before that. I am certain that <u>many of these students will NEVER be able to use Windows 8.</u> So in conclusion, Microsoft has shot themselves and all of the rest of us in the foot by producing an operating system which is basically non-functional. What in the world were these guys thinking? Instead of spending hundreds of millions of dollars on marketing, Microsoft should have hired a few teachers and we could have warned them that simplicity is more important than glitter. What will happen when users around the world discover that Windows 8 is nothing at all like Windows 7?

Largely due to huge upgrades in computer hardware (both storage and speed), the average person replaces their computers every three to five years. This means that in the next five years, nearly one billion folks are going to gradually learn that Microsoft has stuck a knife in our backs. I predict that many of those folks are going to do exactly what I have done. First, they will continue to use Windows 7 as a temporary solution. Second, they are going to start looking around for other alternatives – and by other alternatives, I am not talking about Mac. I am talking about other alternatives that will work well with Windows based programs and are not controlled by the NSA. This is why we all need a review of all of the available operating systems. It is because at some point, we all are going to have to find another option.

How much do we spend on commercial programs and how much will we save by moving to open source tools?
It has been estimated that there are around two billion internet capable personal computers in the world today. It has also been estimated that over 300 million new personal computers have been sold each of the past two years. Thus, it is believed that the average user replaces their laptop every four years. Of the two billion computers, about 45% run Windows 7 and another 40% run Windows XP.

Microsoft has announced that in April 2014, they will discontinue support and security updates for Windows XP. This means that more than 600 million Windows XP users will suddenly find their computers basically unprotected in April 2014. Microsoft has warned that "using XP after April 2014 will be at your own risk."

If you see this symbol on your computer start screen, your goose is cooked in 2014!

On April 8 2013 Microsoft also announced that they would give 15% discounts for Windows XP users who wanted to upgrade to Windows 8 and Office 2013. XP users can get Windows 8 in combination with Office 2013 for $477. Many families have two or three XP computers in their homes – meaning the cost for upgrading could easily reach $1,000 or more. What will these 600 million people do? If you are Microsoft, your hope is that everyone will upgrade to Windows 8. However, as word gets out that Windows 8 has major problems, some people will opt for Windows 7 – which Microsoft has said they will support until 2020.

Most folks are not aware that computer manufacturers pay Microsoft to install the Windows operating system on their computers. This cost varies from model to model. But it is reasonable to assume that the average cost is about one hundred dollars per computer. Manufacturers pay this fee not because they think that Windows is such a terrific operating system. Believe me, they get an earful every time one of their Windows based computers crash. But they realize that Microsoft currently has a monopoly on the computer market and that the only way they are going to sell a computer is if Windows is installed on it. So they pay the hundred dollars and add it to the price of their computers. In other words, when manufacturers offer computers with free open source operating systems, each of us will save $100 per computer. While Microsoft offers a "deal" to manufacturers to get them to install Windows on their computers, Microsoft is much less generous to those who already have Windows 7 on their computers. Upgrading from Windows 7 to Windows 8 Pro will cost an incredible $200. Thankfully, there is no need to upgrade to Windows 8 since Windows 7 is actually better than Windows 8. But the cost of the Windows operating system does not end there - because your computer will not work without additional software for everything from games to word processing and accounting. These Windows based programs can cost several hundred dollars. These programs need updating every year which is why folks typically spend hundreds of dollars per year on Windows based programs.

Thankfully, Linux Mint is capable of running Windows programs. But more importantly, Linux offers thousands of free alternatives to Windows programs. In many cases, these free programs are actually better than their expensive commercial cousins. Then there is the cost of lost productivity and computer repair to consider. The average person is forced to either spend hundreds of dollars on computer repair when their laptop crashes – or spend hundreds to thousands of dollars buying a new computer. Having a more reliable computer which does not require constant updates and virus protection programs can save a person hundreds to thousands of dollars every year. But all of this is nothing compared to the loss of productivity associated with a computer crash. This problem can literally cost you a week's wages – or even put you out of business. So the real savings of learning to use open source tools can be much higher every year.

Public Schools and the Coming Windows 8 Train Wreck
One group in particular that is concerned about price is our public schools. School districts all over the country are turning to portable computers as a way to provide students with a better high tech learning opportunity. They are also looking at computers as opening the door to lower cost and more current electronic text books as well as other new online learning opportunities. However, school districts are on a very limited budget.

One school district in Washington State, the Lake Washington School District, recently spent $500 per student to buy every secondary school student in their school district a portable laptop. This school district which is located in Redmond, the home city of Microsoft, obviously had Windows 7 and Microsoft Office installed on all 20,000 of these computers. The total cost was $10 million. But had they used an Open Source operating system and an open source Office program, the cost would have likely been closer to $300 per student or $6 million for all 20,000 students. **The difference of $4 million dollars could have paid for 80 additional teachers in their school district!**

A Lake Washington School District administrator recently announced that they will likely be "upgrading" to Windows 8 this summer. At a cost of about $100 per student times 20,000 students this will be another $2 million – or another 40 teachers!

The real issue will come when students are unable to use Windows 8 and their classrooms come to a grinding halt. At some point, I see even the Lake Washington School District moving towards open source tools so they can hire more teachers instead of throwing money down the Microsoft drain.

> *"They'll get sort of addicted, and then we'll somehow figure out how to collect some time in the next decade."* Bill Gates July 2 1998

We are reaching a turning point. This turning point is only in part due to price. Many folks would gladly pay an extra few hundred dollars per year just to have a reliable computer for saving and processing documents. But what they are likely not willing to do is pay a few hundred dollars for a system which is less usable and less reliable. Safety is a major reason why the vast majority of web servers in the world, including the Google Servers, run on Linux open source programs and operating systems. Obviously, price is not an issue to Google. Their primary concern is keeping their servers and their websites up and running. The real tipping point comes when folks realize that Windows is neither reliable nor functional. All that is needed is a catalyst to force users to take that crucial first step towards open source. I predict that the April 8 2014 deadline cutting off support for Windows XP will be that catalyst. Instead of forcing folks to pay them for Windows 8, what Microsoft will really be doing is slitting their own throat. Once folks learn how much easier open source is, and how much money they can save, they will happily move to open source tools such as Linux.

Waiting for another update... I sure wish there was an alternative to this slow buggy computer...

Linux is better for Innovation
Another reason open source has pulled ahead of commercial rivals is that open source programmers are allowed to be more creative than private, commercial programmers. Commercial programs are based on patents and monopolies which are the enemies of innovation.

Open source has fewer rules and fewer obstacles. Open source programmers do not have to worry about whether they are violating someone else's patent or how to prevent someone else from violating their patent. They therefore can focus on simply designing a clear and safe program – rather than a complex, bloated program intended more to create or protect a patent than to help the end users.

Open source tools promote better compatibility
Another benefit of open source is compatibility. There are many ways to create, open, manage and send MS Word documents and PDF documents with Linux and its free word processor Libre Office. You can even automatically save documents in several formats at the same time with Libre Office Writer.

Open source tools offer better migration between formats
An increasingly important benefit of open source is safer and easier website and Ebook migration. Microsoft loads literally pages of programming garbage into the beginning of every Word DocX document. This extra code has to be eliminated when pasting Word documents into website pages – or it will slow down your website and even crash it. Libre Office allows easy conversion to HTML and/or Ebook formats!

Open Source Tools are as User Friendly as Commercial Programs
It used to be that open source tools were only for computer geeks who built their own computers and installed an open source operating system because it was free. One often had to know computer programming just to work with open source tools. However, in the past few years, there have been major advances in open source tools such that today, open source tools are actually better and more user friendly than their commercial rivals. They are safer, more reliable and offer more features and functions. We therefore predict that it is just a matter of time until more people realize this and make the move to open source tools.

Linux isn't a for-profit company. It's a not-for-profit community
You are less likely to need help with Linux. But if you do, there are many active forums to help users overcome obstacles. No waiting on the phone for hours to talk with someone who knows less about computers than you do.

Free Open Source Options to Expensive Commercial Programs
The open source tools we cover in the following articles include the **Linux Operating System** (which replaces MS Windows) and **Libre Office** (which replaces MS Office). In our other educational websites and books, we cover more open source tools including Joomla web building tools and VirtueMart online store building tools. Other examples of free open source tools include the Moodle Learning Management System. In fact, there are now thousands of free open source tools available for download with more tools available every day.

How can something free be better than something that costs 500 dollars?

In the following articles, we will explain why the Linux Operating System combined with Libre Office word processor is better than the Windows 8 operating system with Microsoft Office. But the first question we should address is how is it possible for something that is free to be better than something that costs $500? When people first hear about Linux as an option to Windows, their first reaction is that they need something that can process their normal Word documents and run their Windows programs. They are shocked to find out that Linux can run Windows programs and even more shocked to find out that Libre Office can open and process their Word documents. The next most common reaction is to claim that there must be a catch. Anything free cannot possible be as good as something that costs $500. But consider other important things which are free and useful: The Google Search Engine, which runs on Linux, is free and is the most popular website in the entire world. Public libraries are also free and do a great job of helping people gather information.

Some things belong in the public domain. Things like public schools and public roads are too important to charge for. Many in the open source community build and promote open source tools because they believe that open source tools should be like a public library – free and open to all regardless of income.

But if you still have trouble believing that Linux can be better than Windows, give it a try. Very few who make the move to Linux ever go back to the insecure Windows operating system.

Hidden Costs of the Microsoft Windows Monopoly

Microsoft updates and bloated code and vulnerability to computer viruses mean that all of our computers will slow down and crash over time. This means we will be not only required to buy new Windows programs – costing hundreds of dollars per year – but we will also needlessly be required to buy a new computer every 3 to 5 years. This doubles the profit Microsoft gets due to its monopoly. Assuming there are more than one billion computer users in the world today and that each one is forced to needlessly spend an extra thousand dollars to buy a new computer once their Microsoft computer finally crashes, **the real direct cost of Window 8 will eventually exceed one trillion dollars from us to Microsoft!**

But even a trillion dollars is a drop in the bucket compared to other hidden costs of the Microsoft monopoly.

First, consider the horrific working conditions that Microsoft imposes on workers around the world. Microsoft and Apple have both shot themselves in the foot by outsourcing both their manufacturing and their customer service to sweat shops in China and India. On May 22, 2013, Microsoft announced that they would hire "several thousand workers." All of the new hires will be in China – where they already have thousands of workers. Steve Ballmer said at a press conference in Shanghai, "I visited China last about one year ago in May and it is remarkable to me how much has changed. At Microsoft this is an incredibly exciting time."

Monopolies harm the entire world economy by destroying the rights of workers Microsoft alone sucks $70 billion per year out of the economy. Add Apple and other monopolies and the total loss is over $200 billion per year. Moreover, the computer monopolies are just part of a much larger corporate monopoly system that has grown like a cancer on the US and world economy and political system in the past 30 years.

Monopolies harm everyone in the world

Microsoft is just like the predatory monopoly banking system where just a few mega banks control over half of the world's wealth and like the energy monopoly where just a few mega oil companies control nearly all of the world's energy resources. And just like the information monopoly where just a few families control most of the world news distribution on TV, radio and print. As a direct result of this concentration of wealth and power in the hands of a few, the State and National tax burden has transferred from the rich to the poor and what is left of the middle class. As a percent of income, since 1980 and the rise of monopolies like Microsoft and Apple, the federal tax burden on the average middle class family has increased by over $1,000 per year in current dollars. The State tax burden has also increased by about $1,000 per year.

And if you or a member of your family has the audacity to want to go to college, that hidden tax burden has tripled to the point where the total college debt is over $1 trillion. This does not even include skyrocketing costs for everything from gasoline to health care – all due to the concentration of wealth and power in a few corporate monopolies controlled by a few wealthy crime families which control our economic and political systems. This is why our nation and planet are crippled by the worst economic crash since the Great Depression.

But the greatest hidden cost of continuing to support the Microsoft monopoly is the harm that Microsoft has done to our Democracy. Microsoft billionaires have used their extreme wealth to buy State and National elections, and evade paying billions of dollars in taxes by hiding their profits in offshore tax havens. If they are not going to be loyal to the American consumers who created their wealth, then why in the world should we continue to give them our hard earned money?

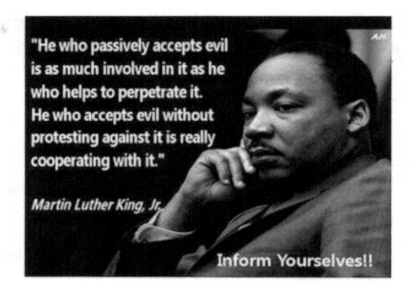

"He who passively accepts evil is as much involved in it as he who helps to perpetrate it. He who accepts evil without protesting against it is really cooperating with it."

Martin Luther King, Jr.

Inform Yourselves!!

The Silver Linux Lining behind the dark Microsoft Cloud
There is a silver lining to this dark cloud. If all one billion Microsoft Windows users decided to use Linux and Libre Office instead of Windows 8 and Office 2013, that would be a savings to the general public of more than $500 billion dollars. This is a savings of $100 billion per year for the next five years for all of the world's computer users! The only question remaining is what should we use to replace Windows 8? In the next article, we will provide a brief history of the evolution of open source operating systems. We will then provide a comparison of three open source operating systems to three closed source commercial operating systems.

Chapter 4... Linux to the Rescue

Chapter 4 includes the following four sections:

4.1 A Brief History of Linux Operating Systems
4.2 Benefits of Linux Mint over Linux Ubuntu
4.3 Four Steps to the Freedom of Open Source Tools
4.4 Install Linux Mint in a Virtual Machine

In this chapter, we will first learn about open source tools. Because open source is more about building communities over the long term rather than maximizing profits over the short term, novices often have a hard time understanding the huge diversity of open source options – which is the opposite of closed source monopolies. Diversity does add to the learning curve of open source tools. But it also is the reason that open source tools are leading a whole new wave of innovation in computer technology.

We will then review how to "experiment" with the Linux Mint 15 operating system by installing it onto a free virtual machine within you current Windows operating system on your current computer. This will allow you to see for yourself the benefits of Linux Mint before installing it as a dual boot (or dual operating system) on its own portion of your computer's hard drive.

4.1 A Brief History of Linux Operating Systems

> **We worked very hard on creating a name that would appeal to the majority of people, and it certainly paid off: thousands of people are using Linux just to be able to say "I've got Linux. What a cool name".**
> Linux Torvalds Developer of the Linux Operating System, March, 1993

While 99% of us were going through the ordeal of trying to work with either the Microsoft horizontal monopoly or the Apple vertical monopoly, there has been a third option growing in the weeds. Free open source tools, such as Linux, began in the early 1990's when some very forward thinking computer programmers insisted on freedom from the rigid patent structure imposed by commercial outfits like Microsoft and Apple.

The free software movement began in 1984 when Richard Stallman left MIT and founded GNU in order to create free software programs. GNU is a recursive acronym for "Gnu is Not Unix." Richard Stallman stated that GNU is a "technical means to a social end." The social end he was referring to was freeing knowledge from the clutches of private corporate monopolies – much as Thomas Jefferson advocated for public schools as being an essential foundation of our Democracy.

Richard was following the example of Henry Ford, who had challenged patents that had been used in 1911 to monopolize the development of the automobile. After overcoming this patent restraint on innovation, the automobile was able to develop rapidly. Richard Stallman argued that the same freedom from patent restrictions would lead to innovation in the software industry that would benefit everyone. Richard also argued that scientific advances were best accomplished in a process of openness and cooperation rather than corporate secrecy.

His goal was to bring a free software operating platform into existence. Stallman wanted computer users to be free to study the source code of the software they use, free to share the software with other people, free to modify the behavior of the software, and free to publish their modified versions of the software. In 1989, GNU published the first General Public License (GPL) under which software is legally shared freely.

One thing missing from the GNU project was a stable "kernel" or core which is at the heart of the operating system. The kernel can also be thought of as the foundation of a house. GNU had made all of the components of the house, such as the walls and the roof and the plumbing and electrical devices. But the foundation they had built it on – a kernel called HURD – was too complex and too unstable.

In 1991, a simple, stable kernel was created by Linus Torvalds. The kernel was called **Linux** since it was based in part on the Unix operating system. The Unix operating system was a private system owed by AT&T which for many years had allowed folks to use their program for free, but in 1979 AT&T decided to start charging to use their UNIX program. Most programmers paid the fee. But some, including Linus Torvalds, decided to create their own operating system.

> I believe Open Source is the right thing to do the same way I believe science is better than alchemy. Like science, Open Source allows people to build on a solid base of previous knowledge, without some silly hiding... you can never do as well in a closed environment as you can with open scientific methods.
> **Linus Torvalds 2007**

Linus Torvalds developed the Linux Operating System in 1991. This is Linus with the Linux Penguin. Linus now works for the Linux Foundation in Beaverton OR.

The proper name for the Linux operating system is **GNU/Linux.** However, as this is difficult to say and remember, most people simply refer to it as Linux and refer to the project which supports much of what goes into it as the GNU project.

> Open Source Math
> GNU + LINUX = GNU/Linux Operating System = Linux

Richard Stallman protests that calling GNU/Linux just Linux fails to recognize the role that GNU plays in building the entire operating system. However, in this book we will use the simple term Linux as our goal is to spread the use of this operating system and a simple term is more likely to spread usage than a complex term.

BSD, another free open source operating system is developed – and also paid for by the public

While Linux was the world's first free open source operating system, it was soon joined by another free operating system called BSD which stands for the Berkeley Software Distribution. This project started in the 1980's with a nearly finished free open source operating system released in June 1991. It was also based in part on the Unix operating system and therefore is a cousin of the Linux operating system. However, lawsuits by similar commercial operating systems, held up release of BSD until 1994 when a court decision held that over 99% of the BSD system did not violate any patents. There are currently several versions of the BSD free operating system.

What is important to understand about both the Linux and BSD operating systems is that both of them were initially funded primarily by public tax payer dollars. The BSD project was at the University of California at Berkeley. Nearly all of the funding therefore came from taxes paid by the citizens of the State of California with some help from the US federal tax payers. Linux Torvalds also points out that the only reason he was able to devote several years to creating the Linux operating system was that the citizens of Finland paid for his college education. In Finland, citizens can attend college for only $500 per year. Linus spent 8 years getting his Master's Degree (and working on the operating system). So we really should thank the citizens of Finland for the fact that we all can now benefit from the world's safest operating system.

Microsoft and Apple take advantage of free open source operating systems

While Microsoft and Apple have both accused each other of violating their patents, the irony is that they have both used free open source components to improve their own operating systems. The Apple operating systems in particular is based almost entirely on the BSD operating system. Thus, Apple is a close cousin of the Unix and Linux operating system.

Because BSD and Linux are shared over the internet, both projects had a strong interest in developing the internet networking portion of their free operating systems. As the importance of the internet grew in the 1990s, Microsoft adopted most of this free open source networking code into their own commercial operating system. Therefore, regardless of the operating system you are currently using, you are already using some free open source code. There are many other examples of technological development paid for by the public. The entire internet was built by public universities with public taxpayer dollars. The wireless WIFI system was also created using public taxpayer dollars. Even current development of open source programs is done largely by programmers at public universities who want to share code with programmers at other public universities. The only question is why any of us should continue to pay for products which were all created by our tax dollars. When products are created by the public, they ought to remain free and in the public domain. So there is something wrong with the current system of the public paying the costs and private monopolies taking the profits.

Open Source Initiative versus the Free Software Foundation
Despite the fact that the GNU/Linux operating system was free and was the safest and most versatile operating system in the world, adoption and refinement of the GNU/Linux operating system grew slowly. The first complete version, Linux 1.0, was not released until 1994. Ironically, there is a drawback to the word "free." Businesses and the general public tend to think of the word "free" as in no cost or "cheap" or "not very good." Richard Stallman tried valiantly to clarify that **the term "free" meant free as in "freedom"** and that freedom from patent restrictions was and still is important. But businesses and the public failed to recognize that their freedom was being taken away by the Microsoft and Apple monopolies. Many business owners thought that free open source programs were a communist attack which threatened their belief in capitalism.

To encourage wider adoption of the Linux operating system, a group split off from the Free Software Foundation in the mid-1990s and formed the **Open Source Initiative**. Instead of emphasizing the fact that the software was free, they pointed out the benefits of the software being open source – meaning that the source code was free of patent restrictions and could be freely shared. This led to businesses such as Google, Amazon and Facebook adopting version of the Linux open source operating system. These groups then devoted some funds back to the further development of open source operating systems. However, this new organization led to a split between Richard Stallman and Linus Torvalds – a difference of opinion which still exists today.

Open Source Desktop Interfaces

One problem with the Linux operating system in 1992 was that you had to know computer programming to use it. Therefore several groups began working on open source Graphic User Interfaces or GUIs so that a person could simply click on a series of buttons with a mouse rather than typing a bunch of computer programming with a key board – thus making Linux more user friendly. The interface appears on a computer screen which is also called a desktop. At some point, this interface became called a "Desktop Environment" or DE.

The first open source desktop interface, called **KDE for K Desktop Environment**, was started in 1996. Because some parts of KDE were not open source, a second and fully open source operating system, called **GNOME,** was started in 1997. GNOME stands for GNU Object Modeling Environment. This was the first major fork in the road for the Linux operating system. Even today, there are still Linux Systems based on GNOME and others based on KDE. A branch off of the Linux tree is called a fork:

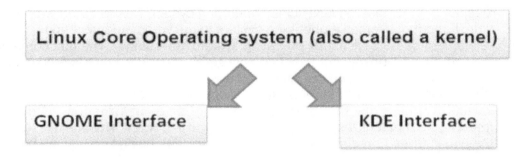

Linux takes over the Web Server Market

Because any computer programmer can do whatever they want with Linux, there quickly became many forks of Linux. Most of these forks were special branches intended to run servers. Servers are special computers that host websites and control traffic on the internet. The main reason most servers use the Linux operating system is that it is safe and dependable. Unlike a personal computer which is usually on only a few hours a day, web servers are typically on 24 hours a day. You therefore need an operating system that does not crash regardless of what it is confronted with. You also need an operating system which is safe from viruses and hacker attacks.

Because servers are built and run by experienced computer programmers, most of them chose to use Linux. But they also forked Linux into highly specialized versions which are not that appropriate for the average person to use to run their own personal computer.

GNOME 1 and 2 Shells

The GNOME project developed a free open source graphic user interface which is used to display the free open source Linux operating system on a normal personal computer. Gnome 2 was started in about 2002 to improve the appearance and structure of Gnome 1. These incredibly smart people were interested in long term cutting edge innovation more than short term quarterly profits. For years, Linux had been a tool used mainly by Geeks and computer programmers who would build their own computers from scratch. It is actually easier than you might think to throw together a few computer components and create a low cost high powered computer. Because they wanted freedom, they would also install their own operating systems – which were nearly all offshoots of Linux. But to use these early Linux operating systems, you pretty much had to be good with computer programming. While some of the computer could be controlled using the GNOME interface, many functions still required entering computer commands into a portion of the GNOME interface called the "terminal." Think of terminal as in deadly illness. Requiring any computer programming at all eliminates 99% of us who will never learn computer programming. I personally know several computer programming languages and have taught computer programming. So I am not really talking about myself. I am talking about my students. It takes real focus and dedication to get good at computer programming and most people simply do not have the time or interest to really learn it.

Distributions – also known as Distros

Distributions are packages of free open source programs that are built on top of the Linux foundation. The package includes a word processing program, an image processing program and any of thousands of other possible programs. Some distributions use the Gnome Shell, some use the KDE shell and/or several different shells. When you download a Linux operating system, what you are really downloading is one of the many distributions of Linux. The oldest of these distributions is Debian – which began in 1993 using a very early version of the Linux operating system. Fedora was introduced a couple of years later. This distribution is sponsored by a commercial Linux based company called Red Hat which has revenue of over one billion dollars per year. Below is a 2013 June list of the five most popular distributions (or open source software packages) based on number of page hits per day according to distrowatch.com:

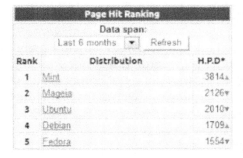

Linux Mint is the first Linux distribution to average over 4,000 page hits per day. It has been the leading Linux distribution for the past two years. Ubuntu is a fork of Debian that was started in 2004 to offer a consistent release and update cycle. It was the most popular distribution until about 2011 when it was replaced by Mint. Mint is a fork of Ubuntu that was started in 2006 to offer users a more Windows-like operating system.

Linux Distributions Family Tree

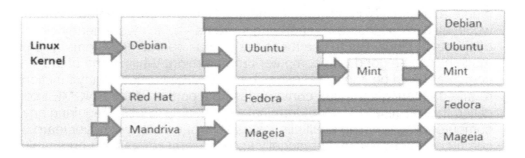

Above are five of more than one hundred Linux distributions. Mageia is a relatively new open source distribution which was started in 2010 and is based on a commercial Linux distribution called Mandriva. Mandriva was liquidated by a French court in 2010 and all of their programmers were fired. Some of these programmers formed a new company called Mageia to carry on with the Mandriva distribution. But Mageia is not as well organized or as simple to use as the Linux Mint distributions - which is why we recommend Linux Mint.

Linux Ubuntu
Ubuntu was started in 2004 by a South African businessman named Mark Shuttleworth. His company is called Canonical and his goal was to create a more user friendly operating system. He chose the "Debian" version of Linux as his base and added more friendly user interfaces over time. Like Debian, Ubuntu is based on the Gnome shell. While Ubuntu and Mint are technically called "distributions" or "distros", they can also be thought of as "skins" with Linux as the brain. Ubuntu released a version called Warty Warthog in 2004. This was the first widespread public adoption of an operating system other than MS Windows and Apple Mac. The main benefit of Ubuntu back in 2005 was that it was free. It was therefore used in cheap computers in schools and in poor countries, which often could not afford hundreds of dollars per student every year for Windows based operating systems and related software. Sadly, Ubuntu was not very stable and it crashed a lot. It was also not very easy to use. Many of the functions are hidden and the file structure is not very logical. Worst of all, to really use it, you still had to learn a series of computer programming commands to operate their "terminal." This meant that Ubuntu was not a good choice for most beginners.

The Linux Mint Project starts in 2006

In 2006, a group of computer programmers, led by Clem Lefebvre, split off from Ubuntu and began the **Linux Mint** project. The Mint interface and file structure are much more like the Windows interface and file structure. This was a huge improvement over Ubuntu – but nowhere near as mature as Windows XP, which had a 10 year lead over Linux Mint. Just as Rome was not built in a day, it took several years for the Linux Mint team to create a stable reliable product. Development, appearance and user friendliness accelerated in 2009 with the introduction of the Ubuntu Software Manager. This new tool, used by both Ubuntu and Mint, would eventually put open source operating systems ahead of commercial operating systems which lack this feature. Thanks to a very large community of supporters, Mint was able to close the gap with Windows by 2010. Their latest version, Linux Mint 15 Mate, introduced in May 2013 and featuring Libre Office 4, is in many ways substantially better than Windows 7. We will review these benefits in the section on Linux Mint. But even ignoring the fact that Mate is free, it is better than Windows – and can work with either Windows based programs – or with thousands of free open source programs, such as Libre Office, which easily converts Microsoft Office documents.

Lord of the Rings... GNOME 3 Divides the Open Source Community

Sadly, beginning in 2011, there was a huge controversy in the open source community. This controversy still exists today. The computer programmers who controlled the GNOME 2 project decided to abandon Gnome 2 in favor of a more mobile friendly structure which they called GNOME 3. The introduction of Gnome 3 created havoc as **Gnome 3 eliminated many popular features of Gnome 2.** In particular, it eliminated the tree structure used to organize the file manager. It was therefore not well accepted. In fact, the founder of Linux, Linus Torvalds, issued a statement describing Gnome 3 as a mistake and a step backwards. This debate is still going on today. In many ways, this debate is similar to the controversy over Windows 8 – which abandoned Windows XP and Windows 7 in favor of a more mobile friendly structure.

The problem with abandoning a system which is popular is that it requires millions of people to learn an entirely new and different process. The other problem with any new computer program is that it tends to be unstable and crash a lot. This is because computer programs are complex and have unforeseen bad interactions with other computer programs. Despite these problems, Ubuntu went along with the GNOME 3 group and released their first GNOME 3 version in 2011. Today, all Ubuntu operating systems are based on GNOME 3.

Linux Mint "Mate" is born

In response to the GNOME 3 crisis in 2011, the Linux Mint team made a rather brilliant move. Instead of placing all of their eggs in the Gnome 3 basket like Ubuntu did – and angering half of their users – they decided to **continue development of Gnome 2 with Linux Mint "Mate**" - and also develop a new operating system, called Linux Mint "Cinnamon" based on Gnome 3.

Linux Mint comes in four different flavors or versions.

In addition, Linux Mint is available in two more versions. These are the KDE project's version of Linux and the XFCE version of Linux:

Mint XFCE is not very good because its file manager is pretty limited. However, Mint KDE is very interesting in that it is very similar to Mint Mate. To make matters more confusing, each of the four options above is available in a x32 bit version for computers with less than 4 GB of RAM and a x64 bit version for computers with 4 GB or more RAM. If this sounds as confusing as the Lord of the Rings trilogy, that is because it is. One of the drawbacks of Open Source is that anyone is free to do whatever they want. So there are lots of open source options and you will need to get use to a diversity of options and opinions if you want the benefits of open source.

Understanding Linux Diversity
One of the perceived drawbacks of Linux is complexity. Linux comes in many different flavors which are called distributions (or distros for short). This is actually a good thing since there is strength in diversity and because diversity helps promote innovation.

There are also many versions of Windows and Mac Operating Systems. But with Windows and Mac, the main purpose of their version changes seems to be to force their customers to pay them for the update to the new version – which is often worse than the old version. With Linux, diversity is more related to meeting different needs – not to create more profits.

Below are just a few of the many branches off of the Linux tree:

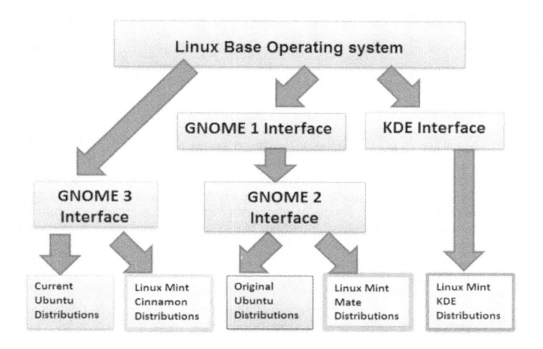

A key difference between the various Linux options is the Graphic User Interface. Other differences include the File Manager and the other free programs that come packaged with each option. We will handle this complexity by recommending what is currently the simplest, most stable and most powerful interface – **Linux Mint 15 Mate.** Its screens look quite similar to Windows 7 and Windows XP screens – so if you have been using Windows 7 or XP, you will feel right at home. In my opinion, **Linux Mint 15 Mate** is currently the best operating system in the world. It uses a very easy file manager called **Caja.**

Linux Mint 15 Cinnamon is also pretty good but it suffers from some minor GNOME 3 issues which are still being worked out. In response to the very bad Gnome 3 file manager, Linux Mint Cinnamon developed a much better file manager called **Nemo**. Linux Mint KDE is interesting and comes with a good file manager called Dolphin. But it also still has some minor issues. Ubuntu suffers from many problems which are discussed further in the next section.

Linux Mint 15 Mate Desktop with Start Menu open

What is important to understand about Linux operating systems is that there is really no need to upgrade or get updates unless you really want to. Some folks have expressed concerns about the rapid release cycles with open source programs such as Linux Mint Mate. New versions are released about every six months. Novices fear it will be difficult keeping up with all the updates and new versions. Others use Linux Mint Maya because it is a "long term release" (or LTS) which will be supported until 2017.

However, unlike Windows, which leaves the back door open to hacker attacks, Linux does not leave the back door open. Thus, there is no need for a monthly "update" and there is no need for an annual "upgrade" just to have a safe and secure operating system. And there is no need for long term support. While Linux Mint 15 Mate will only be supported until April 2014 – you can safely keep using it for the next hundred years if you want. The only reason to upgrade is if you want some new features. Because a lot of people want the most recent version, Linux Mint offers a way to backup and copy all of your data whenever you want to update to a newer version. But try to avoid getting caught up in the craze over the latest gadgets. The primary reason we recommend Linux Mint 15 over Linux Mint 14 is that Mate version 15 comes with Libre Office 4 pre-installed – whereas it has to be added as an update to Linux Mint 14.

Libre Office 4 does have some huge benefits over Libre Office 3. So it is worth using Linux Mint 15 to get these advantages automatically installed. Linux Mint 15 also comes with the UEFI Secure Boot signatures required by Microsoft.

Current Gnome Problems

The difference between Gnome 3 and Gnome 2 was not as great as the difference between Windows 8 and Windows 7. But because many popular features from Gnome 2 were removed in Gnome 3, there was an open rebellion in the open source community and huge resistance to Gnome 3 – much like there is huge resistance against the move from Windows 7 to Windows 8. Even people who are open to change will resist change when it is a step backwards.

What does the future hold for open source computer operating systems? In late 2012, the Gnome 3 team admitted they made a mistake with Gnome 3 and issued a public statement that in 2013, they would re-introduce many of the features they had previously abandoned. In March 2013, the Gnome team introduced Gnome 3.8 which includes a new "Classic mode. " Unfortunately Gnome 3.8 classic mode failed to restore any of the important features many people liked about Gnome 2. In addition, Gnome 3 also got rid of the popular Nautilus File Manager and replaced it with a much worse File Manager which the Gnome 3 team calls "File." Even the "Classic" mode still uses the bad file manager. This thing is so bad that you cannot do even the most basic tasks – such as right click to create a new file or a new folder. So things seem to be going from bad to worse with Gnome 3. On the plus side, the Linux Mint team has actually improved the Nautilus File Manager and renamed it as the Nemo file manager for use with their Gnome 3 based Cinnamon distribution. The Nemo file manager is very similar to the Caja file manager which Linux Mint uses on their Gnome 2 based Mate distribution. Linux Mint Cinnamon is therefore incorporating many of the features which have only been available in Mint Mate.

GNOME MATH...

GNOME 2 + GNOME 3

= GNOME 4!

If they are smart, the Gnome team will follow the Mint project and introduce a new platform called Gnome 4 to make it clear that they are moving away from all the problems caused by Gnome 3. Gnome 4 could bring a reunion of the open source community. This will not affect Linux Mint Mate. But it will mean that Linux Mint Cinnamon will become more similar to Linux Mint Mate. It could be that by 2014, we will see a new operating system from Linux Mint which integrates all of the best features of Linux Mate with the new innovative features of Linux Cinnamon. At the same time, I predict that there is going to be a major shift away from Microsoft Windows. Sales of Windows 8 are down nearly 20% from comparable time period sales of Windows 7. When folks learn that Windows 8 is nothing at all like Windows 7, this gap should grow even greater. The word will eventually get out on the internet no matter how much money Microsoft spends on advertising.

Tipping Points and the Structure of Scientific Revolutions
In the book, <u>The Structure of Scientific Revolutions</u>, Thomas Kuhn explains that revolutions do not happen gradually. People are highly resistant to change. They cling to existing beliefs until something drastic, a triggering event, forces them to consider something new. That triggering event may be the Double Whammy of Microsoft ending support for Windows XP and at the same time trying to force users to adopt the fundamentally flawed Windows 8 operating system.

Once 10% of the people become aware that there is a better option – which is also free – and an option where they can continue to safely use their current computers and current Word documents, change can spread like wildfire to the rest of the population. Only time will tell if this will actually happen. But given how hard it is to learn Windows 8, I am thinking that many people will decide to make the move to Linux.

Because the most widely known Linux distribution is Ubuntu, in the next section, we will look more closely at the benefits of Linux Mint over Linux Ubuntu.

4.2 Benefits of Linux Mint over Linux Ubuntu

The community is the most important asset of a distribution. It provides feedback, ideas, promotion, support, bug reports, artwork, and motivation. It's the living heart of any open-source project. In my opinion you need both clear leadership and good communication with the community.
Clem Lefebvre March 2013

In the last section, we pointed out that Linux Mint uses a better file manager than Linux Ubuntu. In addition, Linux Mint has a user interface which more closely resembles Windows XP and Windows 7. In this section, we will review some other benefits of Linux Mint over Linux Ubuntu.

Linux Mint versus Ubuntu operating system

How to Objectively Compare Operating Systems
Many claim that because Linux operating systems are all free, you should simply set up a free virtual machine on your current computer and install several Linux distributions in order to see for yourself which one you like best. For some, this advice makes sense. I have personally installed more than one dozen different Linux distributions on a virtual machine in order to evaluate them. However, this is poor advice for the general public as many would not even know what to look for in a well structured operating system. It is not efficient for every person to be spending hours, days and even months and years conducting their own research. Therefore, below is a summary of important factors I used to determine that Linux Mint is a better distribution for most users than Linux Ubuntu.

Five Important Characteristics of an Ideal Operating System

Some have claimed that there is an inherent conflict between a simple, fast and lightweight operating system versus a customizable and full featured operating system. However, Linux has solved this conflict by separating the base operating system from the features or additional programs you run on the base system. There are more than 50,000 programs you can install on any Linux distribution.

Linux Mint has also shown that it is possible to have both a fast and fully featured operating system with Linux Mint. Nevertheless, there are a few features which are more important to an operating system that may not be apparent to the casual user. Below we will look at five of these essential features and see how Linux Mint compares to Linux Ubuntu.

#1: Reliability includes stability of the code, not needing frequent updates, protection from viruses and of course not crashing.
#2: Easy Setup means it does not require installing extra tools to operate and can achieve a state of maximum usability with only a few minor adjustments.
#3: File Organized means the file structure can be quickly configured in an open and simple tree structure of folders and files so that all files and all tools can be quickly and reliably accessed.
#4: Easy Use means that there are no hidden files or tools. All files, tools and menus are clearly labeled to assist the novice in learning how to use the operating system
#5: Versatile means that it is compatible with other programs.

Why Linux Mint 15 Mate Won

The reason Mate won is because there is not much wrong with it.

Reliability: Linux Mint Mate is a very stable system which has required almost no updating or revisions in the past 2 years. Ubuntu is less reliable primarily because it is based on Gnome 3 – which is undergoing rapid changes while Mint Mate is based on the more stable Gnome 2.

Ease of set up: Linux Mint and Linux Ubuntu are both fairly easy to install. You just click on a few buttons to install and configure either. We will first cover how to set it up in a virtual machine and later how to set it up as a dual boot so that it can run parallel with the Windows operating system on your current computer.

File Structure: The file structure of Mate is similar to the Microsoft File Structure. Sadly, the biggest problem of Ubuntu is that they recently gutted their file manager such that you no longer have the ability to view your folders in a tree structure. The biggest advantage of Mint over Ubuntu is that it comes with a tree view file manager like Windows XP and Windows 7.

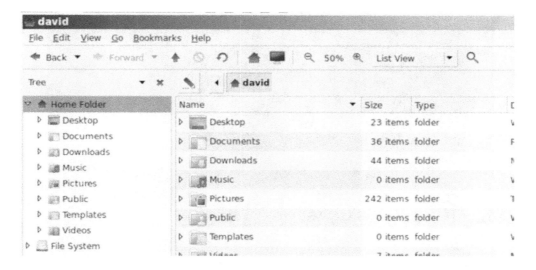

Ease of use

Mate is very easy to use because it is organized much like the Windows XP and Windows 7 operating systems. The Mint Mate desktop and start screen are very similar to Windows XP and Windows 7. This makes Mint much easier to learn for people converting from Windows XP and Windows 7. Ubuntu can be rather challenging because – much like Windows 8 – many important commands are hidden from view. For example, with Ubuntu, it is quite difficult to change the menus and or place shortcut icons on the desktop.

Mint Mate's interface uses a task bar at the bottom of the window. The task bar has a small popup menu that lists most of the applications and settings on your computer. It's **very similar to Windows 7 Start menu**, letting you browse your installed applications by hovering over different categories. When you open up an app, you'll see a button appear on the taskbar, just like in Windows Vista, Windows 7 and Windows XP. You can even add a few shortcuts to the side of your taskbar like Windows' old quick launch.

Mint's menu is much easier to browse, since it lists all your apps by category in a familiar way. It may have a smaller task bar with harder-to-see shortcuts, but beginners should be able to find anything they're looking for just by opening Mint's main menu.

Ubuntu promotes Amazon!

A major benefit of Linux Mint is better respect for your privacy. In October 2012, Ubuntu released version 12.10 which, for the first time, featured a link to Amazon.com in its main menu. Below is the Linux Ubuntu Start Screen:

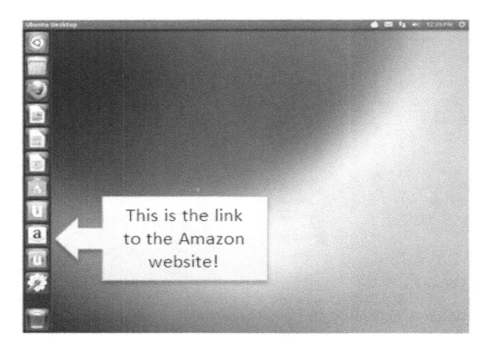

It is easy to delete this link. But what angered many Ubuntu users is that Ubuntu now collects data on user desktop activity and forwards it to Amazon. Many Ubuntu users are now bombarded by ads from Amazon after using the Ubuntu Search Box (which is now linked to Amazon).

Richard Stallman has described the integration of Ubuntu with Amazon as "spyware." See the following 6 minute Youtube video for a fuller explanation of Richard Stallman's concerns about the Amazon/Ubuntu invasion of your privacy:
http://www.youtube.com/watch?v=CP8CNp-vksc

One of the advantages of free software is that users historically have been able to protect themselves from malicious features. To recover our right to privacy, we have to either convince the Ubuntu developers to stop spying on us - or we need to move away from Ubuntu towards a project like Linux Mint which does not spy on us. I should add that even if Ubuntu stopped spying on us, I would still recommend Linus Mint Mate because it has a much better file manager. Also Ubuntu has a problem in that, like Windows 8, many important commands are hidden from view. You can navigate the Dash with your mouse, but it is incredibly complicated for beginners, hiding a lot of your apps under expandable menus and small icons. That means browsing for apps is a pretty bad experience when you are using Ubuntu.

Versatility... Mate, which comes with Libre Office pre-installed, can have a program called Wine added to it. Between Wine and Libre Office, you can use almost any program and process almost any document – outputting the document in almost any form you want.

Using and Installing Apps
Both Ubuntu and Mint come with a set of preinstalled apps that cover most of your needs: an office suite, a web browser, a music player, and a video player. Both Ubuntu and Mint also have their own app stores that make it easy for beginners to find, research, and download new apps.

Customization

Linux Mint Mate also allows you to customize every inch of your computer, from shortcuts to the size of your menus to the way windows work. Ubuntu, however, has done away with a lot of this lately. It does still offer some preferences, but it's much more "what you see is what you get" than Mint, which has loads of settings for tweaking everything down to the minute details of your interface. Many beginners may not care about this, but if you're a tech savvy user looking to learn about Linux, you'll probably find more things to "play with" in Mint. So say goodbye to the daily hassles of Windows and the constant fees for annual updates and say hello to the freedom of open source operating tools! In the following articles, we will begin with a review of installing and using the Linux Mint on a virtual machine.

4.3 Four Steps to the Freedom of Open Source Tools

> "Isn't it ironic that the proprietary software developers call us communists? We are the ones who have provided for a free market, where they allow only monopoly. … the only way to escape from monopoly is to escape from proprietary software, and that is what the free software movement is all about. We want you to escape and our work is to help you escape. We hope you will escape to the free world...Everyone is welcome in the free world, come to the free world, live with us in freedom."
> **Richard Stallman "Free Software in Ethics and Practice" 2008**

Four Steps to the Freedom of Open Source

If you are cautious like me, you are going to want to test the waters gradually before actually taking the plunge to open source. We have the perfect program for you. Thankfully, there is a way to wade into this ocean of freedom one step at a time. The following are four simple steps you can take that will allow you to try out open source tools without changing anything about the operation of your current computer.

Step #1: Use Virtual Box to Create a Virtual Machine

(Note: These directions are intended mainly for Windows XP and Windows 7 users. However, there are similar tools for Windows 8 and Apple users).
In this section, we will show you how to use a free open source tool called Virtual Box to create a virtual computer inside of your normal computer. This will allow you to install any operating system you want inside of your virtual machine so that you can test the operating system and see how well you like it.

Step #2: Install Linux Mint in a Virtual Machine
Using Virtual Box to install a virtual machine on your computer and then installing a copy of Linux Mint into the virtual machine will allow you to experiment with Linux Mint before installing it on your real computer. You can continue to use Windows to run your regular programs while you learn how to use the Linux operating system in a safe test environment. We will also show you how to set up a shared folder which will be accessible to both operating systems. This will allow you to go back and forth and compare the systems directly.

If you would like you can also install Linux Ubuntu in a Virtual Machine
You can also install Linux Ubuntu into a virtual machine on your computer. This will allow you to compare Linux Mint to Linux Ubuntu side by side.

Step #3: Install Linux Mint in a "Dual Boot" on your Real Computer
Third, once you agree that Linux Mint with Libre Office is a better option than what you are currently using, we will show you how to install Linux as a Dual Boot on your real computer. And you still can use your normal Windows operating system to run your Windows programs. Having a dual boot is very useful to help you recover your files in the event that the Windows program crashes – which you know it will eventually do. We will show you how to do all of this in our section on dual booting. You can use the dual boot for as long as you like! At some point, it will dawn on you that you haven't used Windows in years...

Step #4: Ditch Windows and Live Happily Ever After
Once you are confident that Linux Mint with Libre Office and Wine do everything you want to do – and much better than Windows ever did, after say a year goes by and you have never even bothered opening your Windows operating system, then you can delete the Windows program and move forward with a full Linux Mint operating system. When you are ready to let go of the security blanket, we will show you how to take the final steps to freedom. Alternately, if you want to keep Windows around as a security blanket (even though it is not secure), you can install Windows into a virtual machine. Even if you are rich and can afford thousands of dollars for Microsoft programs, you still are going to be very happy you took the time to learn how to use Linux and Libre Office. So let's get started! We will begin with Step 1: Installing Virtual Box on your home computer.

Step #1: Use Virtual Box to Create a Virtual Machine

We will now download a copy of the simplest and most stable version of the Linux Mint operating system which is version 15 Mate. We will then download a virtual machine called Virtual Box to place it in. Using a virtual machine is the safest way to test any operating system before installing it on your real computer.

Download Linux Mint 15 Mate

To visit the main site for Linux Mint go to: http://linuxmint.com/.

Here you will see that the Linux Mint project offers several operating systems. The two most popular are **Mate** and **Cinnamon**. The difference between them is that Mate is the stable version and Cinnamon is the cutting edge version. Unfortunately, Cinnamon was somewhat unstable in Virtual Box. It kept opening new windows. This feature can be disabled. But there will still be problems. For example, it can be difficult with Cinnamon to set a custom background image. Thankfully, there are no problems at all with Linux Mate. It is incredibly stable and easy to use. We will therefore download Mate instead of Cinnamon. Version 15 of Mint is called Olivia (including Olivia 15 Cinnamon and Olivia 15 Mate).

Even with Linux Mint Olivia 15 Mate, there are several versions. We want the version with the codecs. In addition, for a Virtual Machine, we want the 32 bit version which is intended for machines with less than 4 GB of RAM. Our virtual machine will only have 1 GB of RAM. If we were going to install it as a dual boot on a normal modern computer – with 4 to 8 GB of RAM, then we would pick the 64 bit version. To get the Linux Mint operating system, go to the following page: http://www.linuxmint.com/download.php

Download the **MATE 32 bit** version to your Downloads folder. It is a large file so you should be at a high speed internet connection and even then it may take a while. If you have a 64 bit computer with 4 GB or more of RAM, then also download the 64 bit version to eventually put into a dual boot on your computer.

Do the downloads one at a time and make sure one is completed before starting the other. Be patient. Each download will take about 30 minutes and can be found in your Downloads folder when you are done. After clicking on the 32 bit download link, you will be taken to the "mirrors" page. Scroll down to the US and pick one of the mirror locations to actually download the file. Select Save File. Then click OK. Now the download begins. Give it a full 30 minutes to complete the download before downloading and setting up your Virtual Machine.

Download Virtual Box

Before we install the Linux Mint 15 Mate operating system on our laptop, we first need to install and set up Virtual Box on our home computer. This is not much different than installing any other program on our computer. Virtual box can be installed on any computer with any Operating system and allows you to run multiple Operating Systems on the same computer at the same time. For each new operating system we add, we will create a separate "virtual machine" set up specifically for that operating system. For our purpose, we can keep our normal Windows operating system on our computer and learn how to use the Linux operating system inside of Virtual Box. This does require some disk space and memory. If this is lacking, you can also place Linux on a stick or flash drive and practice with it that way.

One option to install Virtual Box is to go to the virtual box website and download the Virtual Box Manual. It is only 324 pages. Thankfully, we can quickly install Virtual Box without reading the manual! Different versions of Virtual Box are available for different host operating systems. We will install the Virtual Box version for a Windows 7 64 bit host. But if you have a 32 bit computer or a Mac, just click on that download option instead.

We will then install Linux Mate Mint 32 bit Operating system as the "Guest" operating system. After setting up the Linux Mint Mate 32 bit operating system, we will install the Virtual Box "Guest Additions" as this will allow us to set up a "shared folder" between our host operating system and our guest operating system.

We will now show you how to do this set up by downloading the guest operating system to your Downloads folder and uploading it to a Virtual Box machine from your Downloads folder. But you could instead place the guest operating system on a Flash Drive and load it into Virtual Box from the Flash Drive.

Installation of Virtual Box

Go to the Virtual Box Downloads page:
https://www.virtualbox.org/wiki/Downloads
The base package includes all of the components. Click on the latest version to download it. It is a big 95 MB folder, so be patient. Do not attempt to start it until it is fully downloaded. Then go to your Downloads folder and start the install.
Right click on the Virtual Box Icon and select Run as Administrator. This will start the installation process. Just click Next:

Then click Install. Then click Finish. After clicking Finish, you will see the following Virtual Box Start Screen:

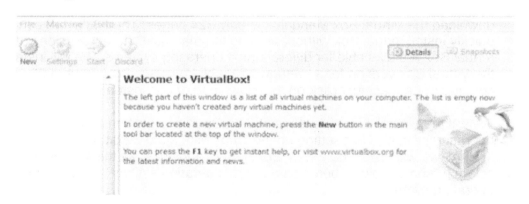

Change your Home Computer BIOS settings

Before creating a Virtual Machine, we need to first change one of the settings in the BIOS section of our home computer. Our task is to enable Virtual Machine Support (SVM support) in our Host computer BIOS settings. First, turn off your home computer. Then push the start button to turn it back on. Immediately hit **the F10 key** after pressing the Start button to bring up the BIOS screen. (This is the key for BIOS start on HP computers. You may need to press a slightly different key for a different manufacturer).

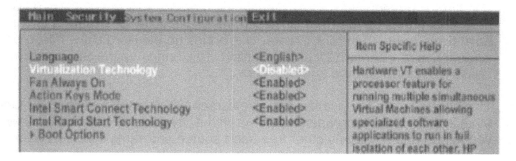

Then click on the right arrow of your keyboard three times to reach the **System Configuration** screen. Then use the down arrow on your keyboard to select **SVM support**. (on some computers it will say **Virtualization Technology).** SVM stands for Secure Virtual Machine. Then press the Enter key on your keyboard to enable SVM Support. Then click on F10 key on your keyboard to save the new settings and Exit BIOS. Your computer should automatically restart. Or you can restart it manually. Either way, log in. Then, when your desktop comes up, you should see a Virtual Box shortcut key on your desktop.

Set up your Virtual Machine
Click on the Virtual Box Icon on your desktop to open the Virtual Box Start screen.

Then click on NEW to create a new virtual machine. You will see this screen:

Use the download arrow to select **Linux** for the type and **Ubuntu** for the version. (Linux Mint is in the same family as Linux Ubuntu). Give your Virtual Machine a descriptive name such as Linux Mint 15 Mate. Then click on Next.

The default memory is 512 MB. Double the memory size to 1024. Then click next. This brings up the Hard Drive screen. Leave it set for **Create a virtual hard drive now**. Then click Create. This brings up the Hard Drive File Type screen. Leave it set for VDI and click Next. This brings up the Storage screen. Leave it set for **Dynamic** and click Next:

This brings up the file location and size screen. 8 GB is the minimum for Linux Mate and all of the programs that come with it. 18 GB is better as this allows you to add and test many other free open source programs that are available for it. Then click Create.

Click on **Settings** to improve the settings. For the General Advanced tab, make the Shared clipboard and Drag and Drop bidirectional.

Increase the display to 128 MB and enable 3D acceleration. Then click OK. Now that we have our virtual machine set up, we are now ready to install Linux Mint 15 Mate on our Virtual Machine. That is the subject of the next section.

4.4 Install Linux Mint in a Virtual Machine

Installing Linux Mint into a virtual machine is a great way to learn more about the benefits of Linux Mint without making any changes to your Windows operating system.

In the last section, we set up a Virtual Machine. In this section, we will install Linux Mint Mate 15 into that virtual machine. Assuming we have already downloaded the operating system ISO file and created a virtual machine in Virtual Box for it, the next step is to open virtual box and select the machine we want to use.

Then click on the Start button:

You have the **Auto capture keyboard** option turned on. This will cause the Virtual Machine to automatically **capture** the keyboard every time the VM window is activated and make it unavailable to other applications running on your host machine: when the keyboard is captured, all keystrokes (including system ones like Alt-Tab) will be directed to the VM.

You can press the **host key** at any time to **uncapture** the keyboard and mouse (if it is captured) and return them to normal operation. The currently assigned host key is shown on the status bar at the bottom of the Virtual Machine window, next to the ⊞ icon. This icon, together with the mouse icon placed nearby, indicate the current keyboard and mouse capture state.

The host key is currently defined as **Right Ctrl**.

☐ Do not show this message again

OK

Click OK:

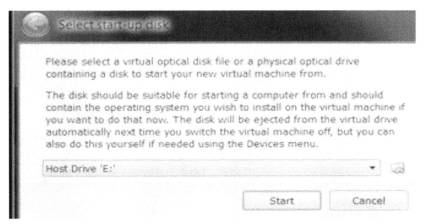

Select start-up disk

Please select a virtual optical disk file or a physical optical drive containing a disk to start your new virtual machine from.

The disk should be suitable for starting a computer from and should contain the operating system you wish to install on the virtual machine if you want to do that now. The disk will be ejected from the virtual drive automatically next time you switch the virtual machine off, but you can also do this yourself if needed using the Devices menu.

Host Drive 'E:'

Start   Cancel

Click on the tiny folder with the green arrow to browse to the Linux Mint install folder. Click on the Downloads folder and scroll to the Mint file to select it:

Please select a virtual optical disk file or a physical optical drive
containing a disk to start your new virtual machine from.

The disk should be suitable for starting a computer from and should
contain the operating system you wish to install on the virtual machine if
you want to do that now. The disk will be ejected from the virtual drive
automatically next time you switch the virtual machine off, but you can
also do this yourself if needed using the Devices menu.

| linuxmint-15-mate-dvd-32bit.iso (1013.00 MB) | ▾ | 🖳 |

| Start | | Cancel |

Then click Start. You may see a couple of Notices. Click OK for each. This will
start the Linux Mint 15 operating system installation process. If a screen
appears with a bunch of "caja" file managers, just click the X by each one to
delete them. This will bring up the following Linux Mint installation screen.
Click on **Install Linux Mint** which is in the upper left corner:

This will bring up the **Install Welcome** screen. Choose the language and click
on Continue. Make sure you are connected to the internet and click Continue:

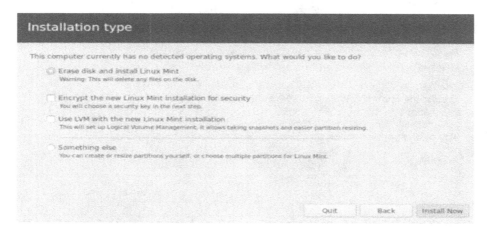

This warning only applies to the E Drive inside of Virtual Box. So leave it set for **Erase Disc** and click **Install Now**. Choose a time zone and click Continue. Select a language. Then click Continue.

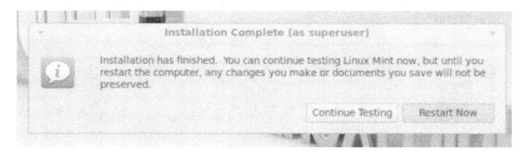

Enter your name, user name and passwords. Setting to log in automatically will save time when rebooting while installing and uninstalling programs. Then click Continue. Now we get the slide show which you can read while Linux is being installed. The slide show explains some of the features that come with Linus Mint Mate such as a web browser, file manager, word processor, software download center, customization options and a help center. There is an entire community of users who can help you solve problems – in addition to lots of tutorials.

When the operating system has been installed, this screen will appear:

Click Restart Now. This will only restart your Virtual Machine, not your actual laptop. After restart, press **Enter** on your keyboard. Close the Help screen. Below is what your desktop looks like. Click **Menu** which is in the lower left corner:

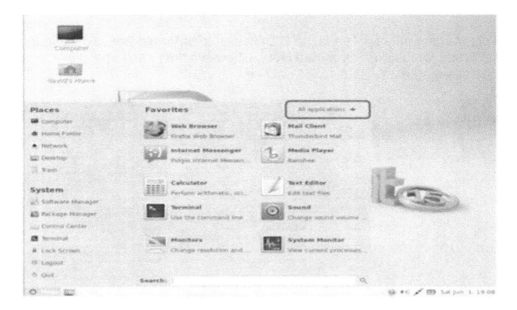

Linux Mate has two Start Menus: With Mate, there are two start menus. Above is the **Favorites Menu**. Click on All Applications to reach the **Applications Menu**.

Install Updates
The first step after installing Mate is updating all of the tools that come with Mate. To do this, click on the Menu icon in the lower left corner. Then click on **the Control Center** which is in the left column**.** Next click on **System,** then **Update Manager.** Enter your password. Then click on **Install Updates**. Click OK to all questions. This one time update will take about 5 minutes to complete. When they are done, you will be returned to the Start screen. To insure there are no more updates, click on Menu, Control Panel, Update Manager again. This time the list should be empty. Close the Update Manager and the Control Center.

When the upload is done, it is a good idea to restart Linux. To do this, click on the Menu:

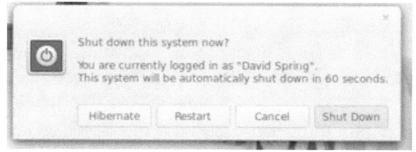

Then click Restart. Congratulations! You now have a fully updates Linux Mint Mate operating system installed. In the next chapter, we will learn how to use it.

Chapter 5... Set up and Use Linux Mint

Chapter 5 includes the following four sections.
5.1 How to use Linux Mint Mate
5.2 Set up and use the Mate File Manager
5.3 Add Free Programs to Linux Mint Mate
5.4 Add a Shared Folder to Linux Mint Mate

In the last chapter, we reviewed how to install Virtual Box and Linux Mint into your Windows based computer. In this chapter, we will learn how to use Linux Mint including how to change the appearance of the desktop, how to use the file manager, how to add free programs to Mint and how to set up a shared folder between Linux Mint and your Windows C Drive.

Nearly all of the steps for using Linux Mint are the same whether you are using Mint inside of a virtual machine (as we discussed in Chapter 4) or whether you have installed Linux Mint in its own separate partition of your hard drive (as we will discuss in Chapter 6). The benefit of setting up a separate partition over a virtual partition is first that programs will run much faster (because they do not have to run through the bloated Windows program), second that you will not need a "shared folder" for transferring documents between Windows and Linux (because Linux Mint in its own partition allows you to access the entire Windows C Drive) and third that should the Windows partition eventually crash, you would have be able to access to all of your data if Linux is in its own separate partition but you would not be able to access your data if Linux is inside of a virtual partition in your Windows partition. So in this chapter we will show you how to use Linux Mint in Windows so you can see how it works. Then in the next chapter we will show you how to install Linux Mint in its own separate partition. Below is what the Linux Mint Desktop will look like when we are done:

5.1 How to use Linux Mint Mate

This section explains how to use the Linux Mint operating system to change the appearance of your desktop and set up quick launch icons on your desktop. One of the big benefits of Linux Mint Mate is the ability to control nearly every aspect of the appearance and function of your desktop – something you have almost no control over with Windows 8!

In our last chapter, we created a virtual machine and installed **Linux Mint 15 Mate 32 bit** version in this virtual machine. In this chapter, we will show you how easy it is to use the Linux Mint Mate operating system. Here is the initial Start screen for Linux Mint Mate:

Click on **Menu** in the lower left corner to bring up the **Favorites menu:**

Our first task will be to install a custom desktop background image.

Add a Custom Desktop Background Image

One of the most important ways to personalize your computer is to install your favorite images to see when your computer first turns on. This can be an image of your family or anything else you like. With Windows XP and Windows 7, it was very easy to change the background image. However, with Windows 8, it is very difficult. Luckily, Linux Mint Mate has a wonderful system for adding any of thousands of background images to your desktop – including your own personal images. To install a new background image, click on **Control Center** in the main menu.

Click on **Appearance:**

Then click on the **Background** Tab:

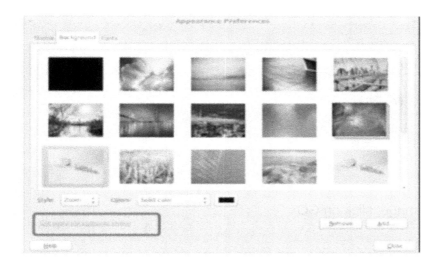

There are about one dozen background images here. But there are thousands more you can get by clicking on the link: **Get more backgrounds online**:

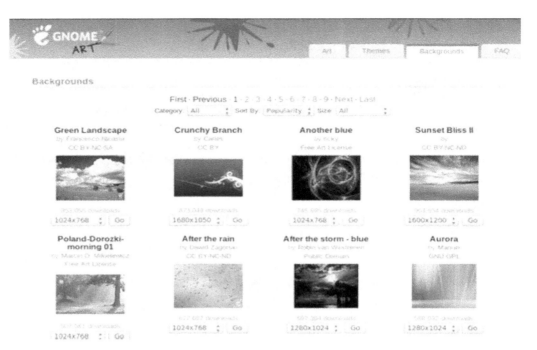

There are 139 pages of backgrounds or over 1400 choices. You can also create your own images 1024 pixels wide by 768 high. Be sure to optimize the file size to keep it under 100KB. Then upload it to your Downloads folder. When selecting a new desktop image, make sure that there are not a lot of graphics on the left side of the image as this is where we will be placing our desktop quick link icons. If you do not get the chance to get outdoors much, choose a light blue image with a lot of sky for your desktop image. On page 11 is one such image. But you can download several images and choose between them later.

To get this image, click on GO:

Then right click on the image and choice **Save Image As**:

This brings up your Mint Mate Downloads folder.

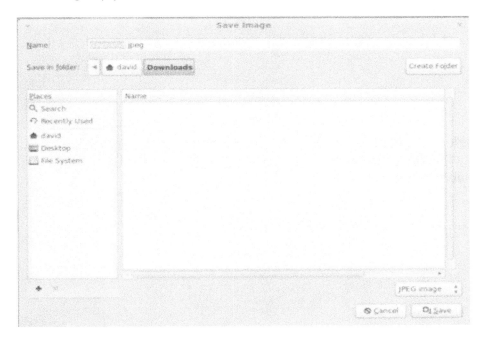

Change the name of the image to something more descriptive and click Save. After downloading all of the images you want to the Mate Downloads folder, exit Firefox browser to go back to the Appearances Preferences Background screen:

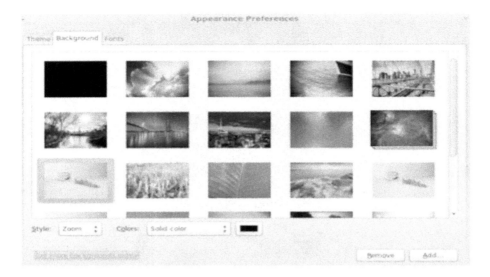

Click Add:

By default, Mate looks in your **Pictures** folder to see if there are any images. Click on **Backgrounds** in the left column above. This is where the default background images are kept:

Then click on **Linux Mint Nadia extra** to open this folder:

This is where all of your default background images are keep. The location is: **File Manager, usr, share, backgrounds, Linuxmint_nadia-extra**. We can right click on any of these images to delete them from our default list. Or we can add images to this list by moving them from the **Downloads** folder to this list. We could also just navigate from this browse function to the **Downloads** folder and leave the images there. But this will clutter up the Mate Downloads folder and run the risk of accidentally deleting your background image in the future.

Next click on your **Home** folder:

Then click on the **Downloads** folder:

Then select the image you want to turn into add to Wallpaper and click Open:

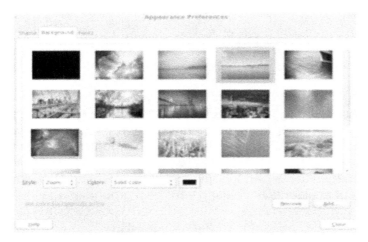

This automatically adds this image to your list of options and applies this image to your desktop. Repeat to add more images to this list. To remove images from the list, click on an image and then click on Delete.

Change your Desktop Theme

In addition to changing the Background image, we can change the "theme" used to display open Windows. Click on the Appearance Preferences **Theme** tab:

We could also get many more themes. But for now, click on Customize which will take us to the pre-installed options.

Mint X is the default theme. But there are several themes inside of Mate you can select. Click on Mist.

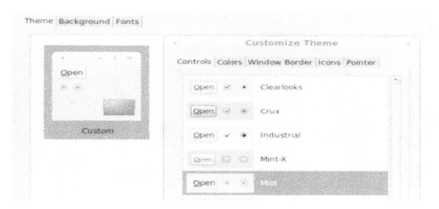

Click on the **Window Border** tab:

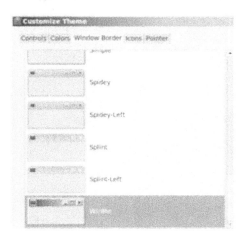

There are about 20 tab display options, To select the option closest to Windows XP or Windows 7, click on **WinMe**. Then click Close.

We now have a Windows like theme and a light blue desktop background. Close the Control Center.

The next issue is to learn how to set up and use the **Mate File Manager**. That is the topic of our next section.

5.2 Set up and use the Mate File Manager

> **This section explains how to set up and use the Linux Mint File Manager. This includes changing the structure of the file manager to make it function just like the Windows XP or Windows 7 file manager.**

In this section, we will review how to set up and use the Linux Mint Mate File Manager. The Mint Mate file manager, which is called **Caja**, is one of the most important reasons to choose Linux Mint Mate over Linux Ubuntu or Windows 8 or Apple. The Caja File Manager is similar to the File Manager that comes with Windows 7 and Windows XP. While this file manager can be added to Linux Ubuntu, it works best with Linux Mint Mate. To open this file manager, click on your **Home** folder in the upper left corner of the Mint Mate desktop. Or alternately, open the Menu in the bottom left panel and click on **Home** Folder. Below is what the Caja file manager looks like using the Winme theme we installed in the last chapter:

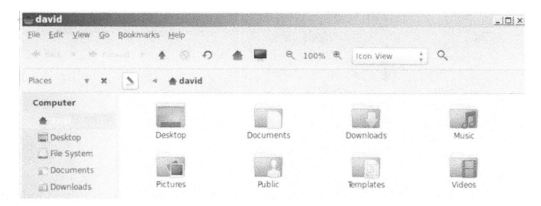

By default, this folder opens in the **Icon View** at 100%. A more efficient view is Compact View at 66%. Click on the Drop down arrow next to Icon View to select **Compact View**:

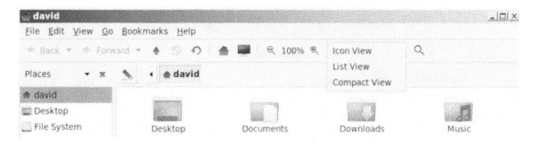

This will bring up the Compact View. This is similar to the "List" view in Windows XP and Windows 7. The Compact View is especially important if you have a lot of files and folders:

Also by default, the Mate Caja File Manager shows the **Places** View in the left column. Click on the Drop Down arrow to the right of Places to select **Tree** View:

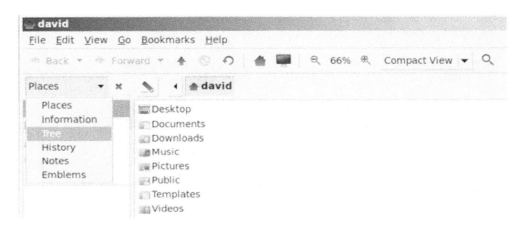

Tree View will cause Caja to look and function like the Explorer File Manager in Windows XP and Windows 7. Changing to Tree View will cause some important arrows to appear to the left of folders in the left panel which have sub-folders:

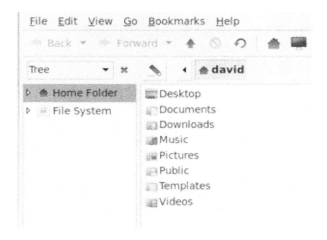

Click on the Home Folder to reveal all of the subfolders in this folder:

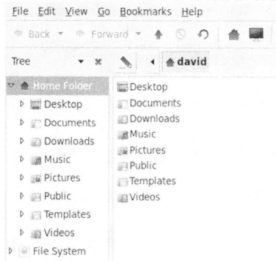

Just as you can do with Windows 7, you can create additional folders and create your own folder structure. Click on the Desktop folder to open it. Then right click on the white workspace to bring up the following screen:

Click on **Create Folder** to place a new folder on your desktop. Give it a name. You can also put a file on the desktop. Right click on the workspace and click on Create Document, Empty File. Give the file a name.

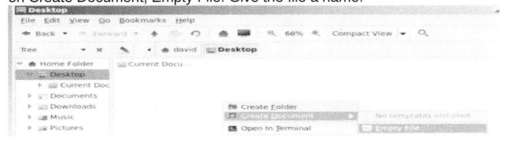

Moving Files and Folders

You could have opened the Current Documents folder first and then created this file in it. However, you can also create the document and then move it into the folder either by selecting it in the file manager and then dragging it to the Current Documents folder in the File Manager:

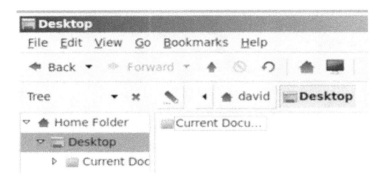

Or you can close the file manager and simply drag the document to the Current Documents folder in the Desktop:

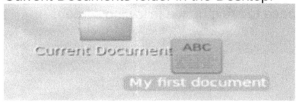

Add Application "Launcher" Icons to our Desktop

We next need to add some Application Icons to the Desktop. This is also done much easier in Mint Mate than in Ubuntu. Click on the Start Menu. This brings up the **Favorites** screen:

Then click on **All Applications** in the upper right corner. This changes the main menu from the Favorites screen to the Applications screen:

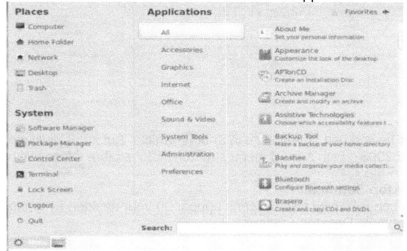

Then click on **Office:**

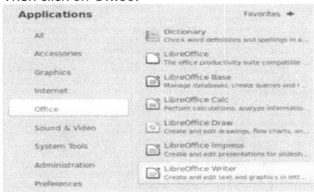

The most important application is LibreOffice Writer, which is the open source version of Microsoft Word. Click on this application. Then hold down on this selection and drag the icon to the desktop.

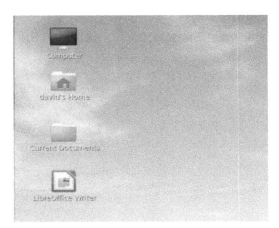

Click on Libre Office Writer quick start icon to make sure it works:

We will cover how to use Libre Office in another article. But it basically works just like Word 2003 – with a fixed menu structure. Close Libre Office Writer.

Change Desktop Settings
You can also control which default icons appear on your desktop by going to Menu, Preferences, Desktop Settings:

We can delete the home or computer quick start icon here if we want less on our desktop. Or add the Trash icon if we want the trash can on the desktop.

Modify the Main Start Menu
To modify the items that appear on the main Start menu, right click on the menu:

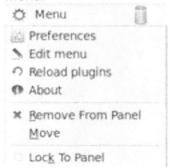

Then click on Edit Menu:

For menu categories to appear in the main menu, they need to have menu items in them. For example, we could select Education, but this menu item will not appear until after we have added some education programs.

Click on each of the Application categories in the left column to bring up a list of possible menu items in the middle column. Select or unselect these to create your own custom menu of the items you are most likely to use.

In the next section, we will explain how to add more free open source programs to your computer and how to add a "shared folder" so you can share documents with one of your normal Windows folders.

5.3 Add Free Programs to Linux Mint Mate

A huge benefit of Linux over Windows is the ability to add thousands of free programs with just the click of a button. This section describes how to add free programs to your Mint system and how to add USB support to transfer files between operating systems in your Virtual Machine.

One of the biggest advantages of Linux over Windows is that there are tens of thousands of free open source programs which you can add to customize your computer. In this article, we explain how to use the Linux Mint Software Manager to add any of more than 63,000 programs to your computer. We will then review how to add a Shared folder so you can share documents between Linux Mint Mate and MS Windows. We will also review how to activate a USB Flash Drive to share documents between Mate and Windows.

Add Free Programs
Go to the Start Menu and click on Administration, then Software Manager:

Linux offers all kinds of free programs for students and schools. Click on **Science and Education.** There is a Ubuntu education primary package and an edu-secondary package.

Both take up nearly one gigabyte.

Click on Install. Then check on the programs to see what was installed:

Activate your USB Flash Drive

This step is not needed when installing Linux Mint in its own partition, but is needed to access your USB flash drive with Mint when it is in a virtual partition. Some folks prefer the convenience of using a flash drive in addition to or instead of a shared folder for transferring data to and from their Virtual operating system. We need to add a special Virtual Box extension called Extension Pack in order to activate our USB. To get this free extension, open the Firefox browser in Linux Mint and go to the following page:
https://www.virtualbox.org/wiki/Downloads

Click on the **Extension Pack, All Supported Platforms.** Then download the file to your Home computer Downloads folder. Next install the **Virtual Box Extension Pack**. This is a different file than the VBox Additions file and must be installed in a different way. Then in the Virtual Box start screen, select the Operating system you want, then click **File, Preferences in the top menu**:

This brings up a different settings screen than we have used before:

Click on **Extensions:**

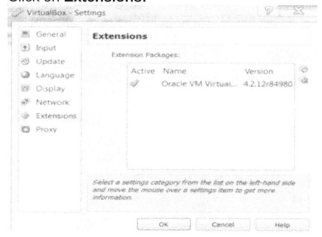

This was automatically installed when I ran the package.

If it has not been installed, click on the upper right icon, called **Install Package:**

Click OK or install. You will see a notice which says:
Virtual Box USB Device Driver Successfully Installed.

Set up a filter for the USB Flash Drive
Next we can install the USB Flash Drive in our home computer. Be sure to put the Flash Drive in a USB 2 port. **NOTE: VIRTUAL BOX DOES NOT RECOGNIZE USB 3 PORTS! The USB Flash Drive must be in a USB 2 port!** Then open Virtual Box and select the Operating System you want to use. Then click on **Settings, USB:**

Right click on the green plus sign to bring up all of the USB devices currently working on our computer:

We want to add a USB Flash Drive to the filters, but we do not want to add other USB items such as our computer camera or mouse. The problem is that if we actually get these transferred to the VM, they will not be available for the computer until the VM is closed. Logitech is my mouse and one of these is the camera for my computer. The question is which one of these is the Flash Drive? To determine this, safely remove the flash drive. Then look at the list again:

Logitech USB Receiver [5700]

Unknown device 064E:D281 [0110]

Unknown device 0A5C:21B4 [0481]

Unknown device 138A:0018 [0078]

Now we know that the device we want to add to the filter is called **USB Flash Memory**. Put the stick back in. Then add it to the USB filter list.

Now that we have the USB filter set and the extension package installed, start up the Virtual Machine. Then in the Mate Top Panel, click on **Devices.** Hover over the USB Flash Drive which shows that it is captured. If it is not already selected, click on the USB Device to select it:

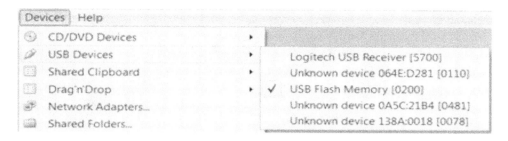

Go to your file manager (Home folder) to see if the USB is active. It will probably not be there. Remove the flash drive and then put it back into its port (making sure you are putting it into a USB 2 port and not a USB 3 port). A USB icon will appear in the lower right corner.

Click on **Open USB with the File Manager**: This should now show an option for the USB Flash Drive. However, depending on the USB device you are using, this option might not show up. There are a couple of things you can do to fix this problem. First, it could be that the USB is recognized, but not mounted. If you hover over it in the USB Devices menu as we did above and it says it is captured, then the USB is recognized. The next step is to see if it is mounted. To determine this, go to **Menu, Applications, Preferences and click on Discs.** Select the USB Device and it will indicate if it is mounted.

This USB is mounted in the Media folder. Sometimes the USB is mounted in the root folder. If it is mounted in a folder, you do not have permission to view, you can add yourself to the folder using the User steps we describe in the next section when we show you how to add a Shared Folder. If the USB is not shown as Mounted, try a different USB stick. To see the USB, open the file manager:

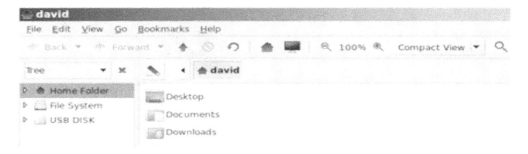

If the file manager is set for Tree View, you should see your USB here. You should also see it in your File System/Media folder:

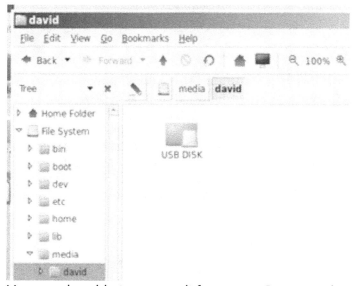

You may be able to access it from your Computer icon:

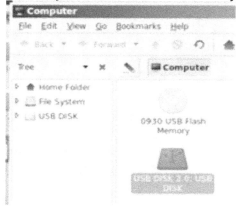

To deactivate the USB in the VM, be sure to right click on it, then click on Eject. Otherwise the USB may not work in your Host computer. Now that we have USB access, in the next section we will review how to set up a shared folder between your Linux Mint and Windows operating systems.

5.4 Add a Shared Folder to Linux Mint Mate

This section describes how to add a shared folder to your Virtual Machine. Adding a shared folder allows you to easily share and transfer documents between operating systems.

Set up a Shared Folder with Virtual Box

Virtual Box offers the ability to share a folder between your Windows operating system and any operating system you have installed in Virtual Box. To do this, the Virtual Box settings for this machine need to be correctly set. Turn off Linux and go to the Virtual Box Start screen. Click on **Settings, General Advanced** and enable Shared Clipboard and Drag and Drop. Set both for Bidirectional:

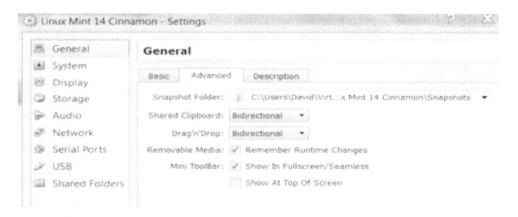

Install Virtual Box Guest Additions

Before we create the shared folder, we need to get and install Virtual box Additions to Linux Mint. First download the latest version of Guest Additions from the Virtual Box website. Then Open Linux Mint. Then in the top panel, go to the Virtual Box menu 'Devices' and select '**Install Guest Additions...**

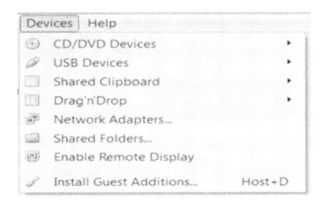

A virtual disc will get mounted in Linux.

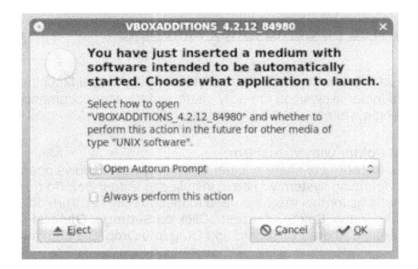

Check Always Perform this action. Then click OK. Then click Run:

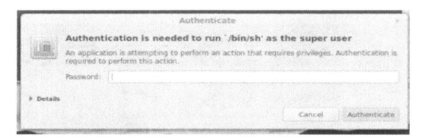

Enter your password. Guest Additions will take some time to install.

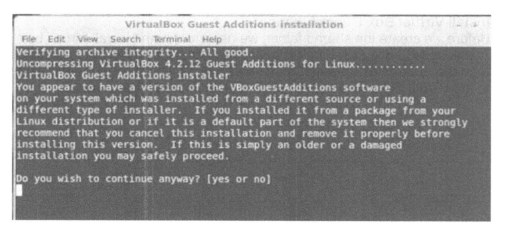

Type in Yes. Then hit Enter. It will take a while to finish. Press return key when it says so (after it's finished). VBOX ADDITIONS is now installed.

The next step is to turn off Linux. Then in the Main Menu, go to the Virtual Box Start screen and select **Settings** (yellow wheel below).

Click on Shared Folders in left column below:

Select **Machine Folders**. Then click the small green **Add folder** icon.

Click on the drop down arrow and select **other.** Then navigate to a new folder called **Shared** on your Windows C drive. Please make sure the folder is named Shared with a capital S.

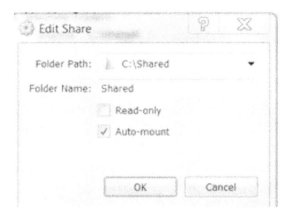

Check Auto Mount. Then click OK:

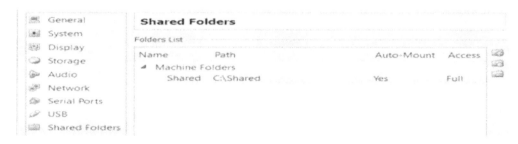

Start your Linux Mint system and open the main menu. Open the Home Folder:

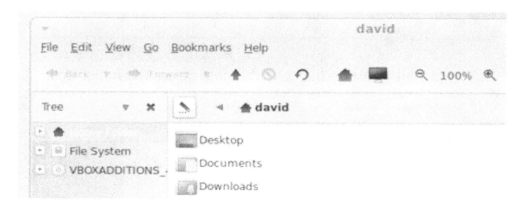

Open the File System. Then the Media Folder:

We could open the shared folder by right clicking on it and clicking Run as Admin then adding our admin password each time. But a better way is to add ourselves as an "owner" of this shared folder. To do this go to Menu, Control Panel, Systems, User Groups:

Click on Users and Groups in the Systems area of the Control Center:

Click on **Manage Groups.** Scroll down to vboxsf (which stands for Virtual Box Shared Folder) and click on it:

Notice that the box to the left of our name is empty by default. This is why we cannot automatically open the Shared folder. Check this box to be added to the vboxsf group. This will bring up the Authorize screen. Enter your password. Then close the screen. In order for Group Change settings to take effect, you need to restart the Mate operating system. Go to Menu, Quit, Restart to activate the change in User Group permissions. Once your operating system is back up again, verify that you have been added to this group by checking it again. You may have to repeat checking the "add to group" box. But it will eventually take. Then go back to your Home folder and open the File System media folder: **Any user within the vboxsf group has full access to any shared folders.** Open Home folder, then file system, then media folder:

Congratulations! You now have access to your Shared folder. Now you'd have a Shared folder working on your Mate operating system and you can share data between your Mate OS and Windows operating systems without the need to use a flash drive. If you want to hide the VBOX Additions Icon which is on your desktop, go to Menu, Control Panel, personal, Desktop settings. Then uncheck "mounted volumes." Then click Close. Now that we have covered how to install and use Linus Mint Mate in a virtual machine, in the next chapter we will learn how to install Linux Mint in a dual boot with its own partition space on your computer. This will allow you to access your data even in the event that Windows crashes and refuses to start.

Chapter 6... Back Up Your Data and Dual Boot

Chapter 6 Back Up Data and Dual Boot includes the following four sections:
6.1 Protect yourself from Windows Booby Traps
6.2 Create multiple backups of your system
6.3 Dual Boot Linux Mint with Windows XP or Windows 7
6.4 Dual Boot Linux Mint with Windows 8

Booting is a computer slang term for starting up your computer. Dual booting means creating two different ways for starting up and accessing the data on your computer. For example, you could start up your computer using the Windows operating system or the Linux operating system.

As we explained at the beginning of the last chapter, the benefit of setting up a separate partition for Linux over a virtual partition is first programs will run much faster (because they do not have to run through the bloated Windows program), second you will not need a "shared folder" for transferring documents between Windows and Linux (because Linux Mint in its own partition allows you to access the entire Windows C Drive) and third should the Windows partition eventually crash, you will still have access to all of your data because Linux will still be able to run.

In a sane world, steps for dual booting would fit on one page. However, Microsoft has spent billions of dollars doing everything they can to maintain their monopoly and prevent you from adding Linux to your computer. This includes placing several booby traps in your way. The purpose of this chapter therefore is to show you how to overcome these obstacles.

6.1 Protect yourself from Windows Booby Traps

> **Microsoft does not want you to use Linux. They have created numerous booby traps which are important to know about. This section reviews how to back up your data and overcome obstacles Microsoft has created to make it harder for you to install Linux.**

Dual booting simply means to install more than one operating system on your computer. The point of dual booting is to allow you to test and experiment with a new operating system, such as Linux, while still keeping your old operating system, such as Windows. In a sane world, not so driven by the profit motive, we could simply add Linux in a simple dual boot next to our Windows operating system with just the click of a couple of buttons. In fact, in a sane world, Linux would come pre-installed by all computer manufacturers and we would not even need to dual boot it. After all, it is free and would cost computer manufacturers nothing to install on all computers and greatly improve safety. The entire process of installing or activating Linux should take more than a few seconds. However, it is important to recognize that we are not living in a sane world. The reason Linux does not come pre-installed is because Microsoft has blackmailed computer manufacturers with hidden "exclusionary" contracts. Microsoft has billions of dollars at stake and has done everything in their power to create obstacles to prevent you from dual booting Linux onto your computer. In this chapter, we will explain some of these traps with the hopes that it will help you better understand why you should not skip any steps – including backing up all of your data.

Benefits of Dual Booting
The first question we should address is why even dual boot in the first place? Why not simply leave Linux in Virtual Box and continue using it inside of the Windows operating system? There are several reasons to dual boot Linux. First, when Windows eventually crashes, if Linux is inside of Windows you will lose both Linux and Windows and all of your data. If Linux is in a dual boot, you can still start and run your computer using Linux. Second, Linux will not be anywhere near as fast inside of Virtual Box as it will be in a dual boot. Third, it is much easier to set up file sharing, USB drive access, CD access and printing access with a dual boot. Fourth, if you want to eventually get rid of Windows, switching to the Linux Boot loader and creating a dual boot is a good first step.

When you should not dual boot
There are a few circumstances when dual booting is not a good idea. The most common problem is if you have an older computer with a limited amount of RAM. You may wind up slowing down your computer with a dual boot. Also, if you have a limited amount of space on your hard drive, you may not want to dual boot.

A dual boot begins by dividing up the space on your hard drive. A solution to this problem is to get a 64 GB USB Flash Drive or a 1 TB USB External Drive and offload data you do not normally need – such as old picture folders – onto one of these. Doing this will free up space on your hard drive which can then be used for a dual boot.

History of the Windows Dynamic Partition Booby Trap
Thanks to Microsoft, we will have to give you two different sets of instructions for creating a dual boot – a relatively simple process if you have Windows XP or Windows 7 installed on your computer, and a second much more complex process for those who have the misfortune of having Windows 8 installed on their computer. Why has dual booting been turned into such a complex process?

We will start with a bit of history. Once upon a time, back in the 1990s, your computer was divided into four simple partitions. The reason for this was to allow you to add operating systems if you wanted. (You can think of a partition like adding walls in a house to create extra rooms. You can either have one big house with no rooms or partition your computer house into two to four rooms). Because Windows is a bit of a bully, it often took up the first two partitions – one for the Windows Start program, called System, and one for the main Windows program which was placed on the C drive. To see what these two partitions looked like on a Windows XP computer from 2003, go to **Control Panel, Administrative Tools, Computer Management, Storage, Disk Management:**

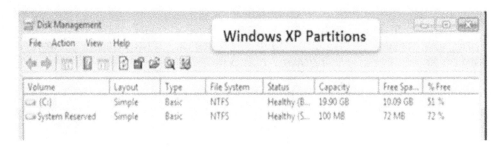

Because there are two partitions left, you could install Linux on one of them. However, because Microsoft really does not want you to install Linux, fast forward to 2010 and look at Windows 7 partitions on a common laptop from HP:

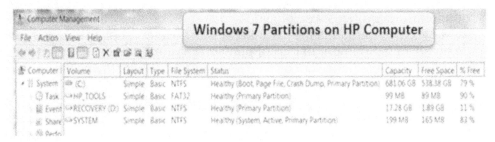

Notice the difference? On a Windows 7 HP laptop, all four partitions have been taken. We now have a partition called HP-TOOLS which controls the BIOS computer start settings – and we have another partition called RECOVERY – which is the backup folder for your Windows 7 program (but not the data on your C Drive). Today, Microsoft will happily allow you to create a fifth partition – even though the limit is four partitions. What will happen if you naively click on ADD PARTITION is that Microsoft will change all of your partitions from Basic partitions to Dynamic partitions.

There are two problems with Microsoft automatically changing static partitions to dynamic partitions. The first problem is that **you cannot install Linux onto a Dynamic Partition.** The second problem is that while it is easy to convert Basic Partitions to Dynamic Partitions, it is very difficult to convert Dynamic partitions back to Basic Partitions. What Microsoft is doing in creating such a devious trap is adding one more hidden obstacle to prevent you from installing Linux on your computer. Clicking on the ADD PARTITION button is one of several Microsoft Booby Traps. "Dynamic" partitions are nothing but a scam to prevent you from installing Linux. This brings us to our first rule:

RULE #1: Never trust Microsoft to do anything associated with backing up your data, partitioning your computer or adding another operating system! If you still think you can trust Microsoft for anything, please reread the preface and first three chapters of this book!

Thankfully, you are reading this book. So hopefully, you will not fall victim to the Dynamic Partition Booby Trap. But let's dig a little deeper to expose what a farce the four used partitions shown in the Windows 7 panel above really are – and how these four partitions have been set up on purpose to prevent you from adding Linux to a Windows 7 computer.

In addition to Basic Partitions, historically, if you wanted more than four partitions, you could turn the fourth partition into an **Extended** Partition. So you would then have three Basic partitions and one Extended partition. On this extended partition, you could have as many "**logical**" partitions as you want.

So imagine that you are HP and you want to take up two additional partitions for HP TOOLS and RECOVERY. The simple and polite option is to create an Extended Partition and put both of these files as logical partitions in the Extended Partition. This would give Microsoft the two partitions that they want, give HP the two partitions they want and still leave one option Basic Partition plus an unlimited number of logical partitions in the Extended Partition created by HP. There is only one reason for HP to take up the last two Basic partitions instead of creating an extended partition and that is to fill up all of the partitions – thus triggering the Microsoft Dynamic Partition Booby Trap should you try to add Linux to your operating system. In other words, what Microsoft and HP did was conspire to prevent you from adding Linux to your computer.

Why would HP help Microsoft sabotage your computer?

It is important to understand that for many years, Microsoft has worked with computer manufacturers to create a Planned Obsolescence program which forces you to buy a new computer every couple of years whether you want to or not. When everyone is forced to buy a new computer every couple of years, both Microsoft and HP make billions of dollars. Once you understand that the only thing that matters to either of these corporations is short term profit, you will be in a better position to protect yourself from the things they do to you to maximize profits. If folks ever started using Linux, it would greatly reduce computer sales. First, Linux is a smaller faster program than Windows. So it works on older computers and helps them run faster and last longer. Second, Linux is a much safer operating system because it does not leave the backdoor open. You do not have to worry so much about super viruses destroying your computer.

But Microsoft and HP will lose billions if you use Linux to extend the life of your current computer. This is why Linux does not come pre-installed on HP computers. It would be like a car manufacturer giving us the option of installing a FREE engine which lasts for one million miles and uses almost no gas! So HP has as much financial interest in preventing you from using Linux as Microsoft does.

Here is how HP added these two partitions. First, let's look at the RECOVERY program. Just a few years ago, when you bought an HP computer, they would ship it with Windows XP on a DVD disc or a couple of CD discs. You then put the disc into the CD player on your new computer to install it. If you wiped out your computer, you could re-install Windows from the Disc. Each of these discs cost less than one dollar to make. So why put did HP install this extra copy of Window 7 in a new partition on your computer – where it is taking up 17 GB of space? Also exactly how will you activate this program if your computer has crashed?

Finally, even if you did find a way to activate the Recovery program from an internal drive on your computer, there is no warning that activating this HP Recovery program will not only wipe out all of the data on your C drive – but it will also wipe out any programs you have installed on your computer AND it will wipe out any additional operating system you have installed (such as Linux) and it will wipe out any data and documents you have installed on your Linux partition. The HP Recovery program is a very dangerous "Destructive Recovery" program which destroys everything in its path.

It short, you do not want a Windows Recovery partition on an internal drive on your computer. Yet if you go to the HP forums, you will see lots of "helpful" tips written by HP experts on how to create a dual boot of Linux with Windows. The questions from innocent novices usually start with: I notice that all four partitions have been taken by Microsoft and HP. Which one should I delete in order to dual boot Linux?

The HP Experts then tell you to do crazy things like deleting your System partition or your HP TOOLS partition. Either of these things will toast your computer. And then guess what... you get to buy a new HP computer – creating even more profit for Microsoft and HP. And with any luck at all, you will give up on trying to install Linux. This leads us to Rule #2:

RULE #2: Never trust HP to do anything associated with backing up your data, partitioning your hard drive or adding another operating system!

The final thing to be aware of is that to have a Dual Boot with Windows, Windows must be given the first two partitions. Windows will not boot well if anything is in front of it. Thankfully, Linux plays much nicer. There is no problem booting Linux from an extended partition. In fact, we recommend it.

Make and follow a Plan to Safely Backup all of your data
Our plan is to first backup the your computer data – using several different methods to backup several different files and folders. This includes the following 8 steps:
Step #1: Gather your backup tools.
Step #2: Organize your files into folders.
Step #3: Clean Up and Defragment your disc.
Step #4: Copy your data on a USB Flash Drive.
Step #5: Create a copy of your C Drive and Data on a USB External Drive.
Step #6: Create a copy of your Recovery Media file onto a USB Flash Drive.
Step #7: Create a USB Flash Drive copy of your HP Recovery Partition.
Step #8: Make a record of all of our Windows program keys.

Once we have backed up all of our data, in the next section, we will delete the Recovery partition and shrink the C drive partition in order to create space to add Linux. We will use the free space to create an Extended Partition for Dual Boot of Windows XP or Windows 7 and Linux using a Linux installation tool. In the final section in this chapter, we will discuss how to install a dual boot with Linux if you have the misfortune of owning a Windows 8 computer. This includes overcoming the latest obstacles Microsoft has placed in our way, a nightmare called Secure Boot – which is not secure but makes it more difficult to add Linux to a computer.

Step #1: Gather your backup tools
While Windows has a backup program, it does not work that well. In case your computer completely crashes and you cannot even restart it, you really want to store your important data in some other place besides on your computer. You also want a system where you can do at least monthly backups and preferably even weekly backups. In the past, we would use CDs and DVDs to back up our data. But these tend to get scratched and many computers no longer even have CD drives. So instead, we will use a variety of USB external drives. We will need to get several tools and follow several steps to back up our computer.

First, we will need a **32 GB USB Flash Drive** to copy all important images and files to. This flash drive can then be used to transfer files to a Shared Partition drive later which will then be available to both the Windows and Linux operating systems after we have installed Linux as a dual boot. If you do not already have a 32 GB USB Flash Drive, this will cost about $30.

Second, at step #5, we need a **1 Terabyte USB external hard drive** to create a complete system backup. My system, shown on the C Drive below, takes up about 130 GB. So in getting a 1 Terabyte USB external hard drive, I can make 6 backup copies before I need to start erasing them to make room for new ones. This is one per week for six weeks or one per month for six months. The point of this backup is to restore your computer to its current state (as opposed to the recovery backup which deletes all of your current files and programs and restore the computer to the state it was in the day you bought it). A 1TB USB hard drive will cost about $70. If you are on a limited budget, you can skip this step as your important data will be on the 32 GB Flash Drive and your Windows Recovery file will be on a separate USB flash drive.

Third, at step #5, we need to install a free program for making backup copies of our complete system. Since Windows 7 Home Edition does not actually allow us to back up the entire Windows operating system, and since the software that comes with our external USB Hard Drive often does not work, we will create this system backup using a free tool called **Macrium Reflect**.

Fourth, in Step 6, we will need **another 4GB or more Flash Drive** to create "recovery media" also using Macrium Reflect. I have used the SanDisk 16 GB for this. But the recovery media file is only 1.7 GB so almost any dependable flash drive will do. This will cost about $10.

If you open "My computer" you will see that the **C local disc** is about 130 GB and the **D Recovery** folder is about 17 GB.

Fifth, we will need **another 32 GB Flash Drive** to create a copy of the Recovery Disc folder which comes with HP. It is important to note that this Recovery disc, if it were ever used, would wipe out all of our programs and system changes we have made – including partition changes and any documents and programs associated with Linux to return the computer back to the initial condition it was in the day we bought it. So this Recovery should be considered the "option of last resort." The benefit of creating this recovery flash drive – which can be done only once – is that we can delete the partition with the Recovery folder which will free up a partition for us to add Linux to our computer. This will cost about $30.

Sixth, we will use a free tool for getting the "keys" to our important Windows programs. After we have completed all of these backup steps, we will be ready to delete the backup partition and begin installing Linux into the resulting empty space. We will also need an 8 GB to 16 GB USB flash drive to put your open source operating system program(s) on. This will also cost about $10.

Step #2: Organize and consolidate your files into folders.
To back up your images, documents, files, folders and other data, first, go to the office supply store and pick up a reliable 32 GB Flash Drive. This is generally enough to hold all your images, videos and documents. If you are like most Windows users, your files will be stored in three or four different places. First, you will have them stored in **My Documents**. But you may also have images stored in a folder called **My Pictures** – and more documents on your C Drive. Create folders and consolidate all files and folders inside of just a few folders.

Step #3: Clean Up and Defragment your disc.
Microsoft Windows does not do a very good job of organizing your files on the C drive. This can make it difficult later on to shrink your C drive. So before you make a copy of your files to a USB Flash Drive, you should take a couple of minutes to clean up and defragment your disc. To do this with Windows XP or Windows 7, go to the Start Menu and click on **control panel**. Then click on **Performance Information and Tools**. Then click on **Open Disc Cleanup**:

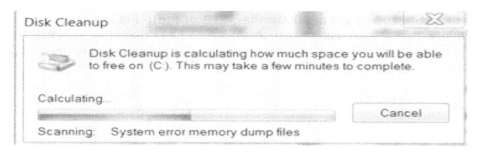

This screen will be followed by:

Click **OK** to delete these unneeded files. When done, go back to **Performance Information, Tools, Advanced Tools.** Then click on **Open Disk Defragmenter**.

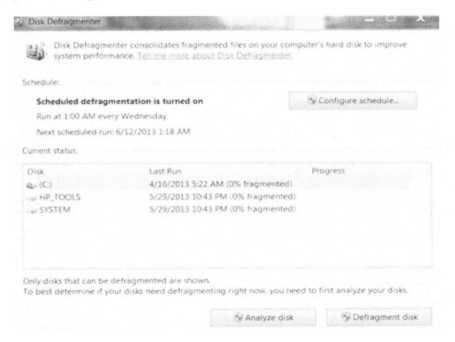

Select the **C Drive** and click on **Defragment Disk**. It will take several minutes to analyze the disc and even more time to defragment it.

Step #4: Copy your important data to a USB Flash Drive

Then insert the 32 GB flash drive in a USB port. Then right click on these folders to copy them to the Flash Drive which is shown below as Removable Disk F:

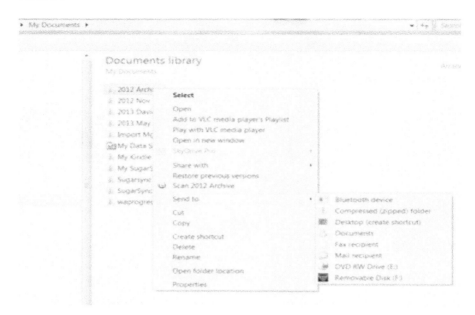

Transfer each folder to the Flash Drive. You should also check the **C Drive** to see if you want to copy any of those folders. This includes any programs you may want to copy. Next check the **Pictures** folder and the **Videos** folder and the **Downloads** folder and the **Programs** folder. When you have all of your folders copied, then safely remove the flash drive and label it with the date of the copy. It is useful to have two flash drives so that you can copy a second one later and then delete the current one – alternating between two Flash drives.

Step #5: Create a copy of your C Drive and Data on a USB External Drive.

There are lots of reliable, compact and economical USB external hard drives. It is useful to get one with a USB 3.0 connection which is ten times faster than USB 2.0. But anything will do. I used a USB 3.0 1 TB External Hard Drive. Next, if you want to use USB 3.0, you need to figure out which USB ports on your computer are USB 3 versus USB 2. If you look very close, the USB 3 ports will have the following symbol:

My laptop has two USB 3 ports on the left side and two USB 2 ports on the right side. Next download the free Macrium Reflect program:
http://www.macrium.com/reflectfree.aspx

After installing this program, the Reflect icon will be placed on your desktop.
Click on the Icon to open the program:

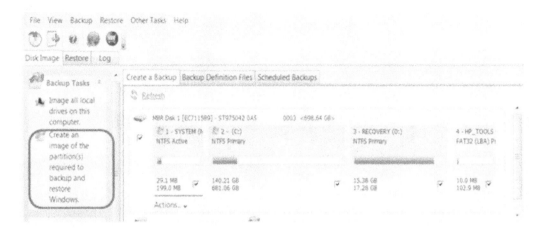

Click on the option '**Create an Image of the partition(s) required to backup
and restore Windows'** located in the top left hand pane of the application
window to start the backup wizard. It is highlighted in red in the previous
image. The wizard should start as shown below. You will note that all partitions
are displayed in the wizard, but only the system partition and the C partition
have been selected because these are what are needed to restore the current
system.

Next select a location for the backup. Assuming your USB external drive is
plugged into a USB port, select it. In my case, the destination was the F drive:

Click Next. It will then take a disc image. Click Finish.

Click OK to run the backup. Assuming the System and C drives are selected, click Next:

To back up 150 GB in data will take about 45 minutes. When the backup has completed click **'OK'** to shut down the message box and then click **'Close'** to close the backup window. Your system is now backed up. Below is what the backup file will look like in the Macrium screen:

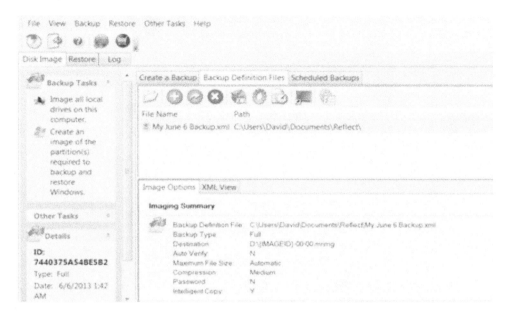

The file is saved as an XML file. Close the Macrium program. To view the backup file in Windows, click on the **Start** Menu, then **Computer**, then click on the **USB Hard Drive**. To eject the USB hard drive, click on the eject icon. When is says Safe to Remove USB, then remove the USB.

Step #6: Create a copy of your Recovery Media file onto a USB Flash Drive.
In addition to creating a complete system backup on your hard drive, Macrium Reflect Free version also helps you create "rescue media" for your Windows 7 backup plan. We will put this rescue media on a separate USB Flash Drive. First, insert the Flash Drive into the USB port. Also make sure you have opened your web browser and that it is connected to a high speed internet connection and that you have at least one hour to complete this task. Then open Macrium Reflect and click on the "**Other Tasks**" tab:

Click on **Create bootable rescue media. Then c**lick Yes:

Leave it as **Windows PE** and click Next.
Put in a 2 GB or more Flash Drive to put the Rescue Media on. We also need internet access to download the following file from Microsoft.

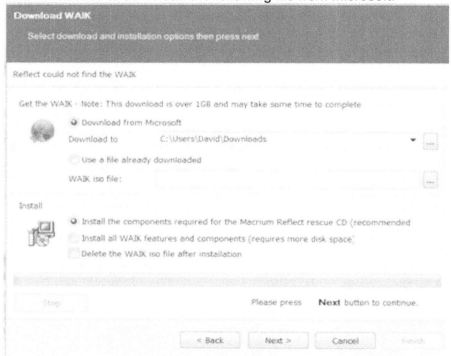

Assuming we are attached to the internet, and that we have a USB Flash drive plugged in to our computer, click Next. The file is 1.67 GB.

After the file has downloaded the following screen will appear:

Windows will want to install this folder inside of program files. Instead click **Browse** and select our Flash drive and install the folder there. Then click Next. After it is complete. Click Close. Then go back to the Rescue Media Wizard screen:

Macrium Reflect needs to initialize this pen drive. All existing data will be lost if you continue – but this warning only applies to any data on your USB drive (which should be blank). So for Proceed with operation? click Yes. We now have a recovery media on our Flash Drive. In the next section, we will make a copy of the HP Recovery partition and also make a record of our Windows program keys.

6.2 Create multiple backups of your system

One of the primary obstacles created by Microsoft is taking up all of the partitions on your hard drive. If you simply add a partition for Linux, Microsoft will convert all of your partitions into a form which can not be used to install Linux. In this section, we will show you how to safely make room for Linux on your hard drive.

In this section, we will remove a Partition. First, let's review our existing partitions. As we noted in the last section, pre-Windows 8 computers typically come with a maximum of four primary partitions on a single hard drive. A dual boot uses one of these partitions to place Linux on after installing Windows 7 on the first partition. Sadly, if you have an HP computer with Windows 7 installed on it, you will likely have an obstacle in that all four partitions have been used by Windows 7 and the HP backup and restore processes. To verify how many partitions are taken on your Windows 7 computer, go to **Control Panel, Administrative Tools, Computer Management, Storage, Disk Management:**

There are already four primary partitions on this HP computer. These are C drive, HP TOOLS, RECOVERY and SYSTEM. Taking up all four available primary partitions is not very polite of HP and Microsoft. It is almost as if they do not want you to install Linux because you might find out you like Linux better.

Let's look at the options for which partition to eliminate:
Option #1: C drive: This not only has your documents, it might also have the Windows Boot files. Do not delete this partition!
Option #2: HP_TOOLS: This has some hot keys support including hardware diagnostics and also the quick web button. Removing this may void your warranty and make it difficult to solve hardware problems. The HP_TOOLS partition contains the BIOS emergency start up program. Do NOT delete this unless you are CERTAIN you have a backup bios on a flash drive that you know will run. There is a special procedure to booting from bios via a flash drive.
Option #3: RECOVERY: You could place the recovery program (17GB) on a 32 GB flash drive or onto 5 DVDs. The 5 DVDs would be a logistical nightmare and the 32 GB Flash drive will cost about $30. But this Recovery program is not that useful because if it is ever used it will destroy all changes to your computer and restore the computer to the original state it was in when you first bough it. We will show you how to create a replacement original state recovery USB below so that we can delete this partition.
Option #4: SYSTEM: According to a Microsoft forum post, Windows 7 will not boot if the System partition is deleted. This partition must be the first active partition and therefore should not be altered or moved.

Our plan is to first create a USB Recovery disc. Then we will delete the HP Recovery partition so we can have room to place Linux on the Extended partition.

Creating a Shared Partition
There is another problem in that all of your data and files are inside of the C drive which right now is only accessible from Windows 7. What we want is a **Shared Partition** which is accessible to both Windows 7 and Linux Mint. Thus at a minimum, we need two new partitions: first, a Linux Partition and then a shared partition. We will later review how to create a shared partition. But if you have a new computer, you should simply completely uninstall Windows 7 and then re-install it so that it takes up fewer partitions. For now, we will show you how to add Linux without uninstalling your Windows 7 partitions.

Create an HP Recovery USB Flash Drive
There are many benefits of the USB Flash Drive recovery option over recovery DVD disks option: The DVD disk option requires 5 disks which could be scratched and corrupted. Also there are many kinds of DVD discs and many of these will not work. Also the discs need to be pre-numbered and then entered in the correct order. This means that the USB option is easier to create and more reliable over time. Just be sure to label this USB when you are done with it and do not try to use the USB for anything else.

Print out these instructions as you will have to close all other programs while creating this Recovery Disk.

Use a blank USB flash drive with at least 32 GB of memory. Use a name brand from a manufacturer you trust. Also temporarily <u>disable Windows User Account Control</u> if User Account Control is enabled. Doing so decreases the chances of encountering problems during the process.

How to disable User Account Control:

User Account Control informs you when a software program is trying to make changes to your computer that require administrator-level permission. User Account Control displays differently for Standard user accounts and Administrator accounts.

User Account Control with Standard user accounts

Enter the Administrator password, and click **Yes** to continue. If you do not know the Administrator password, you cannot continue.

User Account Control with Administrator accounts

If you are logged into an Administrator account, User Account Control asks permission for a program to make changes to the computer.

User Account Control for Administrator

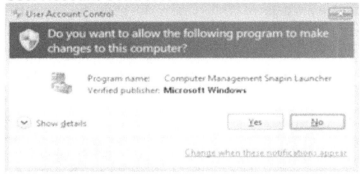

Disabling User Account Control

Click **Start**, **Control Panel**, and then click **User Accounts.** Then click **Change User Account Control settings.**

To turn off User Account Control, move the slider to the bottom (**Never notify**). Then click **OK.** Then restart your computer for this change to take effect.

Save the HP recovery file to a USB flash drive

HP recovery software allows you to make *only one recovery backup* . These backup files contain the original operating system, drivers, and application software that shipped with the computer. Making a copy of this file takes about 30 minutes. Disconnect from the Internet and close all other software. Then insert the flash drive. If a window opens asking you if you want to use the flash drive for files or backup, just close the window. This is not going to be a backup. It will be a recovery tool. From the Windows Desktop, click **Start**, and enter recovery manager into the Search field. Alternately, select **Start > All Programs > HP > HP Recovery Manager > HP Recovery Media Creation**

If a User Account Control message opens, click **Yes** or enter your login password, whichever is required. A Recovery Manager window opens. Click **Recovery Media Creation** NOTE: If Recovery Media Creation is not available (grayed out), then a recovery image has already been created. Due to license restrictions, only one set of recovery media can be created. Any new recovery media must be ordered online or obtained using another method.

Recovery Manager: Recovery Media selection

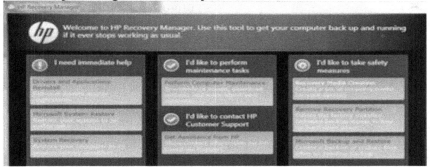

Followed by this screen.

Select **Recovery Media Creation with a USB flash drive** , and click **Next**.

Click **Create recovery media with a USB flash drive** , and then click **Next** .A verification window opens, showing the hard drive locations for removable discs. Select the location for your USB flash drive, and then click **Next.**

A Recovery Manager message opens stating that the flash drive will be formatted. Click **OK** to format the USB flash drive and continue. NOTE: Formatting this flash drive deletes any files on the drive.

Wait while the software creates your recovery media. Recovery image creation happens in two stages. First, the software copies the files to the USB flash drive. Second, the software verifies the files that files were copied successfully. A screen displays for each process. Click **Finish** when Recovery Manager has created the recovery media.

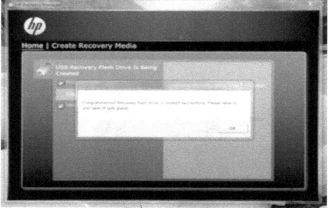

Next, we need to make sure we safely remove the USB. If a warning comes up that the USB cannot safely be removed because it is still running, then turn off the computer before removing the USB. Store the USB flash drive in a safe, protected place. If you attempt to save another recovery image to a USB flash drive after successfully saving one recovery image, a screen displays stating that only one recovery set is allowed. The only choice is to click **OK** and exit the program. To verify that our recovery image has been made, click on the Recovery Manager and attempt to create another recovery. You should see a screen noting that your recovery file was successfully made.

Remove the recovery partition
While you can remove the HP Recovery partition through the Windows Partition Manager, we will instead use the HP Recovery Manager to remove this backup file because the HP tool is safer than the Windows tool. This HP tool is the same tool we used to create the USB Flash Drive of the Recovery file.

To remove the recovery partition, click **Start**, type Recovery in the search field, and click on **Recovery Manager** when it appears in the program list to open the Recovery Manager window. Click **Advanced options**.

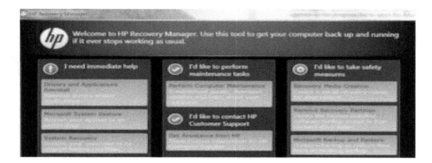

Select the **Remove recovery partition** option and click **Next**.

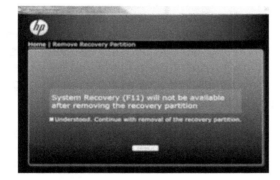

When prompted to verify that you want to delete the partition, select the **Yes** option, and click **Next**. Allow the removal process to continue and restart the PC. Now check to see if the partition was removed. Go to Control Panel, Admin Tools, Computer Management, Storage, Disk management:

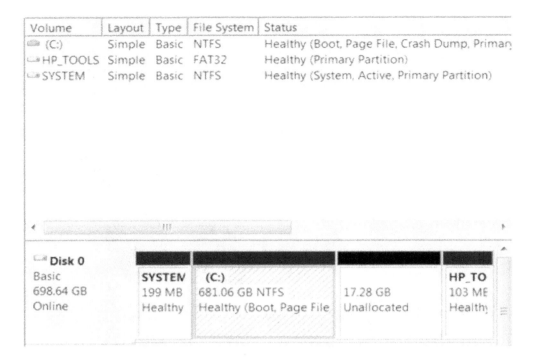

We now have only three partitions! Mission accomplished!

Make and File Product Keys for Windows 7 and Office 2010
The easiest way to get the product keys for Windows and Office is to use the free **Belarc Advisor**. Store these keys on a jump drive - not on your C Drive. This way if the computer crashes completely, we can reinstall everything using the product keys. Having the product keys helps if the original installs were done online and we do not have CDs to reinstall programs from. To download Belarc Advisor, go to: http://www.belarc.com/free_download.html

Then go to Downloads folder and find this file. Right click and select **Run as administrator.** It will create a local screen with all of your software and hardware information – including all product keys. All of your PC profile information is kept private on your PC and is not sent to any Web server.

Now that we have backed up all of our files and removed the HP Recovery partition, we are almost ready to dual boot Linux onto our computer. There are only a couple of things we still need to do. The first is to create a bootable flash drive with Linux Mint Mate on it. The second is to shrink our C drive to create more room for Linux Mint. We will cover both of these tasks in the next section.

6.3 Dual Boot Linux Mint with Windows XP or Windows 7

This section reviews how to add Linux Mint to a computer that already has Windows XP or Windows 7 on it so that you can use either system. This will allow you to keep the Windows operating system on your computer while you are learning how to use Linux Mint.

We will now show you how to create a Dual Boot system on your home computer so that you can have more than one operating system. Dual booting means installing two operating systems on one hard disk and being able to boot into either of them. This article explains how to install Linux Mint 15 alongside Windows 7, but it will also work for any other version of Mint. If you have a Windows Vista or XP computer, the instructions are about the same. Windows XP, Windows Vista and Windows 7 all use a boot process called **BIOS** and a partition table based on the **Master Boot Record** (MBR). However, if you have a Windows 8 computer, you should read this chapter and also the next chapter for how to deal with the problems presented by Windows 8. This is because Windows 8 uses a completely different boot process, called **UEFI** with secure boot, and a completely different partition table arrangement, called **Graphic Partition Table** or GPT.

There are many pitfalls to the dual boot process with Windows and many tutorials on the process fail to adequately warn users about potential problems. So we will provide a more complete set of instructions in this and the next chapter.

The main purpose of this dual boot is to allow you to keep your current Windows system to run your current Windows programs, and then use Linux Mint to run free open source programs and to access files for the rest of your work and play. But a dual boot is also extremely useful if (when) your Windows operating system crashes. Having a second safer and more reliable operating system will allow you to protect your important files and continue getting your work done even if your Windows operating system crashes. Below is what a dual boot startup option looks like with the Windows Boot Manager. We will show you two ways to do a dual boot - one way keeps the Windows Boot Manager and adds Linux to it.

The other way replaces the Windows Boot Manager with a better boot manager called the GRUB 2 Boot Manager which automatically adds Windows to it.

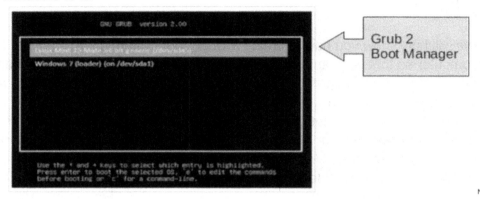

Download the Linux Mint 15 x64 bit ISO file from
http://www.linuxmint.com/download.php

Because I am installing Linux Mint on a 64 bit computer with at least 4 GB of RAM, I have selected the 64 bit version. But if you have a computer with less than 4 GB of RAM which is a 32 bit computer, then select the 32 bit version of Linux Mint Mate. On the next screen, scroll down the list to your country and pick one of the download centers.

This will bring up the Download Notification screen. Click Save. It is a very large 1 GB file and may take up to an hour to download. Be patient and do not try to access the file until it is fully downloaded. The next step is to download UNetbootin to create a Live USB.

Use UNetbootin to create a Live USB Flash Drive

UNetbootin allows you to create bootable Live USB drives for Linux distributions. You will need a USB Flash Drive which is at least 2 GB. It should be empty and in a format of FAT32. To verify that your USB is FAT32, in your Windows computer, go to Start, My Computer and right click on the USB Drive. Then click on **Properties:**

If it is not FAT32, click on **Properties, Format** to reformat it. Once formatted, note the Mount Point (Drive Letter) of the drive (in my case it is D:). You will need to know this later. Remove any other USB drive (including external hard drives) connected to your PC except for the one you want to use for the installation.

Download UNetbootin to your computer

Go to the following link to download it. http://unetbootin.sourceforge.net/
There are three different versions of UNetbootin, one for Windows, one for Linux and one for Mac OS X. The resulting USB drives are bootable only on PCs (not on Macs). Pick the version for your current operating system and download it:
UNetbootin (Download Windows Version or Download Linux Version Download Mac OS X Version)

UNetbootin - Homepage and Downloads

Additional dependencies (*Linux Only*): You will need the packages *syslinux* and *p7zip-full* installed. Click on the Windows Download option.

Then save this file to your Downloads folder. You won't have to install it, it will run directly from the downloaded file. Then go to your Downloads folder and find the file UNetbootin Setup.exe. Right click on the file and select **Run as Administrator:**

Select the **Disk Image** option. Then browse for and select the Linux Mint 15 ISO which should also be in your Downloads folder. Mark sure the Target Type is set for your USB Drive and that the Drive is set for the Mount point (D). Then turn off all other programs. Then click OK. The bootable "live" USB creation process will take a few minutes. Be patient. When it is done, it will show a screen confirming you have a Live USB. **Click Exit rather than reboot** as we need to first change the BIOS boot order. Make sure to label your Live USB and do not use this USB flash drive for anything else. The next step is shrinking the volume on the Windows C partition and then resetting your BIOS boot order (see below).

Special instructions for creating a Live USB if using the Linux version
If using the Linux version of UNetbootin, make the file executable by going to Properties->Permissions and checking "Execute." Then start the application. You will be prompted for your password to grant the application administrative rights, then the main dialog will appear, where you select a distribution and install target (USB Drive), then reboot when prompted.

Shrink the Volume on the Windows C Partition
Our next task is to resize the Windows C partition. This will give us the space we need to add partitions for Linux Mint. We must be careful with shrinking the C drive to not reformat it – as this would cause us to lose all of the data on the C drive. Also be sure to leave much more room in the C drive than you think you need. This is because Windows is not very good about where it puts data and will really slow down if more than 70% of the disc space is taken.

So for example, if you already have 150 GB on the CD, you should give the C Drive 200 GB to minimize slowing down. Alternately, you could defragment you C drive every couple of weeks. (Because Linux is much better at organizing data, it will not slow down just because the disc is getting full).

To use the automatic install method, it is important to resize the C drive before we install Linux. We will therefore use the Windows Partition Manager to resize the C Drive. In Windows XP or Windows 7, go to Start Button and click on the **Control Panel**. Then click on **Administrative Tools,** then **Computer Management**, then **Storage,** then **Disc Management**.

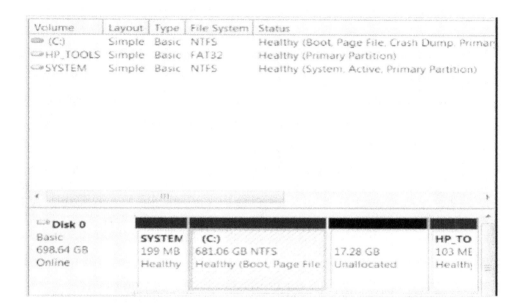

After deleting the Recovery Partition in the last chapter, we have 17 GB of Unallocated space and a lot of GB in the C drive. What we want to do is to move about half of the space from the C drive to the Unallocated space so we can use this to install Linux. Click on the **C drive box** above to select it. Then right click to bring up the **Partition Edit** screen:

Click on **Shrink Volume**. It will take Windows a couple of minutes to figure out how much space is available on the C drive to shrink. It will then display the following screen:

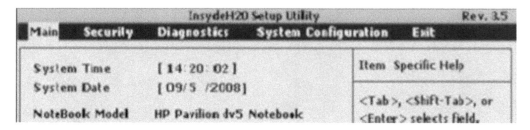

Shrink C:

Total size before shrink in MB:	286102
Size of available shrink space in MB:	123274
Enter the amount of space to shrink in MB:	123274
Total size after shrink in MB:	162828

ⓘ You cannot shrink a volume beyond the point where any unmovable files are located. See the "defrag" event in the Application log for detailed information about the operation when it has completed.

See Shrink a Basic Volume in Disk Management help for more information.

Shrink   Cancel

Do not trust the "size available to shrink space" as it is not accurate. If we actually took all of the space, Windows would quickly slow down to a crawl. Instead only take about half of the space that is indicated as available. After putting in that number, click **Shrink.** It will take a few minutes for the C drive to be resized. When it is done shrinking, the space will be moved to the Unallocated space. Now we can close Windows.

Change the Boot Order in your computer BIOS settings
Our next step is to set the boot order in BIOS to use the USB Live Flash Drive instead of the Windows Boot Manager. This requires turning off and restarting your computer. **BEFORE RESTARTING YOUR COMPUTER TO CHANGE THE BOOT ORDER, PRINT OUT A COPY OF THE REST OF THIS SECTION as you will not have access to this screen while you are installing Linux Mint!**

Now that we have created a Live USB with UNetbootin, leave the Live USB in the USB port or if you took it out, reinsert it. The next step is to change the BIOS Boot Order so that the Live USB is the first item selected. Restart your computer and press the appropriate button (usually F1, F2, F12, or ESC) while your computer is starting to get to your BIOS menu.

| InsydeH20 Setup Utility | | | | Rev. 3.5 |
Main	Security	Diagnostics	System Configuration	Exit

		Item Specific Help
System Time	[14:20:02]	
System Date	[09/5 /2008]	<Tab>, <Shift-Tab>, or
NoteBook Model	HP Pavilion dv5 Notebook	<Enter> selects field.

Then use the right arrow on your key board to select **System Configuration**.

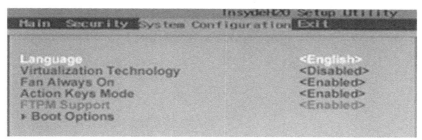

Then use the Down arrow to select **Boot Options**. Then press Enter on your keyboard to start the Boot Options screen.

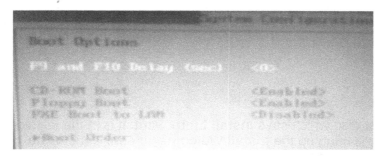

It may appear as if the only options are CD ROM or Floppy Disc. However, select **Boot Order** to bring up another screen. Then select **USB Diskette on Key/ USB Hard Disc.** Click **F6** to raise it to the top of the list. Then click **F10** to save and close the settings. This will change the startup order to boot USB by default. On Restart, the USB screen appears and starts the Linux Mint installer.

Install Linux Mint in a Dual Boot on your computer
We will use the Linux Mint installer to create install Linux Mint. While there are other ways to create partitions, doing it directly with the Linux Mint installer is the most reliable method. After booting from the Live USB, you will go through an installation process which is very similar to the installation process of Linux Mint on Virtual Box. This is another reason to install Virtual Box – to give you a chance to practice installing Linux in a safe environment. The first screen you will likely see after your computer restarts will be the following.

This will start the Linux Mint 15 operating system installation process and bring up the following screen:

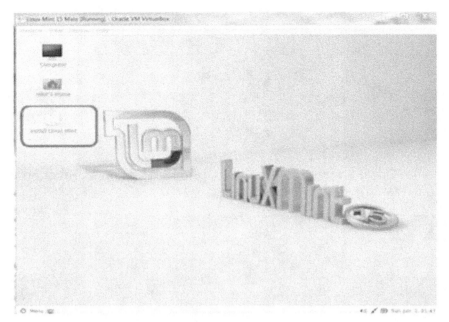

Click on the circular disc which says **Install Linux Mint.** It is in the left side of your screen. This will bring up the **Install Welcome** screen. Choose the language and click on **Continue.** The next screen recommends that you connect to the internet. You do not really need to be connected to the internet as you can add updates later. So click **Continue**.

Installation Type Screen and Options
One major difference between a Virtual Box installation and a real dual boot installation is that when you get to the place in the installation where you are given several options, **do NOT select using the entire disc.** This would wipe out your C Drive and all of your data! Be aware that the Installation Type screen options will be different depending on the operating system you currently have on your computer. Below is the Installation Type screen which appeared when we installed Linux Mint into Virtual Box. Note that there are only four options:

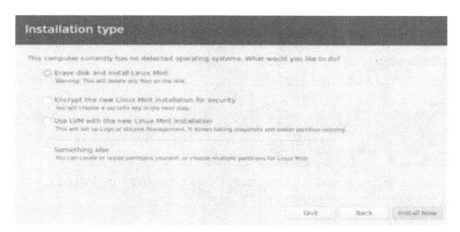

However, when we install Linux Mint as a dual boot with Windows 7, we suddenly have a fifth option called "**Install Linux Mint alongside Windows 7**".

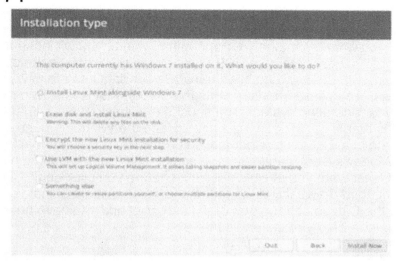

The reason this is the default option is that if you leave it set for this option, Linux Mint will automatically create your new partitions for you and install Linux Mint in whatever free space you have on your hard drive. Let's take a closer look at these options before we select one.

Installation Option 1: The Automatic Install Option
The automatic install method has both advantages and drawbacks. The benefit of the automatic install option is that you do not have to learn about partitions or go through the hassles of creating your own partitions. If you are not very good with computers, this is definitely the option you should take. Just click on Install and then run through the same configuration screens we used to install Linux Mint into Virtual Box. After automatically creating partitions for and installing Linux Mint 15, the new partitions as seen from inside Windows 7 will look a lot different. This image shows the partitions from the computer used for this tutorial after the dual-boot operating has completed.

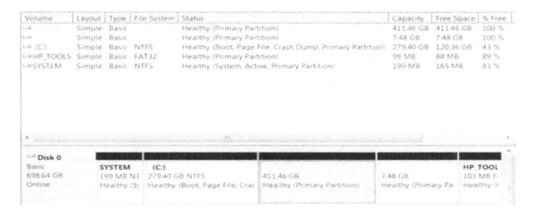

There are however a few drawbacks of the automatic install method. First, it will only create two partitions – one for Linux Mint and another for a "swap" partition. The Linux Boot Manager, called GRUB 2 will be installed into the Linux Mint partition and so will all of your data. (Note that Windows also installs all of your data on its partition which is called the C drive). This means that whenever you want to change your operating system, you will need to make a copy of all of your data on a USB Flash Drive, then replace the old operating system with the new one, then reinstall your data into the new operating system. You would not have to do this if your data was on a different partition than your operating system. The second drawback of the automatic install method is that Linux will automatically replace the Windows Boot Manager with the Linux Boot Manager (called GRUB 2). This is not that big of a loss as the Windows Boot Manager is a piece of junk. But it would be nice if Linux would at least warn you of what it is doing before you click on the Install Now button. The third drawback of the automatic install method is that you need to shrink the C drive before you install Linux Mint and you have no control over the size of any of the partitions.

A fourth drawback is that you do not get a chance to learn how partitions work on your computer. Since knowledge is power, if you really want control over your computer, it is worth learning about partitions. This will also help you better understand some of the major pitfalls of Windows 8 and the UEFI partition manager – which we will be covering in more detail in the next chapter. So even if you decide to use the automatic install method, you might want to take a few minutes to read through the rest of this chapter. We will next show a second more customizable way to install Linux – a way in which you take control over how your computer gets divided up.

Installation Option 2: The "Do Something Else" Method

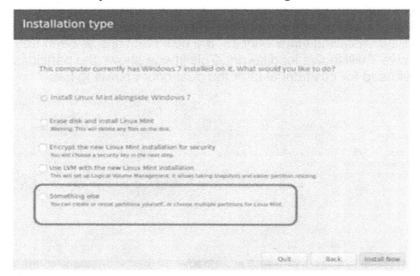

Hopefully, you know that you should not click on the "Erase Disc and install Linux Mint" option as this will erase all of the data on your C drive.

But you can select "**Do something else.**" This will allow you to safely create custom partitions in your partition table. Then click **Install Now.** This will bring up the **Linux Partitioning Tool.** This shows your current partition table and allows you to create your own partitions. Here you can not only create partitions but also resize existing partitions and delete partitions you no longer want. You screen may look slightly different from the following screen:

If you have followed our advice and deleted the HP Recovery Partition, your install screen will look slightly different than the screen above.
Above are two partitions. The first one, sda1 is the Windows System partition with a size of about 100 MB. The second one, sda2, is the Windows C Drive. The C drive above has 320 GB. You should also have some free space where the HP Recovery partition used to be and where we shrank the C Drive. You should also have a partition called sda3 – which holds the HP TOOLS partition. The sda3 partition may be hidden below the free space.

By default, the Linux Mint installer wants to create one root partition and one swap partition for you during the "automatic" installation. But it is much better to have four partitions for Linux Mint rather than two partitions. We will create **a root partition, a separate home partition, a swap partition and a boot partition**. The purpose of the boot partition is to help load the system independently of the operating system – just as the Windows System partition boots Windows. The root partition will hold Linux just as the C Drive holds the Windows operating system. However, instead of placing your data, images and documents on the C Drive as Windows does, we will create a separate **Home** partition for our documents called /home. This way, we can change operating systems without moving our documents. To keep things organized, refer to the following table:

Partition Name	Partition Mount Point	Partition Size	Partition Location	Partition Type
Boot	/boot	500 MB	/dev/sda5	Ext4
Root	/	15 -30 GB	/dev/sda6	Ext4
Home	/home	Most of GB	/dev/sda7	Ext4
Swap		1- 4 GB	/dev/sda8	swap

The file type for all partitions is logical. The boot partition should be created first and be in the beginning position. The mount point for swap should be left blank.

Linux Partition File Location Names

Linux uses different terms for hard drive and partition files than Windows. Windows does not really have partitions but instead calls everything "drives" such as C or D drive. Linux calls the first hard drive /dev/sda and it partitions /dev/sda1 /dev/sda2, etc. "**Dev**" is short for "Device" and "**sd**" is short for Storage Driver. If you have a computer with a second hard drive, the second hard drive would be called /dev/sdb and the partitions would be called /dev /sdb1 /dev/sdb2, etc. The extended partition is always called /dev/sda4 and the first logical partition inside of the extended partition is always called /dev/sda5.

Overview

The objective in setting up our four partitions is to install Linux Mint 15 on the same hard drive, with GRUB, Linux Mint's boot loader, installed in the boot partition of Linux Mint, leaving the Windows 7 boot programs untouched. After creating partitions for and installing Linux Mint, the new partitions as seen from inside Windows 7 will look a lot different. This image shows the partitions from the computer used for this tutorial after the dual-boot operating has completed.

Create your first Linux Partition... The Boot Partition

To create a new partition, select the free space as shown below and click **Add**. **This step will have to be repeated for every partition you need to create**.

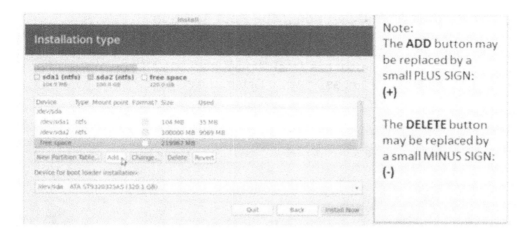

Note:
The **ADD** button may be replaced by a small PLUS SIGN:
(+)

The **DELETE** button may be replaced by a small MINUS SIGN:
(-)

By default, the installer will create the first and subsequent partitions as **Logical** partitions. This is exactly what we want.

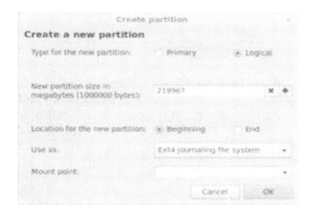

Our first partition will be the boot partition. Use 500 MB to 900 MB for the size and **/boot** as the **Mount point.** Leave the **Use as** value unchanged. Make sure the location is set for the **Beginning.** Then click **OK**.

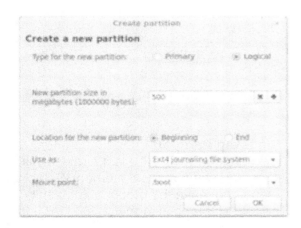

Create your second partition... The Root Partition

Click on the Free Space again and click on **ADD**. For the root partition, the minimum disk space recommended is 8 **GB.** Since resizing the disk on a running system is not an easy task, I gave it 20,000 MB, or 20 GB. After setting the Mount Point as Forward Slash, click **OK**.

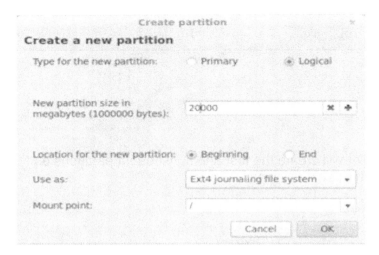

Create your third partition... The Home Partition

Click on the Free Space again and then click on ADD. The partition mounted at /home should be allocated most of the available disk space. Give it a value of 100 to 300 GB. Leave the file system at the default and use **/home** as the **Mount point**. Then click **OK**.

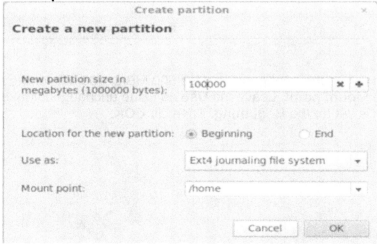

Create your fourth partition... The Swap Partition

Click on the **Free Space** again. Then click on **ADD**. The last partition will be for Swap, disk space that the system may use for virtual memory. Select **swap area** from the **Use as** dropdown menu and leave the mount point blank. Assign it a suitable disk space. The rule of thumb is to match the RAM on your computer. My computer has 4 GB of RAM so I set it for 4 GB. Then click **OK**.

Back to the Partition Table, you should now see the partitions you just created. The partitions should be listed as **sda5**, **sda6, sda7** and **sda8**. Not visible on this screen shot, are the pre-existing Windows partitions, which are **sda1** and **sda2**.

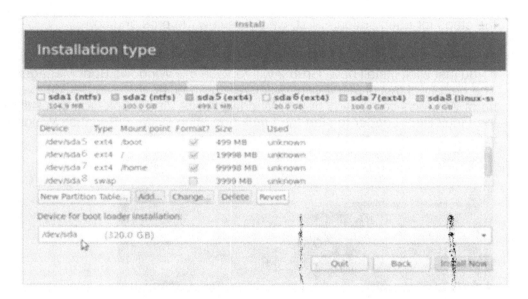

With Windows XP or Windows 7 installations which only use the first two partitions, the Linux boot partition will be listed as sda 3 and the Linux root partition will be listed as sda 5. Also the Linux root partition may be indicated as Linux Mint 14 – even though it is actually Linux 15. Do not worry. This was just a typographical error and will not affect the installation of Linux 15. To format partitions, the sda5, sda6 and sda7 partitions above have the Format boxes checked. If your partitions are not checked, you should click on these boxes to format these three partitions. However, **leave the SWAP partition unchecked.**

Two options for Set the Device to Boot Load the Installation
If you did the "Something Else" option rather than the "Automatic Install" option, you also have the option of deciding which Boot Manager you want to use. This decision comes in the area called "**Device for boot loader installation**."

The boot loader is the program which starts right after BIOS or UEFI and which displays a screen allowing you to choose which operating system you want to load. If you already have Windows XP, Windows 7 or Windows 8 installed on your computer, then you already have a boot loader called **Windows Boot Manager** installed. You can leave Windows Boot Manager in place. Or you can replace the Windows Boot Manager with the Linux Boot Manager which is called **GRUB 2**. (GRUB stands for the Grand Universal Boot Loader and is a tribute to Albert Einstein and his Grand Unified Field Theory). The step of where to put the GRUB 2 boot loader occurs after you have set up all of your Linux partitions. It is the final step just before clicking on Install Now which will begin the Linux installation process. If you do nothing, by default, the Linux installation will replace the Windows Boot Manager with GRUB 2. You can get the Windows Boot Manager back later if you want. But one of my biggest complaints about Linux is the failure to provide users with a clearer choice about their options so that users can make the decision for themselves. In the meantime, we will review the pros and cons of both options and present the steps for each option. First, we will review the pros and cons.

Option 1: Allow Grub 2 to Replace the Windows Boot Manager
If you just click install now, Grub 2 will replace the Windows Boot Manager. The benefit of this is that if Windows ever crashes, or you ever decide to get rid of Windows completely or put Windows inside Virtual Box, you can still use the Linux Boot Loader to start the Linux operating system. Because Windows is far more likely to crash than Linux, this option makes some sense.

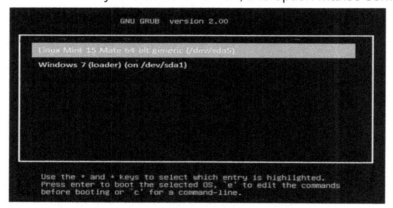

GRUB 2 will give you ten seconds to choose which operating system you want to use. If no choice is made, GRUB 2 will start Linux. The drawback of replacing the Windows Boot Manager with GRUB 2 is that in the hard to believe event that you decide you do not like Linux and you want to go back to Windows, you will have to go through the hassle of replacing GRUB 2 with the Windows Boot Manager. There are several ways to do this so this is not that big of a deal. If the GRUB 2 boot manager is used, it will give you a Start screen allowing you to select Linux or Windows. Should you choose Windows and press Enter, then the GRUB 2 boot loader will chain load or start the Windows Boot Loader. So the Windows Boot loader is still there. It is just hidden away and not in the first position.

Option 2: Leave the Windows Boot Manager alone and allow it to chain load the GRUB 2 boot loader

If you leave the Windows Boot loader in the first position, it will give you a screen at Start Up and allow you to choose either Windows or Linux. If you choose Linux, then the Windows Boot loader will chain load first GRUB 2 for a fraction of a second which will load Linux. In other words, the Linux Boot Loader GRUB 2 is also still there. It is just hidden. There is one extra step you will have to do if you choose this option. You will have to start up Windows and use a free program called **Easy BCD** to add an Entry to the Windows Boot Loader for Linux. Otherwise, the Windows Boot Loader will not even know Linux is there. One added benefit of the GRUB 2 boot loader is that it automatically recognizes all of the operating systems that are available. If there is more than one operating system available, GRUB 2will present you with a list of them at Start Up and let you choose which one you want to load. So you do not need Easy BCD.

How to choose between these two options

If you are not really sure you want Linux, then you should probably choose the second option. However, if you are not really sure you want Linux, you should probably not install a dual boot in the first place and simply keep Linux Mint in Virtual Box. The whole point of our chapter on setting up a Virtual Box and installing Linux in the Virtual Box is to give you the opportunity to see how much better Linux is than Windows. In addition, we had several chapters discussing all of the security problems of Windows. So it is difficult to imagine anyone reading this book and still having doubts about whether they should add Linux to their computer. Nearly everyone who uses Linux comments that the more they use Linux, the less they have a need to use Windows. Entire years will go by without even once opening Windows. So while I can see a need for keeping Windows around "just in case you ever need it," I cannot really see a case for keeping the Windows Boot Manager around. The Windows Boot Manager is so poorly written that it will not work unless it is in the very first partition, called dev/sda1. GRUB 2 will work in any partition. The Windows Boot Manager is so dumb that it cannot tell if there are other operating systems on your hard drive without the help of some other program telling it. By comparison, the GRUB 2 boot loader is not only capable of knowing where the Windows Boot Loader is and the Linux Mint Boot Loader is, it can also automatically detect any other boot loaders on any other operating systems you might install to your hard drive. I do not recommend having more than two operating systems on your hard drive. You are better off testing operating systems with Virtual Box. However, if you have GRUB 2 as your boot loader, you can have as many operating systems as you want and GRUB 2 will automatically find and list all of them. Pretty nice. There are many other problems with the Windows Boot Manager and many other advantages of the GRUB 2 boot loader (for example, GRUB 2 will even let you set a background image to your loading screen). So my advice is to go ahead and replace the Windows Boot Manager with GRUB 2.This is why we present the steps for this option first. But at the end of this section, we will also present the steps for keeping the Windows Boot Manager and adding Linux to it.

Steps to allow GRUB 2 to replace the Windows Boot Manager

Previously, we used the Linux Partition Tool to add four partitions and create a Partition table that looks like the following:

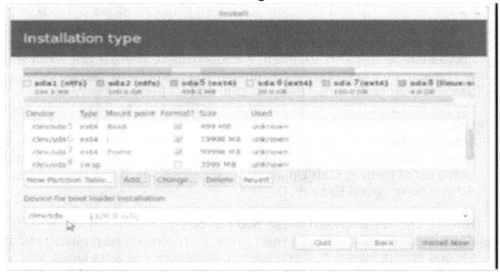

To replace the Windows Boot Manager with the Linux Boot Manager, simply click on Install Now. That's it. You are done. The rest of the Installation is almost exactly like the installation of Linux on Virtual Box.

What does /dev/sda mean?

The term "/dev/sda" above stands for "device – storage drive A". Since your computer has only one hard drive, it is known as Storage Drive A or sda. Whatever is placed in this little box will control the loading process for this entire hard drive. Traditionally, each hard drive has exactly one Master Boot Record (MBR). Each MBR has only two parts. The first part is the Boot Loader or Boot Manager and the second part is the Partition Table. Above we can see the Partition Table. But the Boot Loader is hidden from view. Currently, the boot loader is a device called the Windows Boot Manager – which I believe is actually on the first partition sda1. This is why you should never move sda1 if you want to use Windows. If you click **Install** without making any changes, the Windows Boot Manager (on sda1) will be over-ridden by GRUB 2 (which is actually on sda5). This is not a big deal as GRUB 2 will automatically add the Windows Boot Manager to the GRUB 2 Startup screen and give you a choice of loading Windows if you wish through a process called Chain Loading.

What GRUB 2 is really doing

GRUB 2 takes up more space than is allowed on the Master Boot Record. It therefore uses this space on the Master Boot Record (which is not a partition) to redirect to the partition where GRUB 2 is really at (sda5). The main GRUB program then examines all of the partitions to see if there are any operating systems and any other boot managers (which GRUB calls loaders). What GRUB finds is then listed on the Start Up screen.

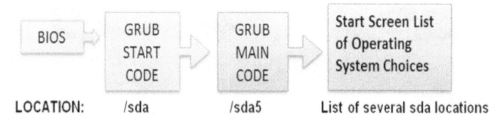

LOCATION: /sda   /sda5   List of several sda locations

The GRUB main code is typically in the first logical partition in the extended partition – which is always sda5. But in reality, GRUB is in whatever partition you called **/boot**. In addition, the GRUB code is also at the beginning of the root partition (/) of any Linux operating system. As for the BIOS program, it is not even on your hard drive. Instead, it is inside of a little memory chip inside of the mother board of your computer that comes just before your hard drive. The main job of BIOS is to turn on other things in the computer and set the correct current. So it is like an On-Off Switch. Once everything is turned on, BIOS looks for the first Boot Manager it can find which will hopefully be at the very beginning of the hard drive – on sda in the case of GRUB or sda1 with Windows.

Finish Installing Linux Mint
After going through the same install screens we went through when installing Linux Mint into Virtual Box, you will come to the restart screen. Click on **Restart Now.** Then while your computer is temporarily off, **remove the USB Live stick.** Otherwise, it will try to install Linux Mint again instead of going to the GRUB 2 screen or the Windows Boot Manager.

Using the GRUB 2 Startup screen
When your computer starts, you will find many entries on the GRUB 2 screen. The first entry in the list will be Linux Mint 15. Press Enter on your keyboard to start Mint 15. The first Windows entry is actually the Windows Boot Manager which is still on the partition called sda1. To start Windows, use the down arrow on your keyboard to select this. Then press Enter to start it. Clicking on this will simply bring up the Windows Boot Manager and you will have to click on Windows 7 again to get to the C drive. The second Windows entry is your Windows Recovery drive. Clicking on this will take you to a series of Windows Recovery steps familiar to those who have tried to recover Windows after it has crashed. So it is best to select the first Windows option on the list if you want to start the Windows operating system instead of the Linux operating system.

Steps to use the Windows Boot Manager instead of GRUB 2
In order to leave the Windows Boot Loader alone, we need to change the Linux installation boot loader to the Boot Loader partition we created which is sda5.
This is what the **Device for boot loader installation** dropdown menu should look like before you click **Install Now**.

Installation type

Device	Type	Mount point	Format?	Size	Used
/dev/sda5	ext4	/boot	☑	499 MB	unknown
/dev/sda6	ext4	/	☑	19998 MB	unknown
/dev/sda7	ext4	/home	☑	99998 MB	unknown
/dev/sda8	swap			3999 MB	unknown

Device for boot loader installation:

/dev/sda5

Notice this was changed from sda to sda5

After installation has completed successfully, the computer should reboot into Windows. Before Windows reboots, it will start checking the resized C drive for consistency. Let the check complete. After the check has completed, login.

Add Linux Mint to the Windows Boot Manager with Easy BCD
Because the Windows Boot Manager is kind of dumb, there is no way to boot into Linux Mint 15 until an entry for it is added to the Windows boot menu. The next task is to download and install EasyBCD. Do a Google search if you want to download this free program. After EasyBCD has been installed in your Windows operating system, start it. Click on **Add New Entry** tab. While there, click on the **Linux/BSD** tab, then select **GRUB 2** from the **Type** dropdown menu. GRUB 2, not GRUB Legacy, is the version of GRUB used by Linux Mint 15.

Edit the **Name** field to match the distribution you are adding it for. Apply the changes by clicking the **Add Entry** button. Click on the **Edit Boot Menu** tab. You should see how the entries will appear on the boot menu. Exit EasyBCD and restart the computer. You can always change, resize or delete partitions later if you need to by booting into Linux Mint and using the free **GParted** partition manager which comes with Linux Mint. In the next section, we will look at how to create a dual boot with Linux and Windows 8.

6.4 Dual Boot Linux Mint with Windows 8

> **Windows 8 is completely different from Windows 7 or Windows XP in that Microsoft has added many more obstacles to prevent you from adding Linux. This section covers precautions you should take in order to add Linux Mint to a computer which already has Windows 8 (with UEFI) on it.**

In this section, we will review your options for dual booting with Linux Mint if you have the misfortune of owning a Windows 8 computer. One of the many problems of Windows 8 is that it uses a new kind of startup program called UEFI.

> **UEFI stands for Unwarranted Elimination of your Freedom and Independence** (or something like that).

One of the more dubious features of UEFI is called **Secure Boot aka the Microsoft Kill Switch.** We covered the history of UEFI in an earlier chapter. Before we review the steps for adding Linux Mint as a dual boot to Windows 8, we will review the problems with Secure Boot and UEFI. These problems are so horrific that our advice is –rather than installing Linux Mint as a dual boot with Windows 8 – we hope you will strongly consider returning your Windows 8 computer to the store where you bought it and insist on a refund. It is likely that you have an old Windows 7 or XP computer sitting around the house. Dual booting either of these older computers would be a much better and safer option than keeping a rather dangerous Windows 8 computer. Here's why:

Problem #1: Secure boot is not secure
Secure boot uses a combination of keys to prevent you from downloading any program Microsoft feels is not safe. The problem is that some of the keys are public and the rest have been hacked in the past – and will be hacked again in the future. So the only one blocked from installing programs to your computer by secure boot is you. Microsoft has left the backdoor to your computer open since 1997. With Windows 8, they have now also left the front door to your computer open. Secure Boot opens up the Startup program to attack because it uses the same top down easily copied digital image system the Microsoft Windows uses to protect its open back door. This lulls users into a false sense of security that they are covered when they are not.

Problem #2: Secure boot is dangerous and could crash the entire world economy
Nearly every business in the world uses computers to manage their business and store their data. Imagine what would happen to the economy if all of the computers were brought down due to a secure boot failure.

Even if you are willing to trust that Microsoft will not push the Kill button deliberately – or accidentally – the real problem is that hackers can and will use this Kill button. Think of the Flame virus only much worse. Secure Boot is like a digital nuclear weapon in the hands of economic terrorists.

Problem #3: Secure boot limits your freedom

With every prior version of Windows, Microsoft allowed you to decide whether a program was safe to load to your computer. With Secure Boot, it will be Microsoft who will get to decide what is acceptable to load to your computer. Load the wrong program and your computer might no longer start. Think of it as the police owning the keys to your home and telling you whether you can go in or not.

(Because secure boot is enabled by default on all Windows 8 computers), "it is a bit like if everyone is born with handcuffs on and only if you pay a certain amount of money you get released."
Red Hat Developer Matthew Garrett

Want Freedom? Say no to (in)secure boot.

Problem #4: Secure boot will kill software innovation

Nearly all innovations have come from the thousands of small time programmers who write applications for themselves and then share them with others. These programmers will be tossed out of business with Secure Boot as most will not be able to jump through all of the hoops imposed by Microsoft to get a signed key.

Problem #5: Secure Boot is very difficult for many users to disable

Supposedly we have the option of turning off secure boot. The problem is that there are four major "families" of secure boot and every manufacturer has a different implementation of secure boot. Without any consistency, this means that there are literally dozens of different kinds of secure boot systems.
Below we will show you screen shots of how to disable secure boot with some of the most common systems. But the actual pathway to find and disable secure boot can be much different on your computer. First imagine how hard it would be to disable secure boot without our detailed instructions and screen shots. Then imagine how difficult it would be for your mother to disable secure boot!!

Problem #6: Even if you disable secure boot, UEFI still has huge problems

Secure boot is just the tip of the iceberg in terms of all of the problems of UEFI. UEFI specifications are a secret.

But what is known about them is that they are thousands of pages long. Subtracting the driver code, the size of UEFI is actually larger than the size of the entire Linux Kernel. What is in all of these thousands of files and lines of code? Many of the files in UEFI begin with a "win" prefix – meaning that they were written by Microsoft for Microsoft and Microsoft does not want to let us know what is in this code.

> The UEFI verification mechanism is identical to the MS Windows signing mechanism. These have already been successfully attacked by the Flame virus. All of the coding of the UEFI signing mechanism start with the word WIN.

UEFI is also written with Microsoft back slashes as path separators – just like Microsoft file paths– making it easier for hackers to attack it. Because UEFI is new it is certain to have many bugs and will have unpredictable reactions with many other programs. In particular, most of the new code affects boot loaders such as GRUB 2 and the Windows Boot Manager.

> According to a leading expert on boot loaders, **"UEFI allows thousands of entry points to Boot Services and has an incredible number of bugs... It is clear that nobody has ever tested this code... Secure Boot is just a distraction. The real problem is UEFI.**
> Red Hat Developer Matthew Garrett, The Future is Here and it is Horrible.
> http://www.youtube.com/watch?v=V2ag5M3Q76U

Incredibly, there is no way to know about what is in the UEFI program or what kinds of bugs have been discovered because all members of the UEFI forum must sign an oath of secrecy. Even UEFI documentation is kept under secure files requiring UEFI passwords to access.

This is the exact opposite of how the open source community works – where everyone knows about all bug reports and everyone works together and shares ideas and solutions to fix the bugs.

Problem #7: There is a safer free open source option to UEFI called Core Boot

If either Microsoft or computer manufacturers really cared about safety, they would have installed the Core Boot Start up program. It is faster and safer than UEFI. By placing the passwords and control of the computer in the hands of the actual owner (you), there is no set of keys to be copied. A maker of processors, called AMD, now fully supports Core Boot. So manufacturers do have an easy option. Our hope is that if enough people return their Windows 8 computers and demand a computer with Core Boot, we will eventually be able to put this Windows 8/UEFI/Secure Boot Nightmare behind us.

Problem #8 Claims that there are advantages to UEFI are false

We are currently being subjected to a wave of propaganda trying to convince us that UEFI has some kind of benefit. For example, they claim that UEFI can handle partitions bigger than 2 Terabytes. Well, so can Core Boot. Even the old BIOS can as long as they are divided between partitions. If you have more than two terabytes of data, you should not be putting so much data on a single hard drive anyway. You should use a second hard drive if only for safety reasons.

You will also hear that UEFI allows you to have a much larger number of partitions. This is also not true. Core Boot has the same partitioning ability as UEFI and even the old BIOS system will let you have as many partitions as you want as long as you use the fourth partition to create an extended partition.

You will also be told that Secure Boot protects against Root Kit infections. It does not. Anyone capable of creating a root kit attack is also capable of creating fake keys similar to the process used by the Flame virus. So do not be fooled. The only purpose of UEFI is to maintain and expand the Microsoft monopoly. If you want your system to be safe and under your control, then install and use Linux. If you really want security, then you need to get a computer with Core Boot.

Problem #9: Even if you want to install a Linux Distribution which comes with the UEFI Secure Boot keys, you are better off disabling secure boot AFTER installing Linux.

As of June 2013, several Linux distributions including Ubuntu, Mint 15 and Fedora now come with the necessary Microsoft keys to permit installation with secure boot enabled. However, you should still disable secure boot after the installation has been completed. There are two reasons for this. First, Microsoft can switch keys at any point in the future and there goes your Linux operating system and all of your data with it. Second, the keys may not allow you to install other programs you want with your Linux system. In fact, you should also disable Microsoft Updates as this can also wind up deleting your Linux system. Windows 8 will work (maybe even better) without secure boot enabled and without all of the monthly updates from Microsoft. And so will Linux and all of your other programs. We will therefore review some tips for setting up a dual boot with Linux and Windows 8. We will then show you how to disable secure boot in some of the most common brands

Problem #10: Why not just get rid of UEFI?

Unfortunately, it is quite difficult to get rid of UEFI – or replace UEFI with Core Boot because UEFI is not on your hard drive. The only way you can get rid of UEFI is to return the computer to the store where you bought it, demand a refund and demand the option to buy a computer with Core Boot on it. It is also not likely that Windows 8 will work on anything other than UEFI because UEFI and Windows 8 were basically made for each other.

Why you should install a dual boot of Linux before disabling Secure Boot

There is a great deal of misinformation on Linux forums about how to install a dual boot of Linux with Windows 8. This is because the partition system for Windows 8 and especially the partitioning for Boot Managers with Windows 8 and the UEFI system is completely different than it was with Windows 7 and the BIOS system. As you may recall in the last chapter, with Windows 7 (or XP) with the BIOS system, the Windows Boot Manager was in two places. First, it was in the source of the hard drive (before any of the partitions). The area was called "sda." Then it was also in the Windows System partition at the beginning of the group of partitions. The area was called "sda1."

When we installed Linux in the BIOS system with the "Automatic Install" method, the default installation placed GRUB 2 in the sda slot. In other words, GRUB 2 replaced the Windows Boot Manager. GRUB 2 automatically recognized where the second copy of the Windows Boot Manager was and included it in the GRUB 2 startup screen – allowing us to boot into either Linux or Windows 7 (or XP). With the "Something Else" installation method, we could also create an extended partition and place whatever items we wanted in as many partitions as we wanted. So we could have a separate data partition and boot partition in addition to our normal Root partition and swap partition. Things were pretty simply and pretty flexible. Kiss all of that goodbye with UEFI.

First, the initial partition arrangements are different depending on what version of Windows 8 was installed in your computer. The basic version of Windows 8 comes with two partitions – one for a systems file and the other for your Windows C drive. The Pro version of Windows 8 comes with four partitions. If you are self-installing Windows 8, you do not have to create any partitions because UEFI will create then for you. Below is a 4 partition version of Windows 8:

Name	Total size	Free space	Type
Drive 0 Partition 1: Recovery	300.0 MB	273.0 MB	Recovery
Drive 0 Partition 2	100.0 MB	95.0 MB	System
Drive 0 Partition 3	128.0 MB	128.0 MB	MSR (Reserved)
Drive 0 Partition 4	243.6 GB	243.6 GB	Primary
Drive 0 Unallocated Space	221.6 GB	221.6 GB	

There are three smaller systems partitions and one main Windows 8 (C Drive) partition. The remaining space is called **Drive 0 Unallocated Space**. However, one of the many problems with UEFI is that there is no longer any space to put the Boot Manager in front of the hard drive. In other words, assigning a boot manager to the sda slot no longer works. This is a major booby trap as Linux users have been used to using sda to place the GRUB 2 boot manager in. Instead of placing the boot manager in sda, <u>UEFI places the Windows boot manager in one of the partitions.</u> Technically, it is in a folder called **EFI.**

The second crazy thing to understand about UEFI is that **all of the boot loaders are put in the same partition.** This is the opposite of BIOS where each boot loader was put in a different partition. This is why it is a mistake to disable Secure Boot before installing Linux. On some systems, when you disable secure boot, UEFI automatically converts to "legacy" mode and when you install Linux, this uses the BIOS/MBR partition system. Suddenly, the GRUB 2 boot loader is put in the wrong partition – leading to a nightmare series of problems. Below is the screen of a person who tried to install Linux Ubuntu with Secure Boot turned off:

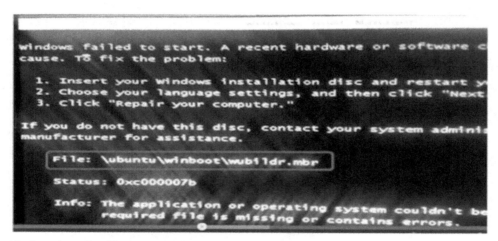

Notice that the file was an MBR or Master Boot Record file. UEFI and Windows 8 have a very hard time with this. So save yourself some grief and **install Linux with UEFI turned on and Secure Boot turned on.** Installing Linux with UEFI turned on is the best way to be sure that UEFI automatically places GRUB 2 in the correct partition. Only after Linux and Grub 2 are in the correct partitions – then we can disable secure boot and live somewhat happily ever after.

First, Shrink the C drive to create unallocated space
In the UEFI partition screen above, there is unallocated space. However, it is likely that you will not have any unallocated space on your computer and that all of the space will be taken up by the C drive. Therefore the first step you should do – before installing Linux – is to select the partition with the C drive and shrink it to create some unallocated space.

Follow the steps and screen shots we used to shrink the C drive in the last chapter. Remember that Windows does not work well without a lot of extra space. So if you have 70 GB of data in Windows, leave at least 100 GB for the C drive. The rest can be left unallocated. This remaining space can be used to install Linux and you can decide exactly how much you want for Linux during the Linux installation.

Second, create the Linux Live USB Flash Drive
UEFI is pretty inflexible. It only works with x64 bit operating systems. So choose a x64 bit version of Linux. Also UEFI will only install versions of Linux with signed keys. This includes the latest versions of Ubuntu, Mint and Fedora (and possibly others by the time you read this book). Our recommendation is to download the Linux Mint 15 Mate x64 bit ISO to your download folder. Then create an installation Live USB with UNetbootin as we described above.

Third, change the boot order to USB
Open UEFI by pressing on the Start button and then clicking F10. Go to the Boot Order screen and Move USB to the top of the list.

Fourth, restart your computer using the Live USB
Place the Live USB Flash Drive in your USB port and restart your computer. It should now boot into the installation screens for Linux Mint 15 Mate. Follow these screens until you get to the Installation Type screen:

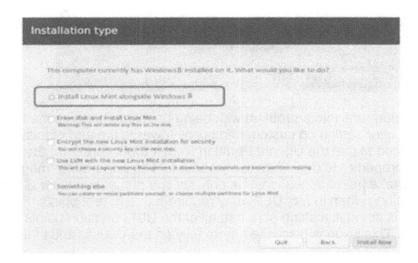

UEFI is so complex that there is really only one way for a normal person to make sure that the Linux Boot Loader (GRUB 2) gets installed into the correct UEFI partition. That way is to use the automatic install method by leaving the Installation Type set for "**Install Linux Mint alongside Windows 8**" and then click on Install Now. This will take you to the same configuration screens we covered for a Virtual Box installation of Linux Mint. **Do not select "Erase Disc" as this will delete all of the information on your C Drive.**

Why you should not use the Something Else Custom Partition option
If you are brave, and want to set up your own partitions, you can click on "Something Else" and then set up your partitions. But do not create a boot partition because GRUB must go in the UEFI boot partition – not in its own partition. Also do not change the Mount Point to sda because this will not work. Even with these precautions, the installation will not result in a dual boot option.

To get this, you will need to open your Linux Mint operating system and click on the Software Manager and install the Ubuntu Disc Repair extension. There is an explanation of how to use this to fix UEFI to create a dual boot. However, if you make even the slightest mistake, your computer's goose will be cooked.

Before attempting the Something Else option, I urge you to watch the following short You Tube video. http://www.youtube.com/watch?v=_cEwj8bBBC4
Practical UEFI Secure Boot Part 3: UEFI dual boot setup with Linux
On Channelintel 5 minutes published on Feb 22 2013

In this video, Brian runs into a problem with being unable to bring up the GRUB 2 menu after setting up custom partitions. Towards the end of this video, he is forced to use the Ubuntu Partition Repair tool in order for the Grub menu to work properly. He describes this Ubuntu tool as performing "magic." I believe the mistake he made was that he only set two mount points for Grub in his custom partition when in fact UEFI may require four different points. I think all Ubuntu tool is doing is making sure that all of the UEFI partition points are made correctly. This issue is discussed more fully on the Ubuntu and Linux Mint forums.

But think about this. If one of the lead engineers from Intel – the group that supposedly created UEFI – is unable to correctly set up custom partitions, what chance does the general public have in setting up custom partitions? I think the odds are close to zero. This is why I recommend only using the custom install option called "Install Linux Mint alongside Windows 8." It is the only way to insure that all of the partitions have been correctly set. So please just use the "Install Linux Mint alongside Windows 8" option above. Then click on Install Now.

After installing Linux Mint and rebooting your computer, you will be presented with the standard GRUB 2 screen which will allow you to select which operating system you want to use. Now that we have installed Linux in a dual boot, we can safely turn off the UEFI secure boot "feature."

How to disable secure boot and remove the digital handcuffs
Secure Boot is enabled by default on all computers that are manufactured with Windows 8. Microsoft's original plan did not include a way to disable secure boot until there was an uproar of protest by open source programmers. Microsoft then changed the specifications to provide a way to disable secure boot. However, the specification did not provide a consistent way to disable secure boot. Thus, each computer manufacturer will have a different process. Our goal with all of the following screen shots is to help you figure out a way to turn secure boot off. Regardless of what brand of computer you have, the general plan is to start your computer and then immediately (within two seconds) press one of the Function keys repeatedly to open up UEFI. The most common keys to launch UEFI are F6, F10, F11 or F12. Once we are in UEFI, we click on tabs until we find something called Security or Secure Boot. We will then disable Secure Boot. Occasionally, we will also need to disable other things for this change to take effect. Then we will save the configuration and restart our computer to begin the Linux Mint installation process.
Note: If you have a Windows ARM computer, you will not be able to disable secure boot and your only options will be to return this junk to the store where you got it or throw it in the dumpster and find a different computer.

Should you enable Legacy Mode?

As we discussed before, having Windows 8 in UEFI mode and trying to install Linux in Legacy mode creates lots of problems. Therefore you should first try to **install Linux while your computer is in UEFI mode** and save Legacy mode for a backup plan. Switching to Legacy typically disables secure boot automatically. So if you are having trouble disabling secure boot, this may be an option. However, Legacy may force you into a traditional MBR partition table. This is why you should try to use UEFI mode first as this will allow you to stay with the newer GPT partition table.

Note: Nearly all Linux distributions now work with UEFI enabled and thus Legacy mode hopefully will not be needed. Some UEFI screens call Legacy mode "Compatibility Support Module" or simply "CSM".

Disable Secure Boot on an HP desktop Computer

While the computer is off, put in your Live USB with Linux Mint on it – created as described in the last section. Then turn on the computer and immediately press the F10 key repeatedly, about once every second, until the Computer Setup Utility opens. Use the left and right arrow keys to select the **Security** menu.

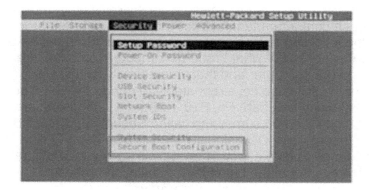

Use the down arrow key to select **Secure Boot Configuration.** Then press Enter. The Secure Boot Configuration warning displays. Press F10 to continue.

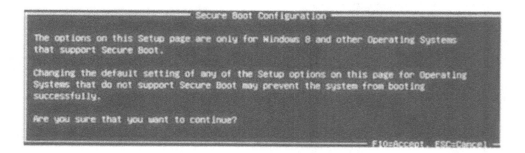

Below is the Secure Boot Configuration screen:

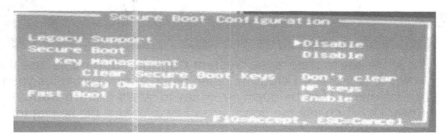

Use the up and down arrow keys to select **Secure Boot** , then use the left and right arrow keys to disable it.

Press F10 to accept the changes. Then use the arrows to select FILE in the top menu. Use the down arrow to select Save Changes and Exit. Press F10 again, then press Enter twice to restart the computer with Secure Boot disabled. As soon as the computer starts, a message appears indicating that the boot mode has changed.

Type the four-digit code shown in the message. Then press Enter to confirm the change. NOTE: No text field displays for the code. This is expected behavior. When you type the numbers, the code is logged without a text field.

Disabling Secure Boot on an HP notebook computer
Most HP notebook computers use the Insyde BIOS. Use the instructions in this section to enable or disable Secure Boot on your HP notebook computer. They are about the same as the steps above only the screens and names are different. While the computer is off, put in your Live USB with Linux Mint on it – created just as described in the last chapter. Then turn on the computer and immediately press the **ESCAPE key** repeatedly, about once every second, until the Startup Menu opens. Use the left and right arrow keys to select the **Security** menu.

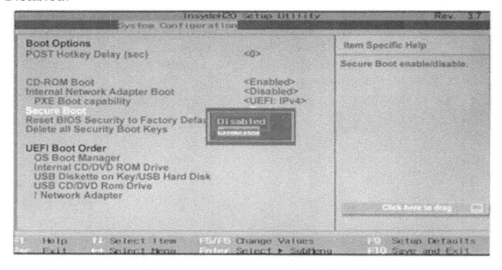

Use the right arrow key to choose the **System Configuration** menu, use the down arrow key to select **Boot Options** , then press **Enter.** This takes you to the Boot Options menu. Use the down arrow key to select **Secure Boot.** Press the **Enter** key, then use the down arrow key to modify the setting to **Disabled**.

Press **Enter** to save the change. Then use the left arrow key to select the **File** menu, use the down arrow key to select **Save Changes and Exit** , then press **Enter** to select **Yes** . The Computer Setup Utility closes and the computer restarts. When the computer has restarted, the Operating System Boot Mode Change screen appears, prompting you to confirm the Boot Options change. Type the code shown on the screen. Then press Enter to confirm the changes.

Why Linux is a much more secure operating system than Windows
At the beginning of this chapter, I promised I would present a more detailed explanation of why Linux is more secure than Windows. I owe you that much since I just encouraged you to turn off secure boot.

Warning: Secure Boot Violation.
Invalid signature detected.
This computer will self-destruct in 60 seconds.

OK

Some claim the reason Linux is more secure is because it is not as much of a target as Microsoft. If a person is a hacker, they are going to go after the operating system with the most computers. While this appears to make sense, it is not why Linux is safer and it is not why those really concerned with security, including the International Space Station and the Los Alamos National Laboratory have moved to Linux. Others have claimed that it is because Linus Torvalds is smarter than Bill Gates. While this may be true, this is also not the reason Linux is more secure than Windows.

Linux is safer because it is open source
On September 15, 1999, one of nation's leading security experts, Bruce Schneier wrote an important article, called **Open Source and Security**, which explained why open source programming will always result in a more secure system than closed source programming. He uses the term "algorithm." But you can think of this as being the passwords and processes by which programmers protect programs from hackers. The term cryptographic refers to processes for securing data such as encryption.

Before an algorithm can really be considered secure, it needs to be examined by many experts over the course of years. This argues very strongly for open source cryptographic algorithms... If an algorithm is only secure if it remains secret, then it will only be secure until someone reverse-engineers and publishes the algorithms.
Bruce Schneier Open Source and Security 1999

What Bruce points out in this article is that open source development provides more feedback to close the weaknesses in a security system. Bruce has written many books and articles on this subject since 1999 and I encourage you to visit his website and read some of these. http://www.schneier.com/

The problem with the Microsoft development model is that it is done in secrecy. There is very little feedback and very little in the way of checks and balances. It therefore results in programs which are easily hacked. This is why I have maintained throughout this book that the entire Microsoft business model is fatally flawed. The Microsoft Monopoly model may make billions of dollars. But it results in extremely poor products such as Windows 8, UEFI and Secure Boot.

Distributed keys and passwords versus centrally controlled keys and passwords
There is another fundamental reason why UEFI and Secure Boot will not work. Both of these programs are top down and controlled from a central point - Microsoft. They therefore have a single point of failure. Linux and Core Boot on the other hand are designed from the bottom up. They are controlled by the local user – you. There is much greater safety in millions of local keys versus a few centrally controlled keys. Imagine if there were only a few keys which could open every lock on every home in America. Thieves would have no problem making copies of these keys and all homes would be in danger. The reason why locks work is because each home has a different key. Even if a crook could copy your key, they would only have access to a single home. They would need to start over and copy a second key to gain access to a second home and a third key to get access to the third home. In other words, the diversity inherent in Linux is a crucial part of the Linux safety structure.

The "Home" for your data is your computer – and Microsoft with UEFI and Secure Boot creates exactly that unsafe centrally located key structure. Even worse, these are digital keys - making them even easier to copy.

The benefit of Linux is that there is no single key. When you install Linux, you create your own key to access your own Linux system. Even if a cyber-thief could break your password, they would only have access to a single computer. This is the benefit of the Linux system – it is that the keys are created from the bottom up whereas with the Microsoft system, the keys are created from the top down.

So one final reason to move towards Linux and open source is that in the long run not only will you have a more secure computer, but we will all have a much safer world.

This completes our chapter on dual booting Linux with Windows. In the next chapter, we will look at adding Libre Office to Windows. We will then look at using Libre Office in either Windows or Linux and comparing it to Microsoft Office. Finally, we will also look at some of the terrific free programs we can add to Linux to help it work even better.

Chapter 7... Benefits of LibreOffice Writer

This chapter includes the following four sections:
7.1 Why Libre Office Writer is better than Microsoft Word
7.2 Customizing the Libre Office Writer Main Menu
7.3 Create your own Custom Template
7.4 More Free Tools for Libre Writer

Libre Office 4 is a word processing program which comes installed automatically with Linux Mint 15 – and can also be installed separately on any Windows or Apple computer. In this chapter, we will review several reasons why Libre Office Writer is better than MS Word.

In Section 7.1, we will first review four different kinds of documents to better understand why different documents require different tools. We will then review the history of Libre Office. We will next describe several benefits of Libre Office over Microsoft Office. Because Libre Office can be used on either Linux or Windows, these tips apply whether or not you are using Linux.

In Section 7.2, we will review how to easily customize the interface of Libre Writer so that it has the word processing tools you like to use most readily available.

In Section 7.3, we will review how to create a custom template for Libre Writer documents. This is very useful if you would like to use Libre Writer to write and organize an E Book or Print Book.

In Section 7.4, we cover several other free and popular tools which can be added to make Libre Writer even better.

7.1 Why Libre Office Writer is better than Microsoft Word

> Even if MS Office 2013 were free, you would still be better off using Libre Office. But the truth is that MS Office 2013 is not free. In fact, it is very expensive. The complete version, with Publisher costs nearly $600.

Why Libre Writer is better than MS Word for creating simple documents
No matter what type of document you are writing, Libre Writer is better than Microsoft Word. In this section, we will first review several different categories of documents and then describe specific benefits of using Libre Writer over Microsoft Word.

LibreOffice Writer is similar to MS Word 2003
On first impression, the Libre Office Writer menu looks very similar to the MS Word 2003 menu. This is in itself a benefit because hundreds of millions of people around the world use the Windows XP operating system with MS Word 2003 to create and edit their documents. You should install and learn Libre Office because, on April 8 2014, Microsoft will be ending support for both Windows XP and MS Office 2003. Shortly after this, hackers will gradually destroy the computers of these users by taking advantage of an open back door to Windows XP which was created by Microsoft in 1998. Microsoft is hoping that killing the Windows XP computers will force users to shell out hundreds of dollars for Windows 8.1 and Office 2013 – programs that are vastly different from Windows XP and MS Office 2003. Thankfully, there is another option. Just install the free program Linux Mint 15 Mate – which comes with Libre Office 4 already installed. Problem solved!

LibreOffice Writer also has Better Tools for creating complex documents
While LibreOffice Writer looks similar to MS Word 2003, there is much more to it! In fact, LibreOffice Writer offers a whole range of tools to create complex documents that are not present on any version of MS Word. To understand how Libre Writer is better than MS Word, we will first cover four different types of documents and then describe several benefits to show how Libre Writer is much better than Word for creating complex documents like 400 page books.

Four Types of Documents
Microsoft Word treats pretty much all documents the same. But LibreOffice comes with different levels of tools for different kinds of documents. Although there is some overlap, documents can be divided into roughly four categories:
Simple Documents like articles under 10 pages in length.
Complex Documents like chapters under 50 pages in length.
Multilevel Books like Print on Demand books under 500 pages in length.
Websites and Ebooks – which are the same length as a multilevel book but which have several additional characteristics.

Different Types of Documents require Different Kinds of Tools
When writing a complex five hundred page book, one of the biggest problems any prospective author runs into is trying to keep their book organized. It is important to understand that different types of documents require different kinds of organizational strategies and different kinds of tools. Below is a table outlining four different types of documents and strategies for creating and organizing each of them. This is followed by a brief discussion of each type of document.

Document Type	Maximum # Pages	# Images Move with	Outline Levels	Style Types
Simple Articles	10	20 Cut/Paste	One Header Type	Manual Format Styles
Complex Chapters	50	100 Cut/Paste	Two Header Types	Default Format Styles
Multilevel PDF and POD Books	500	1,000 Separate Folders	Three Header Types	Custom Format Styles
Ebooks & Websites with Multiple Pages	500	1,000 Separate Folders	Three Header Types	HTML tags and CSS Style Sheet

Simple Documents
Simple documents, like simple websites or a single article, are typically under ten pages and have only a few images. There is not much need for a published outline or table of contents and there is typically one one header type and one style type - such as a single font family and a single font size. Any formatting changes to this default style can quickly be done manually by selecting the text and then clicking on the icon, such as **Bold,** in the Format Toolbar. The article is divided into topics - each with a topic heading in bold. Each topic is divided into one or more paragraphs. This process works well for short simple documents. But it can create bad habits which turn into a disaster when trying to create longer more complex documents. Either MS Word or Libre Writer handles these simple documents in about the same way. The structure of a simple document is:

Article Title
Topic 1... Introduction
Topic 1 Paragraphs Text and Images
Topic 2... Main Topic
Topic 2 Paragraphs Text and Images
Topic 3...Conclusion
Topic 3 Paragraphs Text and Images

Complex Documents

Complex documents are up to 50 pages in length and may have up to 100 images. Complex documents are more likely to come with a simple Table of Contents. Complex documents are more than just a combination of simple documents – because the formatting is now better done by using a predefined template with custom "styles." The Libre Office template manager handles templates and styles much better than MS Word. An example of a complex document is a chapters with several sections. The structure of a complex document is:

Table of Contents... Chapter Title
Section 1 Title
Topic 1.1... Introduction
Topic 1 Paragraphs Text and Images
Topic 1.2... Main Topic
Topic 2 Paragraphs Text and Images
Topic 1.3...Conclusion
Topic 3 Paragraphs Text and Images

Section 2 Title
Topic 2.1... Introduction
Topic 1 Paragraphs Text and Images
Topic 2.2... Main Topic
Topic 2 Paragraphs Text and Images
Topic 2.3...Conclusion
Topic 3 Paragraphs Text and Images

Section 3 Title
Topic 3.1... Introduction
Topic 1 Paragraphs Text and Images
Topic 3.2... Main Topic
Topic 2 Paragraphs Text and Images
Topic 3.3...Conclusion
Topic 3 Paragraphs Text and Images

Multilevel Books

Multilevel PDF or "Print on Demand" books have up to 500 pages. By multilevel, I am referring to the fact that books this long should come with a two to three level Table of Contents – involving at least two different styles of headings. This is where Libre Office Writer excels. It allows us to navigate among the various sections of our book with a unique tool called the "Navigator." Once done, Libre Office helps you export the resulting document as a PDF with full control over both formatting and editing – another set of features not found in MS Word.

The structure of a multilevel book is:
Table of Contents
Chapter 1 Title
Section 1.1 Title
Topic 1.1.1... Introduction
Topic 1 Paragraphs Text and Images
Topic 1.1.2... Main Topic
Topic 2 Paragraphs Text and Images
Topic 1.1.3...Conclusion
Topic 3 Paragraphs Text and Images

Section 1.2 Title
Topic 1.2.1... Introduction
Topic 1 Paragraphs Text and Images
Topic 1.2.2... Main Topic
Topic 2 Paragraphs Text and Images
Topic 1.2.3...Conclusion
Topic 3 Paragraphs Text and Images

Chapter 2 Title
Section 2.1 Title
Topic 2.1.1... Introduction
Topic 1 Paragraphs Text and Images
Topic 2.1.2... Main Topic
Topic 2 Paragraphs Text and Images
Topic 2.2.3...Conclusion
Topic 3 Paragraphs Text and Images

Section 2 Title
Topic 2.2.1... Introduction
Topic 1 Paragraphs Text and Images
Topic 2.2.2... Main Topic
Topic 2 Paragraphs Text and Images
Topic 2.2.3...Conclusion
Topic 3 Paragraphs Text and Images

Websites and Ebooks
Websites and Ebooks are very similar as both are formatted using HTML tags and CSS style sheets. Both websites and Ebooks require precise segregation of images – meaning that the images are actually separate files (such as JPEG files) which are placed in separate folders and then inserted as links inside of the HTML text document. Having spent many years building hundreds of websites and teaching courses in website design and construction, I am acutely aware of how difficult this process can be for the average writer. Libre Office Writer has numerous tools to make this process much easier.

We will provide an overview of Libre Writer tools for creating Print Books and Ebooks in our next chapter. Because this is a somewhat complex topic, we cover how to use Libre Office Writer to create a Print on Demand book and/or an Ebook in our next book - which is called **Create your own Ebook using Libre Office Writer.** However, it is important to know how Libre Writer does a much better job helping you organize a complex several hundred page book than MS Word. The beauty of Libre Writer is that it not only works well for creating simple documents but it also has all kinds of tools for organizing increasingly complex documents. Libre Office Writer is designed to be not only a word processor - like MS Word 2003 - but also an idea organizer.

History of Libre Office 4
Once you learn what a powerful word processing tool Libre Writer is, you might start to wonder where such an incredible tool came from. The answer is that it was created gradually over a period of several years by thousands of programmers working in the open source community. But it all started with a free open source word processing program called Star Office which was created in Germany and brought to the US in 2001 and renamed Open Office. In January, 2011, Open Office became encumbered with commercial conflicts. The majority of Open Office developers left and started a new free open source project called Libre Office. Initially, Libre Office was a clone of Open Office. However, over the past three years, thanks to the work of thousands of contributors, Libre Office has made huge strides in first matching and then passing Microsoft Office. The latest version, Libre Office 4, was released in February 2013 and offers many incredible features.

Five Advantages of Libre Office over MS Office 2013 for simple documents
There are at least five major advantages of Libre Office 4 over MS Office 2013 for creating simple documents.
First, Libre Office costs much less. In fact, it is free.
Second, Libre Office is easier to install and requires much less space on your computer.

Third, Libre Office is easier to use because it uses a single well structured menu (like Word 2003) rather than the ever changing "ribbons" of Word 2007, Word 2010 and Word 2013.
Fourth, Libre Office is the world's most compatible and versatile word processor. It can convert between file formats and open different file formats. It can also run on several different operating systems.
Fifth, Libre Office also offers 650 additional free tools, called extensions which can be added to Libre Office from the Libre Office Extension directory.

Below we offer more details about each of these five advantages.
#1 Libre Office costs much less. In fact, it is free
Even if MS Office 2013 were free, you would still be better off using Libre Office 4. But the fact is that MS Office 2013 is not free. In fact, it is incredibly expensive. The complete version, with Publisher costs nearly $600.

Office Home & Student 2013	Office Home & Business 2013	Office Professional 2013
1 install includes:	1 install includes:	1 install includes:
$169.00	$299.00	$599.00
Buy now	Buy now	Buy now
Learn more	Learn more	Learn more

A big change in Office 2013 compared to past versions of Office is that instead of it being licensed for one user, it is only licensed for one computer. So if you have three different computers in your house, and you want to use Outlook, you are looking at spending $900. This is on top of paying a couple hundred dollars each for Windows 8 and whatever you paid for your computers. To offset this dramatic increase in price, Microsoft is now also offering something called **Office 365.** This allows you to rent Office for $10 per month. Over the normal four year life of a computer, this comes to $480. At this rate, God only knows what they will charge to use the next version of Office. Now imagine you are running a small business with ten employees. To figure out what Office will cost, just multiple all of the above numbers by ten. So the first reason move to Libre Office is to get off of the Microsoft price increase treadmill!

#2 Libre Office is easier to install and requires less space on your computer
One of the biggest advantages of Linux Mint 15 Mate over Microsoft Windows 8 is that Linux Mint comes with the world's best word processor - Libre Office 4 - for free and it is preinstalled on Linux Mint! By comparison, Microsoft Windows 8 does not come with any word processor – and to get MS Office 2013 will cost you hundreds of dollars over and above the cost of Windows 8. To install Office 2013, you need to first go to the Microsoft store and set up an account and give them your credit card number. You eventually get to the Download page and have to load this huge Office program file. If you are using Office 365 you also get the joy of paying monthly bills with your credit card. But with Libre Office, if you are using Linux, it is already preloaded. It comes free with Linux Mint. If you are using Windows and want to add Libre Office, it is a simple matter of clicking on a couple of buttons. As for space, MS Office requires 3 GB on your hard drive. Libre Office is only 545 MB.

Download and Install Libre Office 4 for Windows
There is no need to download or install Libre Office if you are using Linux. It is already there. However, if you want to try Libre Office side by side with MS Office while in Windows, you can easily download it and install it. To get a free download of Libre Office 4 for Windows, go to their website:
http://www.libreoffice.org/

Then click on Downloads. Or go straight to the Downloads page.
http://www.libreoffice.org/download/

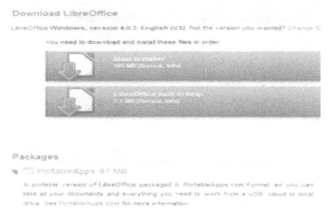

Click on the **Main Installer** to download the file. Then save the file and the help pack in your Downloads folder. Then run the Libre Office file as an administrator to install it onto your Windows computer.

Then click on Writer to create a new document:

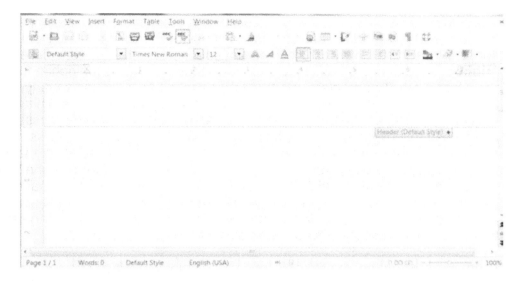

There should now be a Libre Office icon on your desktop. It doesn't get any easier than this!

#3 Libre Office is easier to use because it has a traditional menu

For many years, Microsoft used a simple fixed menu to allow access to important functions. Below is the Office 2003 Word simple Menu.

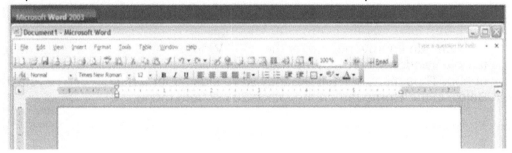

You could customize this menu in many ways to have quick access to whatever tools you used most. Each of the main tabs such as **File, Edit** and **View** offered fixed vertical drop down menus so that it was very easy for even a novice to learn and remember where various tools were at.

With Office 2007, the simple fixed menu was replaced with a complex ribbon:

The **File** tab from Word 2003 was replaced by a Windows icon in the upper left corner. This was very confusing to many novices. Clicking on the Home Tab, the Insert Tab or any other tab displayed a new horizontal menu called a **"ribbon"** instead of the traditional drop down menu. Above is the ribbon for the "**Home**" tab. The problem with the ribbons is that each contains many more choices than the simple 2003 Word vertical drop down menus. This not only meant a steeper learning curve – but also slowed down word processing as you had to look through many choices to find the one you want. Folks describe it as looking for a needle in a rather big hay stack. In addition, many of the functions were indicated only by a very small icon – rather than the text menu items used with Word 2003. Thus, one also had to remember what each icon did. Having been an adult education instructor for more than 20 years and having taught many students both Word 2003 and Word 2007, I can say for certain that Word 2003 is easier for students to learn than 2007.

I can also confirm that the ribbon is one of the stupidest things Microsoft has ever done. Below is the Office 2010 Word Home Menu Ribbon.

This was an improvement over the 2007 Word menu because it replaced the terrible Windows icon with the traditional "File" tab. But it still used the crazy ribbon. Thus many still felt like they were looking for a needle in a haystack. Below is the **Home** tab on the Office 2013 Word menu.

There is a new tab called **Design** which covers some of the functions which used to be in the Insert tab or the Page Layout tab. This is a slight improvement because it places fewer choices on the Insert and Page Layout tabs. But the **SAVE** and **SAVE AS** function have gotten much worse. Clicking on **File** brings up the same options. But click on **File**, then click on **Save** or **Save As** and you will be in for a big surprise. The **Save** function now defaults to Sky Drive (if you do not like Sky Drive, then too bad for you). The **Save As** function adds an almost useless intermediary screen to slow you down.

Below is the Libre Writer Menu in Windows (which uses Times New Roman).

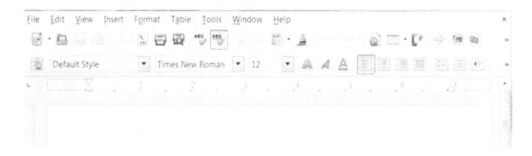

Below is the Libre Writer Menu in Linux Mint (which uses a font called Liberation)

This is the best part about Libre Office. Sanity has returned. If you have a Windows XP computer with Word 2003 – which is the case with one in three computer users today – then you will have a much easier time using Libre Office than using MS Office 2013. Even if you have spent the past three years using Office 2010, you will have an easier time using Libre Office that MS Office 2013.

#4 Libre Office can convert between file formats and open different file formats without subjecting users to a bunch of fake warnings.
Libre Office Writer is not only compatible with all versions of Microsoft Word and Excel, it is also compatible with Microsoft Publisher and Adobe PDF. It is also compatible with HTML formatting used to create websites and e-publishing documents. It has also resolved issues of past open source programs in providing a more consistent display of tables, headers and footers.
You do not even need to install Linux to use Libre Office. Libre Office 4 comes in versions for Windows, Apple and Linux. It is time for all of us to join the 30 million people already using Libre Office!

Libre Office Writer offers many Compatibility Tools
Any time you want to open and work with any document with Libre Office, just click on this icon to open Libre Office. Then click on the "Writer" icon to bring up the Writer document edit screen. You can create the document in Libre Office and then save it as a ODF or a Word document or even an HTML file.

ODF = Open Document Format which is the standard Open Source document. The ending extension for an ODF document is odt. LibreOffice Writer also comes with a Document Conversion Wizard for converting documents between LibreOffice and MS Office. Open any doc or docx document with LibreOffice Writer, then click on File, Wizards, Document Converter.

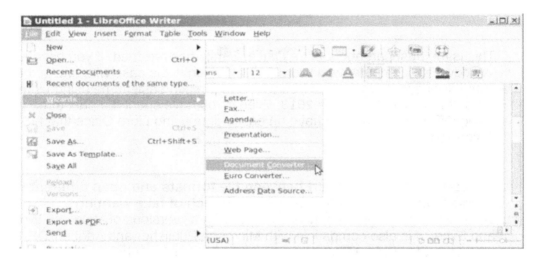

This brings up a simple tool for converting three major types of Word documents.

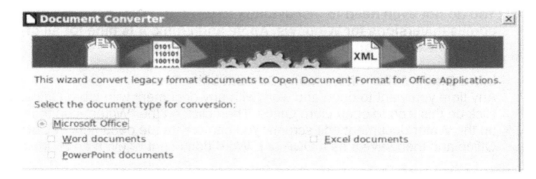

Select Word document and LibreOffice Writer will then create a copy of all MS Word Doc and DocX documents to ODT files – while still retaining all of the MS Word Doc and DocX files. I was able to convert 268 Doc and DocX files to ODT documents in a matter of a couple of minutes using this tool. Libre Office also comes with a Web Wizard which can turn your document into an Ebook. Just click on File, Wizards, Web Page Wizard.

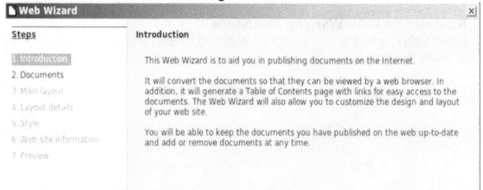

Conversion Issues and MS Office Sabotage
There is almost no problem converting between MS Word 2003 DOC documents and Libre Office ODT documents. The one real exception to this rule is that Word text boxes do not convert well. Text boxes should therefore be changed to images before conversion. There is also not much of a problem using Libre Writer to convert Libre Office ODT documents to MS Word 2007 DOCX documents. However, there are occasionally problems using MS Word to convert DOCX documents to ODT documents. The biggest problem is that DOCX documents handle images in a much different way that ODT or DOC documents. There is no benefit to the way DOCX handles images. Instead it appears to be a deliberate attempt to punish people who use either DOC or ODT documents. It creates compatibility problems which force people to buy the latest version of MS Office. For this reason, if you have friends who you want to share a file with who use MS Office, we recommend that you **create the file as a Word 2003 DOC file rather than a Word 2007 DOCX file.**

With recent advances by Libre Office, you may be able to save ODT documents as Word 2007 documents and have the images turn out okay. Just check the file after you create it. Sadly, Microsoft is also working hard on making DOCX not compatible with Libre Office, so be careful and do not assume anything.
There also seems to be a slight problem converting from one operating system to another. In a recent series of tests I did on file conversion using a very large document with 20 images, I was able to convert documents back and forth between file systems several times as long as I stayed inside of Windows 7 using MS Office 2010 and/or Libre Office 4. I was also able to convert back and forth between file types in Linux Mint using LibreOffice 4. I was also able to import numerous files that had been converted between DocX to Doc and DocX to ODT.

However, one document which had started out as Doc X in MS Office 2010 and then converted to ODT and then converted back to Doc X in MS Office 2010 and then imported to Linux Mint and opened in LibreOffice Writer was corrupted and most of the document was lost. The lesson from this test is to create a backup of any document you want to convert from one format to another – especially if you are exporting a document from Windows/MS Office to Linux Mint/LibreOffice.

Real versus Fake Warning Messages
Libre Office gives you a standard warning when saving an ODF document as a Word document:

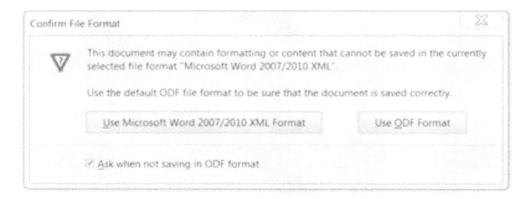

The odds are that the correct formatting is preserved over 90% of the time. So feel free to convert ODT documents to Word documents and Word documents to ODT documents. Libre Office is very compatible with Word 2003 and usually compatible with Word 2007, Word 2010 and Word 2013. If you are working with something really important, first make a copy of the document. Then convert the copy. Then check the document for the correct formatting after you have saved it. However, the warnings are much more ominous when using MS Office. MS Office claims that it can open an ODT document. But just try it and you will get this warning:

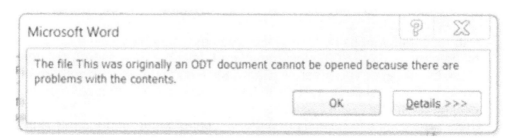

There is actually no problem with the ODT document, but Microsoft is trying to fool you into thinking that Libre Office is not a good program. Click on OK and you will get yet another ominous warning:

Click Yes and the document opens without any problem. However, it does not open as an ODT document. Instead it opens as a Word document! This kind of conduct is revolting because it is worse than dishonest. It is dishonest manipulation. Then try to save a Word document as an ODT document and you will get this warning:

Click Yes and there is no problem saving the document. Then close MS Office and open Libre Office and open the new ODT document. What you will find is that there is no problem at all with the document.
Note: There may be a problem with images when moving to a different operating system due to the way images are stored in MS Office. So always make a copy of files before moving them to a different operating system.

So even though Libre Office and MS Office both claim to be able to open and save documents in many formats, only Libre Office does it without a bunch of ominous warnings. The warnings above are exactly the kind of fake warnings Microsoft used to destroy DR DOS and Word Perfect in the early 1990's. Despite two different federal courts telling Microsoft to stop doing this, Microsoft continues to lie to computer users in an effort to maintain their monopoly. Given that nine out of ten users still use and share Word doc or docx files, I still recommend sharing documents as Word 2003 doc files. This means using the Libre Office **SAVE AS** button and then selecting doc instead of the default open document text file format (which uses the odt extension). Because few people are aware of Microsoft's attempts to sabotage Libre Office, it is best to simply save any documents you want to share as Word 2003 documents in order to avoid frightening your friends.

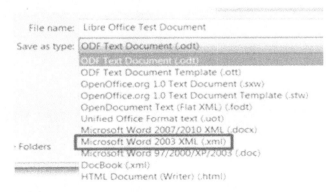

Another option is to save any document you want to share as a PDF and then send that. Both Libre Office and MS Office can save documents as PDF documents – but with Libre Office, it is not done through the Save as type function. Instead it is done through File, Send As and then select PDF.

#5 Libre Office offers 200 additional free tools, called extensions which can be added to Libre Office from the Libre Office Extension directory. These tools, themes and templates allow you to even further customize and expand the ability of your Libre Office word processor. We cover how to add extensions to LibreOffice Writer at the end of the next session.

In the next section, we will first review how to customize the LibreOffice Writer menu bar and tool bars. We will then demonstrate how to add an extension and provide a list of recommended extensions.

7.2 Customize the Libre Writer Main Menu

The benefit of customizing a toolbar is to add any icons you like to use and hide any icons you never use.

In this section, we will describe how to customize the main menu of LibreOffice Writer. After installing Linux Mint 15 and before starting to use LibreOffice, go to the Linux Mint control panel and click on Appearances. Here you can install a better background image – slightly darker so it is not so glaring on the eyes. You can also changed the theme to a Win_Me Theme to make the contrast in the Window screen shots better. You should also right clicked on three applications to put them on the desktop. These are LibreOffice Writer, Firefox Web Browser and Take Screenshot. Then click on LibreOffice Writer to open a new document. Here is my first screen shot of my new desktop – taking while writing this article.

Title Bar, Main Menu, Standard Toolbar and Formatting Toolbar
Before we begin changing the top menu, we should first outline the four rows in the top menu.

The top row is the title bar. The second row is the menu bar. The third row is the standard toolbar and the fourth row is the formatting toolbar.

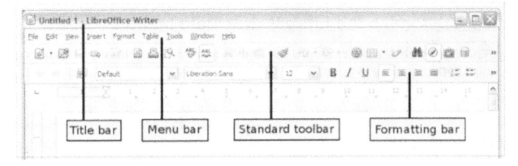

We changed the color of Title bar by clicking on Menu, Control Center, Appearances, Themes.

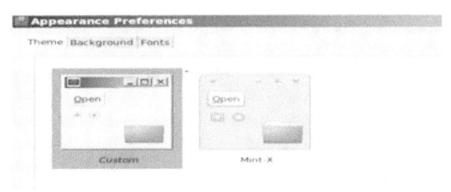

The second row is the Main Menu. It has nine menu items which work in almost the same way as Word 2003. The third row is the Standard Toolbar. The fourth row is the Formatting Toolbar. These last two toolbars can be deleted or modified by going to the Main Menu and clicking on View, Toolbars.

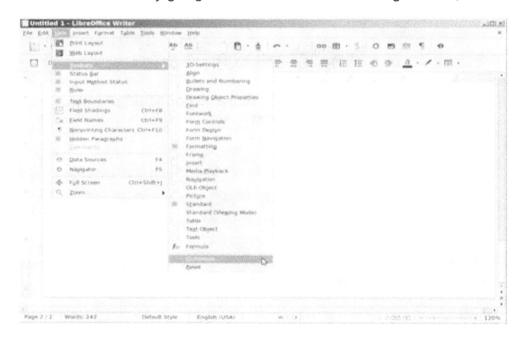

The first thing we will do is turn off the ruler by going to View, Ruler and unchecking the box to the left of the word Ruler. This will give us more space in the Workspace and make our display screen and screen shots less confusing. Next, we will customize the Standard Toolbar. We will then customize the Formatting Toolbar.

Customize the Standard Toolbar
The benefit of customizing a toolbar is to add any icons you like to use and hide any icons you never use. To customize any toolbar, go to View, Toolbars, Customize. This brings up the Customize Window.

Click on the Toolbars tab.

To add a command or icon, check on it. To remove an existing command, uncheck its box. We will remove four commands: Document send as email, Format Paintbrush, Data Sources and Nonprinting characters. Then click OK.

Customize the Formatting Toolbar
To customize the formatting toolbar, click View, Toolbars, Customize to go back to the Toolbars Tab. Then use the Drop down arrow to the right of the word Standard to select the Formatting Toolbar. We will uncheck 8 commands. These are Justify, Left to Right, Right to Left, Numbering, Bullets, Decrease Indent, Increase Indent and Highlighting. Then we will add one very useful command called Select All. Then click OK. We now have a much simpler menu that will be easier to work with.

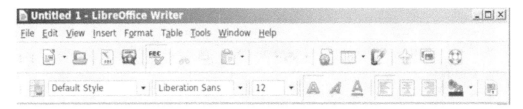

Having fewer icons on the menu also allows us to narrow the screen size of the LibreOffice Writer window. The benefit of this is that we can have two documents open side by side – to transfer content from one document to another. Or we can have one or more documents open in a cascade on the right side of our screen while having our web browser open on the left side of our screen. Below is a screen shot of what my desktop looks like with three documents on the right in a cascade and the web browser on the left.

Being able to have multiple windows open side by side is one of the most important reasons to turn off any unneeded icons. It will also make it easier for you to remember where the remaining icons are on your main menu.

Turn off Word Completion

A common complaint about LibreOffice Writer is the very annoying word completion function. This is a function which tries to complete long words for you. The problem is that most of the time, it guesses wrong and makes it harder for you to type in the word you really want to use. To turn off Word Completion, go to Tools, AutoCorrect Options. Then click on the Word Completion tab. Uncheck Enable Word Completion. Then click OK.

Customize Tools Options

Our next task is to modify a few of the settings on the Tools, Options window. Click on Tools, Options.

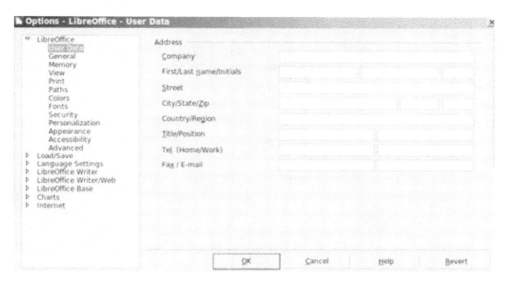

Type in your name. Then click on the Memory tab.

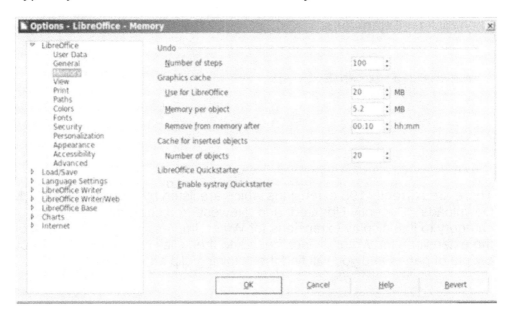

If you insert a lot of images in your documents and write rather large and complex documents, one of the biggest problems with the default settings on LibreOffice Writer is the lack of memory. This can slow down your word processing and even crash the application. Another problem is that LibreOffice will try to remember your last 100 steps. This will also use up memory. To solve both of these problems, reduce the number of steps to 20. Then increase the Graphics Cache to 100 MB and increase the time to 50 minutes. Then click on Load/Save, General and raise the AutoSave time from 15 minutes to 30 minutes.

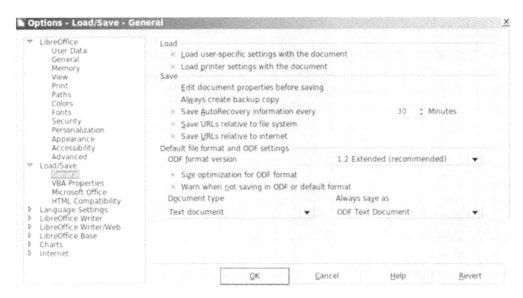

Adding Extensions

Below is an example of how to install a free extension. To reach the Libre Office Extensions directory, go to **http://extensions.libreoffice.org/** Then click on **Extensions.**

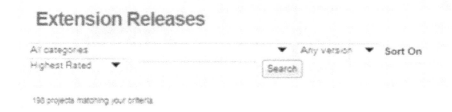

There are currently 198 extensions which are listed by "Highest Rated", "Most Downloads" "Recently Updated" and "Newest" You can also change the category to just display extensions for Writer, Impress or Calc. To check out the extensions for Writer, select these and then click on Search. Scroll down a couple of pages and you will find the following clip art extension:

OpenClipart.org integration

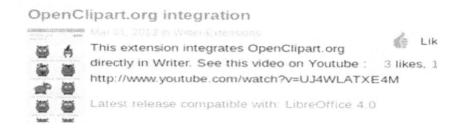

This extension integrates OpenClipart.org directly in Writer. See this video on Youtube : http://www.youtube.com/watch?v=UJ4WLATXE4M

3 likes. 1

Latest release compatible with: LibreOffice 4.0

This extension not only gives you clip art, it also helps improve the appearance of your tool bar icons. Click on the Extension to go to its page. Click on the latest release to download it. Save it in your Downloads folder. Then open Libre Office:

Then select Tools, Extension Manager.

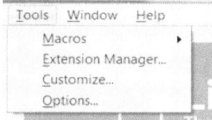

You can also reach the Extension Manager inside of Libre Writer by clicking on Tools, Extension Manager.

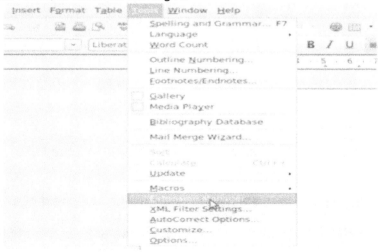

In the Extension Manager screen, click ADD:

This opens up a browser window. Find the extension in your Downloads folder and select it. Then click OK. Then select **All Users**. Then **Accept** the License Agreement. Click on the Close button at the bottom of the screen. You will need to restart Libre Office to access the extension. After installation, the extension will be listed in the Extension Manager which can be reached from the Tools Menu on the Libre Office screen or the Libre Writer screen. After restarting Libre Office, click on Text Document to open Libre Writer:

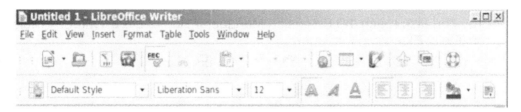

We now have much nicer icons on the main menu – and a bunch of clip art in the "Gallery" folder.

Other popular extension
Below are just a few of the many extensions you can add to Libre Office.

PDF Import
This extension enables you to make minor modifications to the text of existing PDF files when the original source files do not exist or you are unable to open the source files. (Whenever possible, modify the source and regenerate the PDF to obtain the best results.)

When the extension is installed, PDF is listed as a choice in the File Type drop-down list in the File → Open dialog. The best results can be achieved with the PDF/ODF hybrid file format, which this extension also enables. Hybrid PDF/ODF files will be opened in LibreOffice as an ODF file without any layout changes.

Presenter Console
Provides extra control over Impress presentations; for example, the presenter has ability to see the upcoming slide, the slide notes, and a presentation timer —while the audience sees only the current slide.

Professional Template Pack II
Provides more than 120 templates for Writer, Calc, and Impress. Available in several languages. After you have installed this extension, you will find the templates under File → New → Templates and Documents.

Template Changer (for Writer)
Adds two new items to the File → Templates menu in Writer that allow you to assign a new template to the current document or to a folder of documents. All styles and formatting will be loaded from that template and the document will behave as it was created using that template.

Smart Gallery creates graphics:

In the next section, we will review how to create your own custom template for your LibreOffice Writer documents.

7.3 Create your own Custom Template

Even with simple documents, it is useful to use a custom template.

In this section we will review how to create your own custom template – which can then be used as a model for creating all of your future documents.

A Look at the Default Template
Libre Office Writer comes with a predefined template which cannot be changed. It can be found by going to **Tools, Options, LibreOffice Writer, Basic Fonts.**

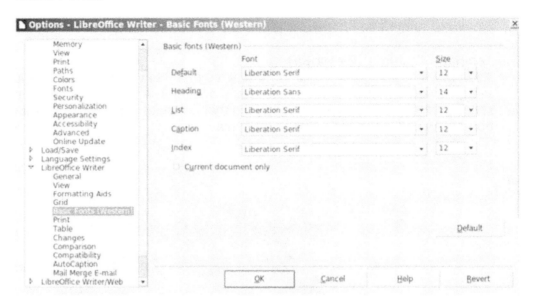

Change the default font from Liberation Serif to Liberation Sans. Then click OK. Now click on Tools, Options to go back to this screen. You will see that all of the settings were changed to Liberation Sans. However, if you click on default, this will restore the initial value of Serif. As Sans is much easier for many people to read, click Liberation Sans, then OK. You will now see that all of the text in your documents has changed from Serif to Sans and that the Default Style in your Formatting Toolbar has changed to Liberation Sans. To make further changes in your default document, we need to create a custom template.

Create your own custom template
A template is a special document which is used as a pattern for creating other documents. To create a new blank template, click on **File, New, Text Document** to open a new blank page. We can turn any document into a template by clicking on **File, Save as Template.**

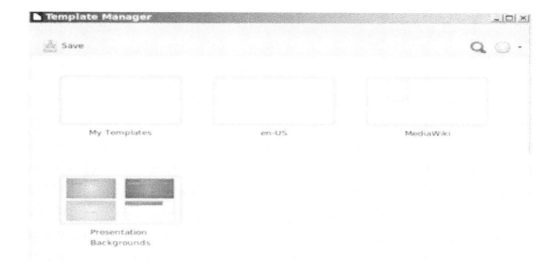

This brings up the Template Manager. By default, there are four categories of templates. However, two of the categories do not have any templates in them. Click on **My Templates** to place our new custom template in this category. Then click **Save**. Give your new template a name and click Accept.

So far our template is the same as the default template we created with Tools, Options, Libre Writer Fonts. To further define our new custom template, click on **File, New, Templates.**

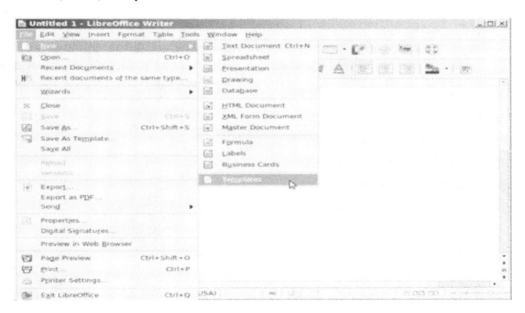

This brings up the Template Manager again - only this is a more complex template manager with four tabs at the top:

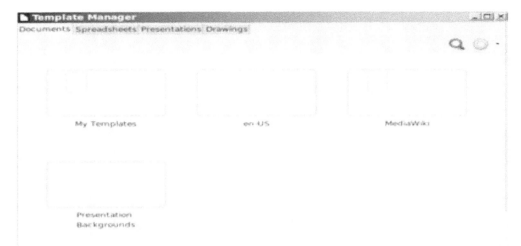

There is now a single template in the My Templates category. Click on My Templates to select it.

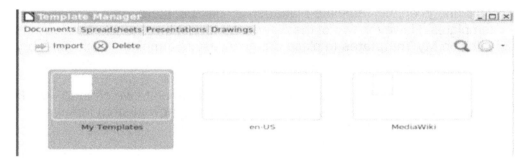

If we want to import a template which was downloaded from the Internet, we could click on Import and then browse to the new template. However, what we really want to do is edit the new template we just made. To do this, **double click on My Templates.**

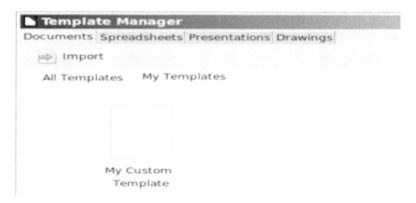

Then click on **My Custom Template.**

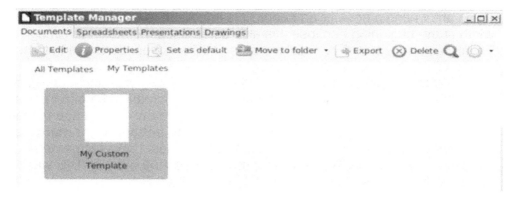

This is the screen where we export any template which we have created in order to use our template on other computers or to post on the internet for other users to copy. To make it the default template for all of our new documents, click on **Set as default**. Then click on **Edit.**

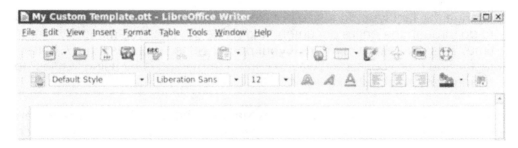

This will create something which looks just like a blank Writer document. But instead of an ODT extension at the end of the file name, it will have an **OTT** extension. To define the page width and margins on our custom template, go to **Format, Page.** Then click on the **Page** tab.

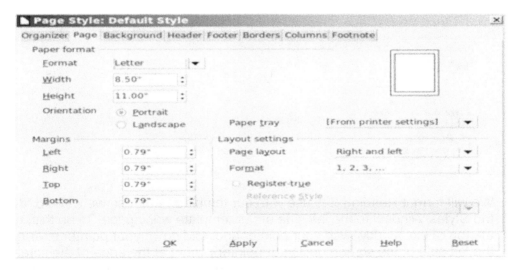

If you are writing a book or an ebook, it is important to set the correct page width at the beginning because this also determines the maximum image size. The default page has very small margins of 0.79 inches. Subtracting twice this amount from the page width of 8.5 inches leaves a text area of about 6.9 inches. Most simple documents have a margins of one inch and a text area of 6.5 inches. However, most ebook readers have a screen width of 6 inches and most books also have a text area of 6 inches. Since my main usage of Libre Writer is to create books and ebooks, I will **set the left and right margins for 1.25 inches**. This will result in a text area of 6 inches. I also recommend increasing the **top and bottom page margins to 1.00 inches**. This will result in a page height of 9 inches. Then click Apply. Then click OK.

Add Custom Styles to your Custom Template (versus manual formatting)
With simple documents, a common way to modify any text is by using the manual icons in the Formatting Toolbar at the top of the page. For example, to change the subject title to bold, you would first select it and then click on the bold icon. The problem with manual formatting is that if you ever want to change the font type, font size or color of your subject titles, you would need to go through the entire document and make the changes manually – one at a time. This can be a nightmare if your document is 50 pages long. A better faster and more consistent way to control formatting is by using "Styles" to change any selected text.

We will cover styles in more detail in the next chapter – because styles are essential for creating complex documents. Here we will simply create a couple of custom styles to add to your custom template as a way to help you get started on using style formatting instead of manual formatting. To create custom styles in our custom template, we first need to open our custom template by going to **File, New, Templates**, then clicking on the template to select it. Then click on **Edit.** To bring up the Styles Window in the template, click on **Format, Styles** and **Formatting.**

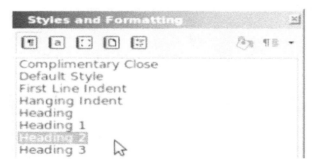

We will format Heading 2 to use with our template. But first, we want to "dock" the Styles Window to the left side of our template workspace. To do this, grab the top of the window with your pointer and hold down your pointer to drag it to the left side of the screen until your pointer is right at the edge of the screen. When you see the guide shadow turn on, release the pointer and the Style Window will snap in place.

In the next chapter we will work more with the various types of styles. But for now, we will customize a "hierarchical" style called Heading 2. We will use Heading 2 to create our Document, Article, and Section Titles. Then we will use a similar process with Heading 1 to create our Chapter Titles. To modify the Heading 2 style, click on it to select it. Then right click and select "**Modify.**" This brings up the Paragraph Style Heading 2 Edit Window.

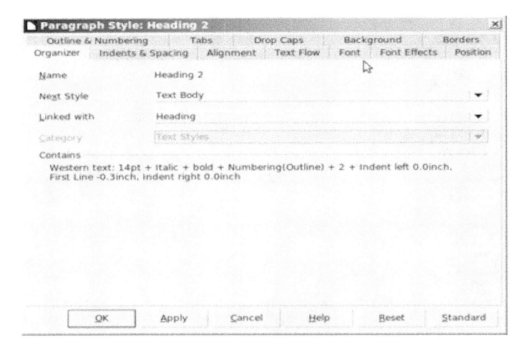

We will first change the font. So click on the Font tab.

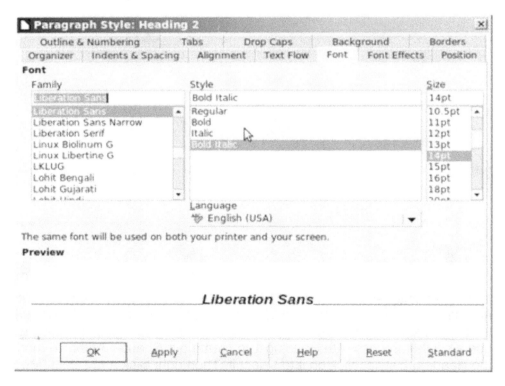

Heading 2 is currently set for Bold Italic 14 point. We want just Bold, but 16 point.

Then click Apply. Next click on the Indents and Spacing tab.

Change Before Text indent to zero and First Line Indent to zero. Also reduce Above Paragraph spacing to Point One inches and increase Below Paragraph Spacing to Point One inches.

Then click Apply. Then click OK. Next, click on **Heading 1**, then right click and select **Modify**. By default, Heading 1 is set for Bold 16 point which is exactly what we want. Click on the Indent and Spacing tab and change these to match the Heading 2 settings except reduce the Below Paragraph setting to zero. Also change the font color to green and make it underline. Then click Apply and OK.

Create a File Reminder

Our final task is to create a reminder that the first step in creating a new document is giving the document a title, then giving it a file name by copying and pasting it into a folder. Below this we will type in a brief first sentence.

Select this Heading 2 text and replace it with your title. Then select it again, copy it and click on File Save to place it in a folder and give it a file name

Begin your first paragraph by replacing this text.

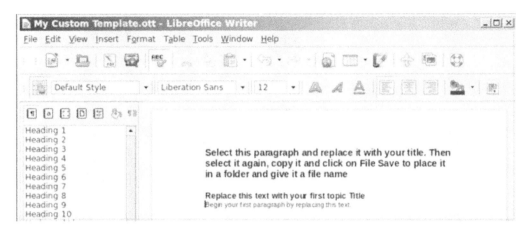

Click **File Save** to save these changes to your custom template. Then **File Close**. Now on any open Writer document, click **File, New, Text Document** to create a new document. To give this document a file name, select the title text and replace it with your title.

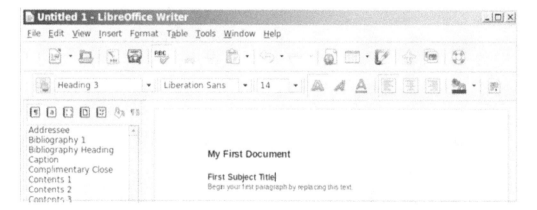

Notice that the template even saves the Style Window being docked. To save this new document, select the title, then copy it. Then click on File, Save. Then select the folder you want to put the document in. Below we have selected the Desktop. But in general, we want to place documents inside of the Documents Folder.

We can create category folders inside of the Documents folder if we want and place the document there.

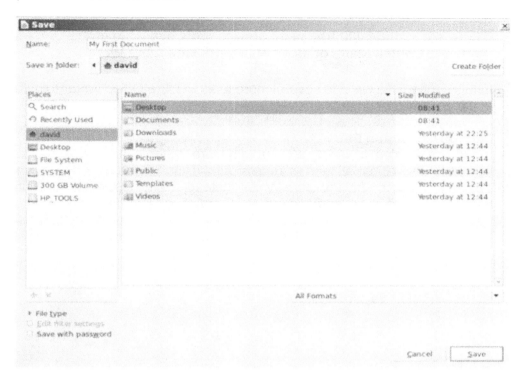

Once the correct folder is chosen, paste the title name into the "Name" box and click Save. As you enter text on your new document, each time you enter a new subject title, just select it and instead of clicking on the **Bold** icon, click on Heading 3 instead. This way if you ever want to change the font on all of your subject title headings to a different color, all you need to do is change the font color on Heading 3. If you placed your document in the Desktop folder, Libre Writer will also place an icon for this document on the Desktop.

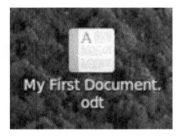

We now have our first custom template and our first document. In the next section, we will add more free tools to Libre Writer.

7.4 More Free Tools for Libre Writer

> **There are over 64,000 free open source tools available in the Linux Mint Software Center. Many of these also work with Libre Writer.**

In this section, we will add several more tools to Libre Office Writer to help make creating documents easier.

Turn off the Touch Pad
A nagging problem in writing articles with Libre Writer is that the pointer and screen and scroll bar all tend to jump around if you have a sensitive touch pad. This is not the fault of Libre Writer. Instead, it is an issue with how Linux Mint handles the touch pad on your keyboard. If you use a mouse like I do, you have two options. The easiest way to stabilize your pointer is to open the **Control Center** in your Mint Menu and click on the **Mouses** Icon which is in the Hardware section.

This brings up the **Mouse Preferences** window.

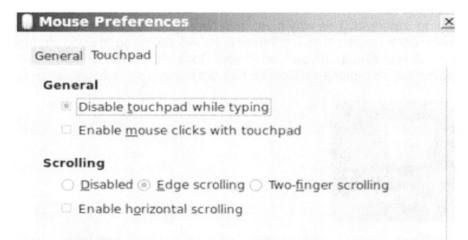

Click on the **Touchpad** tab and then check "Disable touchpad while typing." This will keep the touch pad off while you are typing and about two seconds after you stop typing.

Add a Free Touch Pad Control Tool

Unfortunately, for many of us, this is not good enough. We need the touch pad to be completely off to keep the pointer from accidentally jumping. To get a better tool to control the touchpad, click on the Software Center which is also in the Mint Menu. Then type in "gpointing-device-settings" in the Search Box. This will bring up two results. The i386 version is for 32 bit computers and the unmarked version is for x64 bit computers.

Click install. This adds a new entry to the Control Center called Pointing Devices. First click on Mouse Preferences and turn off "Disable Touchpad while typing" as the Mouse settings override the Pointer settings. Then click on the Pointer icon to bring up the Gpointing Device Settings Window.

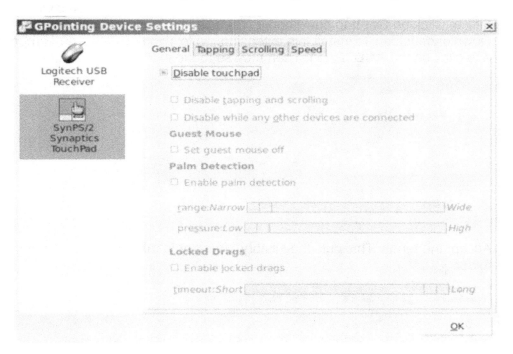

Click Disable touchpad – or disable while other devices are connected. Then click OK. Your touch pad will now stay off for as long as your computer is turned on. Note however, that when you restart your computer, you will need to repeat the process: uncheck Disable Touchpad, then click OK. Then open it again and check Disable Touchpad again. Then click OK.

Use History Master to Increase the Number of Recent Documents
When you first open Libre Writer, it is common to look through a list of Recent Documents to find one you recently worked on and would like to use again. This list is found by going to File, Recent Documents. By default, the maximum number of Recent Documents stored in Libre Writer is ten. Thankfully, there is a simple extension that allows you to increase the number of documents in Recent Documents to whatever you want. To get this extension, go to:

http://extensions.services.openoffice.org/project/HistoryMaster.

Get it!

Note: some browsers may download the extension as a .zip file; if this happens rename the downloaded file from .zip to .oxt

Operating System: System Independent

Version: 1.1.1   **Size:** N/A

View all releases

Like nearly all Open Office extensions, History Manager also works with Libre Office. Click on **Get It** to download it. Then save the extension to your Downloads folder. To install this extension, go to **Tools, Extension Manager** and click on the **ADD** button. Then browse to the extension to select it.

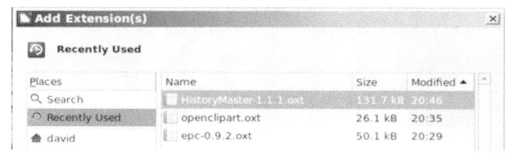

Accept the terms. This puts the History Manager in the Active Extensions folder.

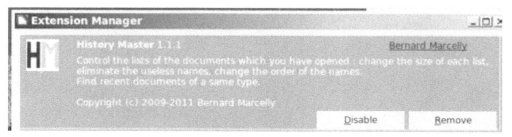

While we are here, we will also add two more extensions from the LibreOffice extensions manager. These are called **Open Clip Art** and **EPC –** which is a flow chart creator. Next, close all documents and close LibreOffice. Then restart LibreOffice Writer and go to **Tools, Add Ons, History Manager.**

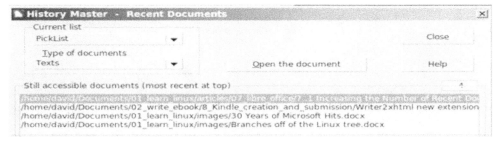

Change the List Size from 10 to 20 so you can have more files in your list of Recent Files. Then click on **Apply Changes** and wait for one minute. Then close History Manager. It will take a while for your list of recent documents to increase. But each time you open and close a document with LibreOffice, History Manager will add it to the Recent Documents list. History Manager also add a new menu item to the File List called **Recent Documents of the same Type.**

Add a Better Screen Capture Tool
The default screen capture tool that comes with Linux Mint has a couple of minor problems. The biggest problem is that it does not really optimize the image file sizes of images very well. Because my instructional guides involve a lot of images, the result is that my article, chapter and book file sizes wind up being too big. In addition, if I post images with large file sizes on my websites, the loading time is slowed down considerably.

Thankfully, there is an excellent screen capture tool called Shutter available in the Software Manager. Using this tool, you can reduce your image file sizes which makes your documents smaller and your web pages load faster. To add this tool to your computer, go to the Main Menu and click on Software Manager.

Enter shutter into the search box. Then click on **Shutter** to reach its screen. Then click on **Install.**

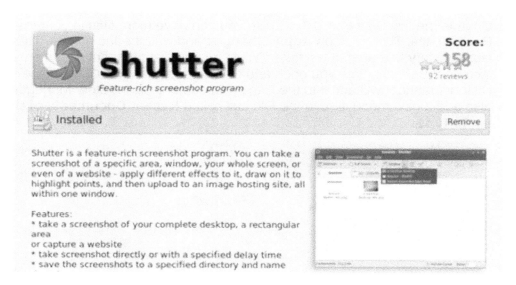

To put Shutter on your desktop, click on the **Mint Menu** and click on **Accessories.** Then right click on **Shutter** and drag it to the desktop. Then click on **Shutter** to open it.

Click on **Edit,** then **Preferences** to open the Preferences window.

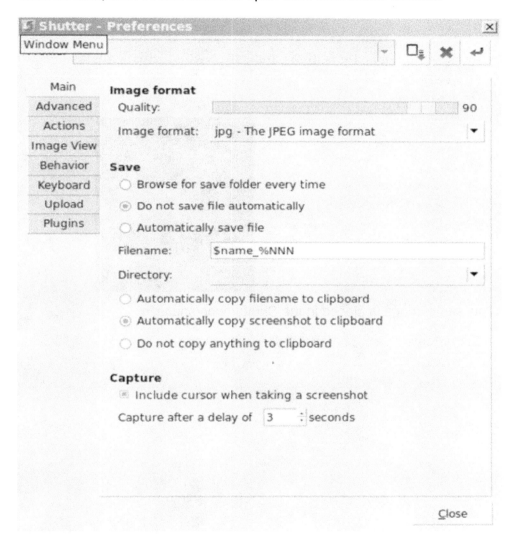

Change the image format to **JPEG** and select **Automatically copy to clipboard.** Then set capture for a delay of 3 seconds. Then click Close.

There are several ways to capture images with Shutter. To capture a region, click on Selection. To capture any particular open window, click on the dropdown arrow to the right of Window. To capture a complex dropdown menu, click on the Menu Item.

Below is an example of shutter capturing a complex menu.

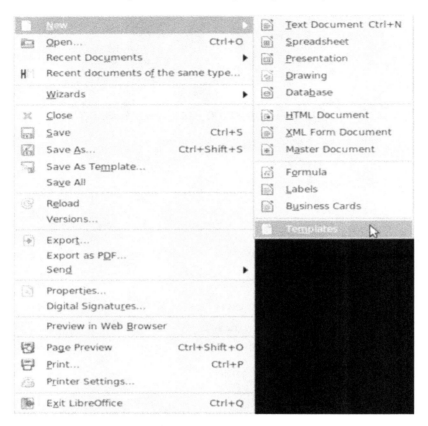

This same image is placed in the Shutter workspace.

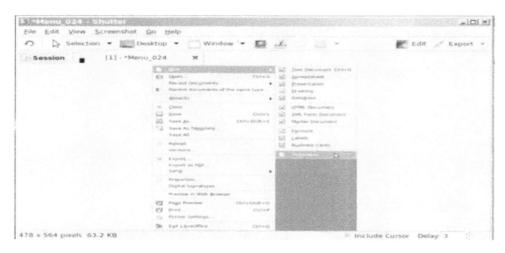

You can also edit images by clicking on Edit.

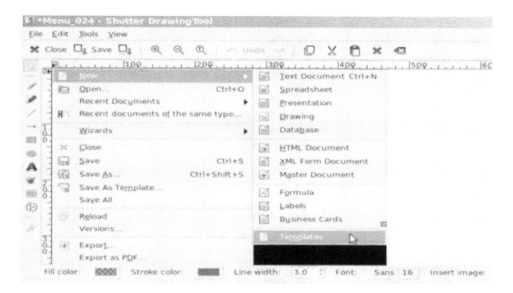

This is what the image looks like after adding some arrows and text to help clarify where a person should click to open the Template Manager.

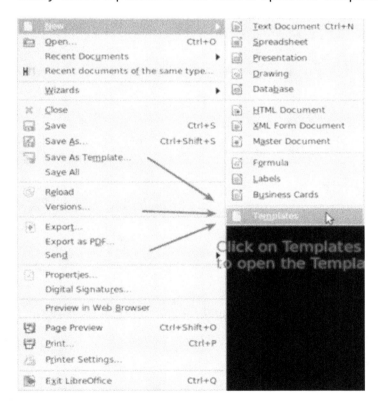

We now have a screen capture tool which saves JPEG images and allows editing of screen captures.

Set Libre Office as Default Editor

The default text editor for Linux Mint, called Pluma, does not have many editing options. If you go to the **Caja File manager** and right click in the workspace to create a new document, Linux Mint will open a text Editor called Pluma:

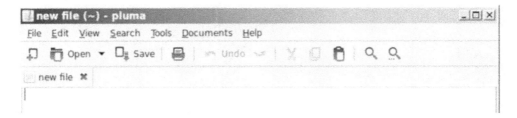

We would rather have the Mint file manager open **Libre Writer because this is the world's best text editor** To make this change, go to **Control Center, Other, Preferred Applications, system tab, set Text Editor for Libre Office.**

Now open the file manager and right click on the workspace and select **Create Document, Empty File.**

Then click on the new file to open it. It should now open in Libre Writer.

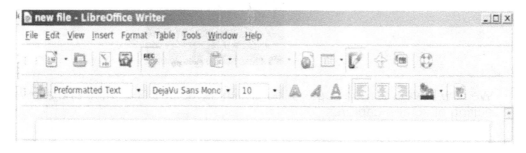

Add your printer to Linux Mint

To install your printer on Linux Mint is usually a pretty simple matter. Go to Control Panel, Printers:

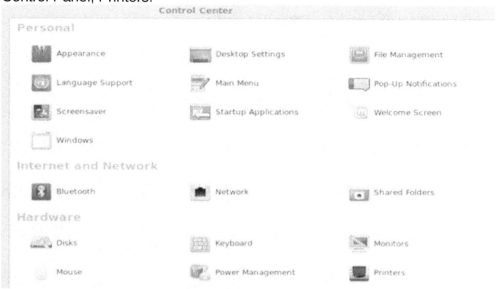

Then click on **Printers.** Then click on **ADD**

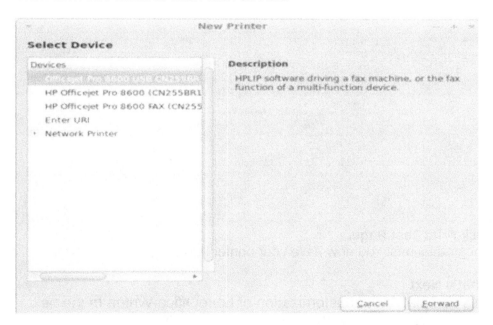

Select the printer you want to use, then click **Forward**. Linux Mint will search for a driver for this printer:

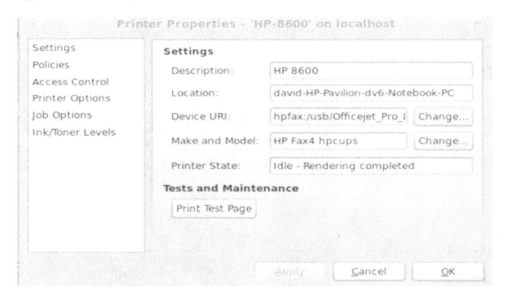

Type in the name you want to use for this printer. Then click **Apply.**

Click **Print Test Page.**
Congratulations! You now have your printer hooked up to Linux Mint.

What's Next
This completes our customization of LibreOffice Writer. In the next chapter, we will review the benefits of Libre Office Writer for creating complex documents, print books and ebooks. We will then take a look at **LibreOffice Calc** to see how easy it is to create a chart with LibreOffice. Finally, we will review how to create a presentation with **LibreOffice Impress.**

Chapter 8... Hidden Benefits of Libre Office

Chapter 8 includes the following four sections:
8.1 Advantages of Libre Writer for Creating a Print or EBook
8.2 Create your own custom styles
8.3 Use Libre Office Calc to create a chart
8.4 Use Libre Office Impress to make a slide presentation

The first section describes seven fantastic tools which Libre Writer provides to help you write and organize a print and/or ebook.

The second section reviews how to create your own custom styles and add them to your custom template.

The third section demonstrates how easy it is to create a chart using Libre Calc.

The fourth section reviews how to make a slide presentation with Libre Impress.

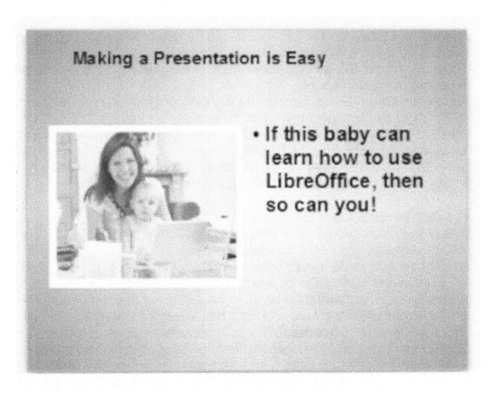

8.1 Advantages of Libre Writer for Creating a Print or EBook

Microsoft Word tends to treat all documents as if they were simple documents. It is like trying to build a house with only a hammer and a saw. Libre Office also includes the hammer and saw. But it also provides you with a set of blueprints for organizing the construction process and a whole team of specialists for doing the foundation, framing, drywall, plumbing and electrical tasks.

The initial interface, tool bars and menus of Libre Writer do a great job of creating and editing simple documents. In addition, Libre Office also offers a whole range of tools for creating, organizing and editing very complex documents such as 400 page books.

Seven Tools Libre Writer offers for organizing complex documents
The following are seven extremely important tools Libre Writer offers to help you organize your Print Book and/or Ebook.
First, the **Libre Writer Master Document** can be used to combine documents into an overall Table of Contents.
Second, the **Libre Writer Navigator** can be used to navigate between files and sub-files in the Master document.
Third, the **Writer Styles Window** which allows precise control over every aspect of every document.
Fourth, the **Page Styles** function allows different formatting of different pages.
Fifth, Writer **Paragraph Styles** can be tied into a Linkable Table of Contents.
Sixth, as of July 2013, Writer 4.1 offers an incredible **image optimization tool** – essential for publishing an EBook or posting your articles to a website.
Seventh, Writer also offers advanced **PDF import and export** functions.
Below, we will review all seven of these tools.

#1 Libre Writer Master Document
One of the major problems of writing a book is that the file size gets so large that it eventually crashes your word processor and/or freezes your computer. This is especially true if your book includes hundreds of images. The benefit of the Libre Writer Master Document is the ability to write each chapter as a separate document and then tie them altogether at the end into an overall Master document. To create a Master document for writing a book, click on **File, New, Master Document.** There is a close relationship between this Master document and the Libre Writer Navigator which is described next. Usage of the Master document and Navigator is beyond the scope of this book. But we do cover it in detail in our next book which is called **Create your own Ebook – with Libre Office.**

#2 The Libre Writer Navigator

The Navigator helps you jump back and forth in a document not just by heading styles, but by any type of object you care to name: tables, frames, images, links, or anything else. For this to work well, you need to keep your tables and images well named and well organized. Moreover, since the Navigator is a floating window, you can place it anywhere on the screen, so that it doesn't reduce the size of the editing window. This is important when editing even and odd paged documents where you want to set up the editing window to display two pages side by side. To open Navigator, go to **View,** then **Navigator.**

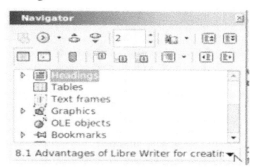

In addition, the Navigator can be used as a multilevel outline and a table of contents for a master document made up of smaller documents. This is very important when you are writing and organizing a print book or an ebook which is 400 hundred pages long and is therefore best divided into 10 smaller documents, files or chapters each of which is about 40 pages long. The longer the document, the more you need the Libre Writer Navigator and Master Document.

#3 The Styles and Formatting Window

Another floating window, Styles and Formatting, places all of LibreOffice's five categories of styles - paragraphs, characters, frames, pages, and lists - within easy reach and allows easy creation and modification of styles. You can easily and quickly apply any style to your document in order to see what it looks like. To reach the Styles Window, go to **Formatting, Styles.**

We will cover style formatting options in greater detail in the next section.

#4 Writer Page Style Options

In Word, you can adjust some limited page features such as margins columns. But all paragraphs have the same alignment and different formatting for different pages is difficult. Writer's addition of page styles gives you far more flexibility. By careful use of the Organizer tab, you can set your document to change page styles automatically, so that a First Page style is always followed by a Left Page and a Left Page by a Right Page. Since headers and footers are also attached to page style, you can also use different header and footer styles automatically to create a different layout for the left or even pages than you have on the right or odd pages. To reach the Page Styles Default Style screen, go to Format, Pages.

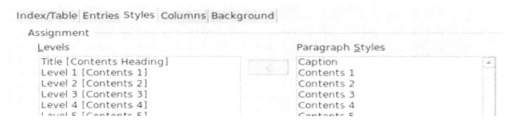

#5 Hierarchical Paragraph Styles linked to your Table of Contents

Word generates tables of contents using existing templates. However, the result is not editable, and invariably looks bad. Writer provides a far wider range of possibilities. You can adjust the position of all the components of a table of contents entry, or determine whether they appear at all. Each level of the table includes its own editable paragraph style, and, while Writer, like Word, assumes you will use heading styles to create entries, you can also manually enter other markers if you wish. The result is a far more flexible set of design options which can be easily edited and updated. To see the window linking the Styles to your Table of Contents, click on Indexes and Tables. Then click on Styles.

#6 Writer Image Optimization Tool

With Writer 4.1, all you need to do to optimize any image in any document is to right click on it.

This brings up a whole selection of image adjustment options. The most important of these for those wishing to publish their information as an ebook or web page is the "compress graphic" tool.

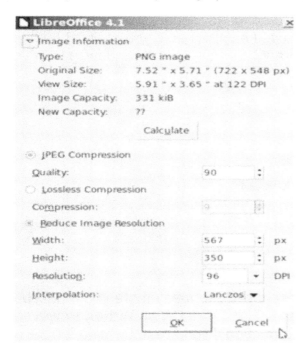

Click on **Calculate** to determine the exact file size after compression.

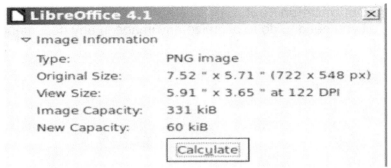

The tool also automatically converts inefficient PNG images into efficient JPEG images. It is typical for image file sizes to be reduced my 80% or more – meaning your web page will load four times faster than if you had used images which were not optimized. In addition, PDF documents can be transferred much more rapidly if the images are optimized.

#7 Advanced PDF Import, Edit and Export Options
Both Writer and Word support saving a file as PDF. However, Word provides only basic options. Writer's Export to PDF function provides an exhaustive set of options for those who want them. Instead of Word's vague options for quality, Writer lets you set the exact image quality and resolution. You can also set exactly how links in the original are handled and set the details of the initial view for the PDF window. Most important, you can add a free tool to Libre Writer which allows you to not only create PDF documents - but also to import them and edit them! Given the importance of PDF creation to modern print on demand publishing, if you are writing a self publish book, you really should use Libre Writer. To reach the Libre Writer PDF export window, go to File, Export as PDF.

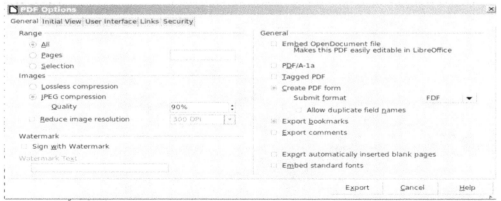

We will cover all seven of these tools plus many more in our next book, called **Create your own Ebook with Libre Office Writer.** However, because Styles are so important even if you are not writing a book, we will spend some more time on this topic in the next section.

8.2 Create your own custom styles

It is a good idea to keep the Styles Window open and snapped to the left side of your document window whenever you are creating a complex document or ebook in order to have quick access to all five types of styles.

You can bring up the Styles Window by clicking on **F11** on your keyboard or by clicking on **Format, Styles** in the **Main Menu**. The top boxes in the Style Window are the five categories of styles on the left and style edit functions on the right:

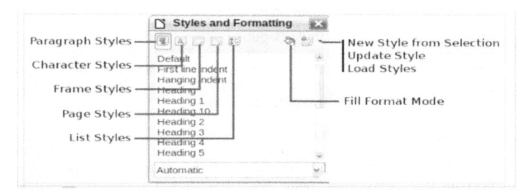

If you plan on writing an E book, or posting your articles on a website, you should consider changing from the traditional way of formatting text (by manually specifying the font weight and size of each line) to using styles to format text. For example, you can have a style called Heading 2 for Section Titles which is defined to be font size 14 and font weight bold. Then instead of selecting the text for your title and selecting the font size and font weight, you simply select the style called Heading 2.

The benefit of using styles instead of manually changing text is that your Ebook will automatically create an outline or Table of Contents based on listing all of the style entries which have been defined as Headings. For example, chapter titles might use a style called heading 1 while sections in the chapter might use a smaller style called heading 2. Another benefit of using styles is that should you decide you want to change the section headings to a larger font - such as 16 - and you want to change the font color to blue, all you need to do is change the style definition and all of the Heading 2 styles will automatically be updated to the new style. A third benefit of getting in the habit of using styles is that your book will have a more consistent appearance and therefore be easier to read and understand. A fourth benefit of using styles is that they can be easily converted to CSS Style Statements for use in creating a CSS Style Sheet – which is the file that controls the appearance of your HTML based ebook.

Before Adding Styles you must first clear all Manual Styles
Manual styles and ebook styles do not mix well. Unfortunately, manual formatting, which is also called direct formatting, can not be over-ridden by applying a style to it. Therefore before applying any styles to your document, you first need to clear or remove all manual styles. To do this, open your document and click on SELECT ALL. Then in the top menu, click on Format, Clear Direct Formatting. Alternately, you can go through your document and individually replace all direct formatting with style formatting. The problem with this is that it is difficult to tell if a particular set of bold text was formatted manually or with a style. After selecting text, you need to pay careful attention to the Style Box. If you have bold text and it still reads "Default Style" then it was manually formatted. If it reads "Heading" followed by a number then it has already been styled with that Heading Style.

Style Categories versus Style Groups
Libre Writer divides styles into five categories. These are page styles, paragraph styles, character styles, frame styles and list styles. Within a given category, styles can be further divided into style groups. Below is a brief description of each of the five style categories.

Create a Custom Page Style
Page styles control the appearance of an entire page. Libre Writer allows us to define different styles for different pages. For example, different sections of the book can have different page styles. The "default" page style is reached by going to **Format, Page.**

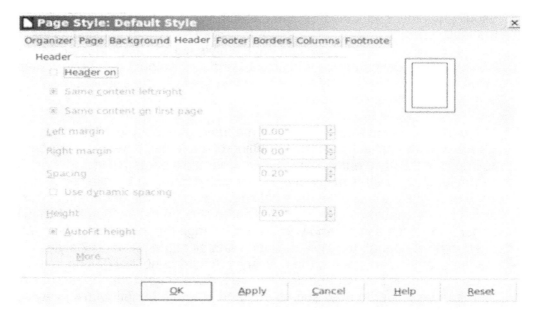

However, you can create a custom page style by clicking on the **Page Styles Icon** in the Styles window.

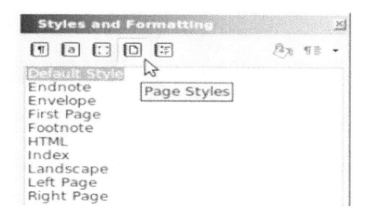

Then right click on **Default Styles** and select **New**.

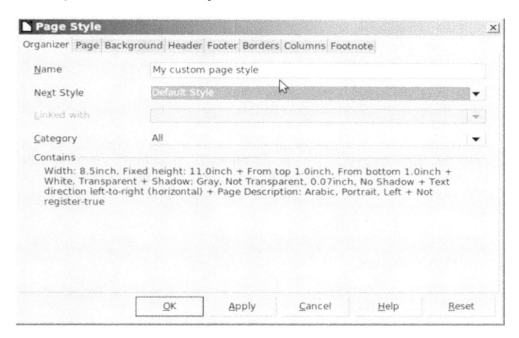

Type in the name of the new page style. Then click **Apply**. Then click **OK**. The new custom page style will show up in the list of page styles in the Style Window.

Create a Custom Paragraph Style

Paragraph styles are the most common type of style. They are styles which can be applied to an entire group of text such as a paragraph or a subject title. One of the most common usages of paragraph styles is to create and format a Table of Contents for your document. However, not all paragraph styles can be used for this purpose. Libre Writer uses "Levels" to structure the Table of Contents. The Title is the Top Level which may be the same of the entire book. This is followed by Level 1 which is likely to be used for the names of chapters. Level 2 is likely to be used for Section Titles.

The following image shows a list of paragraph styles which can be selected and then applied to the Table of Contents Levels. In addition to the styles on this list, any custom styles which you create will also appear on the list. In fact, one of the benefits of creating a custom style is to insure that it shows up on this list. To insert a Table of Contents – or to simply see this list – go to Insert, Indexes and Tables. Then select Indexes and Tables. Then select the Styles tab.

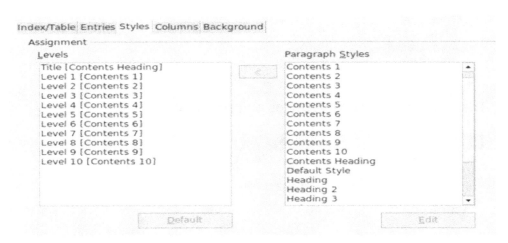

If you want to change a paragraph style for all of your documents, you should make the changes in your Document Template. To change a single document, use the Style Window for that document. To create a new custom paragraph style, first click on Paragraph Styles Icon in the Styles Window to bring up the list of Paragraph Styles.

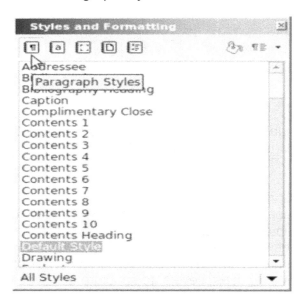

Then right click on the Default Style (or a Heading Style or whatever style you think is closest to the style you want to create). Then select New.

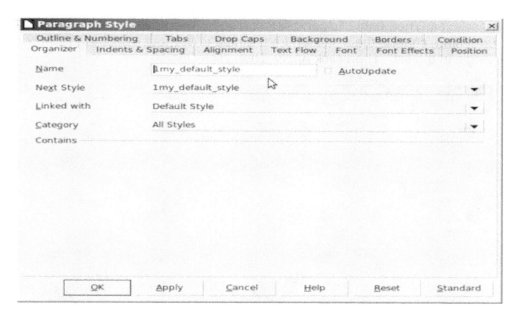

It is important with custom styles to add a number such as 1 to the beginning of the name of your custom style as this will cause your custom styles to always show up at the top of the paragraph styles list.

Create Custom Character Styles

Character styles control special words or phrases within a paragraph. This includes words that you want in bold. To bring up the list of Character Styles, click on the "a" at the top of the Styles window.

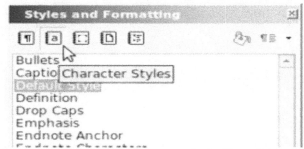

The "Emphasis" character style is like clicking on Italic in the top menu. The "Strong Emphasis" character style is like clicking on Bold in the top menu. The difference is that if at some point in the future, you want to change the style of all bold words, it can be easily done by modifying the character style – whereas if you use manual formatting, you will need to go through your entire document and change each bold word one at a time.

Eliminate the Underline from Internet Links

Character styles are also used to define the style of Internet Links and Index links. So if you want to change your internet links on all of your documents so that they are not underlined, first open your default template by clicking on File, New, Templates, then selecting the default template and clicking on Edit.

Then in the Style Window, click on Character Links. Then click on Internet Link to select it. Then right click and select Modify. Then click on Font Effects. For underling, change the selection from Single to Without (which is just above Single in the list). Then click Apply. Then click OK.

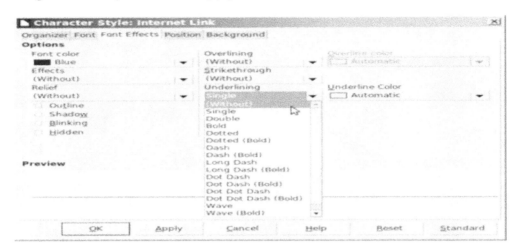

You should also eliminate the underline from the "Visited Internet Links" which is at the very bottom of the list of character links.

Add an Underline Character Style to your Custom Template
There is one common formatting option which is not in the list of default character styles. This is the underline function. To create an Underline character style in your default template, first open the template to the edit screen. Then click on the character icon at the top of the Style Window. Then select the default style and click new.

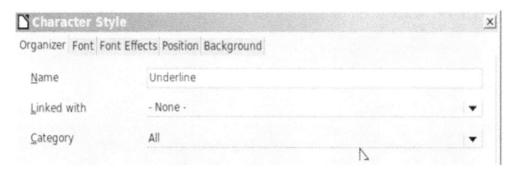

Name the character style Underline. Then set the Linked with to "None." Then click on Font Effects and change the Underline from "Without" to Single. Then click Apply. Then click OK.

Apply Styles Quickly and Easily

The most common way to apply a style is to select the text you want to style and then click on the Styles icon which is at the far left side of the formatting tool bar:

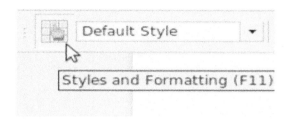

Clicking on this icon brings up the formatting options:

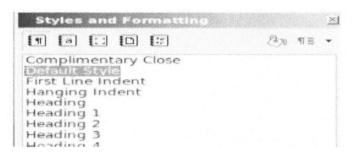

Using the Apply Styles drop down arrow to bring up the current Apply Styles list:. Click on the drop down arrow to the right of the current style box to bring up a list of all styles than have been used so far in your document.

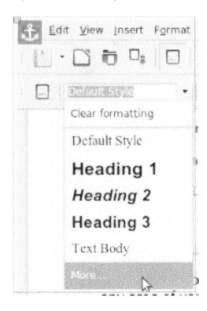

If you want a new style you haven't used yet, click on MORE to bring up the Styles box with all of the styles.

Click on the drop down arrow at the bottom of the styles list and you will see that there are many different "groups" of styles:

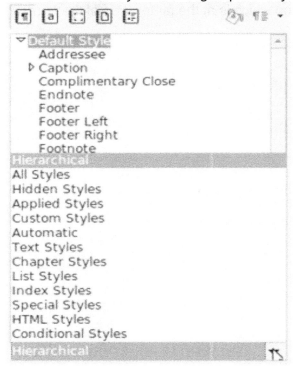

One of the more important groups of styles for an Ebook are HTML styles. While all of these styles are preformatted, meaning that you just need to click on them to apply them, it is useful to know what the preformatting is in case you want to change it to something else. Just click on the style and the font type and weight will be displayed on the formatting tool bar.

Modify an Existing Style
Any style changes you make in any document will only apply to that document. To permanently modify a style, you must edit the template. To change a style from the Style Window, first select the Style Category you want by clicking on one of the five Category Icons at the top of the Style Window. Then, right click on the style you want to change and select Modify. Below we have selected the Paragraph styles category and within this we have selected the Default style:

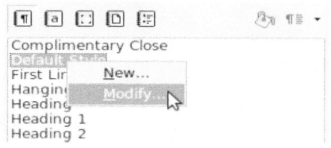

This brings up the Paragraph Styles Edit screen with several tabs that can be changed:

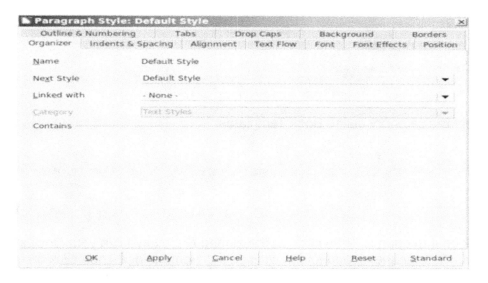

Click on the font tab to change the font family, size and weight. Then click Apply. Then click OK.

Update a document from a modified template
To apply all of the styles of your modified default template to an existing document, first save and close all of your open documents and close Libre Office. Then restart Libre Office and open any document you want to apply the new template to. Before the document opens, the following message will appear.

Note that this message only appears when changing the default template. Click Update Styles to change the styles in the document. Be aware that you only get one chance to update a document this way. If you click Keep Old Styles, the old styles will remain and then must be changed within the document itself.

Adding templates from other sources
Libre Office has lots of templates you can add. To see the list of templates, go to: http://templates.libreoffice.org/template-center

Select the category called Book Templates:

A master document template

A master document template

Latest release compatible with: LibreOffice 3.5

Like

9 likes, 0 dislikes

Click on it to open it: Then click on the zipped file to save it in your Downloads folder. To open the zipped folder, click on the Home folder. Then click on the Downloads folder. Then right click and unzip the folder with Extract Here. Each of the five folders can be opened and then the files inside can be opened one at a time and saved as templates. You can also find more free templates, including Kindle Ebook templates at the Open Office Extension Directory.
http://extensions.services.openoffice.org/
Nearly all Open Office Templates and Extensions also work for Libre Office.

Why a Kindle Template?
The Amazon Kindle is the most popular type of Ebook reader. However, the Kindle has a very narrow six inch screen which is too narrow to read documents that were written on a regular page size (A4 or letter). This template overcomes that problem by using a A6 page size with customized margins that fits well on the Kindle screen. The document can be exported as a PDF in order to be read on the Kindle.

What's Next?
This completes our basic introduction to formatting and using Libre Writer. If you are interested in creating your own Print Book or Ebook, you should consider reading our complete book on this topic called **Create your own Ebook Using Libre Writer.** In this book, we go into more detail on creating a Master document and Table of Contents as well as creating custom styles for an ebook. In the next section, we will review how to use Libre Office Calc to create a custom chart. Then we review how to use Libre Office Impress to create a custom presentation.

8.3 Use Libre Office Calc to create a chart

The Libre Office Calc chart creation process is very similar to the process used with the MS Office 2003 Excel chart wizard. In many ways, it is even simpler.

Having spent many years making hundreds of charts and teaching others how to make charts, and having spent the past three years dealing with the ridiculous process used by the Office 2010 Excel Chart Wizard, I am extremely impressed by the LibreOffice 4 Chart Wizard. It is a much more logical process than the new Office chart wizard. To open Libre Office Calc from the Writer Menu, click on **File, New, Spreadsheet.**

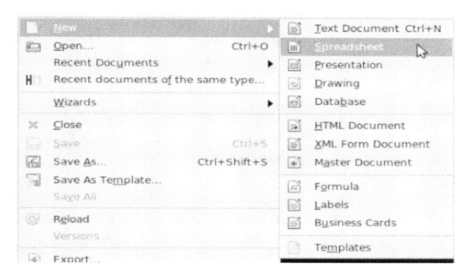

This will bring up the Calc Window.

We will convert the following table to a chart:

Windows Version	Recommended Space on Hard Drive (MB)
Windows 3.1	15
Windows 95	50
Windows 98	500
Windows ME	2,000
Windows XP	2,000
Windows VS	15,000
Windows 7	20,000
Windows 8	20,000

Copy and paste this simple table into the Calc table and save as "Windows OS File Size Increase over Time":

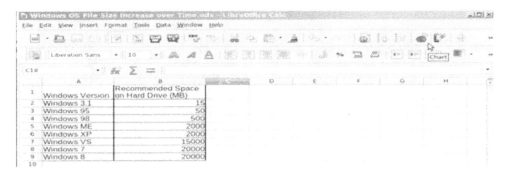

Select the data cells, then click on the Red "Chart" Icon in the top menu. This creates a chart:

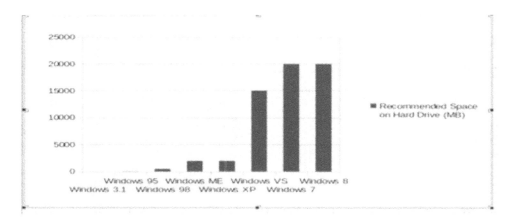

It also brings up a chart editing screen:

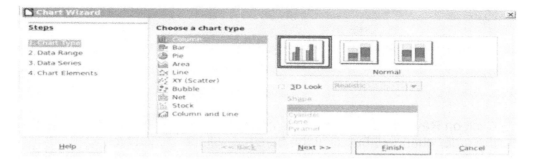

Click on Bar to turn the chart into a bar chart:

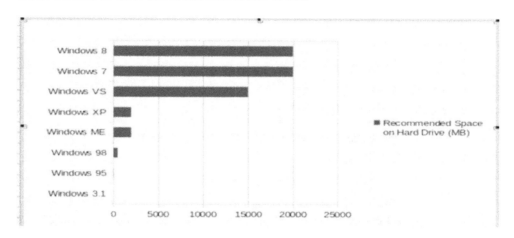

Then run through the four steps. Add a Title, and move the legend to the bottom of the chart. Then click Finish to display the chart:

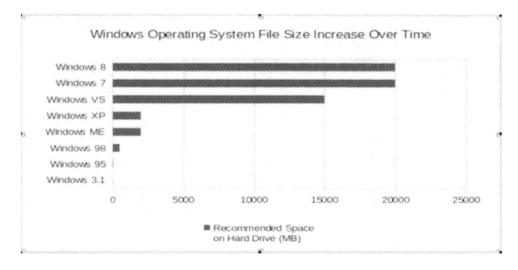

Double click on the chart to edit it. Right click on either axis, then click on **Format Axis** to bring up the following screen:

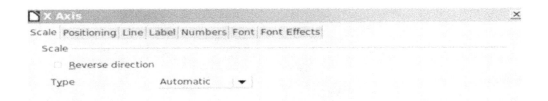

Click on **Reverse Direction**. This changes the order. Below is the chart with the order changed, but all of the bars are still the same color:

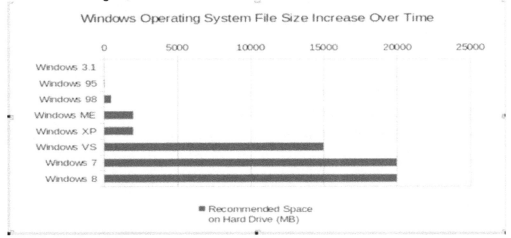

Click on this axis again to increase the font size from 10 Regular to 14 Bold.

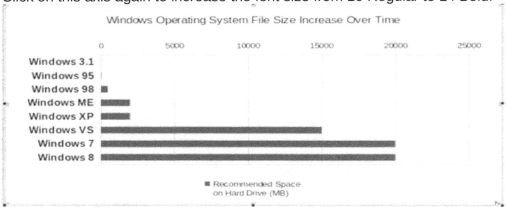

Next, we want to change the color of the Windows Vista, Windows 7 and Windows 8 bars so they are different from the first four bars. To change the color of an individual bar is tricky. First, you have to double click on the bars to select all of them. Then select an individual bar by clicking on it once.

Above we have selected the Windows 8 bar. Note that this brings up some small green bars to indicate that the individual bar has been selected.

Then double click on the individual bar to bring up the edit screen:

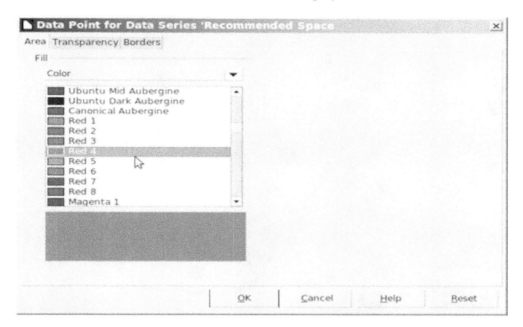

Select the color you want for that bar. Then click OK.

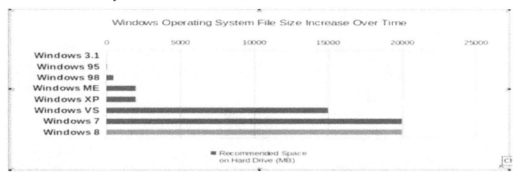

Repeat the steps to change the color of the Windows VS and Windows 7 bars. Next, we want to change the data range from 25000 to 20000. Click on the Horizontal Axis to select it. Then right click and select **Format.** In the scale tab, uncheck Automatic and change the maximum value from 25000 to 20000. Then click OK.

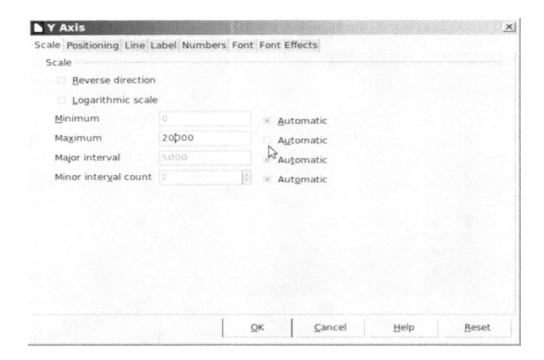

Last, select the Title and right click on it. Then select Format Title. Go to the Font Tab and increase the font to 14 bold. Below is our finished chart.

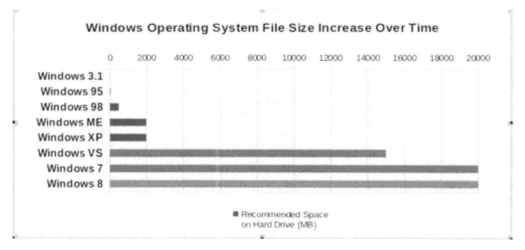

In the next section, we will create a slide show using LibreOffice Impress.

8.4 Use Libre Office Impress to make a slide presentation

The most impressive feature of Libre Office Impress is the ability to define a variety of custom background colors and effects.

Our next mission is to create a Slide Presentation with LibreOffice Impress similar to the following slide.

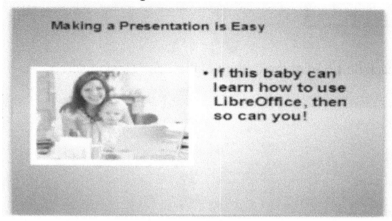

To open LibreOffice Impress from the Writer Menu, click on the Blue box below the Edit Menu item:

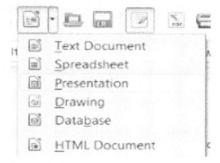

Then click on Presentation:

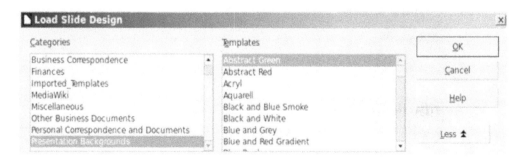

Click on Format, Slide Design and you will see that there is only one design to choose from.

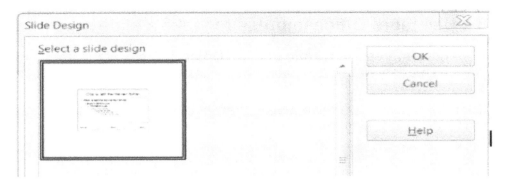

To get more, click on **Load** at the bottom of the Slide Design screen.

Scroll down to the Presentation Backgrounds. Then select one of several backgrounds and click OK to add this background to the list of options. These options are then available under **View, Slide Sorter, Master Pages.**

Changing the Presentation Background Area

Click on the tilted paint bucket:

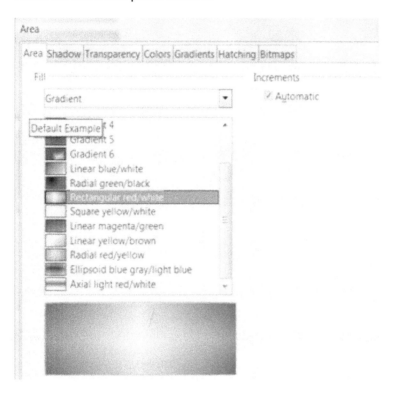

Click on the Colors Tab:

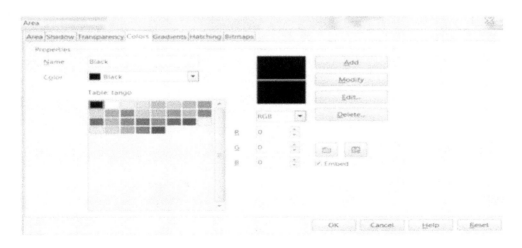

By default, the color selection table is set for a table called Tango. However, there are many other Color Selection Tables we can use. Click on the folder icon to bring up this list:

Click on **Web**, then click Open:

Now we have a selection of web safe colors. Next click on the Gradient Tab:

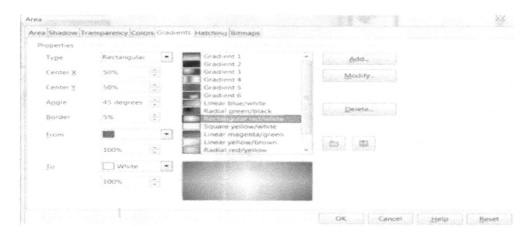

Then click on Add and type in the name of the new background you want to create:

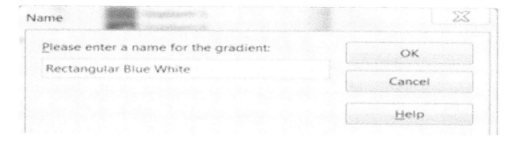

Then click OK

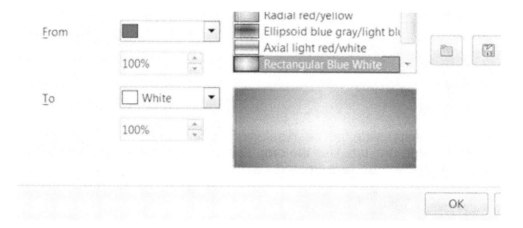

Then change the color from Red to Blue.

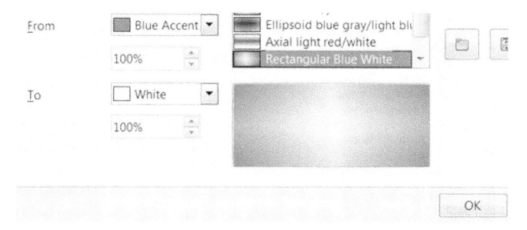

Then click OK, then click Modify, then OK. Now that we have created the background color option we want, we are ready to change the background of the slides. To change the background of a single slide, select View Normal. To change the background of all of the slides, select View, then Master, then Slide Master:

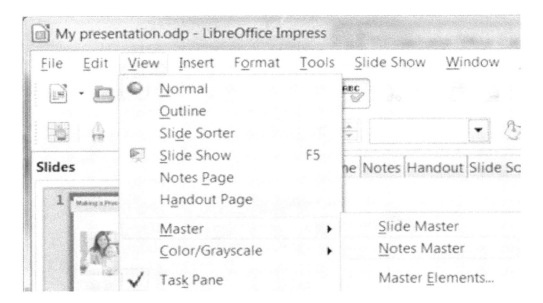

Once the master slide has been selected, click Format, then Page, then click on the Background tab. Use the drop down arrow to select Gradient. Then select the background we created above:

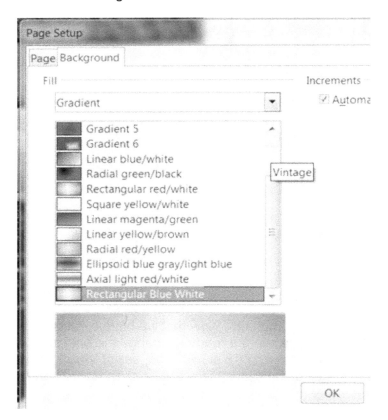

Then click OK:

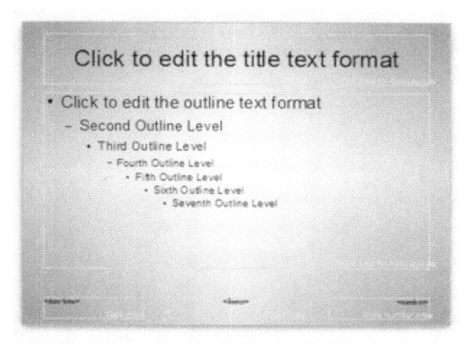

Then click Close Master View. Select a slide and then click on the new master we created to see your newly created background color on an existing slide.

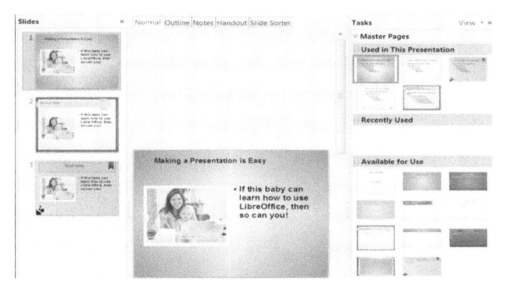

This concludes our chapter on Libre Office tools. In the next chapter, we will look at additional tools which you can use to free yourself from Microsoft and the NSA.

Chapter 9... Additional Free Open Source Tools

Chapter 9 includes the following four sections

9.1 Free Screen recording tools for Linux Mint
9.2 Edit your video with Open Shot Video Editor
9.3 Open Source Alternatives to NSA Partners
9.4 How to use Windows programs in Linux Mint

Section 9.1 describes how to add a free open source screen recording tool called **Record My Desktop** to your Linux Mint operating system. This is an excellent way for teachers to share information with your students and for alternative news groups to post stories to Youtube.

Section 9.2 describes how to use a free open source video editor called **Open Shot** to edit create video introductions, combine video sections and edit videos – including adding sound tracks prior to posting your videos to Youtube.

Section 9.3 describes a variety of other ways to use open source tools to free yourself from Microsoft and the NSA. These include switching from the Google Search Engine to the **Duck Duck Go (DDG)** Search Engine – and switching your email organizer from Microsoft Outlook to a free open source tool called **Thunderbird.** This tool works in combination with a more secure email service called Riseup.net to give you the option of encrypting your emails.

Section 9.4 describes how to use Windows programs with Linux by installing a free program called Play on Linux.

Regain control of your computer
and regain control of your destiny!

9.1 Free Screen recording tools for Linux Mint

Adding a free open source screen recording tool called Record My Desktop to your Linux Mint operating system is an excellent way for teachers to share information with students and for news groups to post stories to Youtube.

In this section, we will review tools for creating your own screen casts.

Tools for creating screen casts.
The Linux Mint Software Manager offers several free tools for creating screen casts. To review these tools, open the Mint Menu and click on the **Software Manager.**

Then click on **Sound and Videos.** The most popular video caster is called Cheese. However, it has some problems. So we will instead install Record My Desktop. If you enter this term in the Search Box, you will see that Record My Desktop comes in two parts. We need both the Graphical Front End and the Recording Back End. Click on each, then click install. If you have an older x32 bit computer, for the back end choose the 386 option (see options below).

We will first install the GTK version of Record My Desktop. Then we will install the normal version of the user interface for Record My Desktop.

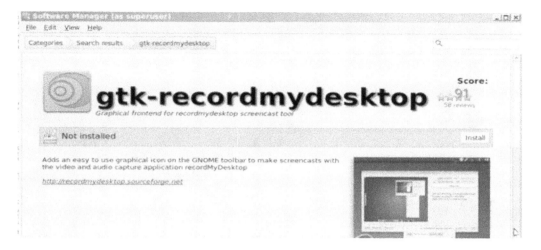

Click Install for each.

Next go to the Mint Menu, Applications, Sound and Video and drag the icon to the desktop.

Click on the icon to open the Record My Desktop window
In addition to the Main Window, there is a small red icon in the system tray which you can also use to control the program.

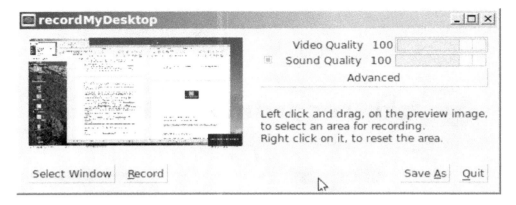

The Main Window

The Main Window includes a preview of your desktop. Note that you can use your mouse to define an area within the desktop preview to record – or select a window to record. If you select a Window, and you want to post the video on YouTube, the window should have a ratio of 16 wide by 9 high. For example, if you create a slide presentation, make the ratio 16 inches wide by 9 inches high. A narrower window will result in black bars on both sides of the video.

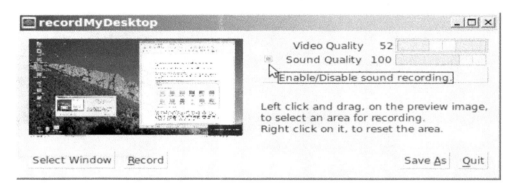

Video and Sound Quality Settings

On the top-right corner of the Main Window, there are two sliders labeled "Video Quality" and "Sound Quality". These control the quality of the encoded file and thus it's file size. To publish videos over the internet, the video quality should be set for 50% and the Sound Quality should be set for 100%. Make sure the Enable Sound Quality box is checked. If it is not, the video will have no sound recording!

Advanced Tab

Beneath the audio and video quality settings, there is a large button named "Advanced". Clicking that will bring a new window, that will allow you to set a vast number of options, and fine tune the behavior of the program. However, we will leave these advanced settings alone.

Save As and Quit

On the bottom-right corner, there are "Save As" and "Quit" buttons. Clicking the "Save As" button will present you with a save-file dialog, which will allow you to pick a destination and file-name for the encoded file. The "Quit" button exits the program. However, to stop the video, use the button in the task bar.

The Task Bar Icon

The other main element of the program is the icon in the Task Bar. Right click on this icon to bring up some options.

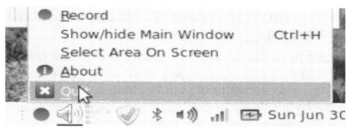

The icon in the task bar will change color and shape depending on what the video recorder is doing. The icon will be a red circle when the video is stopped. It will change to a gray box while the video is being recorded. You can right click on the Gray Square to either Pause the video – in which case the icon will change to a couple of thin bars. Or from the Gray Box, you can click on Stop which will stop the video and bring up the file coding progress window.

There are two ways to start a recording. Either click on Record from the Main Window – or just left click on the Red Circle Icon in the task bar. Either way, the red circle will change to a gray box and you have started recording.

There are also two ways to stop a recording. Either left click on the gray box – or right click on the gray box and select Stop. Below is a summary of the task bar icon changes and actions.

Task Bar Icon	Left Click	Right Click
Red Circle Stopped	Starts a new recording	Shows Tray menu
Gray Box Recording	Stops the recording	Pauses the recording
Two thin bars Paused	Resumes recording	Resumes Recording

Define an area for recording

There are three ways of selecting the area on which you will confine the recording.

Option 1: Use the Full screen preview thumbnail on the main window.
To select on the thumbnail, simply left click on it and drag the mouse. Release it when you have covered the area that you want recorded. Right clicking on the preview will restore the recording area to full screen.

Option 2: Use the "Select Window" button.
To confine the recording to one window, click on the "Select Window" button. The cursor will change to a cross. Now click on the window you wish to record and the area will be selected. Using the "Select Window" button will only set the area. If you move the window, the area will remain unchanged. By default the window decorations will be included in the recording area. This can be changed at Advanced->Misc. **This is the option we will use to display slide presentations we are recording.**

Option 3: Use the "Select Area on Screen" function of the task bar icon.
To select an area with the task bar icon, right click then select "Select Area on Screen". When you do that, a screen shot of your desktop is picked and then over laid as full screen over your desktop. Left click and drag to select an area. When you release the mouse button, the over laid screen shot will disappear. You can also right click to cancel the selection process. After you have finished using any of the above methods, the area you have selected will be shown in the preview window. Depending on your settings, an optional frame might also appear on your real display, around the recording area.

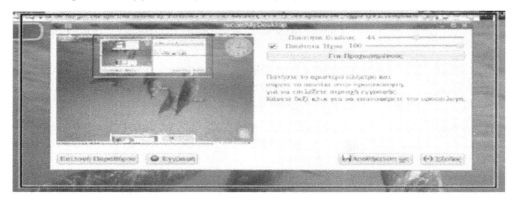

Recording
At this point, you know how to select your screen and then start, stop and pause a recording. You can start a test recording by either left clicking on the tray icon, or left clicking the record button on the main window. When you start a recording session, the main window will hide itself. While you are recording, the Red Dot will turn into a gray folder. While recording, you can pause the recording for any amount of time. When you are done, left click on the gray square in the task bar to stop the recording. This causes a new window to appear, the encoding process monitor.

Recording Process Monitor

By default, Record My Desktop breaks down the overall recording process into two separate steps. First, the video is recorded and cached in a temporary folder in the hard drive. Second, the file is encoded into an OGG video file. The encoding window looks like this:

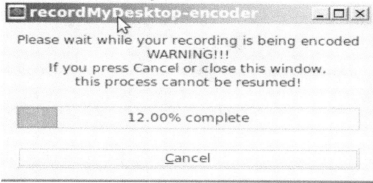

Depending on the video quality you have selected, it could take several minutes to encode your video. But if you have set the video quality to 50%, you should be able to load a 5 to 10 minute video in less than 2 minutes. As the warning reads, clicking on Cancel will irreversibly stop the process and discard the remaining part of the recording. When the encoding ends, the main window will reappear, unless you have manually hidden it through the tray icon pop up-menu.

After that, you can go at the location you chose to save the file (default is out.ogg in your home directory) and watch your session in your favorite media player.

Note that the VLC Media Player by default looks for videos in the My Videos folder. So if the video has been saved in the Home folder, use the File Manager to transfer it to the Videos folder.

Sound recording

Sound recording is the most complex part of any video recording. You have two options. You can either leave the default settings in place, in which case the video will probably use the normal microphone on your computer. The problem is that if the fan on your computer is running, the mic will also pick up this sound.

The first step to sound recording is to make sure that it is enabled. In the main window, as shown in the above picture, the check box in the red circle should be enabled. If not, sound recording will be completely disabled.

If you want better sound quality, then you will need to change the mic setting to your headphone mic. Unfortunately, Record My Desktop does not do a very good job in this area. You can also change the Mint sound settings by going to Control Panel and clicking on Sound. Select and configure your headphones. However, even this may not cause Record My Desktop to recognize your headphone mic. o get better quality sound, you will therefore need to install another tool from the Software Manager called KMIX.

Type in the word mixer into the Software Manager search box to see our choices. Select KMIX and Install it. After installing it, go to the Mint Menu and drag the KMIX icon to the desktop. Click on it to activate it. This places an Icon in the lower task bar. Click on this icon to open it. Then select the Master Channel:

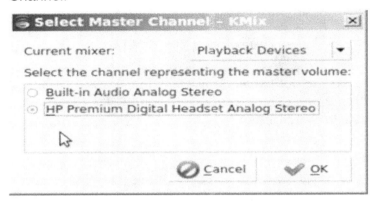

Select the Headset. Then click OK. With Current mixer, select Capture Devices and make sure that the Headset is chosen:

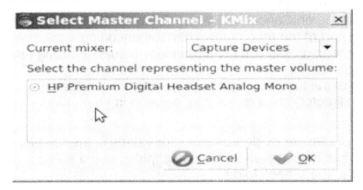

From the icon in the lower task bar, right click and select **Audio Setup**

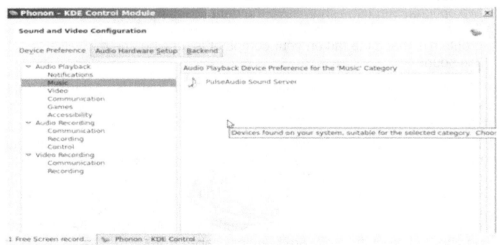

Click on **Audio Hardware Setup** and change the Sound Card to the Headset.

The sound tab lets you configure the quality of the sound capture, or the recorded ports.

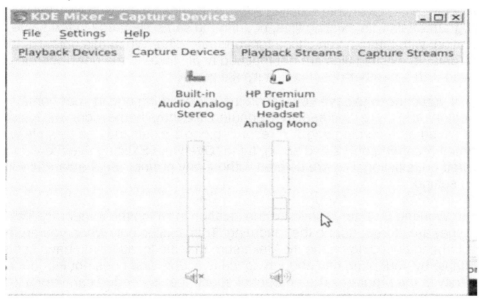

Note that there are separate volume controls for the audio plugs in the back and front of your computer if your motherboard has both. Now make a test recording to see if the headset mic works.

The Advanced Window

There are several settings which can be adjusted with the Advanced Window. However, in general, you should not need to change any of these settings.

Files

The first tab you will encounter is titled Files and looks like this:

The Files tab contains two options; Overwrite Existing Files and Working Directory. The "Overwrite Existing Files" option has to do with how the program deals with existing files, bearing the same file name in the same location, with the one you chose for your recording. When this option is turned off (default) existing files are not touched at all. Instead the new recording is saved with a number post fixed at it's file name.

So, if you choose to save your recording as recording.ogg in your home directory and there is already a file named like that, the new one will instead get saved as recording.ogg.1. If recording.ogg.1 exists too, the new file will be named recording.ogg.2 and so on. If the "Overwrite Existing Files" option is turned on, existing files are deleted without any prompt. So, be careful with this setting.

The "Working Directory" option is the location in which the temporary files (cache) are stored, during the recording. This applies only when you are not performing encoding on the fly. Make sure that the location you have set is writable by your user, has enough space available and does not introduce latency in the program. The amount of space that is needed can vary a lot, depending on the settings of the recording and the amount of activity on the screen. On my setup, at 15fps and a resolution of 1280 x 1024, with average screen activity, there might be needed **3 to 6 GB of space, per hour of recording. If you do videos in blocks of 10 minutes or less, then you would only need 1 GB of space.**

Performance

The Performance tab holds four options that should probably not be changed.

The "Frames Per Second" option controls the frequency with which screen shots are taken. Setting it to a higher value will produce smoother recordings, but it will require more processing power. Leave "Encode on the Fly" turned off. Leave "Zero Compression" turned on. Also leave Quick Subsampling turned off and leave "Full shots At Every Frame" turned off.

Sound

These settings should also probably be left as is. The "Channels" option sets the number of channels in the resulting audio stream. It can be 1 (mono) or 2 (stereo). When your sound source is only a microphone, selecting more than one channel is completely unnecessary and will only increase the size of your files. The "Frequency" setting (or "sample rate" as it is commonly called), is probably the most defining factor for the quality of a recording. The default is 22050, which is more than enough for speech, but if you are recording music, you might need to get it at 44100. The "Device" option should contain an ALSA or OSS sound device, depending on how your copy of recordMyDesktop was compiled. The default is the word DEFAULT, which is an alias for the front end, which means that it won't try to change that setting. Instead it lets the back end determine that, based on the sound system that is used. When using ALSA, the default setting for the device, in the back end, is hw:0,0. This is the hardware plug in and it can only accept channels and frequency values, that the sound card supports natively. This means that while you may have set your recording to mono at 22050 Hz, it might use stereo at 48000Hz. In order to have precise control, you need to use the software plug in for the sound device field, which is plughw:0,0.

The above settings capture sound directly from the sound card. If you wish to use JACK instead, click the "Use Jack For Audio Capture" check box. The channels, frequency and device fields will be grayed out. This happens because these settings are now provided by the Jack server.

Before enabling Jack capture, you should make sure that a Jack server is running. After that you should see a list of available ports. If you see a warning message saying that jack_lsp(which needs to be installed) hasn't found any ports, make sure that you have a running server. To get a more current list of available ports, hit refresh. The initial selection will determine how many capture ports are registered by recordMyDesktop. Of course these ports can later be remapped, with the help of tools like qjackctl.

Misc

The fourth and last tab in the advanced window is called Misc. In this tab you will find various options which are meant to be used less frequently. Do not change any of the settings on the MISC tab.

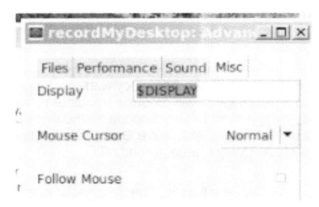

If you can only save videos to your Home folder, then transfer videos from this folder to the videos folder with the File Manager. Then open VLC media player and go to My Videos to play it.

Solving common problems.

If you have no sounds. There is a program called Jack-mixer you may want to try. In order to record sound from a microphone, you have to set it through a mixer like Kmix. Record My Desktop will not set anything itself but rather it will start recording from any preselected source. Another reason for no sound might be the presence of more than one sound card. In that case, make sure you've set the right one. Unless you know that you have more than one sound card, do not change the device setting.

In the next section, we will look at how to edit our video with the Open Shot video editing programming program.

9.2 Edit your video with Open Shot Video Editor

This section describes how to use a free open source video editor called **Open Shot** to edit create video introductions, combine video sections and edit videos – including adding sound tracks prior to posting your videos to You Tube.

The most popular video editing program is called open shot. Another popular video editor is called Pitivi

Then drag the Open Shot Launcher to the Desktop. Then click on it to open it.

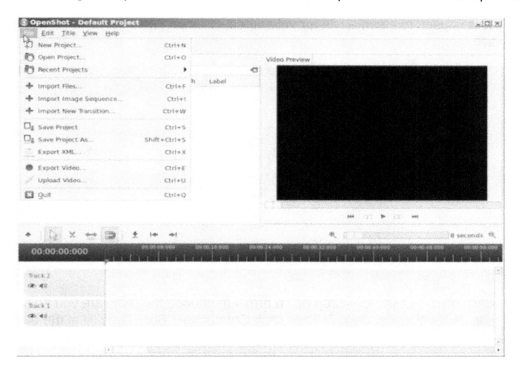

Click on File, New Project to start a new project.

Name the new project.

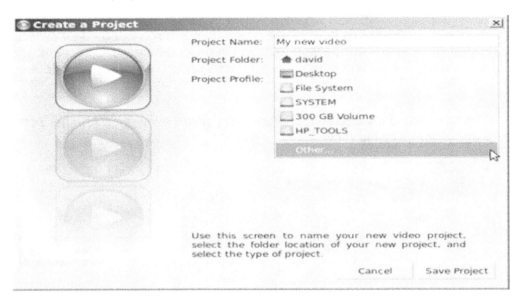

Then click other and place the project in the Videos folder. For project file, select 1024x576 16x9 PAL. Then click on Save Project.

Create a New Title
There is a 5 second Introduction built into the beginning of the new project. This is used to insert a title for your video. Click on Title, New Title to create a title.

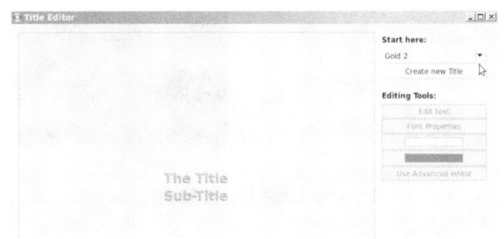

Click on the Start Here drop down arrow to choose the template you want to use. We will select Oval 2. Then click Create New Title. Then fill in the boxes.

You can change the font if you want or even install Inkscape to use the Advanced Editor to make more changes. Then click Apply. Then click on File, Import File and choose a video file to begin. Then click on the Video to start it.

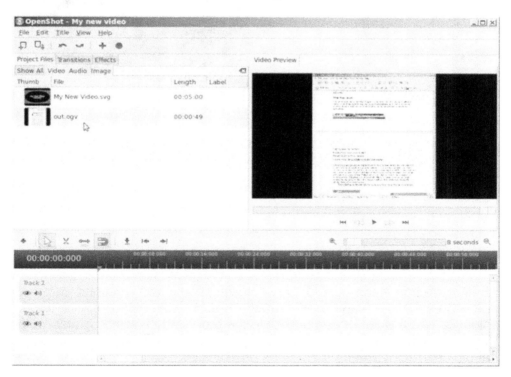

The Title starts out five minutes long. So we will need to cut most of this out. We can also add another Closing screen at the end of the video using the same tool.

To add an audio track to play with the video, first find a free audio track (usually all that is needed is to create the video at the end of the video). This is a link to thousands of options: http://videolane.com/2011/07/free-royalty-free-music-download-sites-for-videos/

Then download the audio track by right clicking on the audio track link and then choose "Save Target As." This should put the audio track in your downloads folder. Next in Open Shot, click on File, Import Files. This will add the audio track to the list. Next, add the screen shot video followed by a closing Title video.

Below are all of the six clips we have loaded for this project.

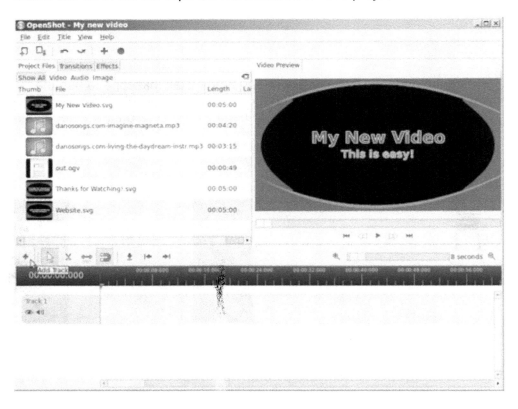

Before we add these clips to the video, we should add a second track so we have an audio track and a video track. To add a new track, click on the PLUS sign. To add a video or audio track to the project track, which is also called the Video Timeline, select the clip and drag it to the Timeline. We will put the audio on Track Two and the Videos on Track One.

The first audio track is too long. To cut a clip, use the scissors. To shorten a clip, use the blue arrows. Below is our finished video with a 5 second introduction, a 50 second video and two closing titles. In the second track, the audio track, there is an audio clip at the beginning and another audio clip at the end.

To view the video, move the red arrow to the beginning of the video tracks. Then click on PLAY at the bottom of the preview screen. To export or upload the video, click on File, Export or File Upload.

Click on **Export Video.** If you want to export the video to YouTube, you should create a YouTube compatible file. To view the video, transfer it to your video folder with the file manager, then open it with VLC Media Player. For more information on using the Open Shot Video editor, visit their online Users Manual: http://www.openshotusers.com/help/1.3/en/

To convert and optimize a longer file, use a video transcoder. A popular free video transcoder is called Transmageddon. In the next section, we will look at free open source tools to further free you from Microsoft and the NSA.

9.3 Open Source Alternatives to NSA PRISM Partners

The NSA now collects phone records on 3 billion private communications per day! In addition, they have access to all of the communications processed by their "providers."

In this section, we will look at free open source alternatives to the top nine NSA providers. In case you do not know what an NSA provider is, the NSA has produced a Top Secret presentation explaining their direct access to the databases of their providers. Please do not share this information with anyone as it is after all Top Secret. On June 29, 2013, the Washington Post published 4 more NSA slides from the documents they had been given by Edward Snowden. These slides referred to several large tech companies as "providers."

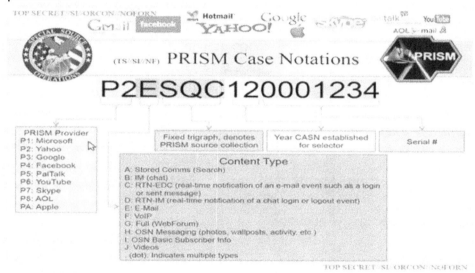

http://www.washingtonpost.com/wp-srv/special/politics/prism-collection-documents/?hpid=z1

Note that Microsoft is provider number one. The slides indicate that the NSA has access to all of each providers servers and databases without any further review from the providers. According to the slides, the NSA/FBI "deploys government equipment on private company property to retrieve matching information from a participating company, such as Microsoft or Yahoo and pass it without further review to the NSA". This is a violation not only of our own US Constitution, but also of universal human rights to privacy and freedom. We therefore propose the following "Freedom Pledge."

"I pledge to take steps to free myself, my friends and my family of NSA providers as soon as possible by finding free open source alternatives to those corporations who give data of innocent people to the NSA."

We will first outline some of the best free open source alternatives in each general category. We will then describe specific steps for moving to a better web browser, search engine, email address, and email organizer.

Free Open Source Alternatives to NSA Providers

Function	NSA Provider	Free Open Source Alternatives
Operating System	Microsoft Apple	Linux Mint 15 Mate http://www.linuxmint.com/
Web Browser	Microsoft Internet Ex Google Chrome	Mozilla Firefox, http://www.mozilla.org/en-US/firefox/new/
Web Search	Google Search Microsoft Bing	Duck Duck Go https://duckduckgo.com/
Email Service	Gmail AOL Microsoft Yahoo	Riseup.net https://help.riseup.net/en
Email Desktop Client	Microsoft Outlook	Mozilla Thunderbird https://www.mozilla.org/en-US/thunderbird/
Email Encryption		Enigmail + GNU Privacy Guard http://www.enigmail.net/home/index.php
Video Conferencing (Voice Over IP calls)	Microsoft Skype Google Talk	Jitsi Encrypted video chat https://jitsi.org/
Social Networking	Facebook Google Plus	Friendica http://friendica.com/
Instant Messaging	AOL AIM Google Talk	Pidgin http://www.pidgin.im/
Web Browser Add Ons		HTTPS Everywhere, https://www.eff.org/https-everywhere
Video Publishing	Google Youtube	MediaGoblin http://www.mediagoblin.org/

We previously showed you how to install and use the Linux Mint operating system. Linux Mint comes with Libre Office Word Processor, Mozilla Firefox Web Browser and Thunderbird Email Organizer preinstalled. So just by installing Linux Mint, you are well on your way towards freedom from Microsoft and the NSA. In this article, we will take four more steps to improve our online security.

First, we will reset our search engine to **Duck Duck Go,**
Second, we will get a new more secure email address from **riseup.net.**
Third, we will use our new email address to set up an account with
Thunderbird.
Fourth, we will add two tools to Thunderbird to give us the option of encrypting
our email. These are **Enigmail with Gnu Privacy Guard.**

Reset your Search Engine to Duck Duck Go
Duck Duck Go is a very effective search engine which does not collect your
data. Linux Mint makes it very easy for you to set Duck Duck Go as your
default search engine, Open your Firefox web browser – which comes with
Linux Mint. Then click on the dropdown arrow on the left side of the search
box and click on Manage Search Engines.

This brings up the Search Engines window.

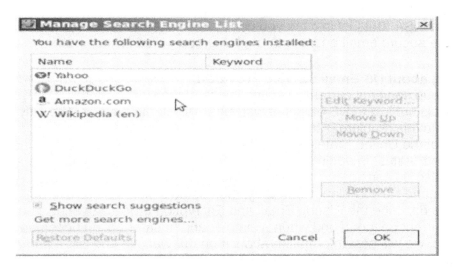

Click on **Duck Duck Go.** Then click on **Move Up** to move it to the top of the
list.
Also in the Firefox menu, click on **Edit, Preferences.**

You can make the Duck Duck Go Search Engine your home page (instead of Linux Mint) by replacing the Linux Mint link with the following link.
https://duckduckgo.com/

Get a more secure email address from riseup.net

A more secure email address simply means an email address that is hosted on a server which is not under the direct control of the NSA. This excludes AOL, GMAIL and YAHOO. If you have a website, you can use an email address associated with your website – assuming the website server is not run by the NSA. But just in case you don't have a website yet, we will add a new more secure email address through a group called Riseup.net.

Warning about US Email Service Providers:
The Riseup server is currently located inside of the United States. This means it is subject to NSA blanket warrants – similar to Lavabit. The only solution to this problem is to find and use an email provider with a server outside of the United States and not owned by a person or corporation inside the United States. In addition, servers in four other NSA partner countries should also be considered "not safe." These are Great Britain, Canada, Australia and New Zealand. Currently, there is no simple option. We will therefore describe the Riseup Email and Encryption process to show you the safest current option. If and when a simpler and/or safer option becomes available, we will post information about it on our website and issue an updated version of our Ebook. Please join our email list if you would like to be kept informed about this evolving topic.

Riseup works directly with Thunderbird. So once we have our secure Riseup email address, we can create our account with Thunderbird. Then Thunderbird works directly with an encryption program called Enigmail – which is in the Linux Mint Software Manager. So Riseup, Thunderbird and Enigmail – together with Linux Mint - make a terrific security team. To get a free Riseup email address, go to their website and click on Request an account.
https://mail.riseup.net/

There are two ways to get an account. If you know two people who already have Riseup accounts, you can get a special code from each of them and then get an account immediately. For the rest of us, fill out the brief form and wait about 24 hours. Hopefully, you will get an email telling you that you have a new account. The Request Form password page can be a challenge. Use special characters such as # and %. The password must contain letters numbers and symbols. Type in a couple of sentences about yourself. Then click Finish.

Another benefit of Riseup.net is that they also sponsor group lists. So you can replace your Yahoo or Google group with a Riseup group. Visit user.riseup.net from there, you can change your password, add email aliases, set up email filters, change your quota, and request help. To create an email list from existing email addresses, log in in mail.riseup.net. Then click on Address Book. Then click on Browse. Click on the email addresses that you wish to add. Then select from the pull-down menu "Create a new contact list in my address book" . Click on Add. Then name the address list

The Confirmation Email, sent to an email address you listed on your request form will look like this.

```
Your account has been approved and is ready for use. You are receiving
this notice because your email address is listed as a contact for this
account.
You can check and send mail by visiting https://mail.riseup.net
For documentation on your riseup.net email account, see
https://help.riseup.net
To edit your account settings, visit https://user.riseup.net
```

Once you have your email address from Riseup, there are two ways you can check your email. First, you can go to Riseup and check your email with Web Mail. Second, you can download the email to Thunderbird and then read it even when you are off line. We will first look at Riseup Web Mail.

Log in to and use Riseup Web Mail
Do not use MS Internet Explorer – Use Firefox. To check your email, go to the Riseup.net home page. https://help.riseup.net/en
Then click on Log in to Web Mail. This will take you to a secure page with the web address: https://mail.riseup.net/

The log in section is on the left with a news section on the right. There are two log in forms. One is called Squirrel Web mail and the other is called IMP Web mail. We will use the Squirrel option. But you can log in using either. When you log in, use only your user name and not the @riseup.net part. Then type in your password.

Your connection is encrypted.

If you want your email to be secure, please
read more on email security.

Webmail Server: fulvetta.riseup.net ▼

Squirrel Webmail

Check your mail using SquirrelMail 1.4.13

User: [   ]

Password: [   ]

Log in

Are you using a public computer? Enter your

password with the virtual keyboard.

This will bring up your Email screen.

Click on options to see the Options window:

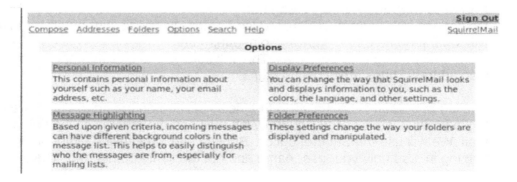

Click on **Display Preferences** to adjust your preferences.

Compose Addresses Folders Options Search Help   SquirrelMail

Options - Display Preferences

General Display Options

Theme: Default

Custom Stylesheet: Default

Language: English

Use Javascript: Autodetect

Mailbox Display Options

Number of Messages per Page: 15

Enable Alternating Row Colors:

Enable Page Selector:

Maximum Number of Pages to Show: 10

Always Show Full Date:

Length of From/To Field (0 for full): 50

Length of Subject Field (0 for full): 50

Here you can set your preferred theme color, font style, and language. There are many additional preferences on this page. When you are done setting up your account, click on Sign Out. We will next set up our Thunderbird Email Organizer.

How to Use the Virtual Keyboard to Check your Web Mail

If you are using a computer in a public setting such as a library, you can enter your password by using the *Virtual Keyboard*. It offers your system another layer of protection from *key-logger* programs. Key-logger programs are designed to monitor a user's physical key strokes to figure out passwords, user names and other vital information. Virtual keyboards allow users to circumvent this security vulnerability, by letting the user enter her/his password using the mouse.

To use the *Virtual Keyboard*, go to the Riseup secure page listed above. Then click on Virtual Keyboard to activate it.

Set up Thunderbird Email Client

Thunderbird is an email organizer similar to Microsoft Outlook but without the connection to the NSA. Thunderbird is automatically installed on Linux Mint and has many features including including: IMAP and POP support, multiple accounts, quick search, advanced spam controls, RSS, virtual folder views, message filtering, address book, and support for OpenPGP encryption.

Start the Account Wizard

Go to the Mint Menu and drag the Thunderbird icon to the desktop. Then click on Thunderbird to open it. It will ask you if you want a new email address. These cost $12 per year. So click on Skip this and use my existing email:

Click on Continue. If the wizard does not open, choose the menu item **Edit > Account Settings. Then click on Add Mail Account. Either way, you will get to the Mail Account.** Thunderbird will pull the incoming and outgoing settings into the next window. Now you need to decide if you want to use IMAP or POP. It will by default pick IMAP. If you want POP to keep your email on your own computer, change the selection to POP. This will change the Incoming setting.

Then click Done. This will add your account to Thunderbird.

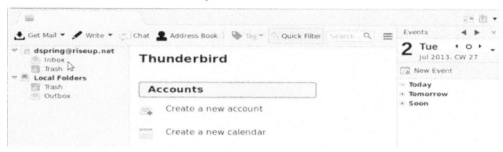

Click on **Get Mail** and select your email address to load your emails. There are two icons in the upper right. Click on the Calendar icon to bring up this screen.

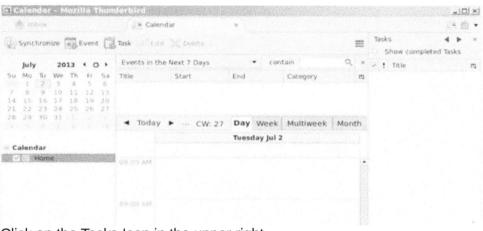

Click on the Tasks Icon in the upper right.

Forwarding other email addresses to your riseup.net email account
Each email address is a little different. But all email accounts allow you to forward existing email accounts to a new email account. As for the existing emails, these are harder to transfer. Consider leaving them and processing them with your old email provider.

Import addresses from your former email box.

First, we need to go to our old email provider and export a copy of our address book as a text or comma separated file. Open you old account and click on Contacts, then Tools, then Export. Then store this on our computer in the Downloads folder. Next, from the Thunderbird Inbox tab, click on Tools Import.

Select **Address Book**. Then select **Next.**

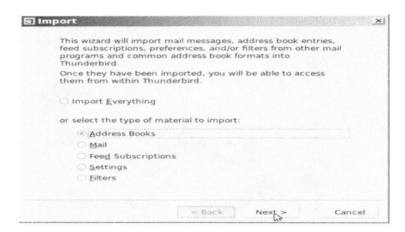

Leave it set for text file and click **Next.**

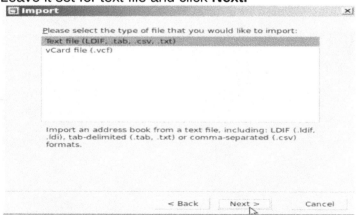

Change the Drop Down arrow at the bottom to All Files. This will bring up the file you want. Then select it. Then click Open. Then for the window called Import Address Book, click OK. Then click Finish. You can now send a test email to your old email address or anyone on your address list. To get help with Thunderbird, go to their help page.
https://support.mozillamessaging.com/en-US/home

Improve your Email Security

From the upper right corner of the Inbox tab, click on the box.

Then click on preferences, then account settings. For enhanced message security, consider setting up Enigmail with Thunderbird to get OpenPGP setup. Enigmail: get started in no time encrypting and decrypting emails and verifying that emails you receive are from the people who you expect them to be

Create an Open PGP key pair using Seahorse

Seahorse is a free tool for creating and managing OpenPGP keys, securely storing passwords, and creating and managing SSH certificates. To get Seahorse, go to the Mint Menu and click on the Software Manager and type Seahorse into the Search box.

There are several versions of Seahorse. We will stick with the main one. Click on it to open it. Then click on Install. Then type **Enigmail** into the Search box.

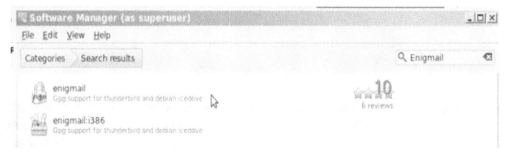

Click on this, then click on Install. Then go to the Mint Menu, Applications, Preferences, then Passwords and Keys and click on Seahorse to open it.

Click on File, New. Then select PGP Key.

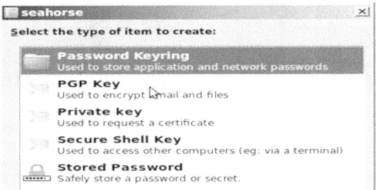

Enter your personal information, select your key encryption type, key strength, and when you want your key to expire. Your name can be anything you want, not necessarily your real name. If you want to use your OpenPGP key for encrypting email, put the email address you want to use with encryption in the "Email Address" box. You do not need to click the Advanced option. Just click Create.

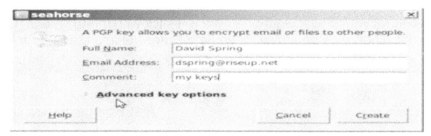

Then type in a strong password twice. However be careful to store this password in a reliable place or use something you can remember. If you ever forget this password, you will lose all emails and data associated with this password.

Type in something and move the mouse to get random data for the key.

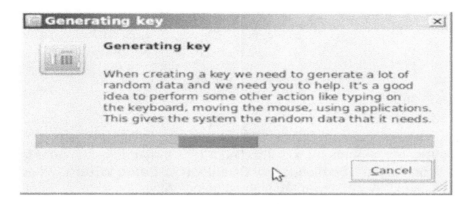

It will take a couple of minutes to generate the key so be patient. Once you have your public private key pair, it will show up at the top of the list.

You can manage the key options, export the public key, change the password, delete and/or revoke the key, and perform other key adjustments through the Seahorse user interface.

When restarting Thunderbird, the black box is now hidden. To get it to show all of the time, right click in the tool bar to bring up the hidden menu bar. Then click on the box to the left of the menu bar.

This is much better.

Install Enigmail and Run the OpenPGP Setup Wizard
After you have generated your key pair, and have downloaded Enigmail, open Thunderbird and from the Inbox tab, restart Thunderbird and get the Menu to show as above. Then click on Tools, Addons, Extensions and verify that Enigmail is installed properly.

If it says "Disable" that means it is installed. Close the Addons Manager tab. Then click on the new top-menu entry **OpenPGP → Setup Wizard.** Select **Yes** and hit **Next.** We just want to sign outgoing emails for some and not all. So click No. Then next. **Signing does not encrypt emails**—it places your digital signature on your outgoing emails to allow others to verify that you sent the email. It is recommended **not to sign all of your outgoing emails** as it strongly links you to everything you send out via unencrypted email directly to yourself. It's best just to encrypt emails to people you know who supports encryption.

Choose whether you want to encrypt all of your outgoing emails by default. **This is not recommended** as it is cumbersome if your recipient doesn't support encryption.

You can setup encryption rules later on, which will enable you to always send encrypted emails under conditions you determine. So leave it set for No. Then click Next. For "Make Open PGP Work More Reliably" click YES. Then click Next.

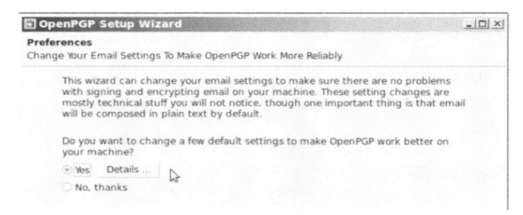

Choosing YES will make changes in Thunderbird recommended by OpenPGP. This will disable HTML composing meaning you will not be able to send HTML newsletters through this account. Clicking next, the following screen appears.

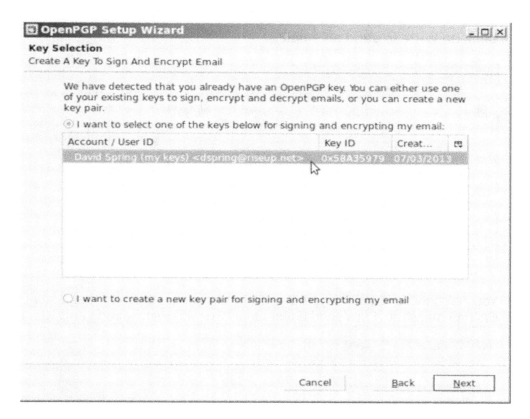

Select an existing key to use. Then click Next.

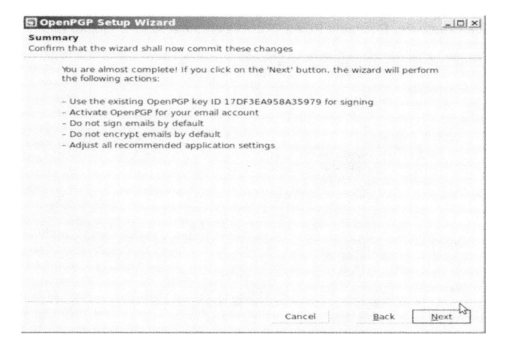

Review the proposed changes. Then click **Next.** Then click **Finish**.

Click on Write to send an email:

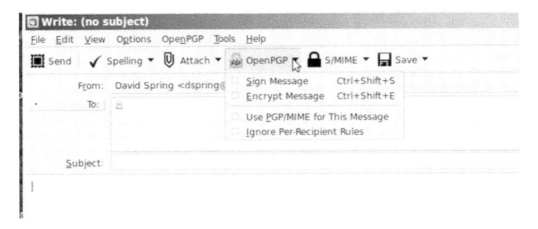

You can now send an encrypted email by clicking on OpenPGP and selecting Encrypt message. Let's send a test email. The following screen appears.

Click Create Per Recipient Rules. This will create a special rule for this person.

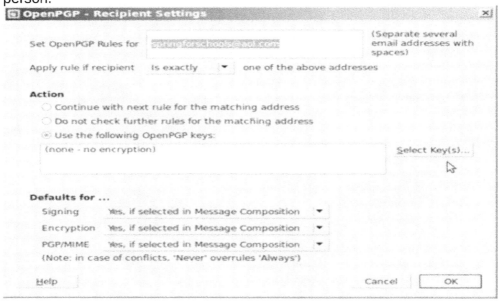

Choose the **Action** to be applied upon matching the rule. For this example, choose **Use the following OpenPGP keys:** and press the **Select Key(s)…** button. In the box that pops up from that button, select the OpenPGP key for the person to whom you're sending email.

If you don't have their public key, press the **Download missing keys** button, at the bottom of the window which will search the key servers for the email(s) you entered in the matching box. There are four possible data bases the key may be stored in. If you try all four and they all say "Sorry" then this person does not have a key and cannot receive your encrypted email. Click Cancel to end encryption for this person. The next thing you need to do is send your friend a copy of this book and encourage them to install Linux Mint on their computer and follow the steps described in this chapter. You can then exchange keys with them – or have both of you post your public keys and then you will be able to exchange encrypted emails with them.

What is all of this about public and private keys?

OpenPGP splits its keys in two parts: **public** and **private** key with different purposes. The public key: used to encrypt a message. It can and should be available to everybody. The private key is used to decrypt a message. It needs to be stored securely. Access is restricted by password.

Key exchange: Before one can send encrypted emails to a peer it is required to have the public key of this person. Therefore before a secure communication can happen between two partners it is required to exchange the public keys of each other. There are multiple ways the public key can be distributed. The most common way is to upload the key to a key server. The second way is to publish the key on a website – like a personal or a club website.

The third way is to send by email to specific correspondence partners. To export a key by any of these three ways, open Thunderbird, then click on OpenPGP. Then select Key Management. Then click File, Send public key by email. Or select the key you want to send, then right click to see several options.

What about sending encrypted emails with Windows or Apple?

There are so many security holes with both Windows and Apple, that this would be pretty much a waste of your time. Below are the comments on this subject from the folks at Riseup.net.

> "Windows is **not recommended** for use as a secure communication platform. The tendencies in Windows lean towards very lax security. There is also a multitude of prebuilt exploits for windows that make it easier for attackers to compromise. These include widespread distribution of malware/trojans/viruses that could log key strokes, bypassing encryption schemes and/or logging other information. Also targeted hacking and malware installation is actively used by governmental agencies with Windows being most susceptible.

Also use of an unencrypted file system, main encryption tool is proprietary and cannot be scrutinized for exploits, back doors, or other weaknesses. Also user accounts are administrators by default. Also since Windows is proprietary and closed-source, there is no outside scrutiny for defects, back doors, or anything that "phones home". You're trusting Microsoft completely with whatever secrets you choose to put on your computer. Microsoft does not have a good track record in terms of protecting privacy.

Mac OS X is **not recommended** for use as a secure communication platform. While there are fewer exploits and a better security model than windows, OS X has demonstrated a poor security patch speed and has a large quantity of proprietary software making it not capable of scrutiny for defects, back doors, or anything that "phones home". Furthermore, it offers features that can be exploited by hackers or abused by governments or corporations. For example the web cam can be remotely turned on, offered as a "feature" if the laptop gets stolen, which could be abused or exploited to violate your privacy. Also the file system not encrypted by default and may have inadequate security."

Now that we have a secure email system, in the next section we will look at how to get a more secure startup program than either BIOS or UEFI.

9.4 How to use Windows Programs in Linux Mint

> *In this section we will review how to use a free Linux program called Play On Linux to install and use Windows based programs such as Microsoft Office in Linux Mint.*

Folks are usually shocked to learn that not only can Libre Office open and manage MS Word documents but Linux can open and manage MS Windows programs. Of course, if you followed the steps to set up your computer in a Dual Boot of Windows and Linux, you may be wondering, why not just use Windows to run Windows based programs? There are several reasons to run Windows programs in Linux rather than Windows.

First, you may not want to take the time to shut down Linux and open Windows. In writing an ebook, you may want to go back and forth between the Amazon Kindle (which is only available currently as a Windows program) and Sigil (which is mainly a Linux program). Play On Linux creates a "virtual Windows machine" inside of Linux which allows you to view Kindle Books inside of Linux.

Second, you may not trust the Windows operating system any more. For example, you have been using Windows XP and it is after April 2014. Because Windows XP is no longer supported by Microsoft, even opening Windows XP after April 2014 will be a risky business. Thankfully, all of the programs you once ran on Windows XP, such as MS Office, can also be run on Linux using Play On Linux.

Third, you may eventually want to get rid of Windows completely – either because you don't want to be monitored by the NSA or you want to free up space for Linux on your hard drive – or you just don't like Microsoft. Learning how to use Play On Linux will make this decision easier once you know that your Windows programs can still be run even if you deleted the Windows partition from your computer.

Play on Linux versus Wine
Wine is the most common Linux program used to play Windows based programs. However, Wine can be difficult to learn and use. Play On Linux has a much better User Interface – meaning you just click on buttons rather than entering computer commands into a terminal. We will therefore use Play On Linux.

Download Play on Linux
Play On Linux is most easily downloaded from the Linux Mint Software Center. Type Wine into the search box but do not select Wine. Instead select Play on Linux.

Then click Install. It is a big program and will take a while to install. Note that Play On Linux will install whatever versions of Wine you need for any Windows program so you do NOT need to also install Wine.

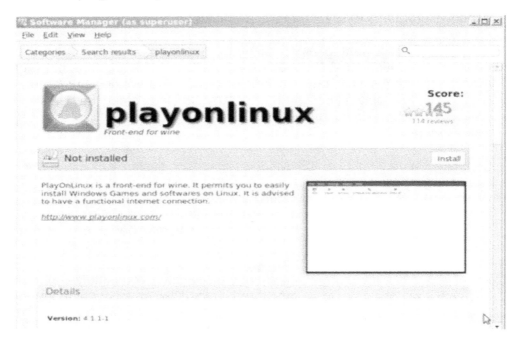

During installation, it will ask you to accept the Microsoft license. Check the box and click Yes to finish the install. During installation, if you have a Libre Writer document open do not worry of the Writer fonts become compressed. This will resolve itself once the install is complete. Also do not worry if the installation progress bar becomes stuck at 67%. Wait a few minutes. Then close the Software Manager. You should now find Play On Linux listed in your Mint Applications Menu under Games.

First, make sure you are connected to the Internet. Then move Play On Linux to your desktop and click on the icon to open it. It may warn you that you are missing a program.

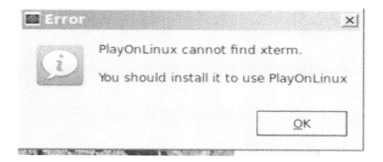

Go to the Software Center, search and install this extra program.

On your first use, the Play on Linux wizard will appear.

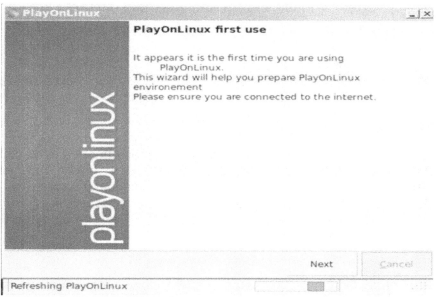

Click Next. Then Next again.

If you are using Linux Mint 15, it may say that an updated version, 4.2.1 is available. For most older Windows programs, it is not necessary to update to 4.2.1. If you are using Linux Mint 16, it may simply come with version 4.2.1.

Install a "Supported" Windows Program... Example Internet Explorer 8

Internet Explorer 8 was and still is a terrible web browser. Firefox, which comes free and pre-installed on Linux Mint is much better. So you may be wondering why we are showing you how to install IE 8 on Linux Mint. The answer is that if you are building websites, you will want to review how they look on Internet Explorer as many people still have and use IE as their web browser.

The other reason we are showing you how to install Internet Explorer is to convince you that it is a stand alone program and does not need to be placed inside of the heart of the Windows operating system for it to work. The fact that Internet Explorer works in Linux is strong evidence that the only reason Microsoft placed a web browser inside of their operating system is to deliberately create an insecure operating system so that NSA could access all data from all Windows computers.

To install any Play On Linux (POL) supported Windows program is very easy. Just open POL and click on the INSTALL button at the top of the screen. This brings up the Install Menu.

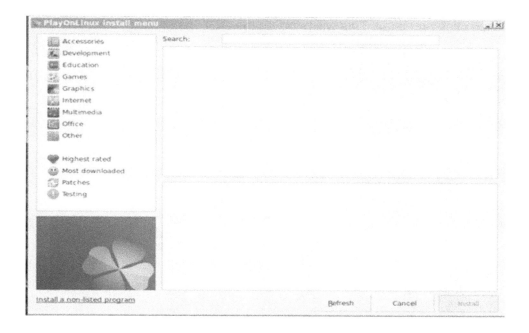

You can review all of the supported programs by clicking on the various categories. There are more than one hundred supported Windows programs – including Office 2003, Office 2007 and Office 2010 (you will need your Microsoft "key" to use these programs. But Internet Explorer 8 is free so we will use this as an example to get you started. Click on **Internet** to view all of the Windows Internet programs you can install. Scroll down and select Internet Explorer 8.

Then click on Install. This will bring up the POL Installation Wizard.

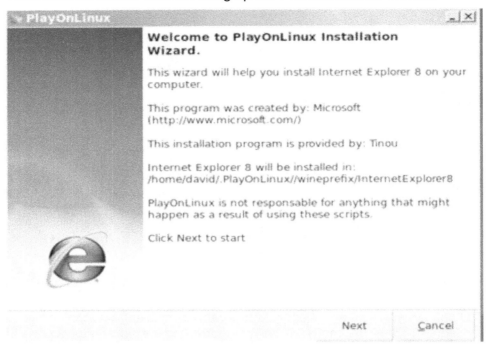

Click Next. POL will first download whatever version of Wine is needed for the Windows program you are installing. POL will then download Internet Explorer 8.

Play on Linux will then open the IE 8 install screen.

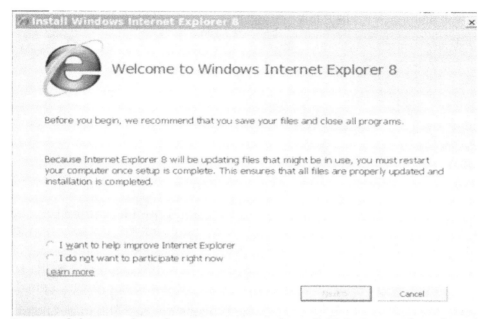

Be careful to read each screen as you install IE 8. Do Not install Updates and the Malicious Software Removal Tool. Uncheck this box:

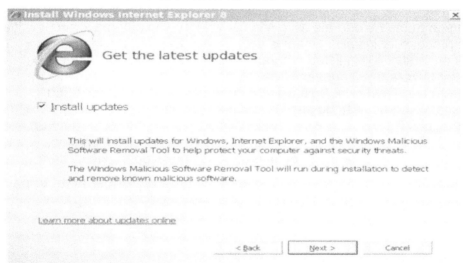

Then click Next. Click on the Restart Now button to finish the process. This will not restart your computer or your Linux Mint program. It will merely restart the POL virtual machine. You should now have an Internet Explorer 8 icon on your desktop.

You will also have an IE 8 link on your Play on Linus start screen.

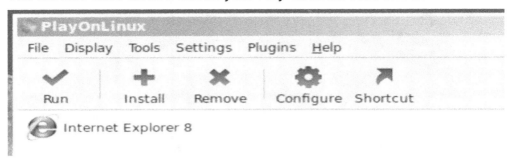

Click on either of these to start Internet Explorer. **When IE comes up, choose custom settings and keep current search engines without any updates. And turn off accelerators. And turn off the smart screen filter.**

You can add Bing Search or Yahoo search to IE 8. Be aware that both of these search engines are basically run by the NSA and are heavily censored.

As a homework exercise, use the same process to install the free Kindle Reader.

Install an Unsupported Windows program

There are some programs which do not yet have an automatic script written. The process for installing them is very similar. Click on the Install button. Then click on "install a non-listed program" which is at the bottom of the next screen. A wizard will appear. Click Next. Then install a program in a new virtual drive. Then click Next. For the program name, type in a short descriptive name, with no spaces, such as KindlePreviewer. Click Next, then Next again. Browse to the installation file which may be a CD, autorun.exe or downloaded .exe file. Then run through the normal installation steps just as you would if you were installing it into the Windows operating system.

What is terrific about Play on Linux is that you no longer need to pay the "Microsoft Windows Tax" just to use Windows based programs.

What's Next?

In the final chapter, we will provide a "Quick Start" review of the most essential steps for installing Linux Mint as a Dual Boot on your computer. We will then cover some important final steps to free yourself from Microsoft and the NSA.

Chapter 10... Linux Mint Quick Start Guide

Chapter 10 includes the following four sections:
10.1 Back up your computer and partition your hard drive
10.2 Dual Boot Linux Mint with Windows XP or Windows 7
10.3 Easy Steps and Free Tools for Using Linux Mint
10.4 Final Steps to Freedom

In the previous nine chapters, we have presented detailed information not only on what steps to take to install Linux Mint, but also why you should take these steps. However, if you are already convinced about why you should install Linux Mint, this last chapter is a condensed version of the book which focuses only on the how of installing Linux Mint. These steps assume that you are part of the 80% of all Windows users who are using Windows XP or Windows 7 and are looking for a safer alternative by dual booting Linux with Windows. If you are using Windows 8, or any other computer with UEFI, as we explained in the last chapter, there really is no safe way to run such a computer and your best bet is to return it to where you bought it and ask for a refund.

Section 10.1 is a condensed version of sections 6.1 and 6.2 which lists the steps for backing up your computer and creating space for Linux on your hard drive.
Section 10.2 is a condensed version of section 6.3 – only instead of providing several options, we describe just the recommended steps for dual booting Linux Mint with Windows XP or Windows 7. .
Section 10.3 is a brief summary of the most important steps to take in using Linux Mint – including a list of important free extensions you should consider adding to Mint from the Mint Software Center.
Section 10.4 describes the most important step we all must take at if we truly want to be free from Microsoft and the NSA. This step is to boycott any computer which has the UEFI startup chip on it – including all Windows 8 computers – and demand that our next computer has the **Core Boot** startup program.

Above is the Award BIOS startup chip. Sadly, thanks to Microsoft, we can no longer buy a computer with this chip. The only safe solution left is to demand that computer manufacturers install Core Boot.

10.1 Back up your computer and partition your hard drive

> The first step before setting up a dual boot with Linux Mint is creating at least one backup of your current computer. Once this is done, we will partition or divide the hard drive in order to create room to add Linux Mint.

Dual booting simply means to install more than one operating system on your computer. The point of dual booting is to allow you to test and experiment with a new operating system, such as Linux, while still keeping your old operating system, such as Windows. Microsoft has billions of dollars at stake and has done everything in their power to create obstacles to prevent you from dual booting Linux onto your computer. In chapter 6, we presented several ways to back up, partition and install Linux as a dual boot on your computer. In this chapter, we will summarize only the most recommended processes for a computer which is currently using Windows XP or Windows 7.

Make and follow a Plan to Safely Backup all of your data
Our plan is to first backup the your computer data using the following 9 steps:
Step #1: Gather your backup tools.
Step #2: Organize your files into folders.
Step #3: Clean Up and Defragment your disc.
Step #4: Copy your data on a USB Flash Drive.
Step #5: Create a copy of your C Drive and Data on a USB External Drive.
Step #6: Create a copy of your Recovery Media file onto a USB Flash Drive.
Step #7: Create a USB Flash Drive copy of your HP Recovery Partition.
Step #8: Delete the Recovery partition.
Step #9: Make a record of all of our Windows program keys.

In the next section, we will shrink the C drive partition and use the free space to create an Extended Partition for Dual Boot of Windows XP or Windows 7 and Linux using a Linux installation tool.

Step #1: Gather your backup tools
In case your computer completely crashes and you cannot even restart it, you really want to store your important data in some other place besides on your computer. We will need to get several tools and follow several steps to back up our computer. First, we will need a **32 GB USB Flash Drive** to copy all important images and files to. If you do not already have a 32 GB USB Flash Drive, this will cost about $30.

Second, we need a **1 Terabyte USB external hard drive** to create a complete system backup. The point of this backup is to restore your computer to its current state as opposed to the recovery backup which deletes your current files and programs and restore the computer to the state it was in the day you bought it.

A 1TB USB hard drive will cost about $70. If you are on a limited budget, you can skip this step as your important data will be on the 32 GB Flash Drive and your Windows Recovery file will be on a separate 4 GB USB flash drive.

Third, at step #5, we need to install a free program for making backup copies of our complete system. We will create this system backup using a free tool called **Macrium Reflect**.

Fourth, in Step 6, we will need **another 4GB or more Flash Drive** to create "recovery media" also using Macrium Reflect. The recovery media file is only 1.7 GB so almost any dependable flash drive will do. This will cost about $10.

Fifth, we will need **another 32 GB Flash Drive** to create a copy of the Recovery Disc folder which comes with HP. It is important to note that this Recovery disc, if it were ever used, would wipe out all of our programs and system changes we have made – including partition changes and any documents and programs associated with Linux to return the computer back to the initial condition it was in the day we bought it. So this Recovery should be considered the "option of last resort." The benefit of creating this recovery flash drive – which can be done only once – is that we can delete the partition with the Recovery folder which will free up a partition for us to add Linux to our computer. This will cost about $30.

Sixth, we will need to use a free tool for getting the "keys" to our important Windows programs. After we have completed all of these backup steps, we will be ready to delete the backup partition and begin installing Linux into the resulting empty space.

We will also need a 4 to 8 GB USB flash drive to put your open source operating system program(s) on. This will also cost about $10.

Step #2: Organize and consolidate your files into folders.
To back up your images, documents, files, folders and other important data, first, go to the office supply store and pick up a reliable 32 GB Flash Drive. This is generally enough to hold all your images, videos and documents. If you are like most Windows users, your files will be stored in three or four different places. Create folders and consolidate all files and folders inside of just a few folders.

Step #3: Clean Up and Defragment your disc.
Before you make a copy of your files to a USB Flash Drive, you should take a couple of minutes to clean up and defragment your disc. To do this, go to the Start Menu and click on **control panel**.

Then click on **Performance Information and Tools**. Then click on **Open Disc Cleanup**:

Click **OK** to delete these unneeded files. When done, go back to **Performance Information** and **Tools** and click on **Advanced Tools.** Then click on **Open Disk Defragmenter**.

Select the **C Drive** and click on **Defragment Disk**. It will take several minutes to analyze the disc and even more time to defragment it.

Step #4: Copy your important data to a USB Flash Drive

Insert the 32 GB flash drive in a USB port. Then right click on these folders to copy them to the Flash Drive which is shown below as Removable Disk F:

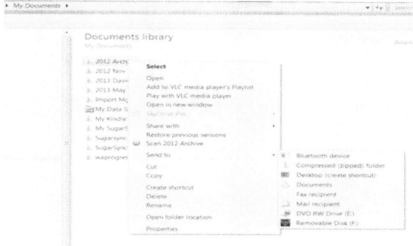

When you have all of your folders copied, then safely remove the flash drive and label it with the date of the copy.

Step #5: Create a copy of your C Drive and Data on a USB External Drive.

There are lots of reliable, compact and economical USB external hard drives. It is useful to get one with a USB 3.0 connection which is ten times faster than USB 2.0. But anything will do. Next download the free Macrium Reflect program: http://www.macrium.com/reflectfree.aspx

After installing this program, the Reflect icon will be placed on your desktop. Click on the Icon to open the program:

Click on the option '**Create an Image of the partition(s) required to backup and restore Windows'** located in the top left hand pane of the application window to start the backup wizard. It is highlighted in red in the previous image.

The wizard should start as shown below. You will note that all partitions are displayed in the wizard, but only the system partition and the C partition have been selected because these are what are needed to restore the current system.

Next we select a location for the backup. Assuming your USB external drive is plugged into a USB port, select it. In my case, the destination was the F drive:

Click Next. It will then take a disc image. Click Finish. Then click OK to run the backup. Assuming the System and C drives are selected, click Next. To back up 150 GB in data will take about 45 minutes.

When the backup has completed click **'OK'** to shut down the message box and then click **'Close'** to close the backup window. Your system is now backed up.

The file is saved as an XML file. Close the Macrium program. To view the backup file in Windows, click on the **Start** Menu, then **Computer**, then click on the **USB Hard Drive**. To eject the USB hard drive, click on the eject icon. When is says Safe to Remove USB, then remove the USB.

Step #6: Create a copy of your Recovery Media file onto a USB Flash Drive.

In addition to creating a complete system backup on your hard drive, Macrium Reflect Free version also helps you create "rescue media" for your Windows 7 backup plan. We will put this rescue media on a separate USB Flash Drive. First, insert the Flash Drive into the USB port. Also make sure you have opened your web browser and that it is connected to a high speed internet connection and that you have at least one hour to complete this task. Then open Macrium Reflect and click on the "**Other Tasks**" tab:

Click on **Create bootable rescue media.** Then click Yes.

Leave it as **Windows PE** and click Next. Put in a 2 GB or more Flash Drive to put the Rescue Media on. We also need internet access to download the following file from Microsoft.

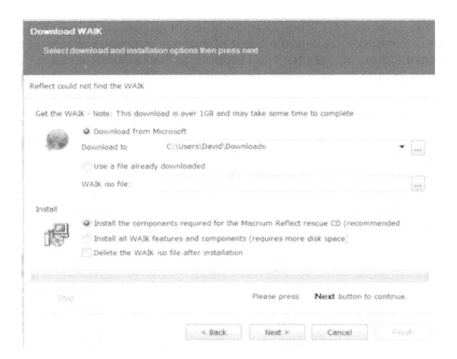

Assuming we are attached to the internet, and that we have a USB Flash drive plugged in to our computer, click Next. The file is 1.67 GB. Windows will want to install this folder inside of program files.

Instead click **Browse** and select our Flash drive and install the folder there. Then click Next. After it is complete. Click Close. Then go back to the Rescue Media Wizard screen. Macrium Reflect needs to initialize this pen drive. All existing data will be lost if you continue – but this warning only applies to any data on your USB drive (which should be blank).

So for Proceed with operation? click Yes. We now have a recovery media on our Flash Drive. We will next make a copy of the HP Recovery partition and then make a record of our Windows program keys.

Step #7: Create a USB Flash Drive copy of your HP Recovery Partition.
If you have a Windows XP computer, you can likely skip this step as your recovery partition is likely already on a separate CD and only two partitions have been taken on your hard drive. To see what your current partitions looked like on a Windows XP computer, go to **Control Panel, Administrative Tools, Computer Management, Storage, Disk Management:**

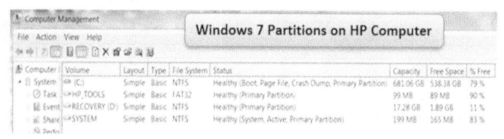

Because there are two partitions left, you could install Linux on one of them. However, fast forward to 2010 and look at Windows 7 partitions on one of the most common laptop from HP:

Notice the difference? On a Windows 7 HP laptop, all four partitions have been taken. We now have a partition called HP-TOOLS which controls the BIOS computer start settings – and we have another partition called RECOVERY – which is the backup folder for your Windows 7 program (but not the data on your C Drive). If and only if all four partitions have been taken, then we need to create a USB Flash Drive copy of this recovery partition in order to delete it from the hard drive. Use a blank USB flash drive with at least 32 GB of memory. Use a name brand from a manufacturer you trust. Then be sure to label this USB when you are done and do not try to use this USB Recovery for anything else.

Disable User Account Control
Temporarily disable Windows User Account Control if User Account Control is enabled. Doing so decreases the chances of encountering problems during the process.

Disabling User Account Control
Click **Start**, **Control Panel** , and then click **User Accounts** .

Then click **Change User Account Control settings.**

To turn off User Account Control, move the slider to the bottom (**Never notify**). Then click **OK.** Then restart your computer for this change to take effect.

Print out these instructions as you will have to close all other programs while creating this Recovery Disk.

Save the HP recovery file to a USB flash drive

HP recovery software allows you to make *only one recovery backup* . These backup files contain the original operating system, drivers, and application software that shipped with the computer. Making a copy of this file takes about 30 minutes. Disconnect from the Internet and close all other software. Then insert the flash drive. If a window opens asking you if you want to use the flash drive for files or backup, just close the window. This is not going to be a backup. It will be a recovery tool. From the Windows Desktop, click **Start**, and enter recovery manager into the Search field. Alternately, select **Start > All Programs > HP > HP Recovery Manager > HP Recovery Media Creation** If a User Account Control message opens, click **Yes** or enter your log in password, whichever is required. A Recovery Manager window opens.

Click **Recovery Media Creation** NOTE: If Recovery Media Creation is not available (grayed out), then a recovery image has already been created. Due to license restrictions, only one set of recovery media can be created. Any new recovery media must be ordered online or obtained using another method.

Recovery Manager: Recovery Media selection

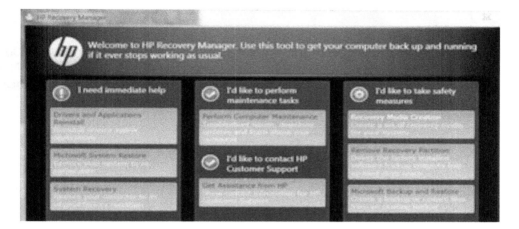

Select R**ecovery Media Creation with a USB flash drive** , and click **Next**. Click **Create recovery media with a USB flash drive** , and then click **Next** .A verification window opens, showing the hard drive locations for removable discs. Select the location for your USB flash drive, and then click **Next.**

A Recovery Manager message opens stating that the flash drive will be formatted. Click **OK** to format the USB flash drive and continue. NOTE: Formatting this flash drive deletes any files on the drive.

Wait while the software creates your recovery media. Recovery image creation happens in two stages. First, the software copies the files to the USB flash drive.
Second, the software verifies the files that files were copied successfully. A screen displays for each process. Click **Finish** when Recovery Manager has created the recovery media.

Next, we need to make sure we safely remove the USB. If a warning comes up that the USB cannot safely be removed because it is still running, then turn off the computer before removing the USB. Store the USB flash drive in a safe, protected place. If you attempt to save another recovery image to a USB flash drive after successfully saving one recovery image, a screen displays stating that only one recovery set is allowed. The only choice is to click **OK** and exit the program. To verify that our recovery image has been made, click on the Recovery Manager and attempt to create another recovery. You should see a screen noting that your recovery file was successfully made.

Step #8: Delete the Recovery partition.
While you can remove the HP Recovery partition through the Windows Partition Manager, we will instead use the HP Recovery Manager to remove this backup file because the HP tool is safer than the Windows tool. This HP tool is the same tool we used to create the USB Flash Drive of the Recovery file. To remove the recovery partition, click **Start**, type Recovery in the search field, and click on **Recovery Manager** when it appears in the program list to open the Recovery Manager window. Click **Advanced options**.

Select the **Remove recovery partition** option and click **Next**. When prompted to verify that you want to delete the partition, select the **Yes** option, and click **Next**. Allow the removal process to continue and restart the PC. Now check to see if the partition was removed. Go to **Control Panel, Admin Tools, Computer Management, Storage, Disk management:**

Volume	Layout	Type	File System	Status
(C:)	Simple	Basic	NTFS	Healthy (Boot, Page File, Crash Dump, Primary
HP_TOOLS	Simple	Basic	FAT32	Healthy (Primary Partition)
SYSTEM	Simple	Basic	NTFS	Healthy (System, Active, Primary Partition)

We now have only three partitions! Mission accomplished!

Step #9: Make a record of all of our Windows program keys.
The easiest way to get the product keys for Windows XP or Windows 7 and Office is to use the free **Belarc Advisor**. Store these keys on a jump drive - not on your C Drive. This way if the computer crashes completely, we can reinstall everything using the product keys. Having the product keys helps if the original installs were done online and we do not have CDs to reinstall programs from. To download Belarc Advisor, go to:
http://www.belarc.com/free_download.html

Then go to Downloads folder and find this file. Right click and select **Run as administrator.** It will create a local screen with all of your software and hardware information – including all product keys. All of your PC profile information is kept private on your PC and is not sent to any Web server.

Now that we have backed up all of our files and removed the HP Recovery partition, we are almost ready to dual boot Linux onto our computer. There are only a couple of things we still need to do. The first is to create a bootable flash drive with Linux Mint Mate on it. The second is to shrink our C drive to create more room for Linux Mint. We will cover both of these tasks in the next section.

10.2 Dual Boot Linux with Windows XP or Windows 7

This section reviews how to add Linux Mint to a computer that already has Windows XP or Windows 7 on it so that you can use either system.

We will now show you how to create a Dual Boot system on your home computer so that you can have more than one operating system. During this process, we will replace the Windows Boot Manager with a better boot manager called the GRUB 2 Boot Manager which automatically adds Windows to it.

Download the Linux Mint 15 x64 bit ISO file from
http://www.linuxmint.com/download.php

Because I am installing Linux Mint on a 64 bit computer with at least 4 GB of RAM, I have selected the 64 bit version. But if you have a computer with less than 4 GB of RAM which is a 32 bit computer, then select the 32 bit version of Linux Mint Mate. Then on the next screen, scroll down the list to your country and pick one of the download centers. This will bring up the Download Notification screen. Click Save. It is a very large 1 GB file and may take up to an hour to download. Be patient and do not try to access the file until it is fully downloaded. The next step is to download UNetbootin to create a Live USB.

Use UNetbootin to create a Live USB Flash Drive
UNetbootin allows you to create bootable Live USB drives for Linux distributions. You will need a USB Flash Drive which is at least 2 GB. It should be empty and in a format of FAT32. To verify that your USB is FAT32, in your Windows computer, go to Start, My Computer and right click on the USB Drive. Then click on **Properties.** If it is not FAT32, click on **Properties, Format** to reformat it. Once formatted, note the Mount Point (Drive Letter) of the drive (in my case it is D:). You will need to know this later. Remove any other USB drive (including external hard drives) connected to your PC except for the one you want to use for the installation.

Download UNetbootin to your computer

Go to the following link to download it. http://unetbootin.sourceforge.net/
There are three different versions of UNetbootin, one for Windows, one for Linux and one for Mac OS X. The resulting USB drives are bootable only on PCs (not on Macs). Pick the version for your current operating system and download it:

Then save this file to your Downloads folder. You won't have to install it, it will run directly from the downloaded file. Then go to your Downloads folder and find the file UNetbootin Setup.exe. Right click on the file and select **Run as Administrator:**

Select the **Disk Image** option. Then browse for and select the Linux Mint 15 ISO which should also be in your Downloads folder. Mark sure the Target Type is set for your USB Drive and that the Drive is set for the Mount point (D). Turn off all other programs. Then click OK. The bootable "live" USB creation process will take a few minutes. When it is done, it will show a screen confirming you have a Live USB. **Click Exit rather than reboot** as we need to first change the BIOS boot order. Label your Live USB and do not use this USB for anything else.

Shrink the Volume on the Windows C Partition

Our next task is to resize the Windows C partition. This will give us the space we need to add partitions for Linux Mint. To use the automatic install method, it is important to resize the C drive before we install Linux. We will therefore use the Windows Partition Manager to resize the C Drive. In Windows XP or Windows 7, go to Start Button and click on the **Control Panel**. Then click on **Administrative Tools,** then **Computer Managemen**t, then **Storage,** then **Disc Management**.

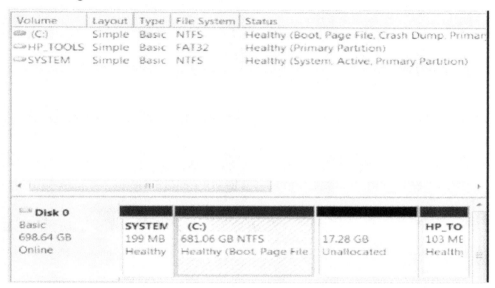

After deleting the Recovery Partition, we have 17 GB of Unallocated space and a lot of GB in the C drive. What we want to do is to move about half of the space from the C drive to the Unallocated space so we can use this to install Linux. Click on the **C drive box** above to select it. Then right click to bring up the **Partition Edit** screen. Click on **Shrink Volume.** It will take Windows a couple of minutes to figure out how much space is available on the C drive to shrink. It will then display the following screen:

Do not trust the "size available to shrink space" as it is not accurate. Instead you should only take about half of the space that is indicated as available. After putting in that number, click **Shrink.** It will take a few minutes for the C drive to be resized. When it is done shrinking, the space will be moved to the Unallocated space. Now we can close Windows.

Change the Boot Order in your computer BIOS settings

Our next step is to set the boot order in BIOS to use the USB Live Flash Drive instead of the Windows Boot Manager. This requires turning off and restarting your computer. **BEFORE RESTARTING YOUR COMPUTER TO CHANGE THE BOOT ORDER, PRINT OUT A COPY OF THE REST OF THIS SECTION as you will not have access to this screen while you are installing Linux Mint!**

Now that we have created a Live USB with UNetbootin, leave the Live USB in the USB port or if you took it out, reinsert it. The next step is to change the BIOS Boot Order so that the Live USB is the first item selected. Restart your computer and press the appropriate button (usually F1, F2, F12, or ESC) while your computer is starting to get to your BIOS menu.

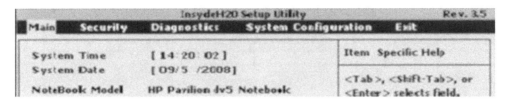

Then use the right arrow on your key board to select **System Configuration**.

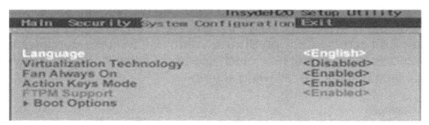

Then use the Down arrow to select **Boot Options**. Then press Enter on your keyboard to start the Boot Options screen.

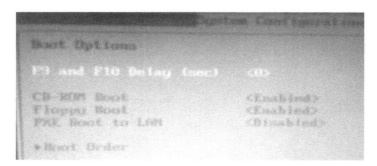

It may appear as if the only options are CD ROM or Floppy Disc. However, select **Boot Order** to bring up another screen. Then select **USB Diskette on Key/ USB Hard Disc.** Click **F6** to raise it to the top of the list. Then click **F10** to save and close the settings. This will change the startup order to boot USB by default. On Restart, the USB screen appears and starts the Linux Mint installer.

Install Linux Mint in a Dual Boot on your computer
We will use the Linux Mint installer to create install Linux Mint. While there are other ways to create partitions, doing it directly with the Linux Mint installer is the most reliable method. After booting from the Live USB, the first screen you will likely see after your computer restarts will be the following.

This will start the Linux Mint 15 operating system installation process and bring up the following screen:

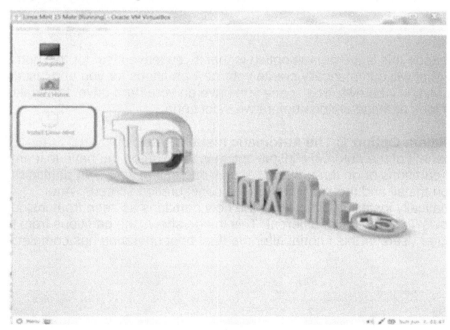

Click on the circular disc which says **Install Linux Mint.** It is in the left side of your screen. This will bring up the **Install Welcome** screen. Choose the language and click on **Continue.** The next screen recommends that you connect to the internet. You do not really need to be connected to the internet as you can add updates later. So click **Continue**.

Installation Type Screen and Options

When you get to the place in the installation where you are given several options, **do NOT select using the entire disc.** This would wipe out your C Drive and all of your data! When we install Linux Mint as a dual boot with Windows 7, we have a fifth option called "**Install Linux Mint alongside Windows 7**".

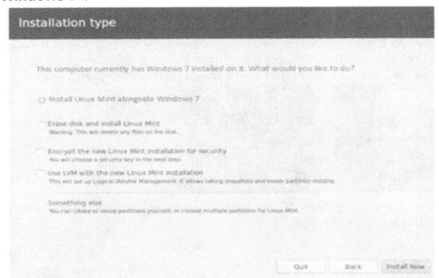

The reason this is the default option is that if you leave it set for this option, Linux Mint will automatically create your new partitions for you and install Linux Mint in whatever free space you have on your hard drive. Let's take a closer look at these options before we select one.

Installation Option 1: The Automatic Install Option

The benefit of the automatic install option is that you do not have to learn about partitions or go through the hassles of creating your own partitions. Just click on Install and then run through the configuration screens. After automatically installing Linux Mint, the new partitions as seen from inside Windows 7 will look a lot different. This image shows the partitions from the computer used for this tutorial after the dual-boot operating has completed.

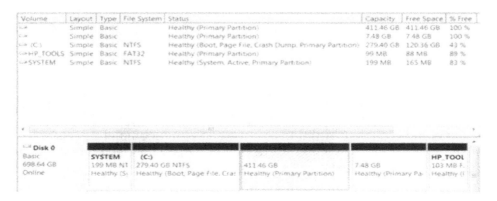

There are however a few drawbacks of the automatic install method. First, it will only create two partitions – one for Linux Mint and another for a "swap" partition. The Linux Boot Manager, called GRUB 2 will be installed into the Linux Mint partition and so will all of your data. (Note that Windows also installs all of your data on its partition which is called the C drive). This means that whenever you want to change your operating system, you will need to make a copy of all of your data on a USB Flash Drive, then replace the old operating system with the new one, then reinstall your data into the new operating system. You would not have to do this if your data was on a different partition than your operating system. The second drawback of the automatic install method is that Linux will automatically replace the Windows Boot Manager with the Linux Boot Manager (called GRUB 2). This is not that big of a loss as the Windows Boot Manager is a piece of junk. But it would be nice if Linux would at least warn you of what it is doing before you click on the Install Now button. The third drawback of the automatic install method is that you need to shrink the C drive before you install Linux Mint and you have no control over the size of any of the partitions.

In Chapter 6, we went through all of the steps of doing a manual installation. However, since we have already shrunk the C drive and we actually want the GRUB 2 Boot Manager to replace the Windows Boot Manager, and since the automatic install is less likely to have errors than a manual install, in this Quick Start Guide we will simply select the Automatic Install option called Install Linux Mint alongside Windows 7 (or Windows XP). Then click **Install Now.**

Choose a time zone and click Continue. Select a language. Then click Continue.

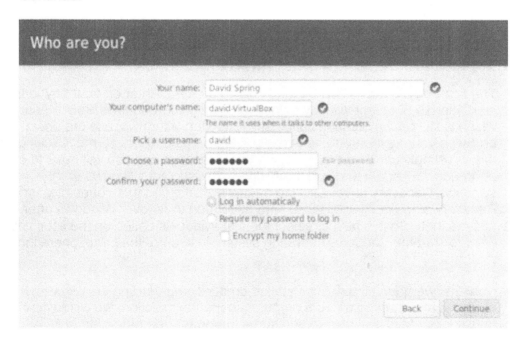

Enter your name, user name and passwords. Setting to log in automatically will save time when rebooting while installing and uninstalling programs. Then click Continue. Now we get the slide show which you can read while Linux is being installed. The slide show explains the features that come with Linus Mint Mate.

Finish Installing Linux Mint
After going through the install screens,, you will come to the following screen:

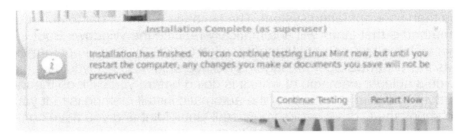

Click on **Restart Now.** Then while your computer is temporarily off, **remove the USB Live stick.** Otherwise, it will try to install Linux Mint again instead of going to the GRUB 2 screen or the Windows Boot Manager.

Using the GRUB 2 Startup screen
When your computer starts, you will find many entries on the GRUB 2 screen:

The first entry in the list will be Linux Mint 15. Press Enter on your keyboard to start Mint 15. The first Windows entry is actually the Windows Boot Manager which is still on the partition called sda1. To start Windows, use the down arrow on your keyboard to select this. Then press Enter to start it. Clicking on this will simply bring up the Windows Boot Manager and you will have to click on Windows 7 again to get to the C drive. The second Windows entry is your Windows Recovery drive. Clicking on this will take you to a series of Windows Recovery steps familiar to those who have tried to recover Windows after it has crashed. So it is best to select the first Windows option on the list if you want to start the Windows operating system instead of the Linux operating system.

Now that we have Linux Mint installed on our computer and we know how to access it after turning on our computer, in the next section, we will review how to use Linux Mint and how to add some important free programs to it.

10.3 Easy Steps and Free Tools for Using Linux Mint

This section explains how to use the Linux Mint operating system to change the appearance of your desktop, set up quick launch icons on your desktop and install important free programs to expand the function of Linux Mint.

Here is the initial Start screen for Linux Mint Mate:

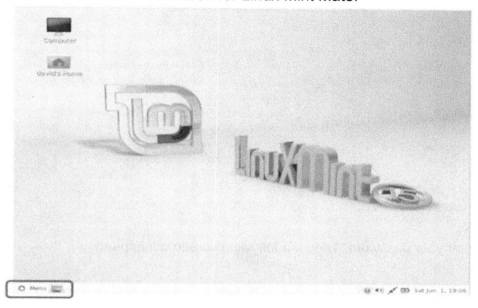

Click **Menu** which is in the lower left corner:

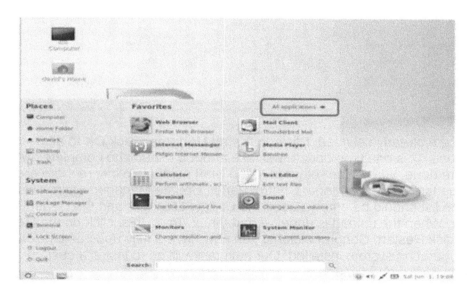

Linux Mate has two Start Menus

With Mate, there are two start menus. Above is the **Favorites Menu**. Click on All Applications to reach the **Applications Menu**.

Install Updates

The first step after installing Mate is updating all of the tools that come with Mate. To do this, click on the Menu icon in the lower left corner. Then click on **the Control Center** in the left column. Next click on **System,** then **Update Manager**

Enter your password. Then the following screen will appear:

These are already selected. Click on **Install Updates**. Click OK to all questions. This one time update will take about 5 minutes to complete. When they are done, you will be returned to the Start screen. To insure there are no more updates, click on Menu, Control Panel, Update Manager again. This time the list should be empty. Close the Update Manager and the Control Center. When the upload is done, restart Linux. To do this, click on the Menu. Then click Restart. Congratulations! You now have a fully updates Linux Mint Mate operating system installed. Our next task will be to install a custom desktop background image.

Add a Custom Desktop Background Image
Linux Mint Mate has a wonderful system for adding any of thousands of background images to your desktop – including your own personal images. To install a new background image, click on **Control Center** in the main menu.

Click on **Appearance.** Then click on the **Background** Tab:

There are about one dozen background images here. But there are thousands more you can get by clicking on the link: **Get more backgrounds online**:

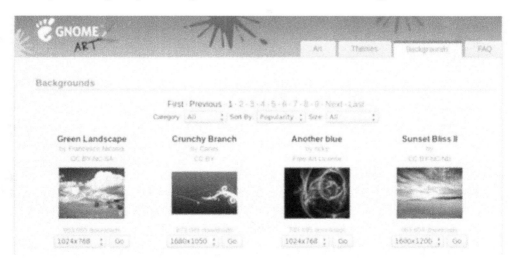

There are 139 pages of backgrounds or over 1400 choices. You can also create your own images 1024 pixels wide by 768 high. Be sure to optimize the file size to keep it under 100KB. Then upload it to your Downloads folder. When selecting a new desktop image, make sure that there are not a lot of graphics on the left side of the image as this is where we will be placing our desktop quick link icons. If you do not get the chance to get outdoors much, choose a light blue image with a lot of sky for your desktop image. On page 11 is one such image. But you can download several images and choose between them later.

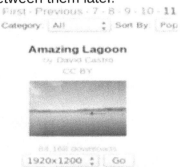

To get this image, click on GO. Then right click on the image and choice **Save Image As.** This brings up your Mint Mate Downloads folder. Change the name of the image to something more descriptive and click Save.

After downloading all of the images you want to the Mate Downloads folder, exit Firefox browser to go back to the Appearances Preferences Background screen and click ADD. By default, Mate looks in your **Pictures** folder to see if there are any images. Click on **Backgrounds** in the left column above. This is where the default background images are kept:

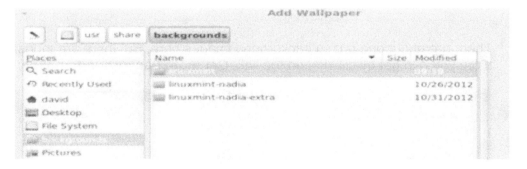

Then click on **Linux Mint Nadia extra** to open this folder. This is where all of your default background images are keep. The location is **File Manager, usr, share, backgrounds, Linuxmint_nadia-extra**. We can right click on any of these images to delete them from our default list. Or we can add images to this list by moving them from the **Downloads** folder to this list. We could also just navigate from this browse function to the **Downloads** folder and leave the images there. But this will clutter up the Mate Downloads folder and run the risk of accidentally deleting your background image in the future.

Next click on your **Home** folder:

Then click on the **Downloads** folder to select the image you want to turn into add to Wallpaper and click Open. This adds this image to your list of options and applies this image to your desktop. Repeat to add more images. To remove images from the list, click on an image and then click on Delete.

Change your Desktop Theme
In addition to changing the Background image, we can change the "theme" used to display open Windows. Click on the Appearance Preferences **Theme** tab. Then click on Customize which will take us to the pre-installed theme options.

Mint X is the default theme. But there are several themes inside of Mate you can select. Click on Mist.

Click on the **Window Border** tab:

There are about 20 tab display options, To select the option closest to Windows 7, click on **WinMe**. Then click Close. We now have a Windows like theme and a light blue desktop background. Close the Control Center.

Add Application "Launcher" Icons to our Desktop
We next need to add some Application Icons to the Desktop. Click on the Start Menu. This brings up the **Favorites** screen:

Then click on **All Applications** in the upper right corner. This changes the main menu from the Favorites screen to the Applications screen:

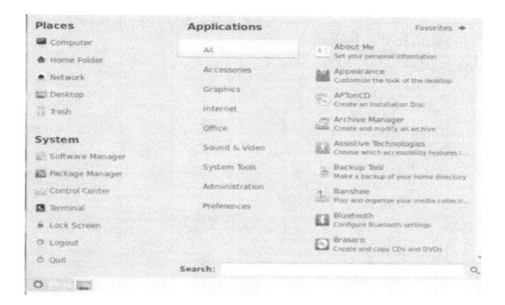

Then click on **Office:**

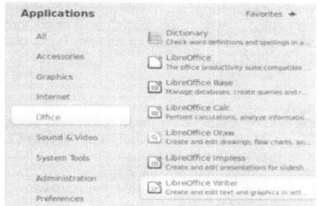

The most important application is LibreOffice Writer, which is the open source version of Microsoft Word. Click on this application. Then hold down on this selection and drag the icon to the desktop.

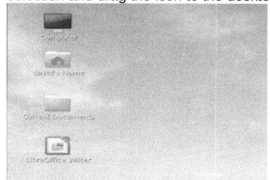

Now add Firefox browser to the desktop using the same process. Click on Menu.

Then click on **Internet.** Then right click **Firefox.** Then click **Desktop. Or just drag the icon to the desktop.**

Change Desktop Settings

You can also control which default icons appear on your desktop by going to Menu, Preferences, Desktop Settings. We can delete the home or computer quick start icon here if we want less on our desktop. Or add the Trash icon if we want the trash can on the desktop.

Turn off the Touch Pad

A nagging problem in writing articles with Libre Writer is that the pointer and screen and scroll bar all tend to jump around if you have a sensitive touch pad. This is not the fault of Libre Writer. Instead, it is an issue with how Linux Mint handles the touch pad on your keyboard. If you use a mouse, you have two options. The easiest way to stabilize your pointer is to open the **Control Center** in your Mint Menu and click on the **Mouse** Icon in the Hardware section. This brings up the **Mouse Preferences** window.

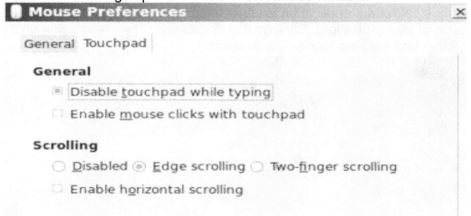

Click on the **Touchpad** tab and check "Disable touchpad while typing." This will keep the touch pad off while you are typing and 2 seconds after you stop typing.

Add Free Programs with the Linux Mint Software Manager

One of the biggest advantages of Linux over Windows is that there are tens of thousands of free open source programs which you can add to customize your computer. To add programs, go to the Start Menu and click on Administration, then **Software Manager:**

Add a Free Touch Pad Control Tool

To get a better tool to control the touchpad, click on the Software Center which is also in the Mint Menu. Then type in "gpointing-device-settings" in the Search Box. This will bring up two results. The i386 version is for 32 bit computers and the unmarked version is for x64 bit computers.

Click install. This adds a new entry to the Control Center called Pointing Devices. First click on Mouse Preferences and turn off "Disable Touchpad while typing" as the Mouse settings override the Pointer settings. Then click on the Pointer icon to bring up the Gpointing Device Settings Window.

Click Disable touchpad – or disable while other devices are connected. Then click OK. Your touch pad will now stay off for as long as your computer is turned on. Note however, that when you restart your computer, you will need to repeat the process: uncheck Disable Touchpad, then click OK. Then open it again and check Disable Touchpad again. Then click OK.

Add a Better Screen Capture Tool

The default screen capture tool that comes with Linux Mint has a couple of minor problems. The biggest problem is that it does not really optimize the image file sizes of images very well. Thankfully, there is an excellent screen capture tool called Shutter available in the Software Manager. Enter shutter into the search box. Then click on **Shutter** to reach its screen. Then click on **Install.**

To put Shutter on your desktop, click on the **Mint Menu** and click on **Accessories.** Then right click on **Shutter** and drag it to the desktop. Then click on **Shutter** to open it.

Click on **Edit,** then **Preferences** to open the Preferences window. Change the image format to **JPEG** and select **Automatically copy to clipboard.** Then set capture for a delay of 3 seconds. Then click Close. There are several ways to capture images with Shutter. To capture a region, click on Selection. To capture any particular open window, click on the dropdown arrow to the right of Window. To capture a complex dropdown menu, click on the Menu Item.

Set Libre Office as Default Editor
The default text editor for Linux Mint, which is called Pluma, does not have very many editing options. If you go to the **Caja File manager** and right click in the workspace to create a new document, Linux Mint will open a text Editor called Pluma. We would rather have the Mint file manager open **Libre Writer because this is the world's best text editor** To make this change, go to **Control Center, Other, Preferred Applications, system tab, set Text Editor for Libre Office.**

Add your printer to Linux Mint
To install your printer on Linux Mint is usually a pretty simple matter. Go to Control Panel, Printers. Then click on **Printers.** Then click on **ADD.** Select the printer you want to use, then click **Forward**. Linux Mint will search for a driver for this printer. Type in the name you want to use for this printer. Then click **Apply.**
Congratulations! You now have your printer hooked up to Linux Mint and you are well on your way to gaining your freedom from Microsoft and the NSA.

What's Next
In the next section, we will review some final steps to gaining and retaining your freedom.

10.4 Final Steps to Freedom

As flowers beneath May's footstep waken,
As stars from Night's loose hair are shaken,
As waves arise when loud winds call,
Thoughts sprung where that step did fall...
A rushing light of clouds and splendor,
A sense awakening and yet tender
Was heard and felt – and at its close,
These words of joy and fear arose...
Rise like Lions after slumber, in unvanquishable number.
Shake your chains to earth like dew, which in sleep had fallen on you.
We are many – they are few... We are many – they are few!

Percy Shelley, 1819, after the slaughter of pro-democracy protesters in Manchester England.

In this section, we will cover steps you can take to continue your progress towards freedom. As I did the research for this book, I often asked myself – how could things have ever gotten this bad? Why have we allowed the Microsoft/NSA monopoly go on so long that this Evil Empire is now on the verge of total control over 90% of the world's two billion computers? It is easy to blame government corruption combined with corporate greed. But we elected the criminals who now run our government and we continued to buy software from a company that has repeatedly ripped us off and sold us out.

I am as guilty as anyone. For years, I taught courses in how to use Microsoft programs without the slightest clue that I was harming my students more than helping them. It was really not until the Windows 8 disaster that I began to realize what was happening. What really woke me up was the research I did on UEFI and "secure boot." By the time the Snowden revelations came out in June 2013, I had already confirmed that Microsoft had colluded with the NSA to create the Flame virus and that there appeared to be a plot to use UEFI to gain complete control of our computers. The Snowden revelations simply turned my concerns from a strong suspicion to an outright certainty.

There are technical steps you can do to move towards privacy and freedom. In Chapter 9, we reviewed several concrete steps to regain your freedom. We will not review them again here. But they included:
First, resetting your search engine to **Duck Duck Go,**
Second, getting a new more secure email address from **riseup.net.**
Third, using your new email address to set up an account with **Thunderbird.**
Fourth, adding two tools to Thunderbird to give you the option of encrypting our email. These are **Enigmail with Gnu Privacy Guard.**

How will knowledge be shared in the future?

This is our last chance to go into detail on how the choice of computer start up programs, and in particular **UEFI versus Core Boot**, plays a crucial role in our ability to create and share knowledge. This issue will determine what kind of future we will have and what kind of future we will leave for our children. Will it be a world where our children control access to their own knowledge and to the tools needed to create knowledge – or will it be a future in which the monopoly of Microsoft and the Big Brother power of the NSA control access to the tools of knowledge and the nature of the knowledge they have access to?

This book is not just about the security advantages of Linux over Windows

Because the connection between Microsoft and the NSA has been in the news recently, there is a tendency for us to look at Linux as a way to regain our freedom from the NSA. There are certainly security advantages in a dispersed system such as Linux over a centrally controlled system such as MS Windows. However, merely putting Linux on your system - without also taking other steps - will not guarantee your safety or security. Even those 600 million people whose Windows XP systems are going to put at risk when Microsoft abandons them on April 8 2014 should look at this as a "blessing in disguise" because this will give them the motivation to get informed – and knowledge is power. As for those who have moved to Linux because of complaints about how difficult it is to use Windows 8, we should look at this as an opportunity to wake up and learn about other important and needed changes that urgently need to be made if we are truly to be free from the control of corporate monopolies.

Sadly, there is an even greater threat to our safety than all of the back doors inside of Windows 8. That threat is **the UEFI Start Up Program** and the tool Microsoft has placed inside of UEFI called Secure Boot. Richard Stallman has more accurately called this "feature" of Windows 8 "Restricted Boot." I am therefore taking this opportunity to explain the dangers of UEFI and Secure Boot and to provide a path forward – specific action we can take now – to insure that our children have control over their own computers and control over their own futures. This future is not only dependent on using Linux and Libre Office instead of Windows and MS Office – it is even more dependent on using a free open source startup program called **Core Boot** instead of using the ultra-secret and extremely dangerous startup program called UEFI.

What is a Start Up Program and Why is it important?

When you push the ON button on your computer, the first program that starts is not the operating system. It is not Windows or Linux. Instead, it is a program which sets up the computer power functions and makes sure everything is running okay. The start up program turns on the operating system's "boot manager" which in turn turns over control of your computer to whichever operating system you have selected with the boot manager.

The reason the Start Up program is important is that, if it does not run properly, you will not have any access to your computer or your data. Think about this. With Windows 7 and Windows XP, both of which use the BIOS startup program, if your operating system crashes, you can still start up your computer and press on F1, F2, F10 or Escape to go into your computer's BIOS Start Up program and try to take steps to repair your computer. You can even use BIOS to install and use a different operating system. However, with UEFI and the Windows 8 system, if your Start Up program fails to start, your computer will become as useless as a big brick – thus the phrase "Microsoft just bricked my computer."

What are BIOS, UEFI and Core Boot?
BIOS is a Start up program that was written in 1975 by Gary Kildall. BIOS stands for Basic Input Output System. With the release of Windows 8 in October 2012, Microsoft's certification requirements now require that all computers include the terrible UEFI startup chip. UEFI is a radically different start up program which is many times larger and more complex than BIOS. The project was originally started by Intel around 1999, but was greatly expanded by Microsoft in 2006. The term UEFI stands for Unified Extensible Firmware Interface. Core Boot is a free open source start up program that was started around 2000 to overcome some of the problems of BIOS and provide a more secure alternative to UEFI.

Where is the Start up Program and who controls it?
The primary processor on your computer is called the Hard Drive. The Hard Drive contains any Boot Loaders, operating systems and all of the programs and data you have on your computer. The hard drive is a little chip which is smaller than your little finger which is made by a chip manufacturer such as Intel or AMD. The start up program is not on the hard drive. Instead, it is on another chip inside of your computer which starts before the hard drive. Below is an AWARD BIOS START UP CHIP detached from its spot on the computer mother board.

When you press on the Power button of your computer and then press on the appropriate function key – which varies from one computer manufacturer to the next – during the first three seconds, you can bring up a user interface to adjust settings in your Start Up Program. Start up chips with their start up programs are made by just a few manufacturers. These include American Megatrends (AMI), Insyde Software and Phoenix Technologies (formerly Award Software).

In 2005, Intel handed over the EFI project to Microsoft who created a "non-profit" corporation called Unified EFI Forum to promote UEFI. The UEFI forum also includes AMD, American Megatrends, Apple, Dell, HP, IBM, Insyde, Intel, Lenovo and Phoenix – in addition to Microsoft. Since Microsoft took over the UEFI project, there have been several versions of UEFI. Version 2.0 was published on October 8 2008. Version 2.3 was published on May 8 2009 and Version 2.3.1 was published on April 8 2011.

Secure Boot is a "feature" Microsoft added to UEFI in Version 2.3. This feature prohibits the computer from working unless it has a "certified signature" which is typically supplied by Microsoft. With the release of Windows 8 in October 2012, Microsoft's certification requirements now require that computers include the UEFI plus secure boot startup program. This is why nearly all computers now come with the UEFI startup program.

Why Core Boot and/or BIOS are better than UEFI
Microsoft (and the NSA) will likely spend more than one billion dollars trying to convince us that BIOS was old and had had to go – while UEFI is new and therefore more secure. However, there is considerable evidence that the move from BIOS to UEFI and the design of UEFI and Secure Boot has nothing to do with security and everything to do with retaining control over our computers and NSA access to our computers. Here we will address several myths about BIOS and then look into the false claims made about UEFI.

The NSA would like you to believe that UEFI is more secure from a RootKit Attack System (RATS) than BIOS. A rootkit attack (or RAT) is an attack whereby the attacker gains access to the Root Administrator Permissions of your computer and therefore has total control over your computer. There is a basic problem with this claim about UEFI being better at stopping these attacks than BIOS. Nearly all of these so-called RATS occur inside of the Hard Drive at either the Boot Loader level or more commonly at the operating system level – for example, by following the path of the Stuxnet and Flame viruses using the Windows open back door to attack computers.

To review, the computer consists of the Start Up Chip which starts the Boot Loader which starts the Operating System which runs the other programs. So RATS occur at the operating system level, not at the Start Up level. There is a simple reason for this. When you are on the internet, you are using the operating system which is on the hard drive. The start up program is on a separate chip which is not even active at this point. There is no access to the start up chip (without disassembling the computer) and it would be much harder to go unnoticed even if you could change the Start Up program.

The many design flaws of UEFI include:
First UEFI was and still is developed in secrecy. As security experts have often pointed out, secrecy has a lack of feedback and is thus a model for failure.

Second, UEFI is an enormous program with over 7000 files and more than 100 MB of code. There is safety in simplicity. More code simply leads to more ways to attack the system.

Third, UEFI has 'call home" feedback loops which were not present on BIOS and are not present on Core Boot. This is perhaps the worst shortcoming of UEFI. BIOS and Core Boot are almost completely separate from the operating system. Therefore attacks on the operating system rarely if ever affect the start up program. However, because secure boot will not work without a "call home" open back door, **UEFI is the first start up program to ever have a call home feedback loop.** This feedback loop would make it possible for an attacker who gains access to the Authorized Certificates to rewrite the code on the start up chip much more easily than could be done with either BIOS or Core Boot.

Fourth, the Secure Boot Authorized Certificate protection method has already been shown to be open to successful attack. This is what Stuxnet and Flame both did with the Windows operating system.

Fifth, UEFI is written in in a simple computer language called C whereas BIOS was written in a more difficult "assembly" language. Think of it as BIOS being written in Latin while UEFI is written in plain English. Which language do you think would be more secure from casual hackers?

Sixth, UEFI uses Microsoft programming languages which use backward slashes for file names. This has also led to easy attacks to the Windows operating system. If one has UEFI, these same attacks could go directly to the Start up chip due to the "call home" open back doors in UEFI.

According to security experts, UEFI is "their worst nightmare." Instead of having to merely replace the hard drive or replace the operating system like they currently do, businesses will be forced to replace their entire computer!

Security expert, Bruce Schneier calls the certificate system "completely broken." *"The problem for all of us, naturally, is if the certificate system was hacked, allowing the bad guys to forge certificates. (This has, of course, happened before.) Are we finally ready to accept that the certificate system is completely broken?"*
https://www.schneier.com/blog/archives/2012/02/verisign_hacked.html

UEFI was successfully attacked before it was even released to the public!
In September 2012, security researchers discovered security shortcomings in Windows 8 (aka UEFI) that create a means to infect the new operating system with rootkit malware. Italian security consultants ITSEC discovered the security hole following an analysis of the Unified Extensible Firmware Interface (UEFI).

> **"The new UEFI platform is as insecure as the old BIOS technology, it's still vulnerable to the old attacks...Writing a bootkit couldn't be an easier task for virus writers with the UEFI framework available, much easier than with BIOS when they needed to code to be written in pure assembly language."**
> Marco Giuliani, Director of ITSEC, in the article:
> Hacking UEFI... New Vicious UEFI bootkit vulnerability found for Windows 8
> http://www.theregister.co.uk/2012/09/19/win8_rootkit/

Linus Torvalds, the founder of the Linux project is also not impressed with UEFI.

> **"The real problem, I feel, is that clever hackers will bypass the whole (UEFI) key issue either by getting a key of their own (how many of those private keys have stayed really private again? Oh, that's right, pretty much none of them) or they'll just take advantage of security bugs in signed software to bypass it without a key at all."**
> Linus Torvalds on Windows 8, UEFI and Fedora June 10 2012
> http://www.zdnet.com/blog/open-source/linus-torvalds-on-windows-8-uefi-and-fedora/11187

Why UEFI is a Trojan Horse

One of the most common tricks used by hackers to gain access to your computer is what they call a Trojan Horse attack. The attack is based on fooling you to download a program which you really should not download. This is the equivalent of inviting the thieves to enter your home. The thieves then change the locks on your doors while you are not looking and then come back later to steal all of your data. The first Trojan attack Microsoft initiated was by inserting Windows Internet Explorer and DLL files (Dynamically Linked Libraries) into the Windows operating system in 1998 with the introduction of Windows 98. We have all seen how many problems this open back door has created for our computers. But the UEFI scam is much worse – because it is taking a start program with no real security problems (BIOS) and replacing it with a start program which is literally loaded with security problems (UEFI) and then trying to convince us that this will somehow improve the security on our computers.

Lack of Choice is a Lack of Freedom

The worst part of all is that we are not even being given a choice of whether to accept UEFI or not. **This is because all Windows 8 and Apple computers are being switched over to the UEFI start program.** We no longer have the choice of buying a Windows or Apple computer with either Core Boot or BIOS. Microsoft is once again using its monopoly power to force all computer manufacturers to use UEFI. So today, we are all being forced to pay for and use an extremely dangerous system.

If nearly all computers now have UEFI, what computer should I buy?

You still have at least four options:

Option #1: Keep your current computer.
Linux works really well in a dual boot with Windows XP and if the Windows XP operating system ever goes down, you still have a terrific Linux operating system. You can even put Windows XP into Virtual Box if you want even more security.

Option #2: Repair any old dead computers you have.
It is likely that your old computer can be made to work like new just by replacing the hard drive chip. I have done this myself and it is not hard. But if you are not thrilled about opening your computer, then take it to a repair store. You can likely get a new hard drive installed for less than $200. This will give you another computer which you can give to your kids to use at school.

Option #3: Buy a Windows XP or Windows 7 computer from a used computer store
There are often very good used computers at the used computer stores. Any BIOS computer – including any Windows XP or Windows 7 computer - will be safer than any Windows 8 UEFI computer.

Option #4: If you really must buy a new computer, consider buying a Google Chrome Book.
Google Chrome Books already come with a version of Linux called Chrome OS. Chrome Books also include a version of the Core Boot startup program. Because Chrome Book computers are only new computers that do not suffer from the UEFI start up program, Chrome Books are the only safe new computers on the market today. Chromebooks are also extremely inexpensive – because you do not have to pay hundreds of dollars for the Microsoft-NSA Monopoly. There are however a couple of drawbacks of Chromebook laptops. The most obvious drawback is that Chromebooks do not come with much storage on the hard drive. The best solution to this problem is to keep most of your data on a 64 GB USB thumb drive (or if you have a lot of data, put it on a one terabyte external USB drive. This is way safer than leaving your data on any computer. The most important drawback is that Chromebooks all come with an incomplete operating system called Chrome OS which is not very good for anything other than browsing the internet. What Google wants us to do is use the Google Chrome Browser to access their online servers and use "Google Docs" for word processing files stored on their servers.
The problem with this is that we now know that the NSA has access to all Google Servers. This is better than Microsoft because at least the NSA cannot brick you computer. But it is still not freedom. Thankfully, there is a free solution to this problem. If you really want privacy and freedom, all you need to do is modify your Chromebook by changing the operating system to the Linux Mint operating system. Because the process for adding Linux Mint to a Chromebook varies from model to model, we do not have instructions for this in this book. But we will provide instructions for how to do this with selected recommended models on our home website, collegeintheclouds.org, along with a special forum where you can ask questions about how to switch your Chromebook to Linux Mint.

There are currently several versions of the Google Chromebook. Unfortunately, some are quite difficult to add Linux Mint to. The two that I recommend are the **Acer C7 Chromebook** and the **Pixel Chromebook.** The Acer C7 is an ideal tool for students. It is inexpensive, costing only $200 and lightweight at less than 3 pounds. It is compact at 11 ½ inches and has a battery life of four hours. The Pixel was released in February 2013 and costs $1300. It features a bigger 13 inch screen with a backlit keyboard. The weight is just over 3 pounds. It uses a fast Intel i5 dual core 1.8 GHz processor. It has 4 GB RAM and 64 GB solid state drive. It has a battery life of 5 hours. Most important, it includes the ability to add a second startup program which makes it easier to install Linux Mint.

Late Breaking News about a Revolutionary New Computer Option
On September 11, 2013, Acer, HP, Toshiba, and Asus introduced new Chrome OS laptops featuring Intel Haswell processors. The new Chromebooks are expected to offer much longer battery life than their predecessors – up to double the battery life. I do not recommend the Toshiba model as there is a problem installing Linux Mint with it. However, HP will be introducing a 14 inch Chromebook, the biggest chrome book to date. The cost will be $299 and have a 16 GB SSD. Acer will be offering a 32 GB Chromebook which will be able to add Linux Mint. There is no question that either of these options, Acer or HP, will be less expensive for public schools than MS Windows computers because Google does not charge a licensing fee to use the Linux operating system.

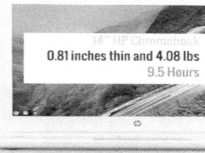

Research firm NPD says Chromebooks represent 20-25% of the $300-or-less computer market. In education, more than 5,000 schools use Chromebooks for their students, representing more than 20% of school districts in the US. An April 2013 study of 12 school districts by IDC found that switching from PCs to Chromebooks saved school districts over $1,000 per year per student.

The study found that Chromebooks reduced the need for additional IT staff to support their deployments, requiring 69% less labor to deploy and 92% less labor to support than desktop PCs or laptop PCs. Chromebooks' high reliability increased actual teaching and educational administration time by reducing the time lost in managing desktop PCs or laptop PCs by 82%.

Finally, the Solid State Drives are obviously more durable and user friendly that the older drives. According to this study, Chromebooks are already the number 2 operating system in schools – right behind Windows 7 and in front of Windows XP. It is my humble opinion that the new Acer Chromebook – with an 8 hour battery life and much faster processor and a weight well under 3 pounds - is going to take the school student market by storm.
Acer has said that this new laptop will be available as soon as November 2013. Since these are new computers, we are not able to provide instructions on how to add Linux Mint to them. However, we will be posting instructions on our website, **collegeintheclouds.org**. We will also provide a forum and email newsletter list where you can sign up for updated information as it is available.

Use Alternative News Sources instead of the Corporate Nonsense Media
If we have learned anything from the Snowden revelations, it is that we cannot rely on the corporate controlled main stream media to keep us informed about what our government is doing to us. This means that we have to consciously seek out alternate sources of information. One key resource for the Snowden revelations has been Glenn Greenwald and **theguardian.com**. Other important sources include **democracynow.org, opednews.com, alternet.com, counterpunch.com, commondreams.org and zerohedge.com**. Some of these are regarded as left leaning websites and others are regarded as right leaning websites. But we need to move away from the left versus right distraction and recognize that the greatest threat to our freedom is not the left or the right, but rather it is corporate fascism – corporate control of government and of people.

There are also several other excellent websites to get information about new developments in open source tools. These include the Linux Mint website and the Libre Office website. Other excellent websites for keeping up on open source technology include:
http://forums.linuxmint.com/
http://ask.libreoffice.org/en/questions/
http://libreplanet.org/wiki/Main_Page
http://en.libreofficeforum.org/
http://techrights.org/?stories
http://www.techdirt.com/

Community Organizing
Another way to become better informed about the evolving story of open source tools is to join or start a local open source community. There are open source communities all over the world being organized through a group called Libre Planet.

To a search on this term to find a group near you and the time and location of their next meeting.
http://libreplanet.org/wiki/LibrePlanet:Local_Teams/List

There are also many Linux forums where you can post questions to and read answers to questions posted by other beginners. http://www.linux.org/forums/ There are also many "linux user groups" - also known as LUGs.
http://en.wikipedia.org/wiki/Category:Linux_user_groups
http://dir.yahoo.com/computers_and_internet/software/operating_systems/unix/linux/user_groups/

A Linux User Group (LUG) or GNU/Linux User Group (GLUG) is a private, generally non-profit organization that provides support and/or education for Linux users, particularly for inexperienced users. The term commonly refers to local groups that meet in person, but is also used to refer to online support groups that may have members spread over a wide area and which may not have physical meetings. These groups may meet at a local library, at a community college, at someone's home or even at a local bar. There is so much happening within the open source community that it is difficult for any one person to keep up with it all. Building a group of friends and a local email list for sharing ideas is an important step for learning about the latest changes. There are several LUG lists on the Web. If you are considering founding a LUG, your first task should be to find any nearby existing LUGs. *Your best bet may be to join a LUG already established in your area, rather than founding one.*

A Linux User Group meeting at a community college.

There are Linux User Groups in all 50 US states plus over 100 other countries, including Russia, China, India, Canada and most of Western and Eastern Europe. Even if you do not have time to go to a local meeting, you can still sign up for their email list. Many of these groups will even help you install Linus operating systems and other open source tools on your computer.

Get involved with your public schools, public colleges and public libraries

There are many ways that you can help introduce and share Linux with the rest of your community. Talk with teachers and administrators at public schools about the financial and educational benefits of using free open source educational tools in the public schools. Attend school board meetings and let school board members know that you would like more course offerings in open source tools in your school district. You can also visit your local community college and ask instructors and administrators for more course offerings on how to use Linux, Libre Office and other free open source tools. You can also visit your local public library and offer to start a once a month discussion group on how to install and use Linux, Libre Office and other free open source tools.

Get Politically Active

Corporate monopolies, such as Microsoft, and the billionaires who own them, have invested millions of dollars buying elections and destroying democracy. The only way we will be able to re-establish a fair and level playing field for small, innovative, new businesses and restore a growing economy is if all of us become more politically active. This means attending local monthly meetings of the political party of your choice. You can either try to help take back the Republican or Democratic parties from the billionaires. Or, if you think the major political parties are beyond help, you can do what Richard Stallman has done and support the Green Party – or any other third party. The reason political activism is so important is that apathy leads to a corporate takeover of our democracy. None of us can be truly free until all of us are free – and that will not happen by sitting on the couch watching the corporate TV brainwashing programs.

Conclusion... Is a better future around the corner?

While Linux is a very small percent of the current overall computer laptop and desktop market, it is likely to become the primary operating system in our public schools in the next three years. The Google Chromebook durable and dependable solid state drive, which does not need a fan, is as likely to drive this change as the $200 price. In addition, the fact that a student can use the laptop for the entire day without recharging the battery is a huge plus for public schools.

For many schools, there will be a temptation to simply stay with the Chrome OS operating system. Sadly, this is a very limited operating system which may give students and teachers a bad idea of the real potential with Linux. Converting the operating system to the Linux Mint operating system has no cost. But it does take about one hour (or less) to run through the steps of changing the operating system to Linux Mint. The benefit is that you not only get a better file manager, but you get Libre Office 4 and access to thousands of other free programs. I am confident that once schools realize how easy it is to convert an economical Chromebook to a powerful full featured laptop, school districts will rush to provide Chromebooks to more students.

Then once students learn how much easier Libre Office is that MS Office, we could have an entirely different future for the sharing of knowledge both in and out of our public schools.

This is an evolving story and I plan on posting updates about changes in free open source technology on our book website and our course website – collegeintheclouds.org.

What's Next?
One of the huge benefits of open source tools is that Libre Office is a great tool for anyone wishing to publish either an ebook or a website. Sadly, the instructions for using Libre Office to do either of these things is pretty limited. I am therefore in the process of completing a book on using Libre Office for writing an ebook. I am also nearly finished writing a book on using another free open source tool, called Joomla for building an educational or business website. Finally, in the coming months, we will start offering online courses on both of these subjects – and on how to install and use Linux Mint. You can learn more about all of these educational opportunities by visiting our main website **collegeintheclouds.org.** You can also post any questions you may have on our course forum which is also on the same website. Thank you for taking the time to read this book. I hope you will consider sharing the link to this book with your family, friends and neighbors.

Regards,
David Spring
September 11, 2013

About the Author

David Spring has a Master's Degree in Education from the University of Washington. He has taught adult education courses for more than 20 years at several colleges in Washington State including Bellevue College, Seattle Central Community College and Shoreline Community College. He lives near Seattle Washington with his daughter Sierra Spring and his partner Elizabeth Hanson, her son Chris Hanson, several cats and four free gnomes.

David Spring, Elizabeth Hanson and our four free gnomes.
(photo by Chris Hanson)

For more information about our other books and courses, visit our website: **collegeintheclouds.org**.

www.ingramcontent.com/pod-product-compliance
Lightning Source LLC
Chambersburg PA
CBHW082108070326
40689CB00052B/3829